BATTLE FOR
HONG
KONG

About the Author

Philip Cracknell was posted to Hong Kong in 1985 whilst working for the UK subsidiary of a major New York bank. He developed an interest in Hong Kong's military history. His archival research was conducted in London and Hong Kong. Living in Hong Kong, he was able to spend a considerable amount of time on the battlefields. He conducts battlefield tours for the Hong Kong Club, Royal Asiatic Society, veterans, schools and charities. He has a blog, battleforhongkong.blogspot.hk, on military history with a special focus on the events in Hong Kong during December 1941.

BATTLE FOR HONG KONG

DECEMBER 1941

Philip Cracknell

AMBERLEY

To my wife Marianne, and my sons, Christopher and Jamie

First published 2021

Amberley Publishing
The Hill, Stroud
Gloucestershire, GL5 4EP

www.amberley-books.com

British Library Cataloguing in Publication Data.
A catalogue record for this book is available from the British Library.

ISBN 978 1 3981 0911 7 (paperback)
ISBN 978 1 4456 9050 6 (ebook)

Typeset in 10.5pt on 13pt Sabon.
Typesetting by Aura Technology and Software Services, India.
Printed in the UK.

Contents

Maps

1

Historical Prelude
1841–1941

When the Pacific War began in December 1941, Hong Kong had only recently celebrated its centenary under British rule. The celebrations were downplayed by the Hong Kong Government due to the war in Europe, the continuing conflict in China, and increasing tensions with Japan. One hundred years earlier, during the First Opium War, a British naval squadron commanded by Commodore James Bremer destroyed a fleet of Chinese war junks and captured the strategically important forts guarding the mouth of the Pearl River. The forts, located at what was known as the Bocca Tigris, the Tiger's Mouth, controlled the river approaches to the trading port of Canton. A ceasefire was agreed, and the terms of a treaty, known as the Convention of Chuenpi, were negotiated. The agreement was formalised on 20 January 1841, at which time Captain Charles Elliot, the British Plenipotentiary, and Qi Shan, his Chinese counterpart, agreed to a number of conditions, which included the return of the forts to China, reparations to be paid by China, and the cession of Hong Kong Island to Britain.

Captain Edward Belcher, commander of HMS *Sulphur*, a hydrographic survey ship, was ordered to sail to Hong Kong and undertake a survey of Hong Kong Island (hereafter 'the Island') and its sheltered harbour. HMS *Sulphur* arrived on 25 January 1841 and anchored off the north-west shore of the Island. Her officers and men landed at a place that later became known as Possession Point. Today, a nearby street still carries the name Possession Street, and a large block of residential apartments, in Kennedy Town facing Belchers Bay, carries the somewhat unattractive-sounding name The Belchers. Captain Belcher, writing in 1843, described how, after landing on the Island as the first possessors of this small addition to the British Empire, his officers and men drank a toast and raised three cheers to Her Britannic Majesty ahead of the arrival of the naval squadron.

On the 26th, the squadron arrived; the marines were landed, the union hoisted on our post, and formal possession taken of the Island by Commodore Sir J.G. Bremer, accompanied by other officers of the squadron, under a *feu de joie* from the marines, and a royal salute from the ships of war.[1]

The Chinese Imperial Commissioner, Qi Shan, despite having agreed to the cession of Hong Kong, failed to get the approval of the Qing Court. The Emperor thought he had conceded too much, and as a result the treaty was not ratified and Qi Shan was dismissed from his position. The British Government was not happy either, feeling that Captain Charles Elliot had not extracted enough. Elliot was recalled and replaced as Plenipotentiary and Superintendent of Trade by Major-General Henry Pottinger. Lord Palmerston, Foreign Secretary, famously dismissed Hong Kong as being a barren rock with hardly a house upon it, claiming it would never be a mart for trade.

Hostilities were resumed, and the de facto possession of Hong Kong was not legally formalised until August 1842 when the Treaty of Nanking brought an end to the First Opium War. Under the terms of the treaty, reparations were agreed, new treaty ports for foreign trade were granted, and Hong Kong Island was ceded in perpetuity to the British Crown. Sir Henry Pottinger became the first Governor of Hong Kong.

In January 1841, when Commodore Bremer took possession of Hong Kong, Japan was still a semi-feudal state. It had been governed since 1603 by a ruling dynasty known as the Tokugawa Shogunate. The Shogun had absolute power and ruled from Edo, present-day Tokyo, whereas the Emperor had symbolic power and lived in seclusion at Kyoto. In the same way that China had restricted trade with the West to the port of Canton, Japan restricted foreign trade to the port of Nagasaki. Just as China had been forced to open trading ports through gunboat diplomacy, Japan was forced to consent to the demands of Commodore Perry, who arrived in 1853 with a squadron of American warships demanding access to Japanese ports for trade. The humiliation of forced compliance and the demonstration of superior Western technology served as a catalyst for the Meiji Restoration, in which, after a civil war, the Emperor wrested power back from the Shogun and set about modernising the country.

The Japanese realised that unless they modernised they would be unable to fend off foreign incursions and would end up sharing the same fate as Imperial China. Kase Toshikazu, a member of the Japanese Foreign Office in wartime Japan, writing in *Eclipse of the Rising Sun*, described the structure of the Meiji Restoration as being inverted in that it was a top-down rather than a bottom-up revolution.

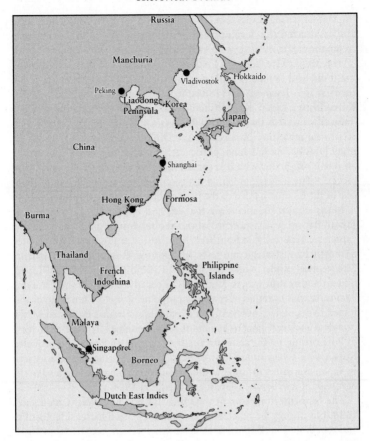

East Asia.

The ruling class of samurai that held power during the Tokugawa period continued to hold power during the Meiji Restoration, acting as government officials and bureaucrats and aligning themselves with the emerging class of merchants and businessmen. Kase postulates that there was insufficient time between feudalism and modernism for any kind of political maturity to develop. The Japanese social structure at that time was characterised by the feudal inheritance of hierarchical relationships, for example between the daimyo and the samurai, the samurai and the soldier, the master and the servant, the protector and the protected. The Japanese psyche had become conditioned to loyalty, and a willingness to serve one's master. People generally accepted their position in the hierarchy and tended towards loyalty and obedience in the face of strong leadership. This interfered with the democratic ideal and facilitated the development of authoritarianism and militarism in Japan.

The Meiji Restoration may not have promoted political development, but it did lead to Japan's rapid modernisation. This was demonstrated in the First Sino-Japanese War (1894–95) when Japan defeated China, seized Korea (then a vassal state of China), and acquired Formosa (present-day Taiwan) as well as the Liaodong Peninsula in Southern Manchuria. This territorial forfeiture imposed on the Qing Government was seen as a great humiliation in China, particularly because they were defeated by an Asian neighbour who had shared their isolationist background until recently. The outrage in China led to attacks on foreigners, and it was one of the factors that led to the Boxer Rebellion four years later.

Many countries, including Russia, had expected China to defeat Japan. Russia was concerned about the territorial gains made by the Japanese, especially in Southern Manchuria, a region in which they had their own strategic interests. In response, Russia led the Tripartite Intervention, under which Russia, France and Germany forced Japan, under the threat of war, to relinquish its ceded territory in the Liaodong Peninsula, and to return sovereignty of the territory to China. Japan was forced to acquiesce, and then, in a move that infuriated the Japanese, the Russians coerced China to lease to them these same territories. The lease of Port Arthur, on the southern tip of the Liaodong Peninsula, provided Russia with a year-round ice-free port. The lease arrangement was seen by Japan as a direct threat, and this among other things would lead to the outbreak of war between Japan and Russia in 1904.

The Manchu Emperors of the Qing dynasty had ruled China since 1644, but during the nineteenth century they faced increasing hostility and rebellion. The Taiping Rebellion, which lasted from 1850 to 1864, had cost the lives of more than 20 million people. In addition to internal dissent and periodic uprisings, Imperial China had faced continual encroachment from foreign powers including Britain, France, Germany, Russia and Meiji-era Japan. Foreign incursions and general dissatisfaction in China led to the Boxer Rebellion in 1899. This was a violent uprising, but unlike previous rebellions, which sought to overthrow the Manchu rulers, this was anti-foreign and anti-Christian, and the Boxers pledged their support to the ruling Qing Government. The Empress Dowager somewhat reluctantly supported the Boxers. They had killed a large number of Chinese Christians, foreigners and missionaries, and laid siege to the foreign legations in Peking. In response, the foreign powers assembled an alliance consisting of Britain, America, Russia, France, Germany, Italy, Austria-Hungary and Japan, known as the Eight-Nation Alliance. The allied forces landed near Tientsin in 1900 and quickly defeated both the Chinese imperial forces and the Boxer militants. Peking was captured, and the fifty-five-day siege of the foreign districts was brought to an end.

Although Japan and Russia had been allied during the Boxer Rebellion, there had been animosity between the two countries since the Tripartite Intervention. In February 1904, Japan launched a surprise naval attack on the Russian Pacific Fleet at Port Arthur. The Japanese Army landed at Incheon on the Korean Peninsula and crossed the Yalu River to attack Russian-occupied Southern Manchuria. Russian warships, blockaded in Port Arthur, were destroyed by Japanese land-based artillery. All attempts by the Russians to relieve Port Arthur were beaten off, and the city surrendered in January 1905. The Russian Baltic Fleet sailed around the world to relieve the siege but arrived after Port Arthur had capitulated. In May 1905, the Russian fleet was defeated by the Japanese Navy at the Battle of Tsushima. Under the terms of the Treaty of Portsmouth, signed in September 1905 with American intermediation, Russia agreed to withdraw from Manchuria, to recognise Japan's control of Korea, and to sign over its lease of Port Arthur. Japan acquired the Russian mining rights in Manchuria and the Russian-owned South Manchuria Railway. Japan had come of age. In a relatively short period of time, she had transformed herself from an isolationist, semi-feudal society to become a modern nation state capable of defeating one of the world's great powers. With its acquisition of part of the Liaodong Peninsula in 1905, the annexation of Korea in 1910 and the acquisition of the Russian mining rights in Manchuria, Japan had established an economic hinterland on the Asian continent.

During the First World War, Japan allied itself with the Triple Entente, consisting of France, Britain, and the old enemy, Tsarist Russia. During the war, Japan captured German territories in China and elsewhere in the Asia-Pacific region, and incarcerated some 4,600 German prisoners of war (POWs). The Japanese treatment of German POWs was generally exemplary, unlike the treatment that they subsequently meted out to Allied POWs in the Second World War, which was generally barbaric. At the end of the First World War, the Treaty of Versailles provided Japan with a mandate to administer the Caroline and Marshall Islands in Micronesia. The fate of the former German possessions in China was not settled until 1922, when under the Washington Treaties it was determined that they should be returned to China. This decision recognised that the Republic of China had also joined the alliance opposing the Central Powers in the First World War, and had sent thousands of labourers, referred to as the Chinese Labour Corps, to assist the war effort in Europe. The Washington Treaties also imposed a limitation on capital ships possessed by America, Britain and Japan, limiting the Japanese to a maximum of 60 per cent of the capital ship tonnage of each of Britain and America. The terms of this treaty irritated the Japanese, who had wanted to take control of the former German possessions in China. They saw it as an example of the Western powers trying to contain Japan.

In November 1930, in a sign of things to come, the Japanese Prime Minister, Hamaguchi Osachi, was shot and severely wounded at Tokyo Station by an ultranationalist protesting against the ratification of the London Naval Treaty, which was an extension of the Washington Treaties. In May 1932, Prime Minister Inukai Tsuyoshi was assassinated. He had tried to rein in the militarists, and as a result was shot at his residence by a group of young officers who wanted to establish a military government to replace what they saw as the corrupt establishment of politicians and capitalists. The militarists argued that since Japan was a relatively small country with limited natural resources, she needed her share of colonial possessions in the same way that European countries did. Many Japanese felt this was necessary for their country's survival. They wanted to go further, in fact, and create a new order in Asia by liberating the European colonies and placing them under Japanese leadership in what they described as a co-prosperity sphere. The idea would be 'Asia for the Asiatics'. Hitler made use of the concept of *lebensraum*, or living space. Germany needed *lebensraum* for agriculture, raw materials and settlement, and for this they looked towards the vastness of Russia. Japan was also looking for living space, for raw materials and for industry, and for this they looked towards China. The Japanese Army in Southern Manchuria, referred to as the Kwantung Army, was a hotbed of nationalist unrest, united by a desire to establish a military government in Japan and seize more territory in China.

In China, the Qing Government finally collapsed following the Xinhai Revolution, which began on 10 October 1911. Sun Yat-sen became Provisional President of the newly formed Republic of China, although he later ceded office to General Yuan Shikai in return for his help in ensuring the formal abdication of Pu-yi, the six-year-old Emperor, and his regents. Pu-yi abdicated in February 1912, and Yuan Shikai became President. Sun Yat-sen for his part became the leader of the Kuomintang (KMT), a political party comprised of former revolutionaries. In 1915, Yuan Shikai re-created imperial rule by declaring himself Emperor in order to strengthen his position in a power struggle with the KMT.

In 1915, Japan issued Yuan Shikai with the so-called Twenty-One Demands, which sought to extend Japanese control over Manchuria, and other parts of the Chinese economy. One of their demands was to insist on the appointment of Japanese advisers in policing and financing departments of the Chinese Government. This was opposed by Britain and America, and as a consequence some of the Japanese demands were modified. However, under the threat of war, China had little choice but to accept the Japanese ultimatum. Japan had her own agenda, and with the Twenty-One Demands had effectively thrown down the gauntlet, signalling an intention to take more control of China and to confront the Western powers if necessary. The Twenty-One Demands were presented several years before the Washington Treaties and the subsequent growth of militarism in Japan, demonstrating that Japan had long held territorial ambitions in China, no doubt inspired by her military success against China in 1895 and against Russia in 1905.

Yuan Shikai died in 1916, and during the period that followed China was thrown into disarray, with feuding between different warlords, and between the Nationalists and the Communists. After Sun Yat-sen died in March 1925, there followed a power struggle between his two protégés, General Chiang Kai-shek and Wang Jing-wei. Chiang Kai-shek emerged as the victor and became Leader of the State Council, equivalent to President, and de facto Head of the Nationalist Chinese Government in Nanking. Wang Jing-wei remained in Chiang Kai-shek's KMT, but no doubt harboured resentment, which may have been a factor in his subsequent defection and collaboration with the Japanese invaders.

In 1931, Japanese troops stationed in Manchuria seized the rest of the territory after blaming Chinese dissidents for the supposed dynamiting of a section of the Japanese-controlled South Manchuria Railway. This pretext, known as the Manchurian Incident, provided the Kwantung Army with the excuse they needed to seize the whole of Manchuria. After capturing Manchuria, the original homeland of the Manchu ruling family, the Japanese established the puppet state of Manchukuo, and in an effort to show some legitimacy installed Pu-yi, the last Manchu Emperor, as a symbolic head of state. In 1933, Japan withdrew from the League of Nations after the Assembly issued a demand calling on Japan to withdraw its troops from Manchuria and to return sovereignty to China. The report was adopted unanimously, with only Japan voting against it. The Japanese delegate insisted that Manchuria belonged to Japan, that they had recovered it from Russia, and that it was the Japanese who made it into what it was. This was a matter of life and death for Japan, and no concession or compromise was possible. The delegate then led the Japanese group out of the hall. Japan's withdrawal from the League of Nations was followed in the same year by Nazi Germany, under their new Chancellor, Adolf Hitler, and then by Italy, under Benito Mussolini.

The Second Sino-Japanese War started in July 1937 following a shooting incident between Chinese and Japanese soldiers guarding a bridge on the Japanese-controlled railway south of Peking. The skirmish, known as the Marco Polo Bridge Incident, led to all-out war. Japanese forces seized Nanking in December 1937, and the following year they landed at Daya Bay, some 40 miles east of Hong Kong. They proceeded inland and captured Canton, and then arrived on the border of Hong Kong. The Chinese Army had fought hard at Shanghai and surprised many international observers by their determined resistance, but they were no match for the well-equipped and well-trained Imperial Japanese Army. The conflict developed into a war of attrition. After the fall of Nanking, Chiang Kai-shek established Chungking as the capital of what became known as Free China.

Russia, now controlled by the Soviets, was worried that Japan might attack Siberia; accordingly, they supported the Chinese, with men and equipment, to keep the Japanese Army engaged and away from Eastern Russia. The US and Britain also supported the Chinese and sent supplies through Hong Kong, Burma and the port of Haiphong in French Indochina. In August 1939, Russia signed a peace treaty with Germany, which created concern in Japan that Russia might attack Japanese-occupied Manchuria. In September 1939, in response to the German invasion of Poland, Britain and France declared war on Germany. After the fall of France, in June 1940, Britain was facing the prospect of a German invasion; had it occurred, Japan might have chosen that time to attack British colonial possessions in Asia. However, British success in the Battle of Britain, which was fought in the skies over England from July to October 1940, prevented Germany from gaining air superiority and led to the postponement of Operation Sea Lion, the planned invasion of Britain.

In September 1940, Japan signed a tripartite pact with Germany and Italy. In the same month, Japanese forces invaded the Vichy French colony of Indochina, ostensibly to stop the supply of arms and equipment to the Nationalist Chinese through the port of Haiphong. Outnumbered, the Vichy French were forced to allow Japanese troops to be stationed in Indochina, and to allow Japanese control of the port, but with a limitation on the number of Japanese troops that could be stationed in the French colony. There had been a long-standing division of opinion within the Japanese military as to whether to strike north and attack Russia, or whether to strike south and attack the European colonies in South East Asia. In April 1941, Japan signed a neutrality pact with Russia, reducing the risk of Russian intervention, and then in June 1941, Germany invaded Russia. With Russia preoccupied, Japan chose to increase the size of its army in Indochina and then occupied the rest of the country. This put Singapore and Malaya within reach of Japanese bombers. In response, America and Britain stepped up their trade embargoes to include oil and steel. America increased her support for the Nationalist Chinese by sending fighter aircraft and a group of volunteer pilots, who were known as the American Volunteer Group, or the Flying Tigers. They served under the banner of the Republic of China Air Force and were initially based in Burma to defend the supply route to Free China along the Burma Road.

By this time, many Japanese leaders felt that war with the West was inevitable if not desirable. There were few moderating voices, especially after the Army Minister, Hideki Tojo, replaced the more moderate Prince Konoe as Prime Minister in October 1941. The Japanese proceeded with their war plan, while their diplomats continued negotiations in Washington to avoid military conflict. The Japanese war plan was ambitious and called for a near-simultaneous attack on Hong Kong, the Philippines, Malaya and the American naval base at Pearl Harbor. The aim was to destroy the US Pacific Fleet in one surprise strike, and quickly seize the South East Asian colonies of Britain (Hong Kong, Malaya and Singapore), the Netherlands (Dutch East Indies) and the United States (the Philippines), and to develop a strong defence of these captured territories. The expectation was that the Western powers would be forced to accept the Japanese conquest of South East Asia as a *fait accompli*.

The Americans were frustrated by the slow progress of the negotiations in Washington, and they had their doubts about Japanese sincerity, believing that the Japanese were just playing for time. As a result, the Americans issued a set of uncompromising demands, referred to as the Hull note, after Secretary of State Cordell Hull. The note was delivered to the Japanese on 28 November 1941. It called upon Japan to withdraw its troops from both China and French Indochina and to recognise the government of Chiang Kai-shek as the sole legitimate government in China. Japan may have been willing to agree to a withdrawal from Indochina in return for an American commitment to cease providing supplies to the Nationalist Chinese, but Japan would never have agreed to withdraw from China and Manchuria. It would have been too much of a humiliation, too much of a climbdown. Kase Toshikazu believed that the Hull note led to war in that it played into the hands of the hawkish militarists who were determined to go to war.

It is difficult to establish how active a role Emperor Hirohito played in the planning for war, and the decision to launch the surprise attack on Pearl Harbor. Many historians claim he urged caution and restraint, but in his constitutional role he could do little to hold back the belligerent and to some extent out-of-control military, whose men were determined to go to war and throw the Western powers out of Asia. He acquiesced and was perhaps surprised by the series of successes achieved by the Japanese military as they quickly overran Hong Kong, the Philippines, Malaya and

Singapore. To his subjects, Hirohito was seen as divine, a god-like person for whom many Japanese soldiers would willingly give up their lives. Many believed that to die for the Emperor was to live forever.

Back in January 1941, Hideki Tojo, then Army Minister, had issued a set of guidelines entitled *Instructions for the Battlefield* or in Japanese *Senjinkun*. This was a supplement to the *Imperial Rescript to Soldiers and Sailors* issued during the Meiji Restoration. The supplement was a pocket-sized leaflet issued to all soldiers, and it called on them to die as soldiers rather than accept the shame of surrender. It also instructed Japanese soldiery to show mercy to those who surrender. It seems that, for the most part, the first was obeyed, as relatively few Japanese soldiers surrendered. The second was ignored by many if not most units of the Japanese Army, as can be seen from the documented atrocities, and from the butchering of surrendered soldiers and civilians across China, Hong Kong and other parts of Asia. The Imperial Japanese Army was generally brutal and inhumane, but in battle their soldiers fought bravely and well. Lt-Colonel Masters, who fought against the Japanese in Burma, writing in *The Road Past Mandalay*, acknowledged their bravery, and those contrasting characteristics in the Japanese military psyche. A sense of honour, the way of the warrior, respect for valour, a willingness to give one's life, an appreciation of nature, of poetry and art, but all this combined with a ruthless and shocking brutality. Kase Toshikazu was considered to have been a moderate member of the Japanese wartime government, but he opposed calls made in 1995 for Japan to apologise for war crimes committed during the Second World War, insisting that Japan had played an important role in overcoming European colonialism in Asia. Some Japanese saw this as a justification for the war and believed that the atrocities were generally exaggerated. Many Japanese considered the war as a matter of survival and self-defence in the face of economic embargoes and containment. Denial, distortion, revisionism, and the perceived lack of genuine contriteness by Japan for its wartime aggression are still sensitive issues for many Asian countries today.

The origins of the Pacific War do not just go back to 1937 and the war with China, 1931 and the capture of Manchuria, nor 1922 and the Washington Treaties, but originate as far back as 1894 and that first war with Imperial China, and the subsequent kindling of territorial ambition in continental Asia. The growth of extremism, ultra-nationalism and militarism in the 1920s and 1930s, and the Japanese desire to free Asia from Western colonialism and replace it with a new order under Japanese leadership, led to the outbreak of total war in December 1941.

When units of the Japanese 23rd Army moved south towards the border of Hong Kong in the first week of December 1941, the die had already been cast. The decision to go to war had received the assent of the Emperor, and the Japanese combined fleet, under the command of Admiral Yamamoto, had already sailed from the Kuril Islands bound for Hawaii. Japan had not known military defeat; war had only brought success and territorial acquisition. However, the act of attacking the US Pacific fleet at Pearl Harbor, and thereby bringing America into the Second World War, whether inevitable or not, eventually led to the near-total destruction of both militarist Japan and Nazi Germany – and for many, but not all, liberation from oppression.

2

Hong Kong before the War
1936–1941

The First World War was thought to be the war to end all wars. Millions were killed, and nobody wanted to see such carnage again. The League of Nations was established in 1920 to maintain world peace through a combination of dispute arbitration, collective security, arms control and disarmament. The Washington Treaty, signed in 1922 by the victors of the First World War, was an attempt to prevent an arms race in the construction of battleships and aircraft carriers. Article 19 of the treaty imposed additional restrictions on Britain, America and Japan, under which each country agreed not to construct any new naval bases or fortifications in the Asia Pacific region. As a result, Britain refrained from adding fixed defences in Hong Kong between 1922 and 1936. After Japan renounced its obligations under the Washington Treaty in 1936, and after the outbreak of the Second Sino-Japanese War in 1937, Britain started to fortify Hong Kong. The Gin Drinkers Line (GDL) was constructed between 1936 and 1938. It was a defensive line that ran from Gin Drinkers Bay on the western side of the Kowloon Peninsula, along the line of hills, to Port Shelter on the eastern side of the peninsula. Some ninety pillboxes were constructed along this defensive line, which was also referred to as the inner line, with the frontier being referred to as the outer line. Artillery Observation Posts (AOPs) were built on dominant hilltops to enable observed, and therefore accurate, artillery fire to be brought to bear should enemy troops approach the inner line.

On the Island, a number of new coastal defence batteries were built and improvements made to existing batteries. Two new 9.2-inch coastal defence batteries were built at Stanley and at Bokhara on Cape D'Aguilar. Three new 6-inch coastal defence batteries were constructed at Cape Collinson, Chung Hom Kok and Jubilee, the latter situated

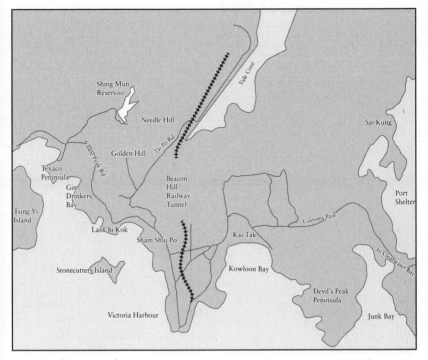

Kowloon Peninsula.

on the shoreline below Mount Davis. Two new 4-inch coastal defence batteries were constructed at Cape D'Aguilar and Aberdeen Island, and military roads were constructed to provide access to the artillery forts and batteries. Splinter-proof shelters, sometimes referred to as bomb-proof shelters, were constructed at battery and infantry positions. These reinforced concrete shelters were used as accommodation blocks, medical dressing stations, stores, and as company or platoon HQs. More than seventy beach defence pillboxes were constructed around the Island shoreline. Each had its own searchlight, called Lyon Lights. The Lyon Light had its own concrete structure and was usually positioned within 50 metres of the pillbox. In addition to the beach defence pillboxes, a number of line-of-gap pillboxes were constructed to defend the vital road passes located at gaps in the range of hills on the Island. Each pillbox generally had a crew of eight to ten men. The pillboxes, batteries, AOPs, platoon and company HQ shelters were equipped with telephone communications.

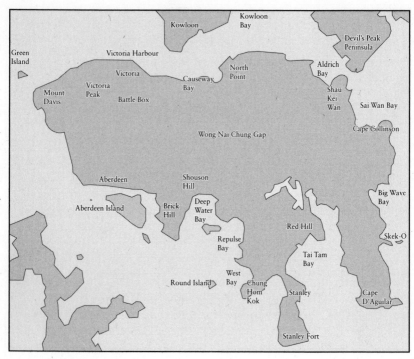

Hong Kong Island.

Outside the built-up urban areas, many of these pillboxes, Lyon Light structures, AOPs, battery buildings, gun emplacements and splinter-proof shelters still exist. Some of the AOPs have been converted into viewing platforms like those at High West, Stanley Mound and Jardine's Lookout. After the war squatters often occupied military structures, and many were bricked up by government authorities or demolished with explosives by the Army to prevent any kind of illegal occupation. Many of the trenches and weapons pits, although overgrown and partly filled in, can still be found in the hills. On the former battlefields, bullet casings, the remains of rusted rifles, bayonets, helmets, military water bottles, webbing buckles, and other similar military items can still be picked up. The headstamp on a bullet casing shows whether it was a British, Canadian or Japanese round. The type of imprint left by the firing pin shows whether the round was fired by a machine gun or by a rifle. The spent rounds indicate where fighting occurred. The precise location in which they are found demonstrates who was where on the battlefield, and the direction of fire. This type of field research helps our understanding of the Battle for Hong Kong.

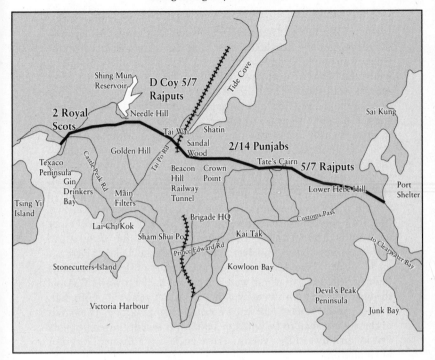

Approximate position of Gin Drinkers Line (GDL).

During the pre-war period when many of the fixed defences were being built, two large ammunition magazines were constructed; one was situated near the village of Little Hong Kong at Shouson Hill, and the other below Lye Mun Barracks at Shau Kei Wan. Some of the magazines at these two locations can still be seen today. The remaining magazines at Shouson Hill have been converted into wine cellars, whilst those at Lye Mun are hidden in the trees on one side of a busy road and remain in their original condition. The underground command post known as the Battle Box, from where the military commander directed the Battle for Hong Kong, was constructed deep below the Military HQ building in Victoria Barracks.

By 1941, although a lot of work had been undertaken in the construction of fixed defences, there were significant weaknesses, most notably the lack of naval and air assets. In the 1938 Defence Plan it was envisaged that the defence of Hong Kong would be limited to denying the enemy access to the harbour. The defence plan called for the military to occupy the inner line for as long as possible, after which they would evacuate south to the Island, which they would hold to deny the Japanese the advantages of the harbour. Hong Kong had been downgraded to the status of an outpost; a delaying action would be fought on the Mainland, whilst the Island was expected to hold out for a period of up to three months until relieved by British forces from Singapore. The defence priorities in the Far East were Singapore and Malaya. Hong Kong was considered too close to Japanese forces in China, and it was within the range of Japanese aircraft bases in Southern China and Formosa.

In July 1939, the Hong Kong Government, following the lead of the British Government, issued a Compulsory Service Order requiring all British male subjects of European descent between the ages of eighteen and fifty-five to register for military service. Those registered formed what became known as the Hong Kong Defence Reserve. The ordinance was enacted several weeks before Britain and France declared war on Germany. Those British subjects not of European extraction were free to volunteer, as indeed many did, but they were not made subject to the compulsory order. A number of British expatriate businessmen, some of whom were veterans of the First World War and the Boer War, and who were over the combatant age-limit of fifty-five, joined a special guard unit known as the Hughes Group. The oldest of these gentlemen to be killed in action was seventy-seven-year-old Private Sir Edward Des Voeux, whose uncle was a former Governor of Hong Kong.

The Defence Reserve was divided into three categories. The first was the 'combatant group', which consisted of British men of military age who were allocated to either the Hong Kong Volunteer Defence Corp (HKVDC) or the Hong Kong Royal Naval Volunteer Reserve (HKRNVR). The second category was the 'key-post group', for those who were in roles considered vital for the normal functioning of the colony. The Governor, Sir Geoffrey Northcote, explained in his introduction of the legislation that this was akin to what was described in the United Kingdom as 'reserved occupations'. In the event of mobilisation, the members of this group would be required to remain at their civil posts. The third category was described as the 'general group' and was comprised of those already in essential services, such as those already acting as members of the Special Constabulary, Auxiliary Fire Service or other such services.

The HKVDC had grown into a sizeable force, and by 1941 consisted of five batteries and seven infantry companies, in addition to specialist units like Armoured Cars, Engineers, Signals and Army Service Corp. The number of personnel, excluding the Nursing Detachment, was approximately 1,700 officers and men, although estimates of the mobilised size of the force vary because of switching from the combatant group to the key-post group and in some cases because of failure to mobilise. The infantry companies were generally formed around national groups. No. 1 Coy was made up primarily of British expatriate businessmen, No. 2 Coy was mainly Scottish, No. 3 Coy was Eurasian, Nos 4 and 7 Coy were Chinese, and Nos 5 and 6 Coy were Portuguese. Many Hong Kong residents of all nationalities including Russian, French, Portuguese and local Chinese volunteered for military service. Hong Kong Chinese served not only with the HKVDC and HKRNVR, but many also served in the regular British Army. In 1941, a machine gun battalion, the Hong Kong Chinese Regiment, was formed and recruited entirely from the local Chinese community. When war broke out, the first batch of recruits had been enlisted, but they were still undergoing basic training; nonetheless, the unit fought throughout the Battle for Hong Kong.

In the summer of 1940, during a period of increased tension with Japan, the Hong Kong Government, acting on instructions from the War Cabinet in London, ordered British women and children to evacuate Hong Kong and relocate to Australia. This order excluded many government employees and others who were involved in essential services, which included nursing. Many women had already joined the volunteer nursing services when war with Germany broke out in September 1939. Many women subsequently joined the Nursing Detachment (ND) of the HKVDC, or the Auxiliary Nursing Service (ANS), in order to be permitted to remain in Hong Kong. On mobilisation, members of the Nursing Detachment of the HKVDC, also known as the Voluntary Aid Detachment (VAD), were assigned to military hospitals, and the ANS nurses to civilian hospitals.

The families of regular members of the armed services were evacuated on Monday 1 July 1940. A second group of British women and children were evacuated on Friday 5 July. In total over 3,400 women and children were evacuated in the first week of July. The evacuees were sent firstly to Manila, and then in most cases on to Australia. A lot of women who were eligible to leave, and should have left, found ways to remain in Hong Kong, some by simply not registering and others by claiming they were running their own business, for which there was an exemption. Others claimed that they had made their own travel arrangements. After a while, the threat of war dissipated, and there was considerable protest both from the wives who had been evacuated to Australia and the husbands who wanted their families to return to Hong Kong. Many people felt that the evacuation had been unnecessary, and complained that the process for exemption was unfair. There were regular and heated protest meetings right up until the start of war. The government announced, in

November 1940, that there would be no further compulsory evacuations, and some two hundred people who had been served compulsory orders were allowed to remain, but those who had already been evacuated were not allowed to return to Hong Kong.

Hilda, the wife of Doctor Selwyn Selwyn-Clarke, the Director of Medical Services, avoided compulsory evacuation by going to Macau on the day registration took place. The wife and daughter of Thomas King, the Commissioner of Police, had also remained in Hong Kong. These and many similar cases caused a great deal of resentment among those who had complied, albeit reluctantly, with the ordinance. Marjorie Elston, the wife of a senior police officer in Hong Kong, wrote a letter in July 1941 to Prime Minister Winston Churchill appealing for his help in allowing them to return to their homes in Hong Kong. A copy of her handwritten letter can be found in the National Archives at Kew. She writes that she had to give up a good job and leave what she regarded as her home to live in a place where she did not feel at home. Although British, she had been born in Hong Kong and had lived there for most of her life. In the letter she is very critical of the Hong Kong Government, citing the fact that the wives of many senior government officials remained in Hong Kong; some, she claimed, by getting jobs in the Government Censor's office, and others by claiming they were nurses. Three hundred women were allowed to remain because they were supposedly running their own business, and while a number of women did own shops, restaurants, and hotels, the total number of British women running their own business would have been far fewer than three hundred. When Major-General Christopher Maltby, the Military Commander, and Sir Mark Young, the Governor, arrived to take up their assignments in Hong Kong in 1941, they came without their wives and families to set an example and comply with the 1940 ordinance.

In the period before the war, a considerable amount of work had been undertaken in respect of civil defence. This work included the construction of air raid tunnels, communal kitchens and food stores. Plans and procedures were drawn up for billeting, transport pools, food distribution, relief hospitals and other such civil defence preparations. Everybody had a role to play in the event of hostilities, and all those who had not joined the Volunteers were involved in some form of civil defence. However, there was still an air of complacency among many in the civilian community. This may have been because the threat of war had been hanging over Hong Kong since Japanese troops first arrived on the border in 1938. There had been periodic increases in tension, but nothing had happened, and so such situations were sometimes dismissed as just another flap, or it was felt that the Japanese were blustering. The precautionary period, during which the military and civil defence were to be mobilised and readied for war, was expected to last a week, but in the event they had just one day. The precautionary period, or state of emergency, was announced on Sunday 7 December, and the war started early the next day.

While serving as Governor, Sir Geoffrey Northcote had at one stage recommended to London that all troops be withdrawn from Hong Kong in the hope of avoiding a Japanese attack on the colony. This was firmly opposed by Major-General Grasett, the Military Commander, who was pressing for more troops to defend Hong Kong. Winston Churchill realised that Hong Kong could not be defended, nor relieved once attacked. He acknowledged this in January 1941 when, in response to a request for reinforcements made by Grasett, he stated in a memorandum that he would rather reduce the number of troops in Hong Kong than deploy more.

> If Japan goes to war with us, there is not the slightest chance of holding Hong Kong or relieving it. It is most unwise to increase the loss we shall suffer there. Instead of increasing the garrison it ought to be reduced to a symbolical scale... We must avoid frittering away our resources on untenable positions... Whether there are two or six battalions at Hong Kong will make no difference. I wish we had fewer troops there, but to move any would be noticeable and dangerous.[1]

Hong Kong was increasingly viewed as a strategic liability. Instead of reinforcing Hong Kong, there had been a policy of draining officers and senior NCOs from Hong Kong to help the war effort by transferring them to other, more important theatres of war. This had a very debilitating effect on the infantry battalions in Hong Kong.

Churchill's view that Hong Kong could not be defended accounts for the paucity of naval and air assets. The RAF in Hong Kong consisted of just five obsolete biplanes that were no match for contemporary fighter aircraft. The Royal Navy included three First World War destroyers, two of which left for Singapore on the first day of the war, and one of which had been converted to a mine-laying role. There were eight motor torpedo boats and four river gunboats, one of which was in dry dock, and there was an assortment of converted tugs and launches that were used for minesweeping and patrolling but of little use militarily. There was a critical shortage of both 2-inch and 3-inch mortars to support the infantry. The Army had virtually no radio communication and relied on telephone lines, which were often cut by mortar and artillery fire; in such cases, they relied on runners and dispatch riders, who were often killed before they could deliver a message.

There was one area of Hong Kong's defences that was both formidable and effective, and that was coastal defence. The coastal defence consisted of three batteries of powerful long-range 9.2-inch guns. These were located on the south side of the Island at Fort Bokhara, Fort Davis and Stanley Fort. In addition, there were a number of 6-inch and 4-inch coastal defence batteries located at intervals along the Island's southern shoreline. The arc of fire provided by these coastal defence batteries covered all the seaward approaches to Hong Kong.

The approaches were also protected by underwater indicator loops. These were cables laid on the seabed that could detect the movement of an enemy ship or submarine. The seaward approaches were further protected with both contact minefields, in which mines detonate on impact with a vessel, and controlled minefields, in which mines could be detonated by remote control from mine-watching stations ashore.

This combination of coastal defence batteries, indicator loops and minefields ensured that the Imperial Japanese Navy stayed well back throughout the coming battle. The big guns, like those in Singapore, were pointing out to sea because they had been installed for coastal defence rather than landward defence. Some of the guns were able to traverse and fire inland, which they did to good effect, but it was not what they were designed for, and most of the shells were armour piercing, suitable for engaging enemy ships but much less effective when used against enemy infantry.

Initially, there were four regular infantry battalions based in Hong Kong consisting of two British battalions – 2nd Bn Royal Scots and 1st Bn Middlesex Regiment – and two Indian battalions – 5th Bn 7th Rajput Regiment and 2nd Bn 14th Punjab Regiment. In November 1941, the garrison was bolstered by the arrival of two Canadian infantry battalions and a Brigade HQ. The infantry battalions consisted of the 1st Bn Winnipeg Grenadiers (WG) based at Manitoba in central Canada, and the 1st Bn Royal Rifles of Canada (RRC) based in French-speaking Quebec. The Canadian infantry brigade, known as 'C' Force, consisted of some 2,000 men. The force was commanded by fifty-five-year-old Brigadier John Lawson, a veteran of the First World War.

The Canadian soldiers made an impressive sight as they disembarked from the troopship TSS *Awatea* and the armed merchant cruiser HMCS *Prince Robert*. The two battalions marched up Nathan Road to their barracks at Sham Shui Po, with Major-General Maltby taking the salute during the march-past. The sight of so many Canadian soldiers coming to reinforce the garrison did much to improve morale among both the civilian and the military community. However, these two battalions were not fully trained. Before being posted to Hong Kong, Brigadier Lawson had served as Director of Training and had been asked to analyse the training and combat readiness of the Canadian infantry battalions. There were three categories: 'A' meant highly trained and combat ready, 'B' meant intermediate, and 'C' indicated troops were not fully trained and not ready for combat. The two Canadian battalions selected for service in Hong Kong fell into category 'C'. Prior to their deployment to Hong Kong, they had been undertaking garrison duties in Jamaica (Winnipeg Grenadiers) and Newfoundland (Royal Rifles of Canada). 'C' Force left Vancouver without their transport, which consisted of some 200 vehicles including trucks, Bren gun carriers and motorcycles. These were sent on another ship that left a week later and failed to reach Hong Kong before hostilities erupted.

Perhaps it was thought that the Canadian force's garrison experience would be appropriate for Hong Kong, where they would be performing a similar role. The best-trained Canadian troops could then be kept for combat roles in the more important theatres of war in Europe and North Africa. Although they were being sent to defend Hong Kong against the possibility of a Japanese attack, many still believed that war would be averted, and few people thought that it would come very soon. It was thought that the two Canadian battalions would have time to train after their arrival in Hong Kong, but in fact they would not have enough time for weapons training, nor would they get the chance to sufficiently familiarise themselves with the terrain and topography of the Island. War broke out just three weeks after their arrival.

There might have been some pre-war discussions with the Chinese Nationalist Government about a coordinated counterattack if the Japanese were to attack Hong Kong. Lt-Col Harry Owen-Hughes, HKVDC, was sent to Chungking on one of the last evacuation flights out of Kai Tak to liaise with the Nationalist Government, which no doubt included discussions on Chinese military assistance to Hong Kong. Maltby wrote in his Report on Operations that Admiral Chan Chak, Head of the Chinese Nationalist Government Liaison Office in Hong Kong, had reported that General Yu Han Mou had radioed a message on 20 December that his 60,000 troops were close to the border at Sham Chun. On hearing this news, Maltby issued the following message to all British and Dominion troops in Hong Kong:

There are indications that Chinese forces are advancing towards the frontier to our aid. All ranks must, therefore, hold their positions at all costs and look forward to only a few more days of strain.[2]

There was no Chinese Army near the border, and the reality was that the Hong Kong garrison would fight a losing battle with no prospect of relief. After their surrender, many would feel they had been lied to.

Professor David Macri, in his book *Clash of Empires in South China*, writes that he believes there was a plan for the Chinese Nationalist Army to come to the aid of Hong Kong. However, when the Chinese High Command saw that Wong Nai Chung Gap, a strategically important central point on the Island, had been lost within twelve hours of the Japanese landings, they realised that the Battle for Hong Kong was all but over, and turned their attention elsewhere. The Japanese kept a large number of troops in reserve across the border in case the Chinese attacked from the rear.

Given Churchill's view that Hong Kong could not be defended, it is surprising that the two Canadian battalions were dispatched to Hong Kong in November 1941, and that there were mooted plans to add a squadron of fighter aircraft. No doubt the senior officers like Major-General Grasett, Military Commander in Hong Kong from 1938 to 1941, and his boss, Air Chief Marshal Sir Robert Brooke-Popham, Commander-in-Chief Far East from 1940 to 1941, were very persuasive, and perhaps the numbers of reinforcements were seen as modest in comparison with the reinforcements already made for the defence of Malaya and Singapore. Perhaps the fact they were being sent from Canada, rather than drawing on stretched British resources, helped sway the decision. Churchill must have been only too aware that while the addition of two infantry battalions would prolong resistance and boost morale in Hong Kong, it would not affect the final outcome. Macri states that the decision was made for geopolitical reasons rather than military ones. It was a show of support to the Nationalist Chinese and also to the Russians, who were facing a devastating attack from Nazi Germany and were concerned about the possibility of a Japanese strike northwards into Siberia. It was also a signal to the Americans that Britain was serious about the Far East theatre, rather than just focusing on the war in Europe, the Atlantic, the Mediterranean and North Africa, which was, of course, Britain's primary focus. The official thinking still seemed to be that if it came to war, Hong Kong would have to be sacrificed, but not without a fight.

There was a large Japanese expatriate population in Hong Kong before the war, variously estimated at around two thousand people, with many working for Japanese shipping companies, trading firms and hotels. Many of them left the colony a few days before war commenced. A large group sailed for Canton, by way of Macau, on the *Shirogane Maru*. By the time war started there were only fifty Japanese nationals left in Hong Kong, and they were quickly rounded up for internment. Five Japanese men were arrested at the Macau ferry terminal on the first day of the war while belatedly trying to escape to neutral Macau. Many of these Japanese nationals had been mobilised for some years, eavesdropping on conversations and feeding back information to Colonel Suzuki, in charge of Military Intelligence at the Japanese Consulate. The work of these Japanese civilian spies was augmented by Chinese fifth columnists, who had also been put to work gathering information and preparing to engage in disruptive strategies once war started.

The fifth columnists included Chinese from Japanese-occupied Manchuria and Formosa, and supporters of Wang Jing-wei, the man who lost the power struggle with Chiang Kai-shek for the KMT leadership. In 1938, following the destruction of Nanking, Wang Jing-wei had advocated a negotiated settlement with the Japanese. In 1940, he was appointed as Head of State for what became known as the Reorganised National Government of China, which was based in Nanking. This resulted in there being two competing Nationalist Chinese states, one supported by the Americans and the British under Chiang Kai-shek, and the other supported by the Japanese under Wang Jing-wei. History has generally condemned Wang as a traitor who collaborated with the Japanese, but Wang's supporters believed that he collaborated to make life easier for the Chinese and to try to save lives in what was an unwinnable war. The Chinese community in Hong Kong was divided, with many supporting the Nationalist Government in Chungking under Chiang Kai-shek, and therefore by extension the British, but others supported the competing government set up by the Japanese in Nanking under Wang. As America gained the upper hand in the Pacific, Wang's position in China became increasingly difficult. He died in Japan in November 1944, where he had gone to seek medical treatment. The Japanese alienated many of the local Chinese in Hong Kong, and elsewhere, by their brutality, and because of this they missed out on the opportunity that they initially had to create broader Chinese support for the new order in Asia.

The Japanese were well organised and had gathered detailed information about British military dispositions, including numbers, barracks, gun sites, warships and aircraft. When the Japanese crossed the frontier into Hong Kong, they were equipped with accurate maps showing British fixed defences. The fifth columnists had been instructed to start their programme of disruption and sabotage ahead of the Japanese invasion. The police war diary records that a series of fifth column incidents, including bomb explosions, started soon after midnight in the early hours of Monday 8 December. During the subsequent battle, they sabotaged vehicles, slashed tyres, damaged engines, mixed sand with rice, and put kerosene in fire water-buckets. Many were armed, and there were several incidents of sniping at British troops, and reports of signalling to the Japanese from the upper floors and rooftops of buildings. When fifth columnists were caught, they were summarily shot without trial.

Before all this, on Saturday 6 December, a fundraising ball was held at the Peninsula Hotel to raise money for the war effort in Europe. The ball was attended by the Governor, Sir Mark Young. The guests included Madame Sun Yat-sen and her sister Madame Kung. At one stage during the evening the music stopped and Thomas Wilson, the Head of American President Lines, made an announcement that all ships' officers and crews should immediately report for duty on board their respective ships. The following day, many ships left harbour including the SS *Ulysses*. One of the passengers on the *Ulysses* was fifty-four-year-old Norman Lockhart Smith, the Colonial Secretary. He was retiring from the Colonial Administration and returning to England with his nineteen-year-old daughter Rachel, who was engaged to Lt Alec Kennedy, a young RNVR officer serving in the MTB (motor torpedo boat) Flotilla. Smith's successor as Colonial Secretary, Franklin Gimson, arrived that weekend on the SS *Soochow*, a 2,000-ton coaster which sailed between Rangoon and China with port calls at Singapore and Hong Kong. The ship had a small number of passenger cabins, and Gimson, anxious to take up his new duties, had boarded the ship in Singapore little realising that the *Soochow* was making her last journey and that Hong Kong would be at war on Monday morning.

While the *Ulysses* was sailing towards Manila on Monday 8 December, her captain, James Russell, heard by radio that war had broken out and that Manila was already under attack. He decided to change course for Singapore, and while heading south the ship was bombed and strafed by Japanese aircraft. Fortunately, there was little damage and nobody was injured, and the ship reached Singapore without further incident. After making repairs, they took on board a large number of women and children evacuees and then sailed to Australia. It was in Australia that Rachel Smith eventually learnt that her fiancé, Alec Kennedy, had escaped from Hong Kong on Christmas Day with the crews of the five surviving MTBs and had reached safety in Free China. The journey home took the *Ulysses* through the Panama Canal and up the Atlantic coast of Florida, where she was involved in a collision with a Panamanian tanker. As a result of damage incurred in the collision, she had to reduce speed, which made her an easy target for German U-boats. Her luck would run out on 11 April 1942, when she was torpedoed and sunk by *U-160* off the coast of South Carolina. She sank slowly, allowing the crew and passengers to abandon ship safely. The USS *Manley*, an American destroyer, rescued the crew and passengers and brought them to Charleston, South Carolina. After escaping from Hong Kong in the nick of time, being bombed, strafed, damaged in a collision and then sunk by a German U-boat, Rachel and her father finally reached home after what had been a truly eventful journey.

On Sunday morning, whilst *Ulysses* was steaming away from Hong Kong, Major-General Maltby was attending the morning service at St John's Cathedral. He read the lesson and returned to his pew. An orderly entered the cathedral and handed the general a written message regarding Japanese troop movements and their proximity to the border. Maltby and several senior officers left immediately. A meeting of the Defence Council was convened, and a state of emergency was declared. The Volunteers were mobilised, and civil defence activated.

Major Charles Boxer was in charge of the joint-services intelligence-gathering unit known as the Far East Combined Bureau (FECB). It had been established in Hong Kong in March 1935. One of its primary functions was intercepting radio traffic from Japanese, Chinese and Russian sources. In 1939, the FECB moved to Singapore because of the perceived risk of a Japanese invasion of Hong Kong. A skeleton staff was left in Hong Kong including Japanese linguists Major Boxer, Wing Commander Alf Bennett and Squadron Leader Max Oxford. On Sunday evening, Boxer and his partner Emily Hahn had been entertaining a small number of guests for cocktails and dinner at Boxer's apartment in the Mid-Levels. Boxer had been in uniform and spent most of the evening sitting by the wireless listening to Japanese radio broadcasts. During the early hours, he went to his office at the Battle Box. At 0445 hours Boxer was listening to Radio Tokyo when the music was interrupted by a coded announcement that units of the Japanese Navy and Air Force were attacking American and British forces in the Pacific.

Some two hours after the attack on Pearl Harbor, the Japanese issued a formal declaration of war signed by Emperor Hirohito, declaring war on the United States of America and the British Empire. China was blamed for provoking Japan, and Britain and the United States were accused of supporting the regime in Chungking, and for seeking dominance in Asia, and for threatening the very existence of Japan with trade embargoes. The collision course between Japan and the West had been determined many years previously and was fuelled in the same way as it was in Germany and Italy by that combination of extreme nationalism and militarism. These three countries were focused on territorial expansion through military conquest, with the aim of creating a new order, in both Europe and Asia, based on racial supremacy and authoritarian control. As of 8 December 1941, the world was at war, and the Battle for Hong Kong began.

3

Battle on the Mainland
8–12 December

Early on the morning of Monday 8 December 1941, Major-General Maltby moved into the underground bunker known as the Battle Box. It was situated under the military headquarters building in Victoria Barracks, and by all accounts was an oppressing place with its musty air, dim lighting, small rooms and narrow corridors. It was from this claustrophobic underground bunker that Maltby commanded his forces in the Battle for Hong Kong. He was fifty years old, a veteran of the First World War, and had served in the Indian Army throughout his career. He was appointed to the role of General Officer Commanding (GOC) British Troops in China in August 1941, just four months before the outbreak of war. His HQ was referred to as HQ China Command, or simply as Fortress HQ. Maltby knew that the most likely direction of attack would be from across the border and into the New Territories, but he had to defend the territory from a possible seaborne invasion, or a combination of both. This meant he could not concentrate his troops and had to disperse them widely. The infantry was comprised of two brigades: the Island Brigade, commanded by Brigadier John Lawson, and the Mainland Brigade, commanded by Brigadier Cedric Wallis.

The Mainland Brigade had been at their war stations on the Gin Drinkers Line (GDL) since mid-November, familiarising themselves with their positions, digging weapons pits, laying wire entanglements and generally improving their defences. At 0545 hours on Monday morning, Brigadier Wallis received a phone call from Colonel Newnham, GSO-1 at Fortress HQ, to inform him that war with Japan was imminent. The brigade staff officers were quickly notified. They included Major Harland, 2 R/S, as Brigade Major; Captain Belton, Yorks & Lancs Regiment, as Staff Captain; and Captain Billings, Royal Canadian Corps of Signals, as Brigade Signals Officer.

At 0610 hours, Maltby telephoned Wallis personally and told him that it was now officially confirmed that they were at war with Japan. Wallis was forty-four years old. He had arrived in Hong Kong a year earlier as commanding officer of the 5th Battalion of the 7th Rajput Regiment with the rank of Lt-Colonel. He had been promoted to brigadier on taking command of the newly formed Mainland Brigade. The brigade consisted of three infantry battalions, including 2nd Bn Royal Scots, commanded by Lt-Col Simon White; 5th Bn 7th Rajput Regiment, commanded by Lt-Col Roger Cadogan-Rawlinson; and 2nd Bn 14th Punjab Regiment, commanded by Lt-Col Gerald Kidd. Additional troops at the brigadier's disposal during the fighting on the Mainland included 'D' Coy, Winnipeg Grenadiers, attached on 10 December as a reserve company; No. 1 Coy, HKVDC, providing defence at and around Kai Tak Airfield; the Hong Kong Chinese Regiment, providing local defence at Brigade HQ; and the Armoured Car Platoon of the HKVDC.

Mobile artillery was provided by three batteries of the 1st Hong Kong Regiment, Hong Kong and Singapore Royal Artillery (HKSRA). The three batteries consisted of the 1st Mountain Battery, 2nd Mountain Battery and 25th Medium Battery equipped with sixteen howitzers deployed as set out below:

- One troop of four 6-inch howitzers towed by Army Scammell trucks. This troop from 25th Medium Battery was under the command of Major Temple. Two guns were positioned at the polo ground on Prince Edward Road, and two were placed further forward near Tai Wai. They utilised the AOP on Golden Hill.
- One troop of four 4.5-inch howitzers towed by hired vehicles. This troop from 2nd Mountain Battery was under the command of Major Crowe. Two guns were positioned forward at Tai Wai, and two guns at the filter beds, known as Main Filters, situated at the southern end of Tai Po Road. They utilised the AOPs at Shing Mun Redoubt and Texaco Peninsula.
- Two troops each consisting of four 3.7-inch howitzers, which were transported by pack mule. One troop from 1st Mountain Battery, under the command of Major de Vere Hunt, with four guns was positioned at Customs Pass, on the right flank, utilising AOPs at Lower Hebe Hill and Tate's Cairn. One troop from 2nd Mountain Battery, under the command of Major Crowe, with two guns forward at Tai Wai and two at Main Filters utilising AOPs at Crown Point and Sandal Wood.

Additional firepower was provided by the 4.5-inch and 6-inch howitzer batteries on the Island, and by the 9.2-inch coastal defence guns at

Stanley, Bokhara and Mount Davis, and from three 6-inch guns and two 60-pounders located on Stonecutters Island. The gunboat HMS *Cicala*, armed with two 6-inch guns and one 3-inch gun, provided naval firepower in support of the infantry on the west flank.

The GDL ran from the west side to the east side of the Kowloon Peninsula, covering a front of approximately 10 miles. It was not a continuous fortified line like the Maginot Line; instead, it consisted of three battalion areas and, within those, company and platoon positions. It had depth as well as breadth. The defensive line included pillboxes, slit trenches, weapons pits, minefields and barbed-wire entanglements. The Royal Scots were deployed on the left flank of the GDL, the Punjab battalion occupied the centre, and the Rajputs held the right flank. Three understrength battalions were insufficient to defend a frontage of that length, and as a result, there were gaps between the battalion positions, and between company and platoon positions. Commanders tried to cover gaps through interlocking fire as best they could. The largest gap was that between the Royal Scots sector, on the left flank, and the Punjab sector in the centre. Wallis addressed this by moving 'D' Coy, 5/7 Rajputs, from the right flank to a position between the Royal Scots and the Punjab sector. 2/Lt Douglas Baird, 2/RS, recalled there being a gap of half a mile between his platoon located in the centre of 'B' Coy's section of the GDL and the platoons on his left and right.

On the right flank of the Royal Scots sector was the strongpoint known as the Shing Mun Redoubt. It was built on high ground above Jubilee Reservoir. The redoubt consisted of a series of pillboxes and open-air firing bays linked by concrete tunnels. It was defended by No. 8 Platoon, 'A' Coy, 2/RS, under the command of 2/Lt Jack Thomson. 'A' Coy was commanded by Captain Cyril ('Potato') Jones, who had established his Coy HQ in the AOP located above and behind the redoubt, and connected to it by the network of tunnels.

On Monday morning, the Mainland Brigade staff moved into their temporary Brigade HQ at Jubilee Buildings in Sham Shui Po Barracks. This temporary HQ was used briefly during the morning while Mainland Brigade Battle HQ, at the northern end of Waterloo Road in an area known as Kowloon Tong, was being readied for use and hurriedly connected to telephone, water and electricity. The temporary HQ was immediately a hive of activity as the brigade staff went about their duties. The infantry battalions, at their battle positions on the GDL, were informed of the outbreak of war. The Royal Engineers commenced the task of blowing up roads leading from the border, including bridges, and cuttings, to delay the Japanese advance towards the GDL.

Air Raid on Kai Tak

The Pan Am Sikorsky S-42 flying boat, known as the *Hong Kong Clipper*, was moored alongside the jetty at the western end of the airfield. Captain Fred Ralph and his crew were getting ready for the early-morning run to Manila. The Kai Tak Airport manager, forty-three-year-old Albert ('Papa') Moss, had tried to persuade Ralph to take off immediately, but the Pan Am Manila office had sent a wireless message advising them not to come. Something was wrong, so Ralph called his boss, William Bond, the Manager of China National Aviation Corporation (CNAC), which was part of the Pan Am Group. William Bond was staying at the scenic Repulse Bay Hotel on the south side of the Island, Ralph quickly explained the dilemma and Bond told him to go back to Papa Moss and find out what was really happening. A short while later, Ralph called Bond back and told him that war had started. Bond told Ralph not to take off, and to get the passengers and crew off the airfield.

On the Island, forty-year-old Canadian stockbroker Benny Proulx was up early riding a horse at Happy Valley. Proulx had been in the Far East for most of his adult life. He had been mobilised in 1939 as a Warrant Officer in the HKRNVR. He was married to Florence Ryder, who had been born in Hong Kong and was of Irish descent. Her stepfather, Albert Simmons, and her mother, Delores, although retired, had continued to live in Hong Kong. Their home was a beautiful villa, named Erinville, at Turtle Cove on the south side of Hong Kong Island. Proulx's early morning ride was disturbed by the noise of aircraft engines. He looked up to see Japanese bombers and fighter formations, and a little later he heard the sound of bombs and gunfire. After the air raid, he arranged for Florence and his two sons, Michael and Roger, to move from their flat in Kowloon to Erinville. He then rushed off to his post at the naval mine control station at Chung Hom Kok.

Forty-nine-year-old Jan Marsman, a Dutch-born US citizen who ran Marsman & Co, a large mining, engineering and construction company with Asian headquarters in Manila, had arrived in Hong Kong on the Pan Am Clipper on 2 December for what he thought would be a short business trip. He expected to be back at home in San Francisco with his wife and family in time for Christmas. He was staying at the Hong Kong Hotel and was scheduled to fly to Manila on the Clipper that Monday morning. The passengers were to board the airport bus outside the Pan Am offices at the Peninsula Hotel on Kowloon side. On Sunday night, the hotels had been asked to wake the Clipper passengers early because the flight departure time had been brought forward by one hour. The Hong Kong Hotel reception desk failed to call Marsman, and when he did wake up, he had to rush to the Peninsula Hotel on the other side of the harbour where the bus was being held for him. The other passengers, having been kept waiting for so long, gave him irritated looks as he clambered aboard the bus with his luggage. Hardly had he sat down when a Pam Am employee anxiously instructed the passengers to get off the bus, saying that the flight had been delayed. The passengers went back to the lobby of the Peninsula Hotel wondering why there was a delay. One of the passengers said that he had heard that war had started in the Far East. He was chastised by the other passengers for spreading such alarmist suggestions, but the man was right: Pearl Harbor had been attacked a few hours earlier, and at approximately 0800 hours Kai Tak was attacked and the Clipper destroyed. Had it not been for Marsman's unintended tardiness, they might all have been killed.

Wing Commander Humphrey ('Ginger') Sullivan was still settling into his new role as commanding officer of the RAF station at Kai Tak. He had arrived in Hong Kong on 30 November to replace Group Captain Thomas ('Horrid') Horry, who was being transferred to a new role with the RAF in Singapore. Horry had left Hong Kong the previous day as a passenger on the ill-fated SS *Ulysses*, which was scheduled to stop at Manila and Singapore. The RAF station in Hong Kong was expected to be reinforced with a squadron of fighter aircraft from Singapore, and Pilot Officer Francis Hennessy had been transferred from Singapore to help set up a Fighter Operations Room at Kai Tak in preparation for the arrival of the new aircraft. When Japanese aircraft first appeared over Hong Kong, some people thought they were the squadron of Buffalo Brewsters expected from Singapore. Maltby stated that the number of Japanese aircraft involved in the attack on Kai Tak numbered thirty-six fighters and twelve bombers. The raid on Kai Tak was achieved with complete surprise, and four out of the five RAF aircraft were destroyed. The *Hong Kong Clipper* was set ablaze and burnt down to the water line. A number of commercial aircraft were also destroyed including two CNAC DC-2s, three Curtiss Condors leased to CNAC, and three Junkers operated by Eurasia Aviation Corporation. After the raid, the airfield was littered with damaged and burning aircraft. The two RAF Walrus amphibious aircraft were sunk at their moorings. One of the three RAF Vildebeest aircraft was destroyed, one was severely damaged, and one escaped all but minor damage. The one remaining serviceable aircraft was not used again and was subsequently put of out of action when the RAF evacuated Kai Tak two days later. The loss of the five obsolete RAF aircraft on the first day of the war made no difference to the outcome of the battle. The RAF contingent was later put to use in radio communications and light anti-aircraft defence, and used in infantry roles to support the Army on the Island.

During the attack, some of the Japanese aircraft bombed and strafed Sham Shui Po Barracks. Captain Peter Belton, Mainland Brigade Staff Captain, recalled in his personal diary that there were around eight direct hits on Jubilee Buildings, with two immediately above Brigade HQ, and that more bombs fell in the barracks area. Captain Belton had been on his way to obtain transport from the Vehicle Collection Centre (VCC) in Kowloon for the move by Brigade HQ from Jubilee Buildings to Waterloo Road. He was just leaving Jubilee Buildings when the air raid commenced. He took cover on the ground floor until the raid was over, and then made his way to the VCC, narrowly missing a second air raid on the barracks. In his diary, he wrote of the difficulty in getting any form of motor transport from the vehicle pool.

Difficulty experienced in obtaining MT, crowds of Chinese around the VCC office and the officer in charge appeared to mistrust me; eventually obtained one staff car, one truck and drivers at the point of a revolver from a group standing idle in Nathan Road. Returned to Sham Shui Po where the HQ staff, of three NCOs and six clerks and orderlies, was ready for deployment to Waterloo Road.[1]

The Imperial Japanese Army Cross the Border into Hong Kong

The 23rd Army, consisting of four infantry divisions, with its HQ in Canton, under the command of Lt-General Sakai Takashi, had overall responsibility for the capture of Hong Kong. Sakai assigned the 38th Division, commanded by Lt-General Sano Tadayoshi, to lead the attack. The 38th Division consisted of three infantry regiments and had a total strength of approximately 13,000 men. The three regiments were made up of the 228th Regiment, commanded by Colonel Doi; the 229th Regiment, commanded by Colonel Tanaka; and the 230th Regiment, commanded by Colonel Shoji. Each regiment comprised three infantry battalions, a signals company and a light artillery company. Each battalion consisted of approximately 1,000 men. In addition to the three infantry regiments, the 38th Division included an artillery regiment, an engineer regiment, a transport regiment, a medical unit and a signals unit. The Japanese invasion force also included the 1st Artillery Group, commanded by Major-General Kitajima. This unit, which numbered approximately 6,000 men, consisted of a number of specialist artillery regiments equipped with 240mm and 150mm howitzers, 100mm and 150mm cannons, 75mm mountain guns and heavy mortars. There are varying estimates of the size of the Japanese force that attacked Hong Kong, some of which suggest that up to 50,000 troops were deployed.

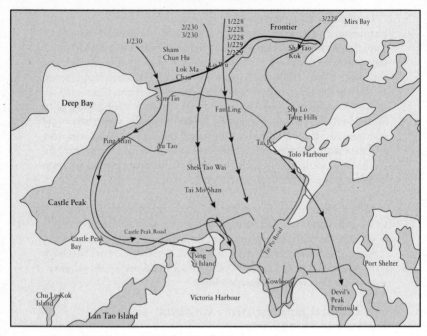

Direction of Japanese advance from the frontier.

It is difficult to be precise, and it depends whether one includes rear-guard troops stationed across the border, but in any event it was not less than 25,000 including Army, Air Force, Marines and Naval units. The 38th Division and the 1st Artillery Group consisted of around 19,000 men. The British forces, including the Royal Navy, Royal Marines, RAF and the Volunteers, numbered approximately 12,500 men.[2]

The 38th Division began its move south on 28 November. They moved at night to avoid their deployment being observed. By 6 December, Japanese advance troops were positioned just across the border at the village of Sham Chun Hu, now the modern city of Shenzhen. Intelligence reports received during the weekend warned of a possible attack by one Japanese infantry division with a further division held in reserve. British forward troops based at Fan Ling had kept a constant watch on the border and had observed the build-up of Japanese troops. This and the intelligence reports led to the general mobilisation on Sunday 7 December.

Colonel Shoji, commanding the 230th Regiment, received orders to cross the border at 1000 hours on Monday 8 December. The 2nd and 3rd Battalions crossed the Sham Chun River near Lo Wu and proceeded south towards Fan Ling. Their objective was the village of Shek Tau Wai in the

Central New Territories, which was situated north-west of Tai Mo Shan, Hong Kong's highest mountain. The 1st Battalion, which was operating under divisional command, crossed the border further west, near the village of Lok Ma Chau. The battalion proceeded in an anti-clockwise direction towards the road bridge at Au Tau. The advance troops arrived at Au Tau in the early afternoon, by which time British sappers had destroyed the bridge, and Japanese motor transport including towed artillery was held up by the demolition. The infantry soon crossed the river and captured the police station, which had been evacuated earlier that morning. Graham Heywood and Len Starbuck, both employees of the Royal Observatory, were taken prisoner while collecting equipment from a meteorological station on the hillside behind the police station. They had the dubious distinction of being the first prisoners of war to be captured in Hong Kong. The 1st Battalion then continued to Ping Shan, and then southward to Castle Peak Bay. They followed Castle Peak Road along the coastline towards the Royal Scots sector of the GDL. They were held up at various points because of demolitions, and by harassing fire from HMS *Cicala* patrolling offshore. On Tuesday 9 December, the 2nd and 3rd Battalions of the 230th Regiment moved south towards the GDL, and by Tuesday evening the two battalions were in line abreast ready to attack the British defence line.

The 1st and 2nd Battalions of Colonel Tanaka's 229th Regiment crossed the border near Sham Chun Hu on Monday morning and proceeded southwards through Fan Ling towards Tai Po. Their objective was to reach Tide Cove and cross the estuary to attack the GDL on the high ground to the south of the inlet. Tanaka's 3rd Battalion crossed the border further east at Sha Tau Kok and followed the main road towards Fan Ling. The battalion turned left before reaching Fan Ling, and then followed hill tracks leading south through the Sha Lo Tung Hills to Tai Po. This was a more direct route and one that enabled them to avoid the multiple demolitions along the main road from Fan Ling to Tai Po. Colonel Doi's 228th Regiment spent the whole of Monday marching 30 miles to reach the Hong Kong border that evening, by which time the other two infantry regiments had already moved well inside Hong Kong territory.

The Forward Troops

Forty-five-year-old Major George Gray, commanding 'C' Coy, 2/14 Punjabs, was responsible for the forward troops out near the border, which included his own infantry company, two armoured cars from HKVDC and demolition units from the Royal Engineers. His orders were to guard the demolition teams and to delay the enemy advance before withdrawing back to the GDL. Gray's troops were all that stood in the way of the Japanese 38th Division as they crossed the border into Hong Kong.

The Armoured Car Platoon, commanded by 2/Lt Mike Carruthers, had mobilised on Sunday 7 December. No. 1 Section, consisting of three armoured cars, deployed to Brothers Point, a road bridge on Castle Peak Road, at 0045 hours on Monday morning. The section commander reported to Major Stanford Burn, 2/RS, in charge of the forward troops on the west flank. Major Burn ordered the armoured cars to patrol along Castle Peak Road through Ping Shan and as far the road bridge at Au Tau. At Ping Shan, they made contact with Captain Slater-Brown, 2/RS, commanding the battalion's Bren gun carrier platoon, which consisted of five carriers. The armoured cars guarded the road bridge at Au Tau while the sappers prepared the demolition. After completing the demolition at 1030 hours, the armoured cars returned to Brothers Point and guarded the demolition team at that location. The bridge at Brothers Point was blown up during the afternoon, after which the armoured cars patrolled Castle Peak Road between Brothers Point and Hong Kong Brewery.

No. 2 Section, consisting of two armoured cars, reported to Major Gray at his Forward HQ at The Pines in Fan Ling. Gray ordered the armoured cars to patrol in a westerly direction from Fan Ling to Au Tau, where early on Monday morning they met up with No. 1 Section patrolling from Brothers Point. On returning to The Pines from their second patrol, they were informed that the war had begun. They then guarded the demolition of the railway bridge at Lo Wu, which was blown at around 0730 hours. The section then withdrew to the Hunters Arms Crossroads at Fan Ling, and during the rest of the day acted as guard for the multiple demolitions being carried out along the Tai Po Road.

During the afternoon, a platoon from Gray's company, covering the left flank, ambushed a Japanese detachment that was reportedly headed by three women. The platoon opened fire, wiping out the entire enemy detachment, including the women, who may have been forced to act as a human shield. Gray anticipated that Japanese troops would approach Tai Po from the Sha Lo Tong Hills. Major Gray and his second-in-command, Captain Ian Blair, had the company positioned so that all their guns were trained on the hill track leading into Tai Po from the north. The Japanese battalion duly appeared, marching in column, with mules carrying their equipment. Captain Blair instructed the troops to hold their fire. He waited until the range was around 300 metres and then gave the order to open fire. The concentrated fire was devastating, and the Japanese incurred a large number of casualties as their troops retreated back over the crest of the hill.

On Tuesday 9 December, Major Gray's company withdrew to Monastery Ridge, a hill feature north of Tide Cove and in front of the GDL. That evening, under cover of darkness, he moved his troops back through British lines and assumed the role of reserve company in the centre section of the GDL. The demolitions had been successfully completed, the Japanese advance had been slowed, and everything had gone according to plan – until later that evening, when the Shing Mun Redoubt fell.

GDL – Royal Scots Sector (Monday 8 to Tuesday 9 December)

The 2nd Bn Royal Scots was under the command of forty-three-year-old Lt-Col Simon White. He was an Irishman who had been awarded the Military Cross while serving in the First World War. The battalion was responsible for defending the left flank of the GDL running from Gin Drinkers Bay, along Pineapple Ridge, up to Jubilee Reservoir and the Shing Mun Redoubt. 'A' Coy was positioned on the right flank of the battalion's sector, which included the Shing Mun Redoubt, 'B' Coy was in the centre, and 'C' Coy was on the left flank, located on the Texaco Peninsula. 'D' Coy was positioned in the rear acting as reserve company. Battalion HQ was located at the Skeet Ground near the sixth milestone on Castle Peak Road and close to Gin Drinkers Bay. The area occupied by the Royal Scots was particularly prone to malaria, and the battalion, which was already well under normal strength, had a large number of men hospitalised with this debilitating illness. On 8 December, there were approximately 150 members of the battalion either hospitalised or in convalescence. Most of the convalescents returned to the battalion when the war started, although many were still in a weak state. Even after these men returned to the line, there were still more than eighty men hospitalised, representing about 10 per cent of the battalion's strength in December 1941.

On Monday morning, the battalion sent out commando patrols, each consisting of three men, one of whom was an NCO. They were to act as reconnaissance patrols, operating in front of the GDL, watching the passes and hill tracks, and reporting back on enemy movements. They were instructed to return after nightfall. At around 1400 hours on Monday, the Bren gun carrier platoon under Captain Slater-Brown, stationed at Ping Shan Police Station on Castle Peak Road, made contact with forward Japanese troops moving westwards from Au Tau. After an exchange of fire, the carriers were ordered to fall back to the east of Brothers Point, on Castle Peak Road.

On Monday night, one of the commando patrols, consisting of Cpl Hale, Pte Peacock and Pte Moore, failed to return. All three were

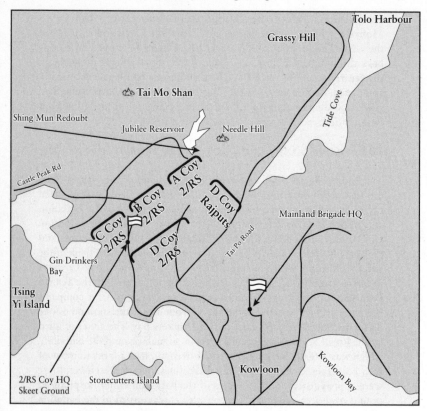

Royal Scots sector on GDL.

members of the Royal Scots Band. The unit had run into a Japanese patrol near the Hong Kong Brewery on Castle Peak Road. Cpl Hale opened fire with his Tommy gun, the patrol became separated, and Peacock and Moore were both killed. Hale was wounded in the shoulder but made it back to British lines. Hale and his patrol were the first Royal Scots casualties in the Battle for Hong Kong. Hale was sent to Bowen Road Military Hospital where he was one of the first patients to be admitted to an otherwise empty ward. Another commando section, led by Cpl Burns from 'D' Coy, made contact with a Japanese patrol on Tuesday morning; in the exchange of fire that followed, Burns killed, or severely wounded, the Japanese officer leading the patrol. On Tuesday morning orders were received for Major Burn's forward troops to return to the GDL.

GDL – 2/14 Punjab Sector (Monday 8 to Thursday 11 December)

The Punjab battalion was under the command of forty-eight-year-old Lt-Col Gerald Kidd. His battalion occupied the centre section of the GDL. The battalion was stood-to at 0600 hours on Monday morning, but apart from observing Japanese aircraft overhead, their sector remained quiet throughout Monday and Tuesday. Fighting patrols were sent out at night, but no contact was made with Japanese troops. On Wednesday 10 December, 'D' Coy, commanded by Captain Mathers, positioned on the battalion's left flank, observed Japanese troops on Monastery Ridge and on the lower slopes of Needle Hill. These enemy positions were engaged by the battalion's mortar platoon. Two Japanese light tanks were observed on 'D' Coy's front, but they remained concealed during the day.

'A' Coy, commanded by Captain Thomson, positioned on the right flank and overlooking Tide Cove, observed Japanese engineers repairing demolitions on Tai Po Road on Wednesday morning. At 1300 hours, troops from Tanaka's 229th Infantry Regiment were seen in strength and with supporting artillery in the vicinity of Kau To, directly across Tide Cove. At 1430 hours, Japanese artillery began shelling the battalion's front, and enemy patrols crossed the inlet in small boats to probe the battalion's defences. At 1600 hours, two sampans carrying

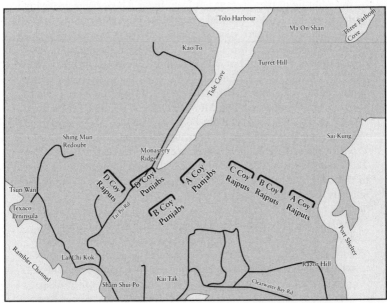

Indian Army positions on GDL.

Japanese troops were destroyed by machine gun fire from Pillbox (PB) 210 while attempting to cross the inlet. During the evening, PBs 208, 211 and 214 were destroyed by Japanese artillery fire, and PB 213 was badly damaged. On Thursday morning, Japanese patrols were probing the battalion's positions around Tai Wai and Shatin and PB 300 was hit and destroyed by artillery fire. At 1100 hours that morning, two lorries containing some thirty Japanese troops were seen at the Shatin level crossing. The lorries were engaged by PB 301, and the enemy detachment was completely destroyed. Later that day, on Thursday 11 December, it became necessary for British forces to withdraw from the Mainland. The two Indian battalions began their withdrawal to Devil's Peak on Thursday evening with the 2/14 Punjabs passing through the 5/7 Rajput lines, and the Rajputs acting as rear-guard.

GDL – 5/7 Rajput Sector (Monday 8 to Thursday 11 December)

The Rajput battalion was under the command of forty-two-year-old Lt-Col Roger Cadogan-Rawlinson. His battalion occupied the right flank of the GDL. The battalion had left India equipped as an Indian Army rifle regiment without Bren gun carriers and without mortars. Mortars were issued to the battalion in August, but that left little time for training and familiarisation. The battalion's strength was increased by the addition of recruits sent out from India. The recruits arrived in Hong Kong in October but had insufficient time for training before battle commenced. There was no enemy activity in the Rajput sector during Monday 8 December, and the battalion spent the time improving their defences, laying additional wire, and completing anti-personnel minefields. On Tuesday morning, 'D' Coy, the battalion reserve company, commanded by Captain Newton was ordered by Wallis to relocate to a new position between Shing Mun Redoubt (2/RS) and Tai Po Road (2/14 Punjabs). On Tuesday night Police Sgt Duncan Macpherson and Sub-Inspector Wong Hi-man, at the request of Colonel Newnham, GSO-1, passed through the Rajput lines in an effort to evacuate villagers from Tai Wai and Shatin. These villages were situated immediately in front of the GDL. The police war diary recounts their efforts to bring the villagers back to British lines.

> The Japanese had collected these villagers … with the intention of using them as a screen during the fighting and also to set off land mines in front of the GDL. … The party reached Shatin Gap at about 0400 hours and passed through the British lines at about 0600 hours. They had to crawl past a Japanese machine gun post to reach Shatin walled village where they managed to warn about 460 Chinese from various New

Territories villages, including ARP personnel, to evacuate immediately. At about 0800 hours the police party started the villagers on their way. Almost immediately the Japanese opened fire with machine guns, and a panic ensued. The Chinese villagers scattered, and in so doing, set off landmines. ... Under heavy fire, Sgt Macpherson and Sub-Inspector Wong managed to bring back 125 terrified villagers, men, women and children, across no-man's-land and back through British lines. The GSO-1 in making his request had stressed the importance of removing the villagers both from a strategic point of view and for their own safety.[3]

On Wednesday 10 December, 'C' Coy, on the left flank of the Rajput sector, reported that pillboxes on their front were being accurately shelled. Orders were issued that half of each PB crew should be in their alternative positions, which consisted of firing pits and trenches set away from the pillbox. On Thursday and Friday, the battalion was in the thick of action while acting as rear-guard for the evacuation of troops from the Mainland.

The Loss of the Shing Mun Redoubt

Colonel Doi, commanding the 228th Infantry Regiment, reached the frontier on the evening of Monday 8 December. The regiment crossed the border early the next morning and followed the main road and railway south through Fan Ling towards Tai Po. The road was still blocked in many places by British demolitions, and Japanese engineers were busy repairing and clearing the road. Doi's regiment turned south-west near Tai Po, and followed hill paths through Lead Mine Pass, between Grassy Hill and Tai Mo Shan, to assume a central position between the other two regiments on a broad front that was closing in on the British inner line.

Doi's regiment was assigned an area south of Grassy Hill and east of Needle hill. The 230th Regiment was on his right flank, in the area of Tai Mo Shan, and the 229th Regiment was on his left flank, in the area north of Tide Cove. Doi had been pressing for his regiment to have a more active role in the attack, and he believed that he had the approval of his divisional commanders, albeit in somewhat vague terms, to make a surprise attack if the opportunity on the ground permitted. During the early afternoon on Tuesday 9 December, Doi took a dozen men with him and set out to undertake a reconnaissance of the British positions.

Feeling the need for personally reconnoitring the enemy situation and terrain if a surprise move were to be made against the enemy,

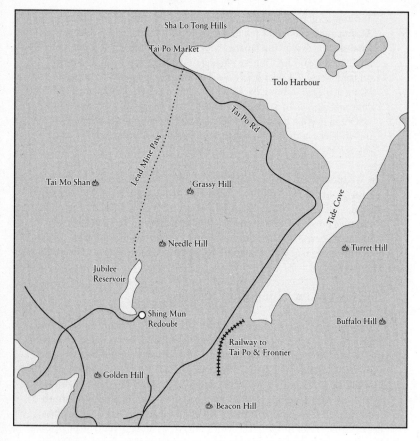

Lead Mine Pass, Tai Mo Shan and Grassy Hill.

I, accompanied by the guard squad and elements of the signal section ... departed from a point south of Tai Po where the road was destroyed and proceeded towards Grassy Hill. We reached the top of the hill ... and found telephone lines, presumably abandoned by the enemy observation party.[4]

During Doi's reconnaissance of the British positions, which included the Shing Mun Redoubt, he had seen what looked like clothing being dried, and he formed the opinion that the British were not at a high state of readiness, and that they had underestimated the depth and speed of the Japanese advance. He saw the chance for a decisive and

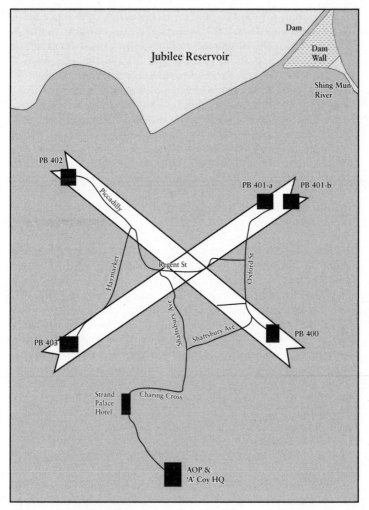

PBs and tunnel layout at Shing Mun Redoubt.

opportunistic attack on this key feature under cover of darkness. He was not sure how well the position was defended, but nonetheless he decided to take the risk and immediately attack the strongpoint, even though this sector was designated for Shoji's 230th Regiment on his right. Doi ordered his 3rd Battalion to lead the attack, and they moved forward at 2100 hours, followed by the 2nd Battalion. The remaining troops were kept in reserve.

I accompanied the 3rd Bn, and the troops marching in single file formation moved stealthily over rough paths, towards Jubilee Reservoir. ... The troops wore rubber-soled canvas shoes and marched silently towards the enemy. The 9th and 10th companies were assigned to make the attack, and the obstacle clearance teams moving ahead succeeded in clearing pathways through the wire entanglements without enemy detection. Meanwhile, the rear element of the 3rd Battalion advanced along the dyke and was assembling under the defilade north of Hill 251 [Shing Mun Redoubt]. The enemy was completely unaware of these movements. ... First, a small number of troops threw hand grenades into the air vents of the connecting tunnels, and then infiltrating teams went into the tunnels and engaged in fierce close-quarter fighting. ... Throughout the night attack, I was near the reservoir dyke [dam] watching the progress of the fighting.[5]

The 3rd Battalion, commanded by Major Nishiyama Haruja, led the assault on the redoubt. The 2nd Battalion, commanded by Major Takeyoshi Inagaki, was ordered to deploy along the north bank of the Shing Mun River, below the dam, in preparation to attack Hill 303, located at the eastern end of Smuggler's Ridge. The 1st Battalion was held in reserve, but ready to push south once the redoubt and Smuggler's Ridge had been captured. Doi had taken the initiative, launched a surprise attack, and captured the all-important redoubt, but it created problems for Japanese divisional command because it was not authorised, and the redoubt was meant to be an objective for the 230th Regiment. Doi was first ordered to move back to his start-line, but that would have led to the reoccupation of the redoubt by the British, so Doi refused to withdraw and held on to the redoubt whilst holding back any further advance by his other two battalions.

Captain Jones, 2/RS, commanding 'A' Coy, had been educated at Marlborough and Oxford. He was the son of a clergyman and had been commissioned from the Royal Scots Territorial Army Battalion. He was a tall man, standing six foot four. Jones had a reputation for hard drinking, socialising and partying, which would not have enamoured him to Brigadier Wallis, who disliked that kind of flamboyance. Jones had assumed command of 'A' Coy in October 1941, and his company occupied the Shing Mun Redoubt from 11 November.

The redoubt has been described as being like a large figure 'X' with two PBs (PB 401-a and PB 401-b) on the right upper apex and PB 402 on the left upper apex. These two positions were about 200 metres apart and were separated by a ravine between the two spurs on which the pillboxes were constructed. These two pillboxes were facing a northerly direction. At the bottom of the figure 'X', higher up the hill and away from the reservoir, were the two remaining pillboxes and the AOP. PB 400 was on the right-hand side, overlooking the steep Shing Mun River valley and figuratively on the lower-right of the 'X'. PB 403 was on the lower-left of the 'X' and was facing a westerly direction. The AOP was situated between these two rear pillboxes, and higher up the hill. Wallis described the area occupied by the redoubt as being approximately 230 metres from north to south and 320 metres from north-east to south-west.

The tunnels linking the PBs and firing bays are still in good condition, although on a recent visit there were a lot of bats and a feral dog to contend with. The tunnels are named after London streets like Haymarket, Piccadilly, Oxford Street and Regent Street. The tunnels reflect the actual roads themselves. Piccadilly has Haymarket running off it and leads to Regent Street just as it does on the ground in London. This made it easier for soldiers from the London-based Middlesex Regiment to find their way around the tunnels when they were assigned to the Shing Mun Redoubt before the war.

Captain Jones chose to locate his Coy HQ at the AOP with Lt Wilcox, HKSRA, who was stationed there with four gunners to observe and direct artillery fire. The redoubt was defended by No. 8 platoon, commanded by 2/Lt Thomson, and consisting of twenty-six other ranks (ORs). The garrison included 'A' Coy HQ personnel, consisting of Jones and nine British other ranks (BORs); and Wilcox with two BORs and two Indian other ranks (IORs). There were forty-two defenders in total, consisting of three officers and thirty-nine ORs. The Japanese deployed one battalion (3/228), utilising two of the battalion's infantry companies, each consisting of around 100 men, to conduct the actual assault on the redoubt. The 9th Company, commanded by Lt Kasugai Yoshitaro, was the first to cross the dam. An obstacle-clearance team was sent up to cut through the outer perimeter wire, and then to cut a path through the wire entanglement around PB 401-b. The assault teams followed closely behind. The 9th Company picketed PB 401-b and later captured PB 402. The 10th Coy, commanded by Lt Wakabayashi Toichi, left the dam a little later to attack the two rear pillboxes and the AOP. They made their way around the hillside from PB 401-b in a clockwise direction to reach PB 400 and the AOP from the rear.

A court of enquiry was conducted at Argyle Street POW Camp in May 1942 to look into the facts and culpabilities relating to the loss of the Shing Mun Redoubt. During the rudimentary proceedings of the court, Wallis referred to a visit he made to the redoubt in November 1941, together with Major-General Maltby, Colonel Newnham, Lt-Col White and Captain Jones.

During this visit, I emphasised the importance of only using the pillboxes and subterranean works as storage and protection in the event of heavy artillery and air attack. ... I pointed out to the Coy commander that the southeast dam and considerable quantities of tactical wire could only be covered by the occupation of outside weapons pits, which needed improvement. I also stressed that whereas by day there might be occasions when long-range machine gun shoots could best be carried out from inside the pillboxes with their fixed mountings, by night the policy must be for every man to be outside in a smaller locality than by day allowing for better control and all-around fire. I also ordered particular attention to be paid to the covering of the dam and the wire obstacles by fire from weapon pits between the redoubt and the dam.[6]

During the afternoon on Tuesday 9 December, Mike Kendall, the leader of 'Z' Force, a specialist unit who were trained to operate behind enemy lines, spotted enemy troops on Grassy Hill. This was probably Doi with his reconnaissance team. On Tuesday evening, Kendall and McEwan, both from 'Z' Force, set out towards the British lines with the intention of reporting their observations to Jones at his Coy HQ. Kendall and McEwan made contact with 2/Lt Fenwick, 'A' Coy, at his platoon HQ below the redoubt, and near the reservoir. Fenwick telephoned Jones to tell him that Kendall was coming up to make a report. Jones sent Pte Wylie, his batman, down to Fenwick's HQ to conduct Kendall to the AOP. However, before Kendall and Wylie could reach the AOP, the redoubt came under attack.

Earlier that day, Jones had gone to see Captain Newton, 5/7 Rajputs, whose company had just deployed to a position about a kilometre from the redoubt at the south-east end of Smuggler's Ridge which overlooked the Shing Mun River valley. The two company commanders agreed to set up interlocking fields of fire and agreed designated patrolling routes. During the day, one of the 'A' Coy patrols had exchanged fire with Japanese troops on Needle Hill. Japanese troop movements had also been observed at Lead Mine Pass and fired on by British artillery. The two company commanders were therefore aware of the proximity of Japanese troops. During the early evening on Tuesday 9 December, Thomson took out a fighting patrol consisting of some nine men from his platoon, leaving Sgt Robb in charge of the remainder of the platoon. Thomson took his patrol along Smuggler's Ridge and made contact with Captain Newton's HQ. After returning from the patrol, Thomson went up to the AOP to report to his company commander. It was while he was at the AOP that the message was rung through to 'A' Coy HQ that Kendall was coming up to report information about enemy movements. Jones recounted these events for the court of enquiry.

When 2/Lt Thomson left my HQ to return to his platoon he found the grille gate was locked. He came back to tell me, and to get out through the trap [door in the roof]. I told him to wait in the AOP and hear Kendall's information before he went. Some little time afterwards I was informed by phone from the Coy Exchange that the enemy had entered the redoubt and captured pillbox 401 and that they were penetrating further. I told the signaller to connect me with No. 8 Platoon HQ where Sgt Robb was in command. The signaller replied that he had already informed Sgt Robb, who was mounting a counterattack with all the men available. He also stated that owing to the approach of the enemy along the tunnel where he was, he would be unable to operate the exchange much longer. I ordered him to connect me with Battalion HQ, lock up the exchange, and to join Sgt Robb. I put my HQ in a state of defence.[7]

On a recent site visit, I crossed the dam from the base of Needle Hill following the route taken by Doi's troops. On reaching the hill on which the redoubt is built I looked for a route to climb up the steep hillside to the redoubt. There is one obvious route, which necessitates moving to the left after crossing the dam before ascending the hill. The path I took was steep, but it could be climbed relatively easily, and following it up one of the spurs of the hill brings you right up to the ruins of PB 401-b. This must have been the same route taken by the Japanese assault troops.

L/Cpl Laird, on sentry duty on the slope below PB 401-b, spotted faint lights and the movement of a group of men working their way up towards the wire entanglement below the pillbox. Laird issued a challenge, and after getting no response, he opened fire with a Tommy gun. The Japanese returned fire and threw hand-grenades. Laird withdrew and informed Cpl Robertson at PB 401-b of the whereabouts of the Japanese assault. He then notified the signaller on duty at the company telephone exchange who immediately advised Jones that PB 401-b was under attack. A short time later Laird entered the AOP through the trapdoor and reported directly to Jones. Jones was in telephone contact with both Lt-Col White and Brigadier Wallis until the line went dead in the early hours of Wednesday. The brigade war diary states that at 2325 hours on Tuesday night Jones reported to Mainland Brigade HQ that the redoubt was under attack and that the enemy was believed to have occupied PB 401-b. In fact, the PB had not been captured and continued to resist until the following day. Wallis was annoyed to hear that Jones was in the AOP, and not where his Coy HQ was expected to have been located, which was at the entrance to the tunnels and close to the telephone exchange. He was also concerned to hear that the commander of No. 8 Platoon was also in the AOP, and not with his platoon, and that platoon members were in the PBs or tunnels rather than in their alternative positions. Wallis ordered Jones to get out of the AOP with his men and to evict the enemy as quickly as possible.

When Pte Wylie left the AOP to meet Kendall, he locked the grille gate at the bottom of the flight of steps leading down from the AOP to the kitchen area, which was known as the Strand Palace Hotel. This gate was referred to as the lower grille. Another grille gate at the top of the steps leading into the AOP was referred to as the upper grille. The lower grille led to an exit by way of an open area, and then through an adjacent portal to the rest of the tunnel system. The lower grille would have been the usual route for entering or leaving the AOP during battle conditions, and it may have been a standard security practice to keep the gate locked. There is a reference in the court of enquiry documents suggesting that Wylie should have given the key to an Indian NCO who was on sentry duty, but instead, possibly in the absence of the sentry, he took it with him down to Fenwick's HQ. The only other exit, during battle conditions, was through the trapdoor in the roof accessed by a steel ladder. After the attack commenced Jones reported to his battalion commander that he intended to leave the AOP to conduct a recce. Lt-Col White suggested Thomson should do this so that Jones could remain in telephone contact with Bn HQ. At about this time a party of two or three ORs, who had been cut off from Sgt Robb's group, entered the AOP through the trapdoor. Jones ordered Thomson, who was preparing to leave the AOP, to take the ORs with him. Thomson tried to get out through the trapdoor but was driven back by gunfire. They had waited too long to get out. Shortly after the initial assault on the redoubt the AOP itself came under attack, and with the Japanese outside and in the tunnel system it soon became impossible for anyone to get out alive.

Sgt Robb attempted to lead a counterattack. There may have been some exchange of fire inside the tunnel system since Doi's account speaks of fighting taking place within the tunnels, but Robb's party was quickly on the surface fighting it out within the wire perimeter. Robb, initially with eighteen men, found himself being attacked from the direction of PB 401 and PB 402 to the north, and then from the east after the Japanese had worked their way around the hillside towards PB 400 and the AOP. Robb's party was pushed back towards the rear of the redoubt. We do not know exactly what happened with Robb's counterattack, how long it lasted, and how it was conducted. Neither do we know where his platoon had been deployed, but it was probably around platoon HQ within the tunnel system rather than in the external weapons pits. His party of eighteen men suffered five casualties and, finding himself under attack from different directions and facing overwhelming numbers, he made the decision to withdraw with the remaining thirteen men along Smuggler's Ridge towards Newton's position.

At 2345 hours, which was about the same time that the redoubt was attacked, Newton's sentries observed some two hundred Japanese troops in the Shing Mun River valley. Newton's company engaged the Japanese in the valley using machine guns and 2-inch mortars, and just after midnight the HKSRA laid down an artillery barrage on the Japanese troops concentrated in the valley. The troops were from Doi's 2nd Battalion, and were forming up at their start-line ready to launch an attack on Hill 303 and capture the ridge. The Japanese had not expected to run up against a company of Rajputs holding the ridgeline with machine guns, mortars and supported by artillery fire. Newton's Rajputs prevented all efforts by the Japanese to move south across the Shing Mun River and ascend Smuggler's Ridge. At 0330 hours Brigade HQ was informed that parties from 'A' Coy, 2/RS, had been coming into Newton's positions from the redoubt during the preceding two hours, and by then totalled 14 ORs including Sgt Robb. Wallis found these reports very disturbing as it suggested to him that a large part of the Shing Mun platoon had withdrawn, with minimal casualties, and left their platoon commander and company commander trapped below ground. Three of the five casualties from Robb's platoon that were left behind at the redoubt were taken prisoner, one was missing in action (and not seen again), and the last, although wounded, made it back to British lines. The Japanese picketed PB 401-b and the AOP. The other PBs had not been occupied. PB 401-b, with its garrison of four ORs, was the only pillbox that was allowed to be occupied at night because of its position on a steep slope and the difficulty of constructing weapons pits on the surrounding terrain.

The trapdoor in the roof of the AOP could be opened from inside or outside. The Japanese troops picketing the AOP were able to open the trapdoor and drop grenades into the AOP. Wilcox and Thomson covered the trapdoor with their Tommy guns to try and ensure that the trapdoor remained closed and prevent the Japanese from forcing an entry. At one stage during the siege, Wilcox called in artillery fire to be brought down on top of their position in an attempt to clear the Japanese. Jones recalled that the Japanese surrounding the AOP later used explosives to blow open the locked lower grille gate.

> I found the bottom grille blown open, and held in force, and covered by two enemy automatics. Bombing through the trap was now resumed but with less intensity. An attempt to blow in the steel door was met by revolver fire [presumably through the observation aperture in the door] and the enemy withdrew after suffering casualties.[8]

The two steel doors in the main compartment had been locked and blocked and were not used in battle conditions. One of these portals still shows fragmentation damage consistent with an effort to force an entry with explosives. A little later the Japanese managed to blow open the steel embrasure shutters at the front of the AOP. They were then able to hurl grenades into the structure through a gap in the damaged embrasure. Jones described the situation in the AOP after this breach.

> The main window [embrasure] had been blown in, a number of the men were unconscious, and some were dazed, and I heard groans from others. I told my CSM to cover the windows with a TSMG. We fired at what we thought were some figures seen outside. We were intending to fight our way through the bottom grille because the AOP was now open to counterattack on two sides and it was no longer tenable. Before we could start, some grenades were thrown through the open window, and 2/Lt Thomson and Pte Martin were badly wounded. Almost immediately afterwards there was a very heavy explosion, when I recovered consciousness, I was lying on the steps leading to the steel door. Only Lt Wilcox, CSM Mead and I got to our feet.[9]

Two IORs, who had been sheltering next to the steel shutters, were killed in the explosion, and Thomson was blinded in one eye from shrapnel when the grenades were thrown into the AOP. With the front of the AOP blown open, and the lower grille gate blown off its hinges, there was no longer any choice, and Jones made his way down to the lower grille where he surrendered the position.

Wallis blamed Jones for the loss of the redoubt. He was of the opinion that there had been insufficient patrolling, no static listening posts, no standing patrol at or near the dam, and that most of the men had been caught underground rather than manning their external weapons pits. Had they patrolled across the dam they may have spotted the Japanese build-up, and had that been the case they may have avoided the redoubt being taken by surprise and so quickly.

It was known that the redoubt was vulnerable to a surprise attack because during an exercise shortly before the war, 2/Lt Fenwick with a small party of men demonstrated it was possible to approach the pillboxes undetected. However, the main problem was inadequate manning. There were simply insufficient numbers of troops, and this was a problem throughout the GDL and throughout the Battle for Hong Kong. One platoon, consisting of 26 ORs, was not enough to defend such a large and complex system of tunnels, firing bays and pillboxes spread over a large area and at the same time maintain static and moving patrols.

Following the loss of the redoubt, Wallis pressed White to mount a counterattack as quickly as possible. Wallis suggested two possible plans, both of which could be effected by using Captain Pinkerton's reserve company. White asked for time to consider, and within an hour came back to say that he thought it was beyond the scope of his battalion. He felt that he had insufficient numbers of troops to launch an effective counterattack without dangerously weakening his defences. He needed Pinkerton's 'D' Coy to prevent any Japanese exploitation south towards Golden Hill.

If a counterattack was to be undertaken, it needed to be done very quickly and before the Japanese could consolidate their defences. The initial inertia and the lack of troops meant the opportunity to make an effective counterattack was lost. By Wednesday morning the Japanese occupied the redoubt in strength and Maltby later acknowledged that a counterattack by one company during daylight hours would have had little chance of success. 'D' Coy, WG, commanded by Captain Bowman, was brought over to support 2/RS. Captain Pinkerton's 'D' Coy was moved up to Golden Hill, and 'C' Coy, with a depleted strength of only thirty-five ORs, was brought forward to act as reserve company. PB 401-b continued to hold out until Wednesday afternoon when the pillbox collapsed following a direct hit by British artillery fire. Perhaps admiring their refusal to surrender, the Japanese somewhat compassionately dug out Cpl Robertson and three ORs who had manned the pillbox.

The court of enquiry, convened during captivity in Argyle Street Camp in May 1942, was presided over by Colonel H. B. Rose, who commanded the HKVDC, and later in the battle became Acting Brigadier and commander of West Infantry Brigade. The original copy of the proceedings was buried for the duration of the troops' internment, and it could not be found when efforts were made to retrieve it immediately after the war. It later transpired that Lt-Col White had retained a copy, and must have secreted it away with great care, as it survived his internment. In 1953, White died in Ireland at the age of fifty-five. Following his death, the copy of the proceedings, which until then was not known to exist, was sent to the Royal Scots and in 1957 came into the hands of Augustus Muir, the regimental historian. Colonel Rose and Major-General Maltby both confirmed in 1957 that this appeared to be a true copy of the original proceedings. The file containing these documents, held by the UK National Archives, was closed for fifty years from the time it took retention in 1958 until 2008.

The copy of the proceedings is useful because it provides the testimony of officers who were present, like Jones and Wilcox, who were recalling details shortly after the actual events. Unfortunately, it does not include testimony by NCOs like L/Cpl Laird, Sgt Robb or CSM Mead as they were interned in a different camp. There were no formal findings issued by the court of enquiry, and in September 1942, when White applied to reopen the enquiry, it was decided not to do so, and the proceedings were dropped. In 1958, Brigadier Latham, Head of the Historical Section Cabinet Office, was commissioned by the Battle Honours Committee to compile a report detailing the actions of 2/RS during the fighting on the Mainland. Suffice to say, and in what many consider an injustice, the Royal Scots were not awarded battle honours for Hong Kong because of the loss of the Shing Mun Redoubt and an unauthorised withdrawal by 'B' and 'C' Coy during the morning on Thursday 11 December.

GDL – Royal Scots Sector (Thursday 11 December)

After the loss of the redoubt, 'B' and 'C' Coy positions on Pineapple Ridge were compromised and came under fire from the area of the redoubt. The GDL was moved back during the evening on Wednesday 10 December in a south-east direction pivoted on Golden Hill. Battalion HQ was moved from the forward position at the Skeet Ground, on Castle Peak Road, to Filter Beds House on Tai Po Road, located a kilometre north-east of Lai Chi Kok. One of the battalion's five Bren gun carriers would not start and had to be blown up and abandoned at the Skeet Ground. Major Stanford Burn supervised the withdrawal of 'B' and 'C' Coy to their new positions. He then established his Rear Battalion HQ at the World Pencil Factory situated near the junction of Castle Peak and Tai Po Roads.

'B' Coy, under Captain Richardson, was deployed with its left-hand platoon astride Castle Peak Road and its remaining two platoons located on the ridge to the east of the road. The ridge extended from Lai Chi Kok northwards to Golden Hill. 'C' Coy, commanded by Captain Rose, was positioned on 'B' Coy's right flank. The northern part of the ridge and the summit of Golden Hill was defended by Captain Pinkerton's 'D' Coy. The summit of Golden Hill was a kilometre south of the Shing Mun Redoubt and separated from Smuggler's Ridge by a steep ravine.

'A' Coy, consisting of No. 7 and No. 9 Platoon, under the temporary command of 2/Lt Fenwick, had remained in their positions near the reservoir throughout Wednesday. Sgt Robb and the remnants of No. 8 Platoon were with Captain Newton's Coy located between Smuggler's Ridge and Tai Po Road. During Wednesday night, 'A' Coy withdrew through 'D' Coy's positions to Golden Hill Road from where they were taken by truck to a new position on Castle Peak Road. The

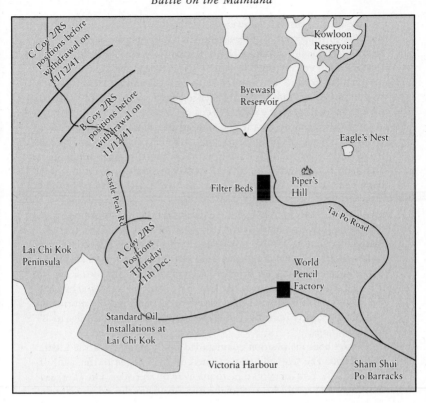

Castle Peak Road and World Pencil Factory.

new position was located at the fifth milestone close to the Standard Oil Depot and close to Lai Chi Kok Hospital, now known as the Jao Tsung-I Academy. In their new position, 'A' Coy provided in-depth support for 'B' and 'C' Coy. Sgt Richard's No. 9 Platoon remained with Captain Newton's company to strengthen his left flank, while Sgt Robb's platoon re-joined 'A' Coy.

These deployments resulted in an untidy front-line running from Lai Chi Kok, up Castle Peak Road, and then up Golden Hill Ridge, then from Smuggler's Ridge towards Tai Po Road and Tai Wai. It was untidy because 'A' Coy was situated behind 'B' Coy, which was situated behind 'C' Coy. It had strength in depth but not in breadth and was therefore vulnerable to exploitation. There were wide gaps between platoons, according to 2/Lt Baird even wider than the gaps between their platoon positions at Pineapple Ridge. There were no pre-prepared fixed defences, no wire, and the disused slit trenches were old and partly filled-in, and therefore provided little protection. Although efforts had been made during the day to lay telephone lines from Bn HQ to the Coy HQs on Castle Peak Road this had not been completed, and there was no telephone communication between 'A', 'B', and 'C' Coy, nor between them and Bn HQ. The only way for a Coy or platoon commander to communicate was to either go forward himself or send a runner.

On Thursday morning, the 2nd and 3rd Battalions of Colonel Shoji's 230th Regiment advanced south and south-east towards Castle Peak Road and Golden Hill. Each battalion consisted of four companies, and each battalion advanced with two companies in front and two companies at the rear. At 0730 hours three of the forward companies attacked 'D' Coy on Golden Hill. 'D' Coy held its position and was involved in close-quarter fighting throughout the rest of the day. The remaining forward company then attacked 'C' Coy positions. Captain Rose, commanding 'C' Coy, was killed after having gone forward to give orders to 2/Lt Haywood commanding No. 13 Platoon. 2/Lt Houston-Boswell, commanding No. 14 Platoon, was killed by a Japanese sword during hand-to-hand fighting. 2/Lt Haywood assumed command of what was left of the company. Their positions were being heavily mortared, and Haywood gave orders to withdraw southwards along the ridge to 'B' Coy's positions.

'B' Coy had one platoon commanded by Lt Stanton astride Castle Peak Road. The Coy HQ was situated on the hillside to the right of the road. The remaining two platoons were on the ridge. On Thursday morning, they could hear machine gun fire from the ridge. Captain Richardson, CSM Matheson and a runner went up the hill to contact the two platoon commanders and undertake an appreciation of the situation. Richardson and his runner were not seen again and were reported as missing in action. They may have been killed by friendly fire, as when 'C' Coy reached 'B' Coy's positions on the ridge they found that 'B' Coy had withdrawn after having come under British artillery fire which was falling short. 'B' and 'C' withdrew, reportedly in a disorderly manner, along the ridge to Lai Chi Kok where they emerged on Castle Peak Road. They continued along Castle Peak Road as far back as the World Pencil Factory. Only 'A' Coy and one platoon from 'B' Coy under Lt Stanton and 2/Lt Baird maintained their positions.

At 0915 hours on Thursday, Lt-Col White called Brigadier Wallis from his Bn HQ at Filter Beds House with the disturbing news that he could see from his HQ that his two left-hand companies ('B' and 'C' Coy) were withdrawing from their positions on Castle Peak Road and the ridge. The line appeared to have broken. Wallis told White that he must stop the retreat and that they must hold their ground; if they did not, the door was open for the Japanese to press forward into Kowloon and for British troops and guns to be outflanked and cut off. It was a potentially disastrous situation, which if not checked could result in the destruction of the Mainland Brigade. Major Stanford Burn, second-in-command of the battalion, was at Brigade HQ at Waterloo Road, having attended a meeting earlier that morning. Burn was ordered to go forward to Lai Chi Kok, to take command of the situation, to rally the two companies, to stop the retreat, and to hold the line at all costs. Wallis made it clear to both White and Burn that the good name of their battalion was at stake.

Once Major Burn arrived back at his HQ, he reported back to Bn HQ on the alarming situation at and around the pencil factory, and his difficulty in rallying the men. When 'C' Coy reformed, they had suffered twenty-two casualties during the fighting that morning from their original depleted strength of thirty-five men. Captain Slater-Brown was ordered to move his Bren gun carriers up Castle Peak Road to prevent any Japanese exploitation southwards. The Japanese concentrated their attack on the high ground around Golden Hill. However, they sent one company southwards along Castle Peak Road. This company proceeded in column formation without scouts. Lt Stanton and 2/Lt Baird waited until they were close and then gave the order to open fire. The six Bren guns and the platoon's rifles took a devastating toll on the Japanese infantry. 2/Lt Baird described the ambush.

> The road was littered with bodies, either dead or wounded. The man who carried the flag was probably one of the first to fall. After a short while when we had held our fire, a Japanese shot out of the gutter, rushed to where the flag bearer had fallen and picked up the flag. He didn't last more than a few seconds before he was shot down. A moment later another Japanese rushed out of the gutter and picked up the flag, and of course went down also. This repeated three times before they gave up their attempt.[10]

Thinking they were facing a much stronger enemy force, the Japanese made no further effort that afternoon to exploit southwards along Castle Peak Road and continued to focus their attention on Golden Hill. Stanton and Baird remained at their position on Castle Peak Road but, realising they were cut off, decided to make an orderly withdrawal. They picked up their weapons and as much ammunition as they could carry. They passed through 'A' Coy's positions further down Castle Peak Road, and were directed to Battalion HQ. There they found Lt-Col White in a state of shock and exhaustion. The adjutant, Captain Cuthbertson, had temporarily taken charge.

Colonel Newnham, GSO-1, had been visiting Mainland Brigade HQ that morning and saw for himself the consternation over the unexpected withdrawal of the two Royal Scots companies, and the weakness suddenly exposed on the left flank of the GDL. He immediately made plans to reinforce the left flank, going forward himself to organise the defence. Newnham telephoned Captain Penn, commanding No. 1 Coy, HKVDC, at Kai Tak, and asked him to send all his available Bren gun carriers to an RV at the junction of Prince Edward and Waterloo Roads. The three available carriers, under the command of 2/Lt Edwards, arrived at the RV at 1045 hours. Newnham and Major Gordon Neve, GSO-2, met the carriers and proceeded with them to the World Pencil Factory at Lai Chi Kok. Newnham continued to a point on Castle Peak Road, forward of the pencil factory, where he came across one of the HKVDC armoured cars, which he ordered to patrol up Castle Peak Road. He then returned to the pencil factory where he met Major Burn.

> Major Burn was very excited, so I took him aside and tried to calm him down. I emphasised the present danger and also the very urgent necessity of holding present positions. ... Major Burn had the greatest difficulty in getting any man to obey him, and I had again to speak to him and warn him that unless he could give calm orders the men could not possibly work for him.[11]

Newnham took charge of deploying both the 2/RS troops at the pencil factory and the Canadian reserve company into tactical defensive positions. He then deployed the Bren gun carriers and armoured cars before returning to Mainland Brigade HQ.

> There I found the situation better because information was to hand and the line, in general, was stabilised. I reported personally by telephone to the GOC and recommended withdrawal that night in view of the precarious situation on the left flank and the consequent risk of losing guns, and the very disquieting state of 2/RS.[12]

Later that day Maltby gave the order for the evacuation process to begin. The next day, Friday 12 December, Major Burn, perhaps blaming himself for being unable to rally and control the men at the pencil factory, took his own life. He was discovered by CSM Matheson, who informed 2/Lt Baird. Baird found him in a sitting position, leaning against a tree, a gunshot wound to the side of his head, his service revolver lying near his right hand, and a letter in his lap presumably addressed to his wife, Ursula. The letter was passed to Lt-Col Simon White. I wonder whether she ever received it. They were both aged thirty-seven. Ursula died in India in May 1942.

The Loss of Kowloon

On Wednesday 10 December, some twenty-five survivors from the Shing Mun Redoubt, some of whom were wounded, were marched off to become the first military prisoners of war. Old film clips, with Spanish commentary, show the prisoners, guarded by Japanese troops, marching down a rough track. One can immediately identify Jones, tall, dark-haired, moustachioed, and marching ramrod straight. Thomson, wearing a black patch over his injured eye, can be seen supported by two other soldiers. They were taken to the Japanese HQ at Tai Po where they were interrogated. The next day they were moved to a large private residence in Fan Ling, which had been the home of William Stanton, a wealthy American businessman. The villa was used as a temporary internment camp, until the internees were moved to Sham Shui Po Camp in January 1942. Captain Jones cut an imposing figure when he entered the camp wearing a fur coat that must have been purloined from Mrs Stanton's wardrobe.

Following the evacuation of the Royal Scots from the Mainland on Thursday evening, the Japanese Army moved into Kowloon on Friday 12 December. Doi's 228th Regiment was ordered to halt and consolidate in the vicinity of Filter Beds and Piper's Hill. They remained at this location until 16 December, perhaps held back by a Japanese divisional command still irritated that Doi disobeyed orders and jumped the gun at the Shing Mun Redoubt. Some units from Doi's 3rd Battalion were allowed to participate in the entry to Kowloon, but the main role fell to Shoji's 230th Regiment. Shoji's 2nd and 3rd Battalions were ordered to enter Kowloon utilising two companies from each battalion. Shoji described their entry into Kowloon on Friday morning and a subsequent firefight at Kowloon Railway Station.

> The four companies of the 2nd and 3rd Battalions, in company column formation, advanced into the city and mopped up enemy units in the Kowloon Railway Station, on wharves and piers, at oil storage tanks and other places. During the mopping-up operations, one company was opposed by a squad of British troops positioned in a watchtower at the railway station. After a sharp two-hour skirmish, the company took the station after suffering several casualties. The enemy troops escaped to Hong Kong by landing barge.[13]

The British troops defending the railway station and the adjacent Star Ferry pier were led by Lt Forsyth, 2/14 Punjabs. Forsyth had been in the rear of the battalion during the evacuation. His group comprised HQ Coy and stragglers from other units that had been picked up along the way. When they reached Shatin Pass, Forsyth decided to follow a Volunteer who knew the way down to the Star Ferry terminal. They arrived at the pier late on Thursday night, and during Friday morning held off the advancing Japanese infantry. Forsyth's group was embarked under fire, at around 1030 hours, by a vessel that had been commandeered by the Hong Kong Police. Forty-five-year-old nurse Jessie Holland died on the ferry from a bullet wound during the exchange of fire. After the capitulation, her husband Adam Holland, a civil servant, was interned at Stanley Camp and died as a result of the American Navy's accidental bombing of a bungalow that was used to accommodate internees.

> After waiting without result for guards to arrive for the Star Ferries to prevent crews deserting Inspector Whant, Sgt Wheeler and Mr Mackenzie of the Star Ferry Company decided to proceed over to Kowloon to reconnoitre. Five European civilians insisted on accompanying them over to Kowloon, two were women, Mrs Holland and Mrs Sando, both in ANS uniform and in spite of Inspector Whant's protest refused to leave the ferry. Approaching Kowloon Docks about fifty Indians and a few British troops were observed firing with machine guns under Lt Forsyth. These were taken on board, and the launch left using the machine guns to cover the withdrawal. In spite of the European ladies being made to lie flat on the deck, Mrs Holland received a bullet wound in the abdomen.[14]

By Friday afternoon it was all over, and Kowloon belonged to the invader, except for a toehold held by two Indian battalions on Devil's Peak Peninsula. The Royal Scots were blamed for the loss of the Shing Mun Redoubt and for the withdrawal by 'B' and 'C' Coy on the left flank. However, it should be remembered that the Royal Scots bore the brunt of the fighting on the Mainland. Some fifty-four men had been killed in action, of which thirty-five were from the Royal Scots. Casualties in the Indian battalions and other units had been relatively light. The fighting defence by 'D' Coy on Golden Hill was legendary. They were attacked by three Japanese infantry companies but held on throughout the day until they were ordered to withdraw. Also, the battalion more than made up for any shortcomings on the Mainland during the subsequent fighting on the Island. At Wong Nai Chung Gap they would fight with great tenacity and gallantry against much stronger Japanese forces.

The Mainland had been lost after only four to five days of fighting. One may ask what the battle had achieved. It caused some delay in the Japanese advance, but not much. Battles had been won and battles lost, but the evacuation was by any measure a great success.

The evacuation – by sea – of an infantry brigade and its supporting artillery was a masterpiece of good planning and good fortune. The Japanese had expected the British to capitulate after the loss of Kowloon, but for the British this was part of a set plan in which they would withdraw to the Island fortress, which they would seek to hold for as long as possible. For the Japanese, it meant they would have to carry out a massive bombardment of the Island, with artillery and aircraft, to weaken the resolve of the defenders. If that did not work, they would have to carry out an opposed landing and fight their way to the finish.

4

Evacuation from the Mainland

8 to 13 December

Although groups of civilians, for example the families of members of the Hong Kong Police and HKVDC, were evacuated from Kowloon to the Island during the first week of the war, there were two principal evacuations from Kowloon in December 1941 which stand out for their audacity and achievement. Firstly, there was a civil evacuation in which nearly three hundred civilians were flown out of Hong Kong during the first two nights of the battle, and secondly, there was the military evacuation, in which the Army was taken off the Mainland in a variety of small boats, launches, ferries and naval craft and brought back to the Island. They were both remarkable achievements. The first involved pilots flying the only serviceable aircraft left at Kai Tak, overloaded, in long-distance relays, by night, without lights and over enemy territory, to safety in Free China. The second involved troops breaking off the fighting, withdrawing under fire, and undertaking long marches by night on mountainous trails while carrying their weapons and equipment in a rear-guard retreat, with the Japanese pressing relentlessly behind them.

Civil Evacuation

After hearing that war had started, William Bond, the CNAC manager in Hong Kong, hurriedly left Repulse Bay Hotel for Kai Tak hoping to save his aircraft, several of which were parked on the apron, fully fuelled, and ready to fly that morning. After nightfall, he planned to fly the CNAC Curtiss Condors and the Douglas Dakotas to safety in Free China.

The Pan Am Clipper would be flown to Kunming where it could land on the large lake in the centre of the city. While Bond was on his way to Kai Tak the air raid commenced, and by the time he reached the airfield the raid was over, and the Clipper and several of the CNAC aircraft had been destroyed. However, the large hangar had survived the bombing, and inside were two of CNAC's DC-3s and a DC-2 completely undamaged. There was also a Curtiss Condor in the hangar which was under repair. The Curtiss aircraft were leased to CNAC and were used for transporting freight. Three other Condors on the apron had been destroyed. The Condor in the hangar, although undamaged, could not be repaired in time and was later put to use by the Japanese. A Vultee aircraft parked outside the hangar had also escaped damage, and was later flown to Free China.

After the first air raid, many of the airport workers absconded, fearful that there would be further raids and worried about their families. As a result, the CNAC pilots and airline staff had to tow their aircraft out of the hangar using towing tractors they had never used before. They bulldozed the perimeter fence, moved the aircraft onto the small fields outside the northern part of the airfield, and then camouflaged the aircraft with shrubbery to conceal them from further air attacks.

Later that morning, Bond received a radio message from Mr H. H. Kung, the Minister of Finance for the Chungking Government. He was anxious about his wife Madam Kung (formerly Soong Ai-ling), his two daughters, and his wife's sister Madam Sun (formerly Soong Ching-ling), the widow of Dr Sun Yat-sen. The Nationalist Government was the main shareholder of CNAC, holding 55 per cent of the share capital to Pan Am's 45 per cent. Mr Kung asked Bond to ensure that his family got safely out of Hong Kong. Bond immediately telephoned Madame Kung at her suite in the Gloucester Hotel, but she was reluctant to leave, not realising the seriousness of the situation, and not thinking for a moment that Hong Kong would fall. She believed that Japan had made a suicidal move by declaring war on America and Britain, and that Allied forces would soon relieve Hong Kong. She felt that it was safer for her family to remain in Hong Kong than to fly at night over Japanese-occupied territory. However, after some cajoling she agreed to fly out with her family on Tuesday night. The Soong sisters got out of Hong Kong, and back to Free China, on one of the last evacuation flights during the early hours of Wednesday morning. If they had remained in Hong Kong, they would have become high-profile hostages in what would have been a propaganda coup for the Japanese.

On Monday evening, the remaining three serviceable CNAC aircraft left for Free China. All three aircraft, although heavily overloaded, made it safely to Namyung. After having flown the 200 miles there, the aircraft were quickly unloaded and refuelled. One of the aircraft needed repairs, but the other two flew straight back to Hong Kong. Another DC3, which had been operating in Burma, was flown to Hong Kong to assist with the evacuation. The three aircraft, refuelled, took on passengers and equipment and then flew to Chungking. On Tuesday, Albert Moss, the airport manager, told Bond that the British military authorities planned to blow up the airfield because they were concerned about the possibility of a Japanese airborne assault using gliders or paratroops. Bond managed to persuade Moss to leave a landing strip 300 feet wide so that the CNAC aircraft could continue to operate.

On Tuesday night, the aircraft returned to Hong Kong from Chungking and picked up other passengers including Bond, Madame Kung and Madame Sun. On Wednesday 10 December, Kai Tak was closed down, the RAF personnel withdrawn, and as a result CNAC was unable to make further evacuation flights, but Bond had saved his airline. They still had aircraft, and they were able to get most of their employees, aircrews and families out of Hong Kong, as well as much of their equipment, tools and spares. They had evacuated the two Soong sisters and other Chinese and American VIPs to safety in Free China. The VIPs included Manuel Fox of the US Treasury and eight members of his staff including some senior members of the Chinese Central Bank. They also took out a Chinese general, and a senior British officer, Lt-Col Owen-Hughes, HKVDC, who had been ordered to liaise with the Chinese Nationalist forces in Chungking.

Military Evacuation from Kowloon

There was always going to be a military evacuation of Kowloon; it was contemplated as part of the defence plan. It was a question of *when* rather than *if*, and of how long they could hold out on the Mainland. Maltby thought the defence would last at least a week, while Wallis had initially expected to hold Kowloon for at least a month. On Wednesday 10 December, the Senior Superintendent of Police in Kowloon informed Brigadier Wallis of a possible police evacuation from the Mainland at any time after 1800 hours that night. Notwithstanding the loss of the Shing Mun Redoubt, Wallis expressed surprise, and stated that he could hold Kowloon indefinitely. The police remained in Kowloon overnight, but at 0530 hours on Thursday morning police families were evacuated to Hong Kong Island on Star Ferry launches.

At first light on Thursday, Lt-Col White reported to Wallis that things were quiet on his sector of the GDL. A conference was held that morning at Brigade HQ to discuss evacuation and embarkation plans that had been drawn up by Fortress HQ in the event that a military evacuation was ordered. The meeting was for the seconds-in-command of the three infantry battalions, and included Major Burn, 2/RS, Major Browning, 5/7 Rajputs, and Major Gray, 2/14 Punjabs. Wallis felt uncomfortable discussing a withdrawal; it went against his nature, and at that stage, despite the loss of the Shing Mun Redoubt, he still felt he could hold the GDL, and therefore Kowloon, for a lot longer. He emphasised at the meeting that there was no thought of withdrawal, and that the embarkation plan should only be discussed with the battalion commanders, and that it was important to ensure that no rumours were spread of an imminent withdrawal.

The Hong Kong Police intelligence network was very effective, and reports were coming into Kowloon Police HQ from their various police stations from which they could see there were problems on the left flank of the GDL. At 0900 hours, Sub-Inspector Wallingford, the police liaison officer with the Royal Scots, reported to Police HQ that some Royal Scots located near the World Pencil Factory, at Lai Chi Kok, had told him that the Japanese were between there and Lai Chi Kok Prison. This was treated with some alarm, but was not correct. Although by that time 'B' and 'C' Coy had withdrawn to the pencil factory, the Japanese had not yet exploited the weakness in that sector. The police were suspicious that the Army were planning to evacuate the Mainland but for security reasons were not letting on, and the police wanted to make sure that they were not caught on the back foot.

After the withdrawal by the two left-flank companies in the Royal Scots sector, Wallis issued an order for all available men at Whitfield Barracks, consisting of HQ personnel under Major Pirie, 2/RS, and Lt Flynn, 2/14 Punjabs, to report to Mainland Brigade HQ in fighting order, and to be ready to reinforce the front line on the left flank. These HQ personnel, referred to in military parlance as 'odds and sods', comprised cooks, clerks, stores personnel and other troops in non-combatant roles. At this point, a strange incident is reported by Wallis in the Mainland Brigade war diary, which may have been caused by strained nerves, lack of sleep and the pressure of battle, and which Captain Belton euphemistically referred to as the Flynn incident.

Lt Flynn, 14th Punjab Regt, OC Details in Whitfield Barracks, had been moved up to Mainland HQ by motor transport with some fifty ORs as a further reserve. On reaching Mainland HQ, in lorries, in readiness to receive orders, Lt Flynn met the brigade commander who had just taken off his belt and arms. Lt Flynn looked excited and had a strange look in his eyes. He spoke incoherently saying, 'are you sure this is necessary'. The brigade commander noticed Flynn's hand creep to his revolver. … From the look in his eyes the brigade commander realised this young officer was about to shoot him. He rushed Flynn and knocked the pistol from his grip as he drew it, placed him under guard, and ordered him to hospital.[1]

It is not clear what happened to Lt James Flynn after this incident, and whether he played any further role in the fighting. He survived both the battle and the period of incarceration, and retired from the Army in 1951 in the rank of Major, and therefore presumably his rather puzzling misdemeanour was not held against him.

After having helped stabilise the situation on the west flank around the World Pencil Factory, Colonel Newnham, GSO-1, had recommended to Major-General Maltby that a full withdrawal from the Mainland should be initiated, and Maltby concurred. The mobile artillery was ordered to commence the immediate withdrawal of their forward batteries at Tai Wai, after which all remaining batteries were instructed to proceed to the vehicular ferry for embarkation to the Island. Only Major de Vere Hunt's troop of four 3.7-inch howitzers, located at Customs Pass on the east flank, was to remain on the Mainland to provide fire support for the two Indian battalions, which were to commence their withdrawal to Devil's Peak Peninsula after nightfall on Thursday 11 December.

The Royal Engineers were ordered to carry out a demolition at the Beacon Hill railway tunnel to prevent Japanese troops from using it to gain access to Kowloon. The railway had connected Kowloon and Canton until it was blocked off at the border during a period of increased tension with Japan in June 1940. In December 1941, the railway ran from the border at Lo Wu in a south-east direction to Tai Po from where it followed the shoreline of Tolo Harbour before turning south-west along the north bank of Tide Cove. It then passed through the Shatin level crossing and entered the tunnel below Beacon Hill, emerging on the north side of Kowloon City and terminating at Kowloon Station near the Star Ferry Pier. During the evacuation, one section of two 3.7-inch howitzers, which had been positioned at Tai Wai, withdrew under orders through the railway tunnel. As they reached the Kowloon end of the tunnel, they found the sappers had completed their demolition task and the tunnel was completely blocked. They had to retrace their steps back through the tunnel, and then take hill tracks through Railway Pass, east of Beacon Hill, to Kowloon. At some stage during their withdrawal a shell exploded among their section, causing injuries to both mules and gunners, and resulting in the loss of one 3.7-inch gun. This was the only gun that was left behind during the military evacuation of the Mainland.

The Royal Engineers were ordered to complete the planned demolition of pre-selected vital installations and infrastructure in Kowloon. However, some of these installations, for example the Standard Oil Depot at Lai Chi Kok and the Texaco Oil Depot at Tsun Wan, were not destroyed. Employees reported having seen demolition equipment including wires and dynamite at both installations, but for some reason they were not blown. It provoked a lot of criticism at the time, as the Japanese were able to seize large quantities of oil at both these installations. Colonel Clifford, the Chief Engineer, China Command, wrote in his war diary that the failure to blow these installations was due to tactical considerations.

> The tactical situation developed in such a way that combined with a westerly wind which would have carried the smoke from the oil depot across our front, the demolition parties were ordered by the Commander Kowloon Infantry Brigade to withdraw without firing.[2]

The Royal Navy storage tanks in Kowloon were destroyed by British gunfire. Japanese bombing and shelling destroyed the Asiatic Petroleum Company (APC) storage tanks at North Point. The burning APC tanks caused a pall of thick black smoke, which was of some assistance to the Japanese during their landings on the Island on the night of 18 December.

On Thursday 11 December, Captain Penn's Bren gun carriers and Vickers machine gun sections were assigned to Major Burn at Lai Chi Kok. The Bren gun carriers were ordered to move forward to a position near the Standard Oil Depot, and hold Castle Peak Road to prevent any Japanese advance towards Kowloon. The carriers had an exchange of fire at long range with Japanese forward troops. The Vickers machine gun sections were deployed in front of the World Pencil Factory. Captain Pinkerton, 'D' Coy, 2/RS, was ordered to start thinning out his forward positions at 1800 hours. After last light, the battalion was to pass through the rear-guard positions comprised of 'D' Coy, Winnipeg Grenadiers, the 2/RS composite company under Major Pirie, and the HKVDC armoured cars and Bren gun carriers. The Royal Scots were ordered to embark at Kowloon City Pier at 1930 hours. The armoured cars and Bren gun carriers were evacuated on the vehicular ferry after the Royal Scots had broken off and withdrawn. 2/Lt Jimmy Ford, 'D' Coy, 2/RS, was one of the last to withdraw. His platoon of twenty-six men had been depleted to a handful of men as a result of deaths and injuries incurred during the fighting on Golden Hill. After the war, he recalled the surreal nature of their withdrawal, one moment in close-quarter combat and the next moment on a bus to Kowloon as if returning from a night exercise.

On Thursday evening, the Indian battalions were ordered to commence withdrawal along the line of hills to Devil's Peak Peninsula. Captain Newton's 'D' Coy, 5/7 Rajputs, and the Punjab battalion were to withdraw in an easterly direction through the Rajput lines with the Rajputs providing a rear-guard to cover the withdrawal.

The Rajput battalion would be the last to leave. Captain Mathers, commanding 'D' Coy, 2/14 Punjabs, was positioned near Tai Wai on the left flank of the battalion's sector. His company became involved in a firefight with forward Japanese troops just as they commenced their withdrawal.

Received orders to withdraw at once leaving the ammunition and supplies, the men took their weapons and the ammunition that could be carried. On withdrawal, two Japanese light tanks and two lorry loads of troops advanced along Tai Po Road towards our position. They were fired on by our anti-tank rifles, and LMGs and very heavy casualties were inflicted on the Japanese.[3]

'C', 'D', and 'HQ' Coy of the Punjab battalion proceeded to Shatin Pass, then down the military road known as Jat's Incline, reaching Devil's Peak pier at 0730 hours on Friday 12 December. At 1900 hours on Thursday evening, it was reported that the AOP on Tate's Cairn, previously manned by the Royal Artillery, had been occupied by Japanese troops, demonstrating how closely the Japanese were pressing on the two Indian battalions. 'C' Coy, 5/7 Rajputs, commanded by Captain Sandilands, was Cadogan-Rawlinson's most forward company, and by 2200 hours they were exchanging fire with Japanese troops on their front. A short while later, the Rajputs began to disengage and fall back, one company covering another, to their pre-prepared positions on the Ma Lau Tong line which ran east to west across the northern part of Devil's Peak Peninsula. Cadogan-Rawlinson evacuated his Battalion HQ at Customs Pass at 2350 hours and established a new HQ at Hai Wan Gap, just south of the Ma Lau Tong line. 'A' and 'B' Coy Rajputs occupied their Ma Lau Tong positions at around 0200 hours in the early hours of Friday 12 December.

The Mule Corps had been assigned to the Indian battalions to help move equipment and stores. In addition, there were some fifty mules at Whitfield Barracks in Kowloon. On Thursday 11 December, Major Arthur Dewar, RASC, was advised that the plan referred to as 'W/M' (Withdrawal from Mainland) was to be implemented that day. He arranged for two of the RASC lighters to be converted to carry mules. These were towed across the harbour to the RN basin in Kowloon where the mules from Whitfield Barracks were loaded and then brought back

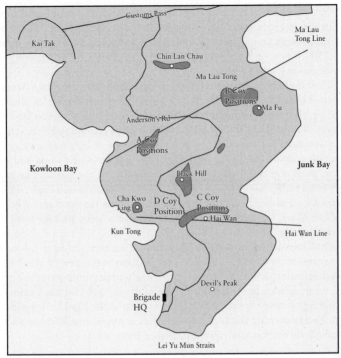

Devil's Peak Peninsula showing rear-guard positions of 5th/7th Rajputs.

across the harbour. Dewar then made his way to Lye Mun to supervise the RASC fleet of lighters and launches which were to be used for the evacuation of troops from Kowloon City on Thursday night, and the evacuation of the Indian battalions from Devil's Peak scheduled for Friday night.

Brigadier Wallis and his Brigade HQ staff departed from their Waterloo Road shelters at 1830 hours on Thursday evening escorted by two Bren gun carriers provided by 5/7 Rajputs. They proceeded to Kowloon City Pier where WDV *French* and two of the Star Ferry launches were standing by to assist in the evacuation. The first troops from 2/RS began to arrive between 1900 hours and 1930 hours. The battle-weary troops, many of them wounded, were embarked and taken across the harbour to the RN Dockyard under the supervision of Captain Belton. Wallis boarded WDV *French*, alighting at Devil's Peak Peninsula at 2130 hours where he established his new Brigade HQ. At midnight, the brigadier, accompanied by some of his staff officers, started the steep climb up Devil's Peak to Hai Wan. At approximately

0400 hours on Friday 12 the brigadier met up with Cadogan-Rawlinson who was preparing his new battalion HQ at Hai Wan Gap. The first of the Punjab companies ('A' and 'B' Coy) reached Devil's Peak jetty at 2300 hours on Thursday evening having gone through the Rajput positions at Customs Pass.

Captain Belton, having returned to the Island with the Royal Scots, spent Thursday night at the Battle Box. The next morning, he drove to Lye Mun from where he was able to get a sampan across to Devil's Peak. Belton found troops and mules on open ground near the jetty. He arranged for the mules to be moved to the nearby quarries, and redeployed the men, who because of the danger of air raids had to wait until nightfall before being taken across to the Island. Having reported to Wallis on Friday morning, Belton then crossed back to the Island with orders to set up a new Brigade HQ at Tai Tam Gap. Whilst at Lye Mun, he had a narrow escape when a stick of four bombs straddled his car.

On Thursday night, de Vere Hunt moved his troop of four 3.7-inch howitzers from Customs Pass to a new position to the west of Hai Wan. During Friday, over 1,000 rounds of 3.7-inch ammunition were brought up from the jetty to the howitzers. The AOP on Black Hill was manned, enabling observed fire to be put down in front of the Ma Lau Tong line. On Friday evening the Japanese launched a major attack in battalion strength on the Rajputs' newly established front line.

At 1745 'A' Coy reported enemy in strength, about five companies, emerging from a re-entrant on his right flank to attack. A few minutes later 'B' Coy reported enemy in strength about one Coy with MGs attacking his front. 1st Battery HKSRA applied SOS tasks [defensive fire barrage] on 'A' Coy Front. 'A' Coy reported enemy withdrawing in some disorder never having got through his wire and having suffered heavy casualties.[4]

The Japanese troops withdrew, taking shelter in ravines to escape the barrage. Artillery fire was then laid down in the ravines from both the 3.7-inch troop at Hai Wan and from the 6-inch howitzer sections on the Island. The Japanese attack was broken up, and they were unable to press forward, which facilitated an orderly withdrawal of troops during Friday night.

Major Dewar collected the WDV *Victoria* from Tai Koo docks. The Commodore had supplied RN personnel to act as coxswains and engineers. Dewar allocated these to *Victoria* and the other War Department and Harbour Department vessels. Captain Belton boarded a private speedboat owned and driven by Dr Frank Molthen, an

American chiropractor, who had volunteered his services to assist in the evacuation of troops. The vessels departed from Tai Koo Docks for Devil's Peak at dusk. The journeys back and forth across the harbour were hazardous because of heavy loads, and the lack of lights in pitch-dark conditions. The Punjab battalion was taken safely across the harbour, and the Rajputs were ordered to evacuate one of their rifle companies together with the troop from 1st Mountain Battery. The rest of the battalion was ordered to fall back to the Hai Wan line, the second line of defence. The original intention was that the Rajputs would continue to maintain their positions on Devil's Peak. However, Lt-Col Cadogan-Rawlinson was asked by Brigadier Wallis, at 0400 hours on Saturday 13 December, whether he was able to evacuate his whole battalion that morning. Cadogan-Rawlinson agreed to do this, but he knew that it was a difficult and dangerous task as by that time there were only two or three hours of darkness left. He had to move his three remaining rifle companies, the 'HQ' Coy, the MMG sections, and all their equipment to the embarkation area, and then to get the men and equipment across the harbour before enemy aircraft appeared at daybreak.

The forward troops started breaking off from their positions and falling back to the embarkation area. One of the machine gun sections, on the left flank of the Hai Wan line, remained in action until 0500 hours having not received the order to withdraw to the jetty. This facilitated the withdrawal because it led the Japanese to think that a strong force still remained on the Hai Wan line. This section managed to withdraw carrying their Vickers guns and their ammunition a distance of 1.5 miles to the jetty. During the evacuation, the lighter that was meant to pick up the mules was damaged. As a result, the mules which had been corralled in the quarry were left behind and later put to use by the Japanese. The loss of the mules was an unfortunate setback because the mules were used to transport the 3.7-inch howitzers. Had the mules been available, more guns might have been saved when the Japanese landed on the Island.

With daylight approaching, the GOC issued orders for the Royal Navy to send the destroyer HMS *Thracian* and the MTBs to assist in the evacuation effort, which had initially been carried out by War Department and Harbour Department launches and lighters. The final crossings were made in broad daylight, which made them vulnerable to aerial attack, but fortunately Japanese aircraft did not appear that morning.

The evacuation was fully completed by 0800 hours, and Brigadier Wallis and Major Harland boarded the last departing MTB. Two Indian soldiers, who were inadvertently left behind, managed to swim across the strait, whilst another group of ten Indian soldiers made their way back by sampan, and reported to their unit that evening. The military evacuation of the Mainland had been a remarkable success. In a Dunkirk-style operation, an infantry brigade, plus its supporting artillery, having conducted a fighting retreat, was evacuated by sea in a variety of launches, naval craft and civilian vessels. As the last British troops left the Mainland, the garrison hunkered down to defend the island fortress, and the siege of Hong Kong Island began.

5

The Royal Navy
8 to 18 December

In December 1941, British naval assets in the Far East were concentrated in Singapore. The battleship HMS *Prince of Wales* and the battlecruiser HMS *Repulse* arrived in Singapore with their escort destroyers on 2 December. The task force, referred to as Force Z, should have included the new aircraft carrier HMS *Indomitable*, but she was undertaking repairs having run aground in the West Indies. This powerful array of warships was expected to help deter the Japanese threat to British territories in the Far East. The naval presence in Hong Kong was comparatively weak. It included three First World War destroyers, HMS *Thracian*, HMS *Scout* and HMS *Thanet*. *Thracian* had been converted to act as a minelayer by removing her rear gun and clearing the afterdeck. The remaining two destroyers were ordered to sail to Singapore on the first day of the war. There were eight MTBs, which made up the 2nd MTB Flotilla. The boats were numbered 07, 08, 09, 10, 11, 12, 26 and 27. The MTBs were armed with torpedoes, depth charges and Lewis guns. The first six boats were constructed by Scott-Paine, and were relatively new, whereas MTBs 26 and 27 were older boats built by Thornycroft, both of which had been acquired from the Chinese Navy.

There were four gunboats: HMS *Cicala*, HMS *Tern*, HMS *Robin* and HMS *Moth*. *Moth* was in dry dock undergoing repairs and played no part in the battle except firing her 3-inch high-angle gun and her 2-pdr pom-pom at Japanese aircraft as opportunity presented. *Robin* had been assigned to boom defence and was based in Sai Wan Bay together with the two gate vessels HMS *Aldgate* and HMS *Watergate*, and the boom-servicing vessel HMS *Barlight*. The gate vessels *Aldgate* and *Watergate* were specialist ships used for opening and closing the anti-submarine boom gates. The boom blocked the eastern entrance to the harbour. It ran from Sai Wan Bay, on the north-east shore of the Island, across the harbour to Junk Bay on the Mainland. Any vessel proceeding in or out of the harbour, through the Lye Mun Straits, had to pass through the boom gates.

HMS *Redstart*, a minelayer, was utilised for laying mines and indicator loops. Indicator loops were cables laid on the seabed, which could pick up electromagnetic emissions from surface vessels or submarines passing over the cable. This data would then be transmitted by cable to a shore station, from where the information could be relayed to the mine control stations, which could then detonate remote-controlled mines to sink an intruding vessel. Alternatively, the information could be passed to the coastal defence batteries and the intruding vessel sunk by gunfire.

After the departure of *Thanet* and *Scout*, the Royal Navy was left with one destroyer, three serviceable gunboats and eight MTBs. The opposing Japanese naval force consisted of the 2nd China Expeditionary Fleet, commanded by Vice Admiral Niimi Masaichi, who flew his flag in the light cruiser IJN *Isuzu*. This ship was armed with 140mm (5.5-inch) guns which were occasionally used under cover of darkness to bombard targets on the south side of the Island including Aberdeen and Mount Davis. In addition to the cruiser, the Japanese fleet included three destroyers, three gunboats, four torpedo boats and a variety of minesweepers, patrol ships and fleet replenishment vessels.

The biggest threat to the Japanese Navy was the presence of the 9.2-inch coastal defence guns located at Fort Davis, Fort Stanley and Fort Bokhara. The 9.2-inch guns had a range of up to 20,000 yards, which was greater than the gun range on any of the Japanese warships assigned to support the invasion of Hong Kong. Major Robert Templer, commanding 30th Coast Battery, RA, based at Fort Bokhara, recalled periodic shoots with their 9.2-inch guns.

The period 8 December to 19 December was fairly uneventful. We had one shoot at extreme range at a Japanese trawler. ... From 12 December, onwards we engaged land targets mostly at night in Customs Pass area with unobserved fire. On 16 December, a large Japanese destroyer came just within our range. We engaged her and fired about ten salvoes. Immediately on opening fire, she started to zigzag and put out a smoke screen. ... The last round fired at extreme range 20,000 yards fell right behind her counter. I saw her stern lift in the air, and she proceeded much slower but still out of range.[1]

The Japanese naval force had been expected to carry out bombardments and to conduct diversionary raids on the south side of the Island, but because of the array of British coastal defence batteries, minefields and the presence of MTBs they stayed well back, limiting their activity to occasional shelling of land-based targets by night. Their principal role was to blockade the approaches to Hong Kong and to prevent reinforcement, replenishment or extrication.

The Wavy Navy

The Royal Naval Volunteer Reserve (RNVR), and their counterpart in Hong Kong, the HKRNVR, was known as the 'Wavy Navy' because of the wavy stripes officers wore on their uniform sleeves. The HKRNVR was responsible for mine warfare and minesweeping, and for conducting war patrols using a variety of converted tugs and launches referred to as auxiliary patrol vessels (APVs). The HKRNVR had been formed in 1933, initially with fifty recruits, many of whom were members of the Royal Hong Kong Yacht Club and therefore familiar with boat handling and navigation. The first commodore was Andrew Shields, a prominent businessman and LEGCO member. In 1934, the Royal Navy provided the newly formed HKRNVR with HMS *Cornflower*, a former *Arabis* class sloop, which was used as a depot and training ship. The RN had previously considered using her as a floating battery, but it was thought that this would contravene the Washington Naval Treaties.

By 1939 the HKRNVR mustered eighty-six officers and 150 men, and due to increasing numbers, consideration was given to forming a shore establishment. *Cornflower* had dragged her anchor a few times and was in need of a major refit. In March 1940, it was decided to sell and break up *Cornflower*, and a new ship, SS *Tai Hing*, was provided by Sir Robert Hotung and renamed HMS *Cornflower*.

The HKRNVR was mobilised in September 1939 following the outbreak of war in Europe. The force expanded rapidly, and officers and ratings served seamlessly with their Royal Navy counterparts on a variety of ships, but their main focus was mine-warfare and patrolling with the APVs. The indicator loops stretched in an arc from Lantau Island in the west to Port Shelter in the east. The indicator loops were connected by cable to a shore station at Tai Tam. The approaches to Hong Kong harbour were defended with contact minefields. Contact mines were cabled to the seabed and contained 350 pounds of TNT, and would detonate on the spikes being compressed by contact with a ship or submarine. Controlled mines had been placed across the Tathong Channel and across the East Lamma Channel. These mines could be detonated by remote control from shore stations at Chung Hom Kok (Mine Control Station, Lamma) and Shek-O (Mine Control Station, Tathong).

The Mine Watching Branch of the HKRNVR was established in August 1938. The HKRNVR carried out minefield and war patrols utilising a variety of APVs. The APVs were slow and lightly armed

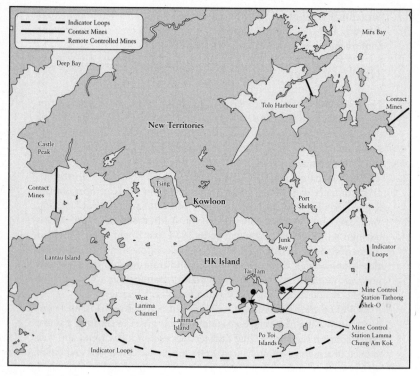

Indicator loops, minefields and mine control stations.

and relied heavily on locally recruited Chinese crews. Two or three HKRNVR officers were assigned to each vessel. There were four naval war patrols, referred to as the Beaufort Patrol from the southern point of Po Toi Island to the south-east point of Lamma Island, the North Ninepins Patrol from Basalt Island to Ninepins Island, the Tathong Patrol from Ninepins Island to Waglan Island and the South Lamma Patrol from south-west Lamma Island to Cheung Chau. The objective of the war patrols was to control shipping entering or leaving the harbour, and to investigate any reported crossings of indicator loops. Minefield patrols were carried out to prevent ships entering the minefields, to check the light-buoys on the minefield borders, and to track down any mines that had broken adrift which, once located, could then be rendered safe and recovered. Mines often broke loose from their anchors, especially in typhoons or stormy weather. Nearly four hundred drifting mines were recovered by APV crews in the period from 1939 to 1941.

Naval Operations (8 to 18 December)

Commodore Collinson, the Senior Naval Officer (SNO) in Hong Kong, received a signal from Singapore at 0500 hours on Monday 8 December stating that war had begun and that Japanese forces were carrying out landings in Malaya. HMS *Cicala* was moored alongside the north wall of the RN basin. She was a large gunboat with a displacement of 625 tons. She was built during the First World War and was designed to serve as a gunboat on the River Danube, but after the war ended she was dispatched to the China Station to patrol the Yangtze River. She had a normal complement of two officers, thirty-eight RN ratings, and eighteen Chinese ratings. Her two engines could produce a top speed of 14 knots. Her twin screws made her very manoeuvrable. She was a small ship, but she packed a surprisingly powerful punch. She was armed with two single 6-inch quick-firing guns located fore and aft, one 3-inch high-angle anti-aircraft gun, one 2-pdr pom-pom gun and eight Lewis guns. One complication was that not all the guns could be manned and fired at the same time. She could adopt any of three combinations: two six-inch; one six-inch and the 3-inch; or both the AA guns. *Cicala*'s commanding officer was forty-one-year-old Lt-Cdr John Boldero, a veteran of the First World War. In April 1941, he lost his right arm in an accident when one of the MTBs collided with *Thracian*. Early on Monday morning, Boldero received a telephone call from the Commodore instructing him to raise steam and to prepare for action. A little later he was warned of an imminent air raid, and the ship adopted the AA combination.

Near *Cicala*, alongside the north arm of the RN basin, was the HKRNVR base ship HMS *Cornflower*. Later that morning, HMAPV *Poseidon* took her in tow and moved her off the dockside, and then followed in her wake with the other APVs as she proceeded to her war station at Aberdeen Harbour. The HKRNVR flotilla was later moved to the naval anchorage at Deep Water Bay, and a shore base was established in one of the houses overlooking Middle Island. HMS *Moth* was a sister ship to *Cicala* with the same armament. When war started, she was undergoing repairs in the dry dock at the RN Dockyard. HMS *Tern* was smaller than both *Cicala* and *Moth*, with a displacement of 262 tons and a complement of fifty-five officers and men. She was armed with two 3-inch AA guns. Her commanding officer was Lt John Douglas, RNR. On that Monday morning, *Tern* was patrolling along the west coast of the Kowloon Peninsula north of Lantau Island. HMS *Robin* was the smallest of the four gunboats in Hong Kong. She had a displacement of 85 tons, and a complement of twenty-five officers and men. She was acting as depot ship for the boom defence vessels and was lying at her moorings in Sai Wan Bay. Her commanding officer was Commander

Hugh Montague, who was serving as Boom Defence Officer and later became Senior Naval Officer (Aberdeen).

Forty-three-year-old Lt-Commander Collingwood-Selby was on board his ship, HMS *Redstart*, at the Kowloon naval basin. The previous evening, Collingwood-Selby had attended a farewell dinner at the Hong Kong Hotel for an American friend, Mose Kelly, a mining engineer, who was one of those passengers due to fly out on the Clipper that morning. The MTBs were also berthed in the Kowloon naval basin. The eight boats which formed the 2nd MTB Flotilla were under the command of Lt-Commander Gerrard Gandy. The MTBs were armed with torpedoes, depth charges and Lewis guns. Each boat had a crew of nine including two officers. During the raid on Kai Tak, the MTBs dispersed in the harbour before moving to their war station at Aberdeen. Once hostilities commenced the officers and crews were accommodated on the MTBs except for the two Thornycroft boats, MTBs 26 and 27, which had no accommodation space. The crews for these two boats were accommodated on *Robin*, initially in Sai Wan Bay, and later at its mooring in Aberdeen Harbour.

At the RN Dockyard, the Royal Marine Detachment, commanded by Major Farrington, had been stood-to since the early hours of Monday 8 December. The marines were manning the dockyard anti-aircraft guns, consisting of a 4-inch AA gun, pom-poms and Lewis guns equipped with AA mountings. Later that morning, the venerable HMS *Tamar* was towed out from the west wall of the RN basin to No. 8 buoy, situated to the west of Kellett Island. A care-and-maintenance party had been left on board while the rest of her ship's company were moved to the China Fleet Club and later to Aberdeen Industrial School (AIS), which was taken over by the Royal Navy to act as the main naval base. *Tamar* was a Victorian-era troopship that had been launched in 1863. She had been permanently located in Hong Kong from 1897 as receiving ship and naval headquarters. *Thracian*, commanded by Lt-Commander Pears, had sailed to Port Shelter, where she was laying mines guarded by HMS *Thanet*. HMS *Scout* was in dry dock at Tai Koo Dockyard having her bottom plates scraped. At 0740 hours, *Tern* was attacked by two Japanese seaplanes while on patrol in the North Lantau Channel. *Tern* opened up with her AA guns and reported that one of the planes appeared damaged and broke off from the action with smoke trailing. HMS *Tern* received four near misses from aerial bombs, incurring no damage but earning the distinction of being the first British warship to engage with Japanese forces in Hong Kong waters.

At 0800 hours, Kai Tak and Sham Shui Po barracks came under attack. *Cicala* was ordered to relieve *Tern*, which returned to Hong Kong Harbour to take up her war station in Kowloon Bay from where

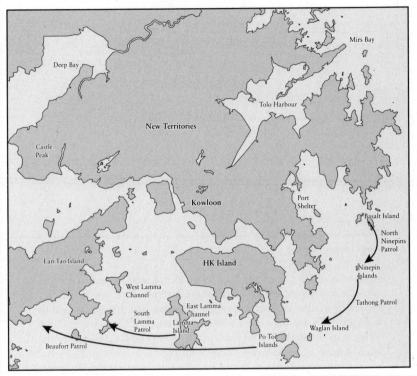

Naval war patrols.

she could provide AA defence for Kai Tak Airfield. *Cicala* and MTB 11 patrolled the west coast of the Mainland from Castle Peak to Tsun Wan. At 1100 hours, *Cicala* was attacked by two seaplanes which carried out six bombing runs. The aircraft were engaged by the ship's 3-inch HA gun and her quick-firing pom-pom guns. At 1430 hours, *Cicala* was attacked for the second time that day, again by two seaplanes which made five bombing runs.

Scout and *Thanet* were ordered, by the Commander-in-Chief, Eastern Fleet, to sail for Singapore where they were to join Force Z. HMS *Scout* was taken out of dry dock and moved to the RN Dockyard where her torpedoes and ammunition were reloaded. Preparations were made for the departure of both ships, which would take place after nightfall. *Scout* and *Thanet* passed through the anti-submarine boom gates at Lye Mun at around 2100 hours bound first for Manila and then Singapore. While on passage to Manila they searched for any sign of SS *Ulysses*. The Blue Funnel Line ship had left Hong Kong

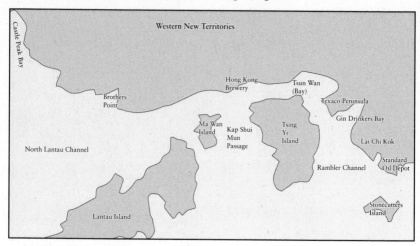

North Lantau Channel.

on Sunday 7 December and had sent out a distress signal reporting that she was under attack by Japanese aircraft. The two destroyers arrived in Manila on Wednesday 10 December and then proceeded to Singapore. *Thanet* was sunk a few weeks later, on 27 January 1942, by a Japanese cruiser, but *Scout* made it safely back to Colombo after the fall of Singapore in February 1942.

At dawn on Tuesday 9 December, *Cicala* was patrolling between Castle Peak Bay, Brothers Point and Hong Kong Brewery. Lt-Cdr Boldero observed a large number of Japanese troops attempting to repair the road bridge at Brothers Point, which had been partially demolished by the sappers. *Cicala* opened fire with her 6-inch forward gun at a range of 8,000 yards. The fire was seen to be effective. At 0900 hours, two seaplanes attacked *Cicala*, but the two sticks of three bombs went wide. At 0930 hours, *Cicala* was ordered back to Brothers Point to check that the road demolition was still effective. They noticed piles of timber stacked by the roadside to facilitate the repair work. Using her 6-inch guns, *Cicala* fired at the road bridge, and at a bus and lorry to the west of the bridge, thought to be carrying troops, which had been held up by the demolition. The gunfire was seen to be effective. Meanwhile, *Thracian*, having completed the minelaying at Port Shelter, returned to the RN Dockyard to convert back to her normal armament.

On Wednesday 10 December, the Royal Navy suffered its biggest loss in the Far East when the battleship *Prince of Wales* and the battlecruiser *Repulse* were sunk by Japanese aircraft off the east coast of Malaya.

The *Prince of Wales* was a newly completed battleship. It had been built in compliance with the tonnage and gun calibre restrictions set out in the Washington Treaties. *Repulse* was a First World War-era battlecruiser that had been refitted and recommissioned in 1936. The loss of these two capital ships was a serious setback for the British, and the news of their destruction was demoralising not just for British forces in Singapore and Malaya, but also for those defending Hong Kong as it closed any prospect of relief coming from Singapore. During Wednesday afternoon *Cicala* was attacked by nine aircraft. One bomb hit her stern quarters without exploding but nonetheless caused considerable damage by passing right through the ship from top to bottom. She returned to the harbour escorted by *Tern*, and later proceed to Tai Koo Dockyard for repairs.

Thracian completed her conversion work on Thursday 11 December and sailed to the East Lamma Channel where a number of junks and sampans had been observed. There was concern that these vessels might be used to carry Japanese troops from Lamma Island to Hong Kong Island. Lt Ralph, commanding HMAPV *Shun Wo*, was anchored near Sandy Bay, on the south-west side of Hong Kong Island, when he was fired on from Lamma Island.

> We saw puffs of smoke on the shores of Luk Chau Wan on Lamma. It was then obvious that the Japanese had landed a field gun on Lamma and that they were firing at my ship. ... I at once moved to the east of Magazine Island and sent in a signal. This raised a hornet's nest as destroyers as well as all our APVs were instructed to sink all junks in the East Lamma Channel. I only sunk one at my end and rescued all the crew who were obviously Chinese including women and children.[2]

There were a large number of casualties among the boat people who lived and worked on these junks. Lt-Commander Gandy wrote about this incident in the MTB war diary suggesting that it may have been a contributory factor in the subsequent desertions by Chinese naval ratings from many of the APVs.

> About noon HMS *Thracian* and all APVs were ordered to shell all junks out of Picnic Bay on Lamma Island as the Japanese were thought to have a party on the island ready to come across in junks. Some junks were sunk. I consider that the Chinese HKRNVR crews of the APVs did not relish this work against their own class of junk-men, this may have been a contributory cause of their defection which gradually took place, until on 19th December when the APVs were scuttled there was practically no Chinese HKRNVR ratings left.[3]

While *Cicala* was undergoing repairs at Tai Koo Dockyard on Thursday 11 December, one bomb landed quite close to the ship, causing splinter damage and leading to the desertion of her eighteen Chinese ratings. *Cicala* was instructed to make up the shortfall from the crew of HMS *Moth*. *Moth* and HMAPV *Margaret* were both sharing the dry dock at the RN Dockyard. It was found impossible to effect repairs to these vessels with the lack of dockyard labourers and the constant shelling of the dockyard, and a decision was taken to scuttle both vessels, by removal of their bottom plates, after flooding the dock. During the late afternoon on Thursday, *Tern* and the MTBs were ordered to Kowloon Bay to guard the withdrawal of 2/RS from Kowloon City Pier. Star Ferry launches manned by naval personnel also assisted in the evacuation. During the afternoon, before the evacuation commenced, the Commodore utilised MTBs 08 and 09 to allow him to move around the harbour. HMS *Tamar* had been evacuated earlier that day, and while the Commodore was embarked on MTB 08, he ordered the boat's commander to fire a torpedo at *Tamar* lying at its mooring off the Wan Chai waterfront. The torpedo was launched but did not explode, probably due to insufficient depth of water. The following day, on Friday 12 December, *Tamar* was scuttled at her buoy. Recently, what appears to be the bottom plate of *Tamar* and various other artefacts linked to *Tamar* have been found during reclamation work off Causeway Bay.

On Sunday 14 December, *Thracian* was ordered to sail to Kowloon Bay to destroy two steamers that were thought to be carrying troops. The destroyer sailed anticlockwise around Lamma Island and through the East Lamma Channel to Victoria Harbour. While rounding the southern tip of Lamma Island, *Thracian* grounded on Un Kok Point. The ship floated off and was able to complete the mission by destroying the Japanese vessels in Kowloon Bay. However, after returning from the raid in the early hours of Monday 15 December, *Thracian* was ordered to proceed to Deep Water Bay where dockyard technicians examined her damaged bows and decided that she would need to be put into dry dock in order to effect repairs.

During the evening, Aberdeen was shelled at extreme range by Japanese warships. At 2130 hours, MTBS 10, 11, 12 and 27 were dispatched to locate and attack the enemy vessels. The MTBs proceeded in pairs towards Lantau Island. The sea was calm and the night was dark, which were ideal operating conditions for the MTBs. The Japanese must have heard the sound of the engines as the first pair of MTBs were suddenly illuminated by searchlights and then came under fire. The first two MTBs withdrew from range. The second pair of MTBs proceeded to attack from a different direction, but again the searchlights picked out the leading boat, which came under heavy fire. However, the second boat, which was not picked up by the searchlights, continued the attack, while the first two boats returned to make a simultaneous attack from another direction. Four torpedoes were launched at the Japanese warships, which were thought to be either destroyers or minesweepers. A Tokyo newspaper later reported that Japanese naval vessels had been attacked in Hong Kong and casualties incurred on that day.

On Tuesday 16 December, there was a very heavy air raid on Aberdeen Dockyard carried out by high-altitude bombers, which were thought to be targeting *Thracian*. The dockyard sustained considerable damage. MTBS 10 and 26, which were lying alongside *Robin*, were damaged by bomb fragments. MTB 08, which was on the slipway, was hit by bomb splinters and set ablaze and completely burnt out. The naval armament tug *Gatling* was hit and destroyed with several fatal casualties among her Merchant Navy volunteer crew. Following the damage to the Aberdeen dockyard, it was not possible to repair *Thracian*. On Wednesday 17 December, *Thracian* was undocked and, with a skeleton crew on board, sailed under her own power to Repulse Bay where she was beached at Round Island. The naval party on *Thracian* was picked up by the launch WDV *French*, which was manned by the crew from the burnt-out MTB 08. The following evening, Japanese forces crossed the harbour and landed on the north-east shore of the Island.

6

The Island under Siege
12 to 18 December

The infantry was initially divided into two brigades: the Mainland Brigade under Brigadier Wallis, and the Island Brigade under Brigadier Lawson. The Mainland Brigade consisted of the two Indian battalions, the Royal Scots and No. 1 Coy, HKVDC. The Island Brigade consisted of the two Canadian battalions, the HKVDC (less No. 1 Coy), and the Middlesex Regiment. The Middlesex manned most of the beach defence pillboxes situated around the Island shoreline. After the evacuation of the Mainland between Thursday 11 December and Saturday 13 December, the two infantry brigades were reorganised into the East Infantry Brigade under Wallis, and the West Infantry Brigade under Lawson. Wallis established his Brigade HQ in an underground bunker at Tai Tam Gap, which had once been the Fortress Plotting Room (FPR) for Eastern Fire Command. A new FPR for Eastern Fire Command been established at Stanley Fort. The FPR for Western Fire Command was located at Mount Davis. Eastern and Western Fire Command were responsible for the coastal defence batteries in the east and west sectors of the Island. Wallis provides a good description, in the East Brigade war diary, of the Brigade HQ at Tai Tam Gap. He occupied this underground bunker from 13 December, following the evacuation of the Mainland, until 19 December, when East Brigade and its supporting artillery withdrew to Stanley following the Japanese landings.

> The room was largely occupied by a huge steel table which was useful to work on with maps, but hampered movement. In this room were located: the brigade commander, Brigade Major, Staff Captain, half the Brigade Signals Exchange (two operators), Brigade Intelligence Officer and three Brigade Clerks. In a tiny side room was the large telephone exchange. In another small room was the emergency lighting plant.

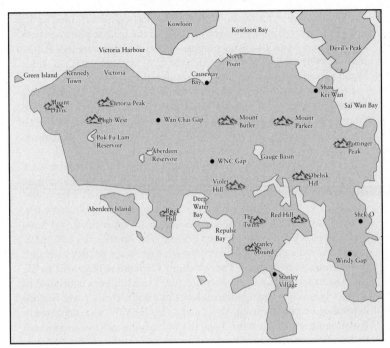

The Island.

The room was reached by a long winding narrow passage into which the sappers were busy fitting sleeping bunks for staff and signals personnel. This passage was very dark and crowded at night, and it took me some six minutes to leave my maps and numerous telephones and reach East Group, RA, and 'D' Battalion [RRC] HQ in the shelters up above mine, after threading my way through a maze of camouflage nets and nervous sentries. The atmosphere was heavy, and even with the emergency plant working, and the air-vent (emergency exit) open the air was unhealthy and oppressive and made clear thinking difficult. One became flushed and had bad headaches. The useful guiding sounds of battle which are so helpful in telling a commander of progress when he is located in a well-selected field position were denied to one. The only advantage was immunity from shell fire and air attack.[1]

The Tai Tam Gap military HQ structures, situated at the junction of Tai Tam Road and Shek-O Road, close to Obelisk Hill, still remain. They include two line-of-gap pillboxes and some seventeen splinter-proof concrete shelters. The site is overgrown, and the structures are dilapidated, but one can still enter the underground bunker that Wallis used as his HQ. The underground passageway leads to the former plotting room which is now home to a large number of bats. The concrete legs for the plotting table are still there, although the large steel table top, on which Wallis spread his maps, has long been removed.

Brigadier Lawson continued to occupy his existing Brigade HQ located in a cluster of splinter-proof shelters just north of Wong Nai Chung (WNC) Gap. Lawson's HQ found itself on the front line when the Japanese Army converged on WNC Gap. The concrete war shelters, including Lawson's bunker, still remain.

After the evacuation of the Mainland, the 2/14 Punjabs were transferred to West Brigade and were responsible for the north-west sector of the Island. The Royal Scots were initially deployed on the north-east shore in East Brigade sector but later transferred to West Brigade. The 5/7 Rajputs took over the north-east sector from the Royal Scots and remained there as part of East Brigade. The Royal Rifles of Canada continued to be responsible for the south-east sector of the Island and came under East Brigade. The Winnipeg Grenadiers remained in the south-west sector as part of West Brigade. The Middlesex continued to man their beach defence pillboxes and came under the relevant brigade depending on their location. Nos 1 and 2 Coy HKVDC were deployed in East Brigade sector, the remaining HKVDC infantry units were deployed in West Brigade sector.

The mobile artillery was split into East Group, RA, which provided artillery support to East Infantry Brigade, and West Group, RA, which supported West Infantry Brigade. The mobile artillery was equipped with 3.7-inch, 4.5-inch and 6-inch howitzers. The 3.7-inch howitzers were capable of being stripped down and transported by pack mules. The larger howitzers had to be towed by trucks. In reality, the mobile artillery was not very mobile, because they were generally located in pre-prepared sites with concrete ammunition shelters, gun pits, splinter-proof battery buildings, and in some cases, light AA defence, but more critically because of the shortage of both mules and towing trucks. This lack of mobility resulted in a large number of guns being lost on 19 December, when during the chaos and confusion following the Japanese landings on the Island, many of the guns found themselves unexpectedly on the front line and unable to withdraw because of the lack of dedicated transport near the gun positions. The most mobile of the artillery units were the 40mm Bofors guns operated by 5th AA Regiment, and the 2-pdr anti-tank guns operated by 965 Defence Battery, which with dedicated rather than pooled transport were frequently moved around.

East Group, RA, HQ was co-located with East Infantry Brigade HQ at Tai Tam Gap and utilised AOPs at Stanley Mound, Braemar Hill, Pottinger

Peak, Mount Parker, Red Hill, and Jardine's Lookout. Two additional AOPs were opened on 15 December, one at Sai Wan AA Fort and one on Mount Butler. West Group, RA, HQ was initially located at Wan Chai Gap but later moved to West Infantry Brigade HQ shelters at WNC Gap. West Group utilised AOPs at Victoria Peak, High West, Matilda, Middle Spur, Mount Nicholson, Kennedy Town, and Wan Chai Gap.

The *Jeanette* Incident

On Friday 12 December, Commander James Jolly, the harbourmaster, notified Fortress HQ that they were going to ship 9 tons of dynamite by launch from the magazines on Green Island to the vehicular ferry pier on Hong Kong Island. The police were asked to clear civilians from No. 9 Air Raid Tunnel, located in an area known as Smithfield, near Belchers Street. The air raid tunnel was to be used to store the dynamite, which was needed to create firebreaks in the urban areas, particularly in the vicinity of Kennedy Town in the north-west sector of the Island. The vessel designated to transport the dynamite was the launch *Jeanette*, a passenger tender belonging to P&O, which had been requisitioned by the Harbour Department. She had a volunteer crew, which included several European police officers and Harbour Department staff. It was agreed that the vessel would leave Green Island at midnight, and would then proceed along the north-west shore to the ferry pier. The Army notified the pillboxes situated on that section of the Island shoreline of the launch's route and timing. The launch left for Green Island without incident, and on arrival loaded the cases of dynamite, fuses and detonators. At 2138 hours, the Harbour Master telephoned through to Fortress HQ with a message that *Jeanette* was now leaving Green Island at 2200 hours, and not at midnight as previously advised. The Army authorities hurriedly started calling the pillboxes to notify them of the new departure time.

PB 63, with a ten-man crew from 1/Mx, was under the command of Cpl Charles Heather. The pillbox was situated on the vehicular ferry pier. Tiredness, the darkness of the blackout, the periodic sound of gunfire, and strained nerves must have all contributed to the men being on edge, and seeing things differently than they were. At 2230 hours, PB 63 reported that a large launch full of enemy troops was approaching their location. At 2245 hours, PB 59 in the RN Dockyard reported seeing, and engaging, a number of small craft full of troops in the harbour. The sound of gunfire on their right may have led the crew of PB 63 into thinking that a landing was being attempted. Major Gray, 2/14 Punjabs, was duty officer for the north-west sector that evening and he described receiving an urgent call from PB 63.

At 2250 hours Fortress informed that the launch had left Green Island (two hours before time). I immediately started to inform PBs of this fact, starting from the left (PB 72), as that would be the first to be passed. As instructions were being given to PB 66 an urgent call from PB 63 to the effect that the enemy launch previously reported was now very near, bearing directly at the pier, and that it carried no lights. The speaker was very agitated, and while he was still reporting this, another voice was heard over the telephone giving an order to fire, and the noise of firing was then heard. Suddenly there was complete silence and communication appeared to have broken down. I at once informed Captain Kampta Prasad at Garden Road and ordered him to take a platoon ... and clear up the situation in the vicinity of the vehicular ferry. I then called for reports from PBs 64, 65 and 66 who all reported nothing suspicious. After attempts to regain communication with PB 63 for several minutes, I finally gained contact with a L/Cpl who appeared to be quite calm and reported that everything was alright.[2]

PB 63 had hit *Jeanette* and her cargo of dynamite. The explosion was enormous, blowing out windows and causing damage all across the central area of the city. It must have shocked, deafened and disorientated the crew of PB 63. The L/Cpl who spoke with Gray did not mention that his section commander, and at least two others, had left the PB after the resulting explosion in a panic, perhaps thinking the PB had been destroyed and convinced that they were under attack. At approximately 2330 hours, Captain Prasad rang through to Bn HQ and informed Major Gray that everything appeared normal on the north shore. However, the story gets more bizarre.

A commotion was heard outside Battalion HQ, and a civilian ARP man was brought in by a Cpl of 1/Mx who said he had found him rushing about in a state of panic. ... Captain Flood, 1/Mx, recognised the corporal as Cpl Heather, the commander of PB 63. On being questioned the Cpl stated that PB 63 had been destroyed and that enemy soldiers had landed and were firing in the streets. During this interrogation, two Ptes of 1/Mx arrived in a state of exhaustion and panic and confirmed all that Corporal Heather had said about the enemy landing and said that one of them had been wounded by rifle fire whilst escaping from the PB and pointed to blood on his face. All three stated they were the only survivors of PB 63. The NCO and men were immediately placed under arrest. I then ordered Captain Flood to go to the area and take over general command.[3]

Later that night, PB 59, situated on the north arm at the RN Dockyard, and PB 58, located near the China Fleet Club, both reported the presence of small boats and again opened fire. Major Gray stated that he believed that enemy boats were operating, possibly testing the defences on the north shore. The firing of flares and machine guns went on intermittently from 2300 hours until the early hours of Saturday 13 December.

John Monro, Brigade Major Royal Artillery, was asleep in his apartment at Courtlands on Kennedy Road. He was woken up to take a telephone call from Staff Captain Harry Bramble, RA, who was on duty at Fortress HQ. Bramble asked him to return to the office in the Battle Box because the Japanese had apparently effected a landing. When Monro arrived, he found the HQ in a state of confusion. In his memoirs, held at the Imperial War Museum, he describes taking part in a patrol with a party of military police.[4] Around the harbour front they found windows blown out and the streets covered in broken glass. They came across military and police patrols but found no sign of the Japanese. The next day, a party of Japanese did cross the harbour.

The First Peace Mission

After the massive explosion and the rumours of Japanese landings during the previous night, Saturday morning began quietly. The last troops to be evacuated from the Mainland had already left Devil's Peak. The Japanese were in full possession of the Mainland. American news reporter Gwen Dew, staying on the Island, had got up early to take photographs of the damaged buildings along the harbour. She glanced across towards Kowloon and saw a boat emerging from Holt's Wharf and heading for the Island. Its occupants bore a large white banner with the words 'Peace Mission' emblazoned on it. The boat, the *Ma On*, which belonged to the Hong Kong and Yaumati Ferry Company, was initially fired on before the white flag was observed. The boat arrived at Queens Pier, where a party of three Japanese officers and two European women disembarked. One of the ladies was Mrs Mavis Lee, the wife of Charles Lee, the Governor's Private Secretary. Mrs Lee had brought her two dachshunds with her. The second woman, Mrs MacDonald, was a pregnant Russian lady. The three Japanese officers were Colonel Tada of Military Information, Lt Mizuno, and Lt Othsu, who acted as an interpreter.

Gwen Dew was busy taking photographs and interviewing both Mrs Lee and the Japanese military officials. One of her photographs, showing the three Japanese delegates and Mrs Lee standing behind a barbed-wire barrier with British soldiers in the background, was published in the next day's edition of the *South China Morning Post*. Mrs Lee had been working at an ARP post and was unaware that Kowloon had been evacuated, only discovering this late on Thursday 11 December, by which time the ferries had stopped running.

The Japanese had entered Kowloon the next morning. Mrs Lee had been staying at the Harbour View Hotel with a group of about fourteen people, which included Mrs Winifred Gardiner, the proprietor of the hotel, and James, her twenty-nine-year-old son. The Harbour View Hotel was located in the Lei Yu Mun Building on Chatham Road. The building also included the Arlington Hotel. Mrs Gardiner was the proprietor of both hotels.

While Mrs Lee was waiting with the Japanese delegation, Major Charles Manners, a retired Army officer who was General Manager of Hong Kong & Kowloon Wharf Company, brought her some cigarettes and arranged for a tray with tea and sandwiches to be delivered from the nearby Hong Kong Club. Mrs Lee explained that the Japanese had arrived at the hotel on Friday evening and had treated them courteously. They asked her to act as a hostage for the peace mission, which she agreed to on condition that Mrs MacDonald, who was heavily pregnant, would be allowed to accompany them and be permitted to remain on the Island. Major Boxer, in charge of the intelligence unit known as the Far East Combined Bureau, arrived and received a letter addressed to the Governor from the Japanese commanders that called for an unconditional surrender, and warned that if this was not forthcoming the artillery and bombing raids on the Island would be escalated. Boxer took the letter to the Governor, Sir Mark Young, and returned with the Governor's response, which was an outright rejection. The Japanese delegation returned to Kowloon, with Mrs Lee and her dogs, and in the afternoon war resumed.

The Siege of the Island

The aerial bombing and shelling of the Island intensified. An artillery duel developed with shells raining down on both sides. Some of the larger buildings in Victoria stood up well to the bombardment, in particular the newly built head office of the Hongkong and Shanghai Banking Corporation. The large hotel buildings in the city, including the Hong Kong Hotel and the Gloucester Hotel, also withstood the shelling with relatively light damage. Mount Davis came under particularly heavy bombardment, and on 13 December, Western Fire Command at Mount Davis was hit by three 240mm (9.45-inch) shells. These rounds were fired by a Type 45 siege howitzer, which was the largest gun used by the Japanese in the Battle for Hong Kong. The Type 45 howitzer fired a 440-pound shell with a range of up to 6 miles.

On Sunday 14 December, a 240mm shell hit the uppermost 9.2-inch gun at Mount Davis. The shell failed to explode but still did enough damage to put the gun out of action. This gun, being the highest of the three 9.2-inch guns, was particularly useful for landward firing. During the same bombardment, one of the two 3-inch AA guns on Mount Davis was put out of action, and the other gun damaged following a direct hit on the nearby magazine. On the same day, the Lower Belcher's Battery, consisting of two 4.7-inch guns, was destroyed and set ablaze by a combination of aerial bombing and shelling. The next day, Monday 15 December, Pinewood AA Fort, which was situated in an exposed position on the north-facing slopes of the Peak, was put out of action following accurate shelling and bombing. One of the fort's two 3-inch AA guns was destroyed and the other badly damaged, and with both guns out of action the fort was abandoned. The ruins of the gun emplacements and battery buildings can still be seen today.

As a consequence of the very heavy shelling being directed at the Island, a counterbattery HQ (CBHQ) was established under the command of Major Proes at WNC Gap. Directly under his command were the 6-inch howitzers at Tiger Balm Gardens, which were subsequently moved to Stanley Gap Road on 16 December, and the 6-inch howitzers at Caroline Hill, which were moved on 17 December to the area near the Jockey Club Stables. He also had a call on the other medium (4.5-inch and 6-inch) howitzers from both East and West Group to provide counterbattery fire as required. Reports of shelling and flash spotting were sent through to CBHQ from the AOPs, BOPs and PBs. Some Japanese guns were destroyed by counterbattery fire but the position of the 240mm siege howitzer, which was reportedly located near Shatin, was not identified. Japanese observed artillery fire was very accurate, and two 18-pdr beach defence guns, belonging to 965 Defence Battery, were destroyed following movement of the guns on the north shore. However, none of the British howitzers from the mobile artillery were hit by Japanese counterbattery fire.

During the evening on 15 December, there were reports of an attempted landing by Japanese forces around Lye Mun. One of the main searchlights at Pak Sha Wan was switched on, illuminating the channel between Devil's Peak and Lye Mun. On being told that an attempted landing was taking place, Wallis ordered an artillery barrage to be laid down both on the channel and on the foreshore at Devils Peak. Japanese records do not mention an attempted landing on that day, and this may have been another false alarm. The reported landing and subsequent firing may have been in response to the movement of civilian junks and sampans. Japanese reports only indicate that prior to the invasion of the Island, reconnaissance patrols were landed on the Island by night to reconnoitre the landing areas and shore defences.

On Tuesday 16 December, Mount Davis, with two of its three 9.2-inch guns still operating, was subjected to a very heavy bombardment.

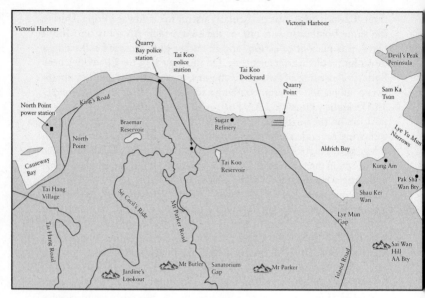

North Shore from Causeway Bay to Shau Kei Wan.

The Fortress Plotting Room was hit by a shell and destroyed. There were twenty men inside the plotting room, but only one injury was sustained because the shell failed to explode. RSM Ford describes the damage caused to the plotting room.

> BSM Barlow and myself established order in the plotting room amid smoke, fumes and picric acid. Our lights are out and the blower plant disabled, and daylight is visible through the roof. This roof was once a thickness of fifteen feet of earth and concrete. A shell penetrated right through this, through a steel door, ripped all the bricks from one wall ploughed through another wall and finished up in the telephone exchange without exploding.[5]

Mount Davis was temporarily evacuated after the bombardment, and the gunners spent the next day at Felix Villas, located at the base of Mount Davis. The fort was reoccupied after nightfall on 17 December. Western Fire Command was re-established at the Royal Navy Port War Signal Station on the mid slopes of Mount Davis. The bombing and shelling of the Island was relentless until a lull occurred on Wednesday 17 December when a second peace mission was sent across to the Island.

This time two launches flying the white flag of truce crossed the harbour, but without hostages, and bearing a similar message as before, calling on the Governor to surrender the colony to avoid further bloodshed. Once again, the letter was addressed to the Governor and was signed by Lt-General Sakai, Commander of the 23rd Army, and Vice Admiral Niimi, the naval commander.

Maltby thought that this second demand to surrender, coming so quickly after the first, suggested that the Japanese were reluctant to launch an attack across the harbour and that they were concerned about the Nationalist Chinese Army threat to their rear. This was not the case. The Japanese had sufficient forces in southern China to deal with any threat from the rear. The Japanese knew that the outcome of the battle was a foregone conclusion; they never doubted they would quickly capture Hong Kong, and they knew exactly what they were up against. It is more likely that they thought that the heavy bombardment of the Island would have weakened the will to resist, and they no doubt wanted to spare the infrastructure of the city they were about to capture. It was also important for the Japanese to expedite the capture of Hong Kong so that their forces could be deployed elsewhere. After the battle, Lt-General Kitajima's 1st Artillery Group was dispatched to the Philippines, and the 38th Division was moved to the Dutch East Indies, and later participated in the fighting in New Guinea and Guadalcanal. The Japanese delegates landed at Queen's Pier and once again were met by Major Boxer, who carried their proposal to the Governor. Once again the Governor defiantly refused to consider the surrender of the colony, and like a Roman general burning his bridges, sent the Japanese delegation away, but this time closing the door to any further such entreaty by stating that he was not prepared to receive any further communication on the subject.

During the evening on 17 December, the Royal Artillery was ordered to sink by gunfire three freighters anchored in Kowloon Bay. The vessels ranged in size from 3,000 to 5,000 tons. It was thought they were being utilised by the Japanese as observation posts or staging posts for an attack on the Island. Lt Vintner, HKSRA, was given the responsibility of carrying out the operation after nightfall. He was allocated a 60-pdr field gun which had been in storage for many years together with an 8-ton Scammell towing truck and fifty rounds of ammunition. The only shells available for this First World War-era field gun were of the anti-personnel variety rather than armour piercing. However, notwithstanding this, all three vessels were damaged, and one was reportedly sunk at her mooring. After having fired some thirty rounds, the detachment was forced to withdraw after Japanese counterbattery fire homed in on their position on the North Point waterfront.

During the morning of Thursday 18 December, there was a heavy air raid in the central area of Victoria. Shelling continued all along the north shore, but particularly from North Point to Shau Kei Wan. The Japanese had been systematically and accurately shelling the pillboxes along the north-east shore so that by Thursday afternoon more than half the PBs in this sector had been knocked out. In the early evening, the Japanese Army moved to their embarkation points. The siege of the Island was over, and the invasion of the Island was about to begin.

7

Invasion of the Island
18 to 19 December

The Japanese landings took place during the night of Thursday 18 December along a broad stretch of shoreline from North Point to Shau Kei Wan. All three infantry regiments of the 38th Division were deployed in the initial landings, with each regiment utilising two of their three battalions. The remaining battalion from each regiment was operating under divisional command and was deployed to the Island at a later stage. The infantry battalions were the first to land, with other units including artillery, gendarmerie, and engineers landing once the beachhead had been secured. The 229th Regiment, under Colonel Tanaka, was assigned to the left flank and was to land at two locations in Aldrich Bay. The 228th Regiment, under Colonel Doi, was assigned to the centre and was to land in Quarry Bay and Tai Koo Docks. The 230th Regiment, under Colonel Shoji, was to land on the right flank at North Point.

Colonel Doi assigned the 2nd Battalion of the 228th Regiment to cross first, and once they had landed and fired their success signal, they were to be followed by the 1st Battalion. The embarkation point for Doi's regiment was at Tai Wan Tsun, at the eastern end of Kai Tak Airfield. The 2nd Battalion embarked at 1900 hours just after dark. They were to cross the harbour by rowing collapsible assault craft with each boat carrying fourteen men. The Japanese had brought with them rigid assault boats and collapsible boats, but they also made use of commandeered launches, junks and sampans. The men in the first wave of the assault were ordered to paddle quietly, and to take advantage of the half-sunk wrecks in the harbour to conceal their approach for as long as possible. It was estimated that they would take one hour to cross the harbour. The battalion was to land at Braemar Point, with one company assigned the task of capturing the docks and the sugar refinery. Once the first

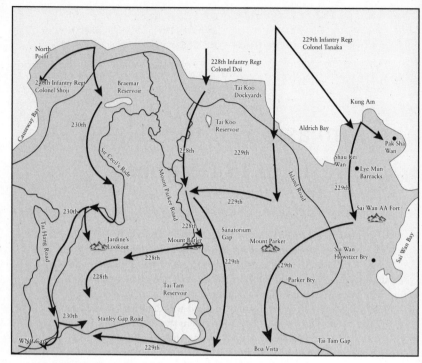

Japanese landing areas and approximate routes taken to WNC Gap.

wave (2/228) had landed, the second wave (1/228) was to proceed as quickly as possible using powered boats, with each boat towing a string of collapsible assault craft. The first wave reached mid-stream without detection, but as the landing craft got closer, they were spotted by the Rajput defenders in their pillboxes and alternative positions along the north shore. Red flares were fired, signalling that an enemy attack was taking place, and the pillboxes commenced firing with their Vickers medium machine guns (MMGs). Doi's account, written after the war, captures the tension of the crossing and the devastating effect of the MMG fire.

> Streams of enemy machine gun fire from the opposite shore and Lye Mun Point slowed the boats, and since they failed to take a straight course, units were either mixed or separated while they were still on the water. The resultant confusion made it almost impossible to maintain complete command of the battalion. Some boats had their

oars broken, and men rowed with entrenching shovels. When exposed to fire on the water, which offers no shelter, it is absolutely useless to turn the boats away from the direction of enemy fire, but perhaps it is only normal human psychology to react that way. It was a spectacular and grim crossing, but for the most part, men went ashore as scheduled.[1]

Once the 2nd Battalion had landed and fired its signal, the 1st Battalion proceeded to cross the harbour as quickly as possible. Doi described how he boarded a barge with some eighty officers and men and led the 1st Battalion in the crossing.

> The harbour was still being illuminated by searchlights and the flare of the burning heavy oil in storage tanks, and the enemy machine gun fire was all the more intense. ... At the spot where we landed there was a wire net fence, something like the one ordinarily found around a tennis court, which blocked our advance inland. Unlike ordinary wire entanglements, the net could not be cut by wire-cutters, and we spent some time going over it with a ladder which was brought along. Enemy machine gun fire was as intense as ever, and the second wave was forced to lie prone at the water's edge for a time after the landing. The anti-tank gun company lost a number of men so that only one gun could be manned, and it took three hours for the commander of the 1st Battalion to regain complete command of his battalion.[2]

The other two regiments had also succeeded in getting ashore. The 230th Regiment, commanded by Colonel Shoji, landed some 500 metres east of North Point at approximately 2000 hours. Shoji disembarked with the second wave of his regiment at about 2100 hours. At around midnight, Shoji established his Regimental HQ on the western side of what he described as a large lake – it was actually Braemar Reservoir – situated on the high ground several hundred metres south of the landing area. Shoji's two battalions proceeded uphill from the reservoir to join a nearby track, known as Sir Cecil's Ride, which led around the north face of Jardine's Lookout to WNC Gap.

Colonel Tanaka's 3rd Battalion (3/229) landed at Aldrich Bay at a location between Tai Koo and Shau Kei Wan. The battalion moved quickly inland, ascending the north-facing slopes of Mount Parker. There are still old stepped paths that lead up from that part of the Island shore to the heights of Mount Parker. The Japanese are thought to have used fifth columnists to guide them through these hill trails, enabling them to outflank and outmanoeuvre the British defenders.

It was pitch dark, and the men stumbled as they manhandled their weapons and equipment up the steep path. When they were about halfway up, they intercepted a level contour path running east to west. Japanese battle maps prepared after the war show the bulk of the battalion proceeding directly to the summit, and while some may have done this, I believe that the main body of the battalion turned right, in a westward direction, when they reached the contour path. The Japanese soldiers would have been relieved to find themselves on a level path which wound its way around the northern slopes of Mount Parker. The trail passed under Sanatorium Gap and emerged on Mount Parker Road just below PB 45. After overcoming the garrison at PB 45, the lead troops proceeded up Mount Parker Road to Sanatorium Gap. After seizing and securing the gap, they continued up a path that led to the summit of Mount Parker which was the battalion's first objective. It was not until the early hours of Friday 19 December that Colonel Doi's 1st Battalion, which had been held up by the strong resistance at Tai Koo, started working their way up Mount Parker Road and ran into units of Tanaka's 3rd Battalion ahead of them.

Colonel Tanaka's 2nd Battalion (2/229), having embarked at Sam Ka Tsun on Devil's Peak Peninsula, landed at Kung Am north-east of Shau Kei Wan. The troops first silenced PB 40, which was situated near the jetty at the bottom of the road leading up to Lye Mun Barracks, then moved quickly up the road to assault the barracks, Pak Sha Wan Battery and the AA fort on Sai Wan Hill.

By midnight, the three Japanese regiments had landed six infantry battalions on the north shore. At Tanaka's war crimes trial, held after the war, he suggested that up to thirty different units were landed on the Island with a total force consisting of more than 20,000 men. However, this would have been over a longer period. It is difficult to quantify with any precision how many troops landed during the night of 18/19 December, but a reasonable estimate would be around the 8,000 mark. The British infantry defending this stretch of the shore totalled fewer than 800 men. They were overwhelmed by the sheer number of the invading force, outnumbered ten to one.

The Defence of the North Shore

The north shore, between North Point and Shau Kei Wan, was defended by three infantry companies from the Rajput battalion. A fourth company was held in reserve, behind the north shore, at Tai Hang. Lt-Col Cadogan-Rawlinson, the battalion commander, had established his battalion HQ at Tai Koo Police Station. 'C' Coy, Royal Rifles of Canada, commanded by Major Wells Bishop, was positioned on the Rajput battalion's right flank with their Coy HQ located at Lye Mun Gap close to Lye Mun Barracks.

At Pak Sha Wan there was a battery of two 6-inch coastal defence guns manned by No. 4 Battery, HKVDC, commanded by Lt Ken Barnett. The battery was located in a very exposed position, facing Devil's Peak, and had been subjected to a very heavy bombardment during the siege of the Island. The Battery Observation Post had been destroyed by a direct hit. The gun emplacements and battery buildings still exist today and still carry the scars of battle. The site of the battery is overgrown, largely hidden from view, and relatively inaccessible. On Sai Wan Hill there was a section of two 3-inch AA guns. It was situated on an exposed hilltop, and like Pak Sha Wan, it had been heavily shelled by Japanese artillery. The AA section was manned by No. 5 Battery, HKVDC, commanded by Captain Lawrence ('Lolly') Goldman. The gun positions and the battery buildings still remain and are easily accessible.

The pillboxes along the north shore, from PB 40 at Kung Am to PB 52 at Causeway Bay, were manned by the 5/7 Rajputs, whereas those to the east of PB 40 and to the west of PB 52 were manned by 1/Mx. Many of the pillboxes had been damaged or destroyed by Japanese artillery fire during the siege of the Island. The PB crews used their alternative positions, which were typically either weapons pits with sandbag parapets or MMG positions constructed inside buildings with firing loopholes drilled through the external walls.

Cadogan-Rawlinson deployed 'A' Coy, 5/7 Rajputs, under the command of Captain Ansari, to the right flank defending the shoreline around Aldrich Bay. He deployed 'D' Coy, under the command of Captain Newton, to the left flank defending the shoreline from Quarry Bay to North Point. Two 3-inch mortar sections were allocated to each of these left and right flank companies. 'C' Coy, under the command of Captain Sandilands, was acting as a support company and was positioned at Tai Koo on the higher ground south of the police station. 'C' Coy's role was to prevent any penetration of 'A' Coy's front and, if necessary, to fill the gap between 'A' and 'D' Coy in the centre of the battalion's sector. 'B' Coy, under the command of Captain Course, was positioned at Caroline Hill, near Tai Hang, away from the north shore. Their role was to support 'D' Coy and prevent any Japanese penetration on the left flank of the battalion's sector. At noon on Thursday 18 December, two subalterns, Ernie Lammert and Eric Matthews, reported to Cadogan-Rawlinson at his Bn HQ. They were both newly commissioned officers from the ranks of No. 1 Coy, HKVDC. They had been given emergency commissions and sent to bolster the officer cadre in the Rajput battalion. They were both killed in action on the north shore within twenty-four hours of reporting for duty.

The heavy bombardment of the north shore intensified on Thursday evening, but at around 2000 hours all enemy artillery and mortar fire ceased abruptly. Shortly afterwards, PB 43 at Quarry Point in Tai Koo Docks and PB 44 at Tai Koo Sugar Refinery reported enemy landing craft approaching their front. The PBs opened fire, sinking and disabling some of the boats, but they were unable to prevent others from reaching the shore, and by 2100 hours the Japanese were landing around the dockyard and the refinery. On the right flank, 'A' Coy reported that Japanese troops were attempting to land at Aldrich Bay. PB 40 at Kung Am and PB 41 at Aldrich Bay commenced firing. On the left flank, 'D' Coy reported landings taking place at North Point. Lt-Col Cadogan-Rawlinson, writing in the battalion war diary, described the landings around the docks and the refinery.

At 2100 hours, PB 44 informed me that the enemy was landing all around him at slipways and the factory, which was corroborated by PB 43 at his end of the dockyard. Both stated they were causing heavy losses. Shortly after this PB 44 was knocked out and the enemy then commenced infiltration across the main road to the high ground between Tai Koo and Braemar. ... Brigade HQ was put in the picture. They replied within five minutes with an excellent 6-inch artillery concentration on the sugar factory and docks area, which did considerable damage and caused enemy delay. It came down actually one hundred yards short causing some casualties to my men but was invaluable for its speed, moral effect and delaying action on the enemy. PB 43 was still in touch and was frequently reporting his action with the enemy who though they had secured a footing on the docks were quite unable to subdue this gallant crew who continued to inflict heavy casualties till about midnight when most of them were killed.[3]

From 2200 hours there was close-quarters fighting around the Rajput Bn HQ, and a decision was made to withdraw the HQ to the higher ground 200 metres to the rear. When the fighting died down, half an hour later, the Bn HQ staff fought their way back and reoccupied their Tai Koo HQ. At that time the battalion commander was in touch with Brigade HQ (Wallis), G-Ops (the Battle Box), and with 'A' Coy, but out of communication with 'B', 'C' and 'D' Coy. At midnight, Cadogan-Rawlinson was again forced to withdraw his Bn HQ because of the overwhelming number of enemy troops in the Tai Koo area. By 0100 hours the docks and the sugar refinery were in Japanese hands.

Lye Mun Barracks

The barracks were originally built between 1890 and 1910, but with more recent buildings added between 1938 and 1939. Lye Mun Barracks were used by the British Army until 1985 when the site was handed over to the Hong Kong Government. Most of the barrack buildings still remain; they are well looked after and in excellent condition. They are now part of Lye Yue Mun Park and Holiday Village. I must confess to having booked myself in for a day, but not for the archery or table tennis – I went there to view the barrack buildings and to gain surreptitious access, by climbing a fence, to Pak Sha Wan Battery.

On the night of the Japanese landings, the barracks were mostly empty because the troops had moved to their battle positions. There was a 3.7-inch howitzer positioned midway between the barracks and the AA fort. The howitzer had been moved earlier that day from the 1st Mountain Battery position at Tai Tam Fork in order to fire at Japanese mortar positions and observation posts that had been seen on Devil's Peak. The gun was commanded by twenty-six-year-old Captain Eric Bompas.

Colonel Tanaka's 2nd Battalion (2/229) got ashore between 2000 and 2100 hours in two locations around Kung Am. Those troops who landed near the jetty, at PB 40, moved up from the landing positions to attack the barracks and the 3.7-inch howitzer position. Those who landed further north proceeded to attack Pak Sha Wan Battery and Sai Wan AA Fort. Lt Buxton, No. 2 Battery, HKVDC, had been sent to Pak Sha Wan from Stanley the previous day to relieve another officer. At some stage during the evening, he led a detachment of men from the battery towards Lye Mun Barracks. His group ran into a Japanese patrol advancing through the barracks area, and in the ensuing melee, Buxton and most of his men were killed. In a double tragedy, Buxton's wife, Alberta, who was working as a military nurse, was killed when Japanese soldiers attacked the relief hospital at St Stephen's College, Stanley. She was one of three European nurses who were raped, mutilated and killed on Christmas morning by Japanese troops.

Sai Wan AA Fort

On the night of the landings, No. 1 Section of No. 5 Battery, HKVDC, comprising forty men, was on duty at Sai Wan Fort. Among its number were Captain Lolly Goldman and Sergeant David Bosanquet. Many of the gunners were locally recruited Hong Kong Chinese, Eurasian and Portuguese volunteers. Although sentries had been posted, they were taken by surprise and killed by Japanese troops infiltrating the fort.

One of the gunners, who had gone out for some fresh air, raised the alarm when he rushed back to the accommodation bunker, below the gun platform, shouting a warning that the Japanese were in the gun positions. Captain Goldman ordered everybody to get out and to follow him. Most of the gunners had been resting off duty. They tried to put on their boots, and grab their helmets and weapons, but they were too late. A grenade was thrown into the accommodation bunker. Some of the men were wounded, but an internal wall had prevented more injuries. Sgt Bosanquet ordered the men to get out as quickly as possible and to make their way across the gun road and down the hillside before any more grenades were thrown. Bombardier Bennett, a regular soldier attached to the battery, went down the gun road with several others rather than down the hillside. Some of this group, including Bennett, were killed on the gun road.

Bosanquet, with a few others who had managed to get out in time, went down the steep slope to Island Road. At the roadside, they joined up with Captain Bompas who with two IORs had escaped down the hillside after their howitzer position had been overrun. The group of gunners made their way along Island Road to the nearby Sai Wan 6-inch howitzer position. They briefed Lt Kenneth Allanson, the section commander, and Captain Feilden, an officer from 3rd Medium Battery who had just arrived at the position with reinforcements from Parker 6-inch Section. Feilden then reported to East Group, RA, HQ that the 3.7-inch howitzer, the barracks, and the AA fort had been overrun and were now in Japanese hands. Bosanquet, and his small party from the AA fort, continued along Island Road where he came across Captain Goldman who was with No. 2 Section who had been on their way from West Bay AA Fort to relieve No. 1 Section. Goldman was shocked to see how few of his section had got away. The gunners, consisting of No. 2 Section and the survivors from No. 1 Section, spent the rest of that night deployed on Island Road to prevent any further Japanese exploitation southwards towards Tai Tam Gap military HQ.

Those gunners who had been unable to escape from the AA fort were taken prisoner and then put to death. Two of the AA gunners, Bombardier Martin Tso and Private Chan Yam-kwong, survived despite multiple bayonet wounds. After the war, they gave evidence at war crimes trials, and it is from their shocking testimony that we learn in detail what actually happened. Martin Tso described their surrender.

> We heard voices in English telling us to surrender, and then Bennett told us to fix bayonets and try and force our way out of the tunnel. We followed him and tried to force our way downhill, but we heard

several shots from the opposite side, and three of us were killed. We then went back to the tunnel and shouted that we were going to surrender, then they told us to come out in single file. There were about twenty-six of us.[4]

After surrendering, the gunners were put inside one of two splinter-proof shelters which had been used to store ammunition. They were held for two or three hours during which time they were counted, searched and relieved of their valuables. The Japanese decided to kill the prisoners. They formed a semi-circle of soldiers outside the doorway. The prisoners were ordered to come out, one by one, and as they came out, they were bayoneted one after the other. Their bodies were thrown over a wall with a drop of some 2 or 3 metres. Chan Yam-kwong described how he lay among the dead and wounded.

> I do not think they were killed instantly, they were all suffering from heavy wounds and calling for water, some for their mothers, and some for God. The Japanese threw stones, and one fired a shot. I remained there for three days and three nights. I escaped on the fourth day.[5]

After feigning death and hiding for three days, the two survivors saw some Chinese civilians going up the hill. The Japanese had left, and the Chinese suggested they discard their uniforms and escape. In mid-January 1942, whilst Bosanquet was imprisoned at North Point POW Camp, he took part in a burial party that was sent to Sai Wan AA Fort. As they proceeded up the gun road from the barracks to the AA fort, they came across the decomposing bodies of those who had tried to escape down the gun road. They found the bodies of the three sentries at the gun positions and finally discovered the pile of bodies of those who had been captured and so cruelly bayoneted and left to die.

Lye Mun Magazine

On Thursday evening, Captain Potts, ASC Coy, HKVDC, had driven out to the Lye Mun Magazines with Lt Andrews, RA, to supervise a large ammunition convoy, which was due to collect howitzer shells from the magazines that night. The magazines were accessed by driving through Lye Mun Barracks and then down a steep hill to sea level where the magazines were located on either side of the road. The road led down to the waterfront where there was a pillbox near the jetty. When the two officers arrived at the magazines, they spoke with Cpl O'Connell, RAOC, one of five ordnance men based at the magazines. O'Connell appeared quite shaken and told them that the magazine area had been under constant shelling all day and had only just stopped. The barrage resumed while they were talking. They took cover in a disused magazine which the ordnance men had been using for their accommodation. After the barrage stopped, Potts went outside to look for any sign of the ammunition convoy. He heard the sound of a lorry descending the steep hill from the barracks. The lorry drew up, and Sgt Gow, HKVDC, reported that the convoy, which consisted of four lorries with ten Chinese labourers on each, had been caught up in the barrage while driving through the barracks. The Chinese workmen, shocked by the intensity of the barrage, had mostly absconded, and Gow had sent the other three lorries back to Major Dewar, RASC, at Tai Tam Gap to pick up more labourers.

While Gow was briefing Potts, the PB near the jetty released a red flare, and commenced firing. Later, while they stood watching this, they observed some fifty men running up the road towards them. They realised with a shock that these were Japanese troops, probably the first to land. Potts and Gow rushed back to the magazine, passing through the grille gate and down the corridor with the Japanese close on their heels. Once inside the main chamber of the magazine, their small group huddled in the darkness with their weapons trained on the steel door. They heard the grille gate being opened, and then the sound of hand-grenades exploding in the passageway. There was silence, and then they heard the sound of two or three Japanese soldiers moving cautiously along the passageway and coming up to the steel door, but they did not try to force an entry, and after a short while they left. As more landing craft arrived, they could hear the sound of Japanese troops doubling up the road from PB 40 at the jetty towards the barracks.

They remained in the magazine that night. The next morning Potts and Gow cautiously went outside to have a look around and discovered to their surprise that there were no Japanese in the vicinity. Sgt Gow's lorry and Lt Andrew's Studebaker car were still parked outside and appeared undamaged. The car started straight away. They all got in, and drove through the barracks, out of the main gate, and up Island Road without seeing a single Japanese soldier. They continued up the steep incline of Shau Kei Wan Hill, passing what had been the Canadian roadblock at Lye Mun Gap, only coming across Canadian troops as they got closer to Tai Tam Gap.

'C' Coy, Royal Rifles of Canada at Lye Mun

At 1945 hours, a sentry on duty at the junction of Island Road and the military road leading to Lye Mun Barracks reported that what appeared to be a truckload of Chinese labourers had driven up the road towards the barracks and the AA fort. Lt Scott, commanding No. 15 Platoon, was ordered to take his men up to the barracks and investigate. At 2030 hours, Scott reported that he had encountered an armed party at the gates to Lye Mun Barracks. There had been an exchange of fire, and Scott had moved his men back to Island Road to report the situation to his Coy HQ. It was a dark night, but Scott stated that in his opinion they were Chinese labourers. They must have been either fifth columnists or Japanese soldiers disguised as Chinese labourers. Major Bishop, the company commander, ordered No. 15 Platoon to move back into Lye Mun Barracks, but first he took a rifleman with him and went up the road through Lye Mun Barracks that led towards the AA fort. On the road leading to the fort, he met a party of gunners, led by a bombardier, who told him that the Japanese had overrun and captured the fort. Bishop was astonished that the fort could have been taken so easily. He returned to his Coy HQ and reported the capture of the AA fort to Bn and Brigade HQ. He then set about organising a counterattack. He ordered two of his platoons to mount an attack from the south-east near the 6-inch howitzer section, and Lt Scott's platoon was ordered to attack through the barracks.

The Sai Wan 6-inch Section, commanded by Lt Kenneth Allanson, was located just off Island Road on the south-east side of the AA fort. The howitzer section was overlooked by the AA fort and by 2200 hours the howitzer position was coming under small arms fire, causing casualties among the gunners. An artillery barrage was laid down on the AA fort, directed by Captain Feilden, but the effort to recapture the fort by the two Canadian platoons proved unsuccessful. The counterattack had resulted in a large number of casualties, including nine men killed. The Japanese held the position in strength and had the tactical advantage of defending higher ground, which included the fortified walls of the old Victorian redoubt.

Lt Scott's platoon had been involved in firefights around the barracks and had been pushed back again to Island Road. Major Bishop went over from his Coy HQ to get an appreciation of what was happening in that area. Bishop, accompanied by Scott, took a party of riflemen with him and proceeded up the road towards the barracks. They ran up against a Japanese patrol coming down the gun road from the direction of the AA fort. The Japanese patrol attacked them with grenades, and Bishop returned fire with his Tommy gun. A firefight ensued, and the Japanese patrol was wiped out. When the Canadians went forward they found seven dead bodies, three of which were in Japanese uniform and four of which were dressed as Chinese labourers. Those dressed in Chinese clothes were probably fifth columnists and may have been part of the lorry-load that was reported to have entered the barracks earlier that evening.

No. 14 Platoon, under Lt Strang, was deployed at Lye Mun Gap acting as left flank guard to prevent any Japanese movement up Shau Kei Wan Hill from the north shore. The platoon reported that a large number of Indian troops had made a disorderly withdrawal, without their weapons, through the Canadian lines. Later that night, No. 14 Platoon came under attack from Japanese troops moving up from Shau Kei Wan to secure their flank. Following the destruction of the Rajput battalion on the north shore that night, Major Bishop's 'C' Coy was the only infantry unit that stood between Tai Tam Gap military HQ and the Japanese forces on the north shore. Bishop asked Bn HQ for reinforcements to make a counterattack. Bn HQ asked for reinforcements from Brigade HQ, but none were available. Bn HQ sent forward a platoon from 'D' Coy, based at Obelisk Hill, to deploy at the food store building on Island Road, which was located between Parker 6-inch Section and Lye Mun Gap. Lt Power, commanding No. 17 Platoon, 'D' Coy, described the platoon's deployment to the food store that night in the battalion war diary.

I arrived at HQ at approximately 2250 hours, Lt-Col Home, Major Price and Major Macaulay being present. As the situation was yet extremely uncertain, I was told to sit down while Major Price got into communication with Major Bishop and with Brigade HQ. At about 2345 hours in accordance with orders received I was detailed to take up a position in the vicinity of the ration store about half a mile from Tai Tam HQ and in the direction of Lye Mun. Major Macaulay was sent with me to guide me to my position. I proceeded back on foot to the ADS where I ordered my men into the truck and then moved down to Bn HQ where we were joined by Major Macaulay in another truck and immediately set off for our destination. Arrived there we quickly got into positions as suggested by Major Macaulay covering the road. Major Macaulay proceeded on down the road to 'C' Coy HQ, and I sent my truck back to 'D' Coy HQ for further supplies of ammunition and grenades. We were completely settled in by 2359 hours with sentries posted on the flanks and in front.[6]

At 0200 hours, the 6-inch howitzers at Sai Wan Section were disabled by the removal of dial sights and percussion locks, and the gunners withdrew down Island Road to Parker 6-inch Section. 'C' Coy was withdrawn along Island Road, passing through Lt Power's positions at the food store, and later falling back to Tai Tam Gap. On Friday morning, the two 6-inch howitzers at Parker, now close to the front line, were also disabled and abandoned. In the early afternoon East Infantry Brigade, together with East Group, RA, and the gunners from the coastal defence forts in the eastern sector of the Island, withdrew to Stanley. The infantry occupied new defensive positions on the line of hills surrounding Stanley.

North Point Power Station

The Hong Kong Electric Company (HKE) power station at North Point was guarded by a unit known as the Hughes Group, which had been formed to provide a special guard for defence against fifth columnists, looters and saboteurs. The unit was part of the HKVDC but recruited predominantly British men from the business community who were over the combatant age limit of fifty-five. These were men who had military experience and were keen to serve but were too old to serve in the combat units of the HKVDC. The unit was named after its founder, Colonel A. W. Hughes. On his departure from the colony in 1941, command of the unit had passed to fifty-five-year-old Major John Johnston ('JJ') Paterson. He had been Taipan of Jardine Matheson, Chairman of Hongkong and Shanghai Banking Corporation and was a member of the Executive Council. He had served with the Camel Corps during the First World War. Fifty-eight-year-old Captain Ronald Burch was second-in-command of the Hughes Group. He had served in both the Boer War and in the First World War. The group included a handful of Free French volunteers led by Captain Frederic Jacosta and Captain Jacques Egal. The Hughes Group undertook training twice a week conducted by NCOs from the Royal Scots. Their war station was to defend the HKE power station presumably from sabotage. This somewhat unusual group of militia, sometimes referred to as the Hughesiliers, were to find themselves in the front line on 18 December when the 230th Regiment landed near the power station at North Point.

At approximately 2030 hours, Police Sgt Bill Morrison, in charge of the HKE Vital Post, which consisted of the power station and the adjoining government stores, noticed ten or more landing craft crossing from Kowloon Bay towards Tai Koo. The troops at the power station opened fire with their machine guns, firing at the phosphorescence created by the boats. Paterson recalled that as the Japanese got ashore in the locality of the power station, they quickly moved inland, and as they did so the firing moved up to the high ground south of their location on King's Road. The pillboxes were designed so that their firing apertures faced the harbour, and they became less effective once the Japanese had got behind the PBs, which were vulnerable to grenade attacks in which grenades were inserted through the loopholes. During the night of 18 December, Captain Newton, 'D' Coy, 5/7 Rajputs, was killed in action in the close-quarters fighting around the power station. 'D' Coy was overrun, with some pushed back onto the higher ground and eventually captured or killed. A few survivors joined the Volunteers defending the power station.

Fortress HQ ordered a mobile infantry platoon to proceed to PB 50 at North Point. The platoon comprised some twenty-five men of No. 16 Platoon, 'Z' Coy, 1/Mx. The platoon was commanded by thirty-six-year-old Lt Ewan Graham. He had been a businessman in Hong Kong before the war, and in 1939 had been given an emergency commission in 1/Mx. At approximately 2300 hours, the platoon left their positions at Leighton Hill in three 15-cwt trucks heading east along King's Road. As they approached the power station, the trucks came under automatic fire from the high ground on their right and from an anti-tank gun emplacement on King's Road to their front. All three trucks were put out of action and many casualties incurred. L/Cpl Coleman, driving the first truck, was killed instantly. Sgt Miller, driving the second truck, and L/Cpl Cavill, driving the third truck, were both lightly wounded, but together with some nine survivors from the ambush they were able to reach the power station. Some survivors from the patrol, including Lt Graham, were able to head back towards Causeway Bay.

Later that evening, 2/Lt Mike Carruthers, HKVDC, commanding the Armoured Car Platoon, reported to 1/Mx Bn HQ. He was ordered by Lt-Col Stewart to proceed eastwards along King's Road and to make contact with Lt Graham's mobile platoon, which was thought to be in the vicinity of PB 50, located just east of the power station. He was then to continue in an easterly direction to ascertain the whereabouts and strength of Japanese troops on the north shore. Carruthers proceeded with No. 4 car, commanded by L/Cpl Harry Long, with a crew consisting of Pte Miller, Pte Smits and Pte Park. At the same location where the mobile platoon had been ambushed his vehicle received a direct hit from the Japanese anti-tank gun. Bill Park, the driver, was killed instantly. In civilian life, Park had been an employee of the Chartered Bank, and his wife Betty was working as an ANS nurse at a hospital on the Peak. Harry Long was seriously injured in one leg, and unable to walk. He described the ambush in his personal war diary.

> We moved slowly into King's Road through the rock cutting at the HK Electric. I was in the turret looking out through the peephole; then we came near the Commercial Press when suddenly there was a loud report in front of us, the car stopped, my driver gave a groan, and the car horn started to sound, then in a few seconds there was another report, and I felt a sting in my left leg. ... I spoke to Lt Carruthers [and told him] that my leg was gone. ... Then he decided to go for help, so he and Henry Smits left leaving Evan Miller with me. My driver was dead lying over the driving wheel.[7]

The engine caught fire and Harry Long was worried that the ammunition carried in the vehicle would explode. He ordered Miller to drag him out through the rear door. As they got out of the vehicle, they came under machine gun fire and lay flat in the road until the ammunition started to go off.

> The ammunition in the car began to go off like crackers. ... I told Miller to ... drag me over to the sidewalk on the harbour side of the road. We had just moved when we received another burst of machine gun fire, at any rate, we got over and got behind some Mimi Lau brick walls, which were built to protect the ground floor windows of the Commercial Press.[8]

Harry Long applied a tourniquet to his injured leg. He and Miller lay where they were outside the Commercial Press Building in King's Road. They were later joined by a severely wounded soldier from 1/Mx who had been a machine gunner in one of the pillboxes on the waterfront. A short time later, they saw the lights of a car coming from the direction of Causeway Bay. The car stopped, and a man got out to try and find a way through the shell craters and debris. He turned out to be an artillery officer trying to make his way to Pak Sha Wan Battery. He obviously had no idea that the Japanese had landed all along that stretch of shore. On hearing the situation, and seeing the condition of the wounded men, he realised it would be useless to carry on along King's Road. He helped the wounded men into his car and drove them to Bowen Road Military Hospital. Harry Long's leg was amputated, but he survived the fighting and subsequent incarceration. Lt Graham and Sgt Fox, both from the mobile platoon, made it back to 'Z' Coy HQ at Leighton Hill. Carruthers and Smits were able to make their way back to British lines, stopping at one of the pillboxes in Causeway Bay to report the incident to Fortress HQ. Carruthers was ordered to report back to Lt-Col Stewart at 1/Mx HQ in Ventris Road. Smits remained with the PB crew in Causeway Bay and was killed in action the following morning.

At the power station, Sgt Miller and Cpl Meakin set about organising the defence of the compound and placing machine guns at strategic points. The defenders had two Lewis guns, two Vickers Berthiers, six Vickers MMGs and a Thompson SMG. The Vickers Berthier was a light machine gun used by the Indian battalions as an alternative to the Bren gun. Meakin and L/Cpl Dooley carried out a recce patrol of the immediate surroundings. They ascertained that there were no Japanese troops in the immediate area other than those on the hillside south of King's Road and those at the anti-tank gun emplacement. Sgt Miller, 1/

Mx, and 2/Lt Lammert, the newly commissioned officer attached to 'D' Coy, 5/7 Rajputs, destroyed the anti-tank gun position at around 0200 hours by lobbing grenades from a veranda located on the top floor of the HKE office building. As dawn broke, and the visibility improved, the defenders at the power station found that they were surrounded on three sides. The only possible escape route was in a westerly direction towards Causeway Bay. During the morning, the defenders fought off all efforts by the Japanese to capture the position. The Japanese used mortars and light artillery at point-blank range from the high ground to the rear of the power station.

The militia group at the power station numbered seventy, and this included HKE and China Light & Power staff as well the Free French contingent. In addition to the militia, there were a dozen regular soldiers made up from both the 1/Mx mobile platoon and from the remnants of 'D' Coy, 5/7 Rajputs. There was a small group of civilians, which included Police Sgt Morrison, and forty-nine-year-old Agnes Duckworth, who was married to Ferdinand Duckworth, the superintendent of the power station. Mrs Duckworth was accompanied by her thirteen-year-old son Frederick, and her twenty-four-year-old married daughter Joan Crawford, whose husband, Ken, was both an engineer with HKE and a sergeant in the Hughes Group. Prior to the Japanese landings, Joan Crawford had been working as a volunteer in the dispensary at the French Hospital in Causeway Bay. During the siege of the power station, she and her mother helped tend to the wounded. Since the group comprised several civilians, including two women and a thirteen-year-old boy, and a number of wounded who needed medical assistance, a decision was made to evacuate the power station at 1000 hours on Friday morning and to try to escape towards Causeway Bay. A rear-guard, consisting of Lammert, Miller, Meakin, Dooley and three members of the Hughes Group agreed to remain behind to cover the withdrawal.

By midday, the Japanese were infiltrating under covering fire on various sides of the compound, and the last of the defenders, who were by now pinned down in the office building on the south side of the complex, were incurring more casualties. Meakin, armed with a submachine gun, stopped a Japanese attempt to rush the west gate. However, other Japanese troops were able to enter the compound from the rear, pushing captured prisoners in front of them as a screen. The Japanese brought up a flamethrower and called out to the small group of defenders to surrender otherwise the building would be set ablaze. In view of the number of wounded and the futility of further resistance, the defenders finally surrendered the position at 1400 hours after destroying their weapons.

The Escape Attempt

The escape party crossed a fence on the west side of the compound and entered a government store area adjacent to the power station from where they were able to get access to Electric Road. A few of the more elderly Volunteers, already exhausted, decided to fight it out where they were. These included seventy-seven-year-old Private Sir Edward Des Voeux, who was killed in action that morning. He was a stockbroker, secretary of the Hong Kong Club, and the nephew of a former Governor of Hong Kong. A number of the escape party were killed or wounded as they tried to make their way towards Causeway Bay. The Japanese had by that time surrounded the installation. Some of the group took shelter both inside and underneath a broken-down bus in the street running between the slipways on the waterfront and King's Road. There was a skirmish around the bus in which fifty-seven-year-old Pte Tam Pearce was shot and killed. Pearce was a well-known businessman in Hong Kong and a member of LEGCO. In the same skirmish, Cpl Dunlop and Pte Roscoe were wounded by swords. L/Cpl Gahagan broke off an attack on the bus by single-handedly shooting a Japanese officer and three soldiers with one clip of five rounds. Police Sgt Morrison described the escape attempt, in a statement made while he was interned at Stanley Camp.

> About 1000 hours on the morning of 19 December it was decided that the position was untenable and that we had better try to make our escape from the position which was surrounded. About sixteen persons, including myself, succeeded in reaching Ah-King's slipway at the cost of three wounded. Here we were held up by machine gun fire from the pillbox at the junction of Causeway Bay and King's Road, causing a number of our party to take shelter in the Chinese tenements, whilst the remainder rested beside two buses in a side street opposite the front entrance to Ah-King's slipway. There followed a lot of sniping and finally a bayonet charge by a small party of Japanese. This we managed to beat off. However, it was at this time that I saw Mr T. E. Pearce, who was inside one of the buses, had been fatally shot in the forehead.[9]

In the late afternoon, the Japanese surrounded the tenements and ordered the survivors to come out and surrender. They were then marched back to the power station and held overnight in a garage. The next day they were taken to North Point Refugee Camp. Those defenders at the power station who were wearing military uniform were sent to POW camps, while those in civilian clothes were held initially at North Point Camp, and later sent to Stanley Civilian Internment Camp. Joan Crawford was interned with her parents at Stanley. Her husband, presumably wearing military uniform, was interned at Sham Shui Po (SSP) Camp. Tam Pearce's wife, Eva, was interned at Stanley; their two sons, John and Alec, who had been commissioned in the Royal Artillery, were interned at SSP Camp. John Pearce later escaped and made his way to Free China.

Of the seventy Volunteers who made up the group of militia defending the power station, there were twenty-one casualties, of which thirteen died in action or died from their wounds. Sixty-year-old Vincent Sorby, the manager of HKE, died from wounds incurred that morning. He was a veteran of both the Boer War and the First World War. Captain Jacosta, leading the Free French contingent, was killed at the power station. Major Paterson paid high praise to the indefatigable group of 1/Mx soldiers led by Sgt Miller, including Cpl Meakin and L/Cpl Dooley, for their gallant conduct throughout the siege. 2/Lt Ernie Lammert was reported to have been beheaded after surrendering because he refused to salute a Japanese officer. His father, Lionel Lammert, a long-term Lithuanian resident of Hong Kong, and proprietor of Lammert Brothers Auctioneers, was interned with his married daughter at Stanley Camp.

The Loss of Mount Parker and Sanatorium Gap

Sanatorium Gap, better known today as Quarry Gap, is the saddle between the summits of Mount Parker and Mount Butler. It was named after the Tai Koo Sanatorium, built there in 1893 and demolished in 1932. There was a road track running up to the gap from Quarry Bay, which was joined by a path from Tai Koo. The track, known as Mount Parker Road, passed through the gap and continued down into Gauge Basin, eventually emerging at the Tai Tam Crossroads (Tai Tam X-Roads) on the south side of the Island. The gap was an important feature because ownership of it allowed access to the reservoirs at Gauge Basin, to Stanley by way of the Tai Tam X-Roads, and to Stanley Gap Road, which led from Gauge Basin to WNC Gap.

At the gap, a track continued up to the summit of Mount Parker. Another path consisting of a flight of steps, known as Jacob's Ladder, led to the summit of Mount Butler. Another path led from Sanatorium Gap to the hill feature known as Boa Vista which overlooked the military HQ at Tai Tam Gap. On the night of 18 December, the gap was defended by a platoon from No. 1 Coy, HKVDC. The nearest friendly troops were a Canadian platoon positioned on Boa Vista, and an AOP located on the summit of Mount Parker.

Captain Harry Penn, commanding No. 1 Coy, HKVDC, had established his Coy HQ at the Tai Tam Bungalow, a house situated on a knoll at Gauge Basin, which had previously been a family residence for senior managers of the Public Works Department. Captain Penn's company consisted of three platoons. No. 3 Platoon, the Bren gun carrier platoon under 2/Lt Edwards, was assigned to Windy Gap and was under the operational control of the Royal Rifles of Canada. No. 2 Platoon, under 2/Lt Redman, was positioned at Repulse Bay View. This is the saddle between Violet Hill and the Twins which would be familiar to readers who know Hong Kong as the junction of paths at the bottom of the one thousand steps leading to the Twins. The saddle overlooked Repulse Bay, and it could be easily accessed by a trail running along the shallow water catchment from Coy HQ at the Tai Tam Bungalow. No. 2 Platoon at Repulse Bay View was situated in between the Royal Rifles of Canada (East Brigade) and the Winnipeg Grenadiers (West Brigade) and was under operational control of the Winnipeg Grenadiers, whose sector originally included Repulse Bay.

No. 1 Platoon, commanded by 2/Lt Carter, was deployed at Sanatorium Gap and was under operational control of 5/7 Rajputs. The bulk of the platoon, including 2/Lt Carter's Platoon HQ, was positioned at the gap. One section of ten ORs, under the command of Cpl Thompson, was deployed at PB 45. This pillbox was situated on Mount Parker Road close to the junction with Sir Cecil's Ride. The PB was equipped with two Vickers MMGs and a light machine gun (LMG). There is no sign of this pillbox today. There is only a small splinter-proof shelter nearby. Local history enthusiasts have searched for any structural evidence of PB 45 but to no avail. Some have suggested that, although referred to as a pillbox, PB 45 may in fact have been a weapons pit with sandbagged parapets rather than a concrete structure.

Carter had thirteen ORs at the gap, which included the MMG and LMG sections. All movement between PB 45 and the rest of the platoon at the gap had to be carried out at night as any movement could be observed by the Japanese on the Mainland and would bring immediate artillery fire. On the evening of Thursday 18 December, Penn was informed by RRC Bn HQ at Tai Tam Gap that the Japanese had landed on the Island. Penn sent a message to this effect to his platoon commanders at Sanatorium Gap and Repulse Bay View. He then decided to go up to No. 1 Platoon's positions at the gap. He advised the RRC adjutant of his intended movement and was informed that the Canadian detachment on Boa Vista had been ordered to move to Sanatorium Gap to provide reinforcement. Penn arranged for an NCO and two men to go along the path from Sanatorium Gap to Boa Vista to help guide the Canadian platoon to their positions at the gap. At 2250 hours, Penn set off for the gap with two orderlies, leaving the CSM in charge at Coy HQ and arriving at the gap at 2320 hours.

The Canadian detachment on Boa Vista included No. 5 Platoon, 'HQ' Coy, RRC, under the command of Lt Gerard Williams, and two sections from No. 3 Platoon, 'HQ' Coy, under the command of Sgt Harold Hughes. Hughes had taken over as platoon commander when Lt Arnold Woodside was moved to West Brigade HQ as Brigade Intelligence Officer. The detachment did not arrive in time to stave off the attack on Sanatorium Gap. The RRC war diary states that the detachment was ordered 'to move from Boa Vista to Mount Parker to reinforce a platoon of No. 1 Coy, HKVDC, in position there'. There may have been a miscommunication in orders because the Canadian detachment was meant to be reinforcing No. 1 Coy at Sanatorium Gap, and not Mount Parker. The summit of Mount Parker is another kilometre up the hill-path from the gap. With the benefit of hindsight, one may well ask why the summits of hills like Mount Parker, Mount Butler, Violet Hill and Mount Nicholson were not better defended. Most of them were left undefended, and these hilltops were the primary objective for the Japanese. Where hilltops were defended, for example at Mount Cameron, the British and Canadians were able to hold out against large numbers of attacking Japanese troops.

The Canadian detachment under Lt Williams and Sgt Hughes arrived at the gap after the HKVDC positions had been overrun. The Japanese had by that time already left the gap and moved up to the summit of Mount Parker. On reaching the gap, the Canadian detachment turned right and continued up the track to the summit of Mount Parker only to find the Japanese were in possession of the summit and in superior numbers. The Canadian detachment was destroyed and its members killed, wounded or captured. Lt Williams and Sgt Hughes were both killed in action. Military history enthusiast Stuart Woods found a large number of spent Japanese 6.5mm Arisaka rifle rounds in a cluster of rocks just below the summit of Mount Parker. These may have been used to fire down at the Canadian troops attacking uphill. Stuart also found a brass shoulder flash bearing the inscription HKS-RA (Hong Kong Singapore Royal Artillery), which may have belonged to one of the gunners from the AOP on the summit of Mount Parker.

Lt Blaver, in command of No. 9 Platoon, 'A' Coy, RRC, was ordered to move from Windy Gap to Boa Vista to replace Lt William's platoon. Shortly after midnight, Blaver's platoon was ordered to deploy from Boa Vista to Mount Parker in support of No. 5 and No. 3 Platoon 'HQ' Coy. It is thought that Blaver's platoon took a wrong turn and as a result did not reach the top of Mount Parker until 0730 hours on 19 December. Blaver's platoon found no sign of the two 'HQ' Coy platoons. Whilst Blaver was deploying his men to attack the summit, his platoon came under machine gun fire from the direction of Tai Tam, which may have

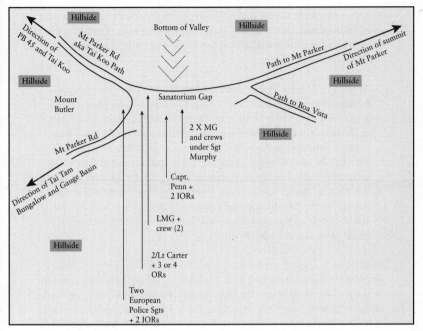

Sanatorium Gap defences.

been friendly fire. This alerted the Japanese that an attack was being mounted. The Japanese entrenched on the summit began firing at the Canadians and lobbing grenades down the hill. The platoon incurred a number of casualties, including Cpl McRae and L/Cpl Harrison who were both killed in action. With the Japanese strongly entrenched and in superior numbers, the attack was eventually broken off.

At Sanatorium Gap, there were only a dozen defenders including Captain Penn and Lt Carter. The two MMGs were positioned on the right flank, and the LMG was placed 25 metres to the front at a point where a grass-cutter's path, leading up from the valley bottom, intercepted Mount Parker Road. Penn sent a message by motorcycle orderly instructing his CSM to send up an additional LMG section from Coy HQ to reinforce their left flank at the gap. At about 0030 hours the LMG section arrived from Coy HQ and was ordered to establish their LMG position on the lower slopes of Mount Butler. At about this time, stragglers from the north shore started coming through their positions at the gap. These included Indian troops from 5/7 Rajputs, Indian police and two British police sergeants from Quarry Bay Police Station. They were unable to give details of what was happening on the north shore except that it was full of Japanese troops. Penn and his men tried to organise the stragglers into their defence line. The two police sergeants agreed to assist, and some of the Indian soldiers and police were also willing to help.

> At about 0045 hours Pte Van Leeuwen arrived from PB 45 with a message that the Adjutant of 5/7 Rajputs [Captain Cole] had arrived at their position, and he suggested withdrawal of the section to the gap as the enemy were infiltrating up the hillsides and would make their position untenable at daylight if not before, and the two MMGs could probably be used to better advantage at Sanatorium Gap. I decided to act on this suggestion, and I sent instructions back by the same runner to withdraw the section to Sanatorium Gap. This message did not get through as the PB 45 section was attacked before he got back to them and the body of the runner was found just above the position, by a burial party sent out from North Point.[10]

Penn sent a second message to his CSM ordering him to bring all remaining ranks, numbering some fifteen men, to help bolster the defence of the gap. At 0100 hours, the defenders at the gap could hear the sound of firing coming from the direction of PB 45. A short time later, three members of the PB section, two of whom had been wounded, reached the gap. They reported that their position had been attacked and overrun and they thought the Japanese were close behind them. Captain Cole then appeared coming up the path, and he also warned that the Japanese were close behind. The survivors of PB 45 stated that immediately before the attack on their position a small group had approached claiming to be ARP personnel. They were not allowed to pass because it was felt they may be fifth columnists, or that they may have been ARP personnel captured by the Japanese and forced to act as a screen. Charles Mycock, who was in charge of the Tai Koo Braemar Refugee Camp, reported seeing the dead bodies of William Seath and Ada Baldwin, both ARP personnel, on Mount Parker Road the following morning. Captain Penn wrote in the company war diary that shortly after Captain Cole reached their defence line, their positions at the gap came under attack.

> I was positioned approximately in the centre of the gap with two Rajputs ORs whom I positioned one on either side of me. On my left was the main path with the LMG team, 2/Lt Carter a few yards behind it with three or four of our own men. The two European police and one or two Indians extended from the path in a line up the lower slopes of Mt Butler for 15–20 yards. On my right, there were the two Vickers MGs, and the rest of the force was extended in suitable firing positions,

with three men watching our rear flanks. Within a few minutes of Captain Cole's arrival, a party was heard in front, and a challenge brought no prompt answer and then a few unintelligible words. Someone on my left, I think 2/Lt Carter, shouted: 'who the hell are you, answer, or we fire'. The party appeared to be 50 or 75 yards in front of us on the main path. There were a few seconds of hesitation, and then fire was opened by the LMG section, and this was immediately taken up generally from our positions.[11]

During a lull in the firing, and in an effort to outflank Penn's position at the gap, the Japanese moved some of their troops off the road and into the dead ground provided by the valley bottom. After ten minutes the firing intensified from the Japanese position on the road. The Japanese were utilising a light machine gun, as well as rifle fire, to provide covering fire for the main attack which came from the valley bottom. The Japanese infiltrated close to the gap and then launched a barrage of hand grenades, many of which failed to detonate. The Japanese Type 97 grenade was activated by hitting the detonator against a hard surface such as a helmet. Sometimes soldiers forgot to do this or did not do it hard enough. This is no doubt the reason why a lot of live Japanese grenades are still found in the hills of Hong Kong.

> Fortunately, many of the grenades proved to be duds or non-effective; otherwise, this grenade shower would have inflicted heavier casualties. ... The grenade bombardment was immediately followed by an attempted rush at the centre of the gap by a small party of the enemy, but which was unsuccessful. At the same, time a rush was made up the main path, and the grass-cutter's path, upon our LMG at the junction of these two paths. The LMG was kept firing by the No. 1 until he and his No. 2 were overrun, one being bayoneted, and the other shot at point-blank range. 2/Lt Carter with those that remained of the party with him, on my left, took toll of this rush, one of the European police and the Indians had slipped away earlier.[12]

Penn was hit on the head by a fragment from a grenade, and although protected by his helmet, he was dazed and knocked unconscious by the force of the blow. When he regained consciousness, he found that one of the Rajputs beside him was dead and the other had left. At this stage, the Japanese who had overrun the LMG position fired off a success signal. The red flare of the signal illuminated the group of Japanese around the captured LMG. They were fired on by both Penn and Carter. After this there followed a lull. Sgt Murphy's MMGs had ceased firing, and there was only scattered rifle fire.

Carter found that only he and one of the European police sergeants remained on the left flank. The ORs had either become casualties or withdrawn. Carter and the police sergeant then moved off, behind Penn, to the MMG position to ascertain why they were no longer in action. Penn had not seen Carter move to the right and assumed that he and his group were still in position on his left. On reaching the MMG position, Carter found Murphy and the gun crews, some of whom were wounded, pulling their guns out having assumed the rest of the defenders had been overrun or had withdrawn. Carter and Murphy then withdrew, with the MMGs, along the Boa Vista Path. At this point, Penn was probably the only defender left at the gap.

> Meanwhile, I was waiting, unaware of these developments, in my original position until the lull was broken by a sudden rush of a number of the enemy from the path on my left front. ... I personally lay doggo and was passed unnoticed. Within a few minutes, I was able to make my way unobserved across the few yards back to the head of the path down to Tai Tam. The enemy party, which broke across the gap, seemed to make their way across our shelters and up the slopes of Mount Parker.[13]

Penn withdrew down Mount Parker Road in the direction of his Coy HQ at Gauge Basin. At the first bend, barely one hundred metres from the gap, he came across his motorcycle orderly with a wounded OR. They were joined by another wounded OR who had come down from the LMG position on Mount Butler. The LMG section had only just got in position when they were attacked and overrun. The Japanese party scaled the north-facing slope from Mount Parker Road and then rushed the position with bayonets. The sergeant, together with four ORs, was killed in hand-to-hand fighting. There was only the one survivor. Penn only had three men with him, two of whom were wounded, so he decided to wait for the CSM's party before trying to retake the gap. Most of the Japanese had continued up towards Mount Parker, but some remained at the gap, and their voices could be heard close by. The CSM's party did not arrive as they had been told by stragglers that the defence line at the gap had been overrun. After waiting to no avail, Penn decided to continue down to his Coy HQ. Further down the road, he met up with Carter's group and both parties made their way back to Coy HQ, arriving just before dawn on Friday 19 December.

The force which attacked Penn's position at Sanatorium Gap was from Tanaka's 229th Regiment. They approached the gap from Mount Parker Road, which they joined close to PB 45. They outflanked PB 45 by going up the hillside and throwing grenades down onto the MMG emplacements. The most forward Vickers gun was rushed from the road. The No. 1 on the second Vickers gun was killed at his gun, and two of the crew were wounded. At this point it was decided to withdraw to the gap. Three of the section made it to the gap, two of whom were wounded. Two more ORs re-joined the company the following day at Stanley, having made their way around the north side of Mount Parker to Tai Tam Gap. Three were killed, and three were taken prisoner. Penn's platoon located at PB 45 and at the gap consisted of two officers and twenty-nine ORs. They incurred nineteen casualties, of which ten were killed. They had put up a good fight but against overwhelming numbers.

Withdrawal of Lt-Col Cadogan-Rawlinson's Bn HQ

A decision was made at around midnight to move the Rajput Bn HQ from Tai Koo Police Station to the higher ground on the track leading up to Sanatorium Gap. At around 0200 hours on 19 December, the new Bn HQ was coming under fire from the left flank, probably from Colonel Doi's 2nd Battalion on Braemar Hill. To avoid this flank-fire, the Bn HQ moved higher up the track to a location on the slopes of Mt Butler which provided better cover. This position was attacked at around 0330 hours by Doi's 1st Battalion as they started to work their way up Mount Parker Road from Tai Koo. After fighting off the attack, Cadogan-Rawlinson decided to withdraw his Bn HQ by way of Jardine's Lookout and to regroup at Tai Hang where 'B' Coy, the reserve company, was positioned. Here, he intended to reorganise what was left of his battalion. Cadogan-Rawlinson took with him a small group of officers and men that would form the nucleus for a reformed Battalion HQ. He instructed the rest of the group to make their way to Tai Tam via Sanatorium Gap.

Cadogan-Rawlinson's party turned right, before reaching PB 45, and went up a path that led to the ridge between Mount Butler and Jardine's Lookout. The rest of his party proceeded up Mount Parker Road, most likely to their death or capture as Tanaka's 3rd Battalion was ahead of them and Doi's 1st Battalion was behind them. After reaching the ridge path, Cadogan-Rawlinson came across a platoon of Winnipeg Grenadiers, commanded by Lt Charles French, in the col between Mount Butler and Jardine's Lookout.

About half an hour after first light having crossed the watershed I came across a platoon of Winnipeg Grenadiers resting below the narrow col joining Jardine's Lookout with the massif of Mount Butler. Their commander stated that they were there to protect it and whilst explaining we were heavily fired on at about 400 yards from Jardine's Lookout. Some thirty minutes were wasted in getting this platoon deployed and into action, and by then all chance of slipping down to Tai Hang was lost as more enemy forces were advancing up the northwest slopes. Having satisfied myself that the Canadians could more or less look after themselves, I took my party and one or two casualties through the enemy positions via Gauge Basin to Tai Tam Tuk and reported by phone to the brigade commander. ... He informed me he was going to withdraw to Stanley and asked me to hold the Tai Tam X-Roads with what personnel I had until his elements were clear.[14]

Lt French must have been surprised to see a battalion commander, with his staff officers, in the hills around his position and was no doubt concerned to learn that the Rajput battalion defending the north shore had been overrun. Lt French was now on the front line with Japanese troops to his left on Jardine's Lookout, to his front on Sir Cecil's Ride, and to his right at Sanatorium Gap and Mount Parker. After holding out for several hours, French was killed in action and his platoon overrun and destroyed. With Japanese troops advancing up the northwest slopes of Jardine's Lookout, Cadogan-Rawlinson had only one way out from French's position, and that was by heading south on a trail called Reservoir Path which led downhill to Stanley Gap Road. He reached Bridge Hill shelters at 1000 hours where he organised the defence around the Tai Tam X-Roads and the dam. After the last troops from East Brigade had crossed the dam in the early afternoon on Friday 19 December, Cadogan-Rawlinson's small group of Bn HQ personnel and various stragglers that had joined along the way were relieved by Canadian troops. Cadogan-Rawlinson left for Stanley, from where he was taken by MTB to Aberdeen so that he could re-join the remnants of his battalion fighting around Causeway Bay and Happy Valley.

The Salesian Mission Building

The Salesian Mission Building was situated on the right-hand side of the road leading up Shau Kei Wan Hill towards Lye Mun Barracks. It was lower down the hill than the Canadian positions at Lye Mun Gap and closer to the fishing village of Shau Kei Wan. On the night of the Japanese landings, the building was being used to accommodate an Army medical store, an Advanced Dressing Station (ADS) and a civilian First Aid Post (FAP). The senior officer was thirty-four-year-old Captain Stanley Banfill, a Canadian medical officer (MO) attached to the Royal Rifles of Canada. Banfill was originally responsible for the ADS in Lye Mun Barracks, but after the evacuation of the Mainland the position became too exposed to artillery bombardment, and on Saturday 13 December he was ordered to relocate his medical facility to the Salesian Mission Building.

His immediate team at the ADS included L/Cpl Harrison and Rifleman Oakley, both RRC, and Pte Kelly, a RASC driver. His previous driver had been killed at Lye Mun during a bombardment. 2/Lt Osler Thomas, HKVDC, a young Eurasian medical officer, joined Banfill's team. Thomas had initially been posted as MO to No. 4 Battery at Pak Sha Wan, but because of the heavy shelling, he had also been asked to relocate to the Salesian Mission Building.

At the FAP there were two European nurses, one Eurasian nurse, and several Chinese nurses. The European ladies included fifty-year-old Eileen Tinson. She was married to George Tinson, a partner in the law firm Johnson, Stokes & Master. Working with Mrs Tinson was thirty-year-old Lois Fearon, an American, whose wealthy parents, William and Elsa Stanton, lived in a large villa near Fan Ling before the war. Their home was by then being used by the Japanese as a temporary military internment camp. The Eurasian nurse was twenty-year-old Mary Suffiad, who later escaped to Free China. There were two or three civilian doctors including Dr Orloff and Dr Tsang, and several St John Ambulance Brigade (SJAB) orderlies attached to the FAP. The FAP was responsible for providing first aid for the civilian population in the Shau Kei Wan area, which numbered some 20,000 people, but the FAP had received very few casualties despite the heavy bombardment around Shau Kei Wan. The Army Medical Store was under the supervision of QMS Buchan, RAMC, with a group of around ten RAMC personnel.

Banfill woke up an hour before dawn on 19 December when two British officers, both holding the rank of captain and both from 5/7 Rajputs, were brought in for treatment, both severely wounded. These were probably Captain Ambler and Captain Sandilands, who were killed that day while serving with 5/7 Rajputs on the north shore. One of the two officers died soon after arrival at the ADS; the other, who had been shot in the chest, was insistent that he should be taken to Lt-Col Home, RRC battalion commander, based at Tai Tam Gap. The wounded Rajput officer had been on his way to deliver an urgent message when he was shot. He told Banfill that he thought he had been carelessly shot by Canadian sentries on Island Road whilst approaching Lye Mun Gap.

They placed both the dead officer and the wounded Rajput officer in the makeshift ambulance together with an injured Chinese civilian. 2/Lt Osler Thomas took charge and was accompanied by Rifleman Oakley and Driver Kelly. They started off in the direction of Tai Tam Gap, but they had only gone a short distance when the ambulance was hit by machine gun fire. The driver jumped out, as did Oakley, who was then shot in the leg. 2/Lt Thomas got into the driving seat and reversed the ambulance back down the road, and into the entrance drive of the Salesian Building. This must have alerted the Japanese that there was a military presence in the building. At 0700 hours, a sentry came down from the top floor and reported that the building was surrounded by Japanese troops. A short time later there was a loud banging at the door and shouted commands in Japanese. The RAMC orderlies, having piled their weapons in the middle of the dining room, opened the doors and came out with their hands raised above their heads. The Japanese troops had come from the direction of Lye Mun and not Shau Kei Wan, indicating that they were most likely from Colonel Tanaka's 2nd Battalion.

The surrendered personnel were lined up in the courtyard with the troops at one end, the nurses in their white uniforms in the centre, and the Chinese and SJAB orderlies at the other end. The soldiers were made to remove their tunics and their boots. The building had a large Red Cross flag flying to denote that it was a medical facility. The RAMC personnel were in uniform but were without Red Cross armbands. They tried to show the Japanese soldiers their RAMC ID cards, but these were taken from them and thrown to the ground. The nurses were taken up to Lye Mun Barracks escorted by a Japanese MO and two soldiers. While they were at the barracks, they witnessed the gruesome sight of the killing taking place across the valley. After having been held for some hours, Eileen Tinson and Lois Fearon were released. They went down the road to Shau Kei Wan where they were robbed of their possessions by looters. They later found refuge in a Chinese convent where they remained until after the surrender. Mary Suffiad made her way to her parents' home in Causeway Bay.

The men were marched up Island Road towards Lye Mun Gap. Cpl Leath, who survived the killing, recalled that they were taken two hundred metres up the road before taking a path leading up into the hills. They were halted in a little valley where Leath estimated there were about one thousand Japanese troops. This would be equivalent to a battalion, and this may have been the RV for the 2nd Battalion of the 229th Regiment after securing the Lye Mun area and before proceeding on to Boa Vista and Tai Tam Gap. Leath described what happened next in an affidavit prepared for war crimes trials after the war.

> We were told to sit down, and some Chinese civilians who were with the troops came and removed our jewellery, rings and watches. ... We were then ordered back down the hill and on reaching a small clearing on a level piece of ground we were halted facing a small nullah, which was about three-foot-deep and also facing the road. Suddenly I heard laughter from behind us and saw a commotion and heard a loud moan from down the line, I saw Sgt Watt fall down, face down on the ground with a bayonet in his back. He was then stabbed several times with the bayonet whilst lying on the ground. I felt a terrific blow on the back of

my neck. The blow shot me into the air, spun me around completely, and I fell to the ground face downwards. ... I then heard further commotion up and down the line followed by shots and a great deal of moaning. I could also hear the Japanese talking and laughing behind me. I then heard people moving behind me and heard someone loading presumably a pistol. There was a single shot fired very close by me after which the moaning from the man next to me ceased. I heard further shots at varying intervals, and after each shot, the moaning lessened.[15]

When Captain Banfill protested that it was a medical facility and that they were non-combatants, the response was, 'Soldier first, medical afterwards.' He was told, 'Order is all captives must die.' When he asked why they were keeping him alive, they responded that he would be killed, but first he had to let them know where the landmines were by walking in front of the Japanese troops. Tim Cheung, who was in charge of the SJAB orderlies, decided to run for his life when he saw the bayoneting commence. He fell into a steep nullah and slid down the hillside before managing to escape to Shau Kei Wan. Osler Thomas also had a lucky escape.

Some of our men had to be bayoneted three times before they would fall and then their bodies were kicked into the nullah. I think at this moment panic must have broken loose as a number of those on the lower end of the line broke and ran and these were shot. These included Dr Orloff. During this pandemonium of shooting, I fell into the nullah as though shot, the bodies of two victims later falling on me and protecting me from the orgy of shooting and bayoneting that followed. I lay in that bloody nullah all day, hearing the groans of the dying and seeing the flow of blood under me, but not daring to move. One RAMC badly wounded in the neck [Cpl Leath] crawled over me down the nullah, and I advised him to lie still but this advice he ignored. That night I escaped down the nullah.[16]

2/Lt Thomas hid in the hills for a few days before making his way to a friend's house in Causeway Bay. Cpl Leath, wounded in the back of the neck by a sword strike, escaped down the nullah and hid in the hills for several days. He worked his way around the hillside to the area above Tai Koo Docks where he could see Japanese troops landing, and proceeding along King's Road, and up Mount Parker Road. After several days, he decided to come down and give himself up because of lack of food and water and the need to get medical attention for his wound. However, by that time the colony had surrendered and the fighting was over, and when he approached Japanese soldiers, they directed him to

North Point POW Camp from where he was transferred to Bowen Road Military Hospital. He was told later that one of the Salesian Fathers had recovered seventeen bodies and buried them at the spot where they were so cruelly put to death.

After the killing, Banfill was taken up the hillside to the water catchment. They walked inside the concrete drain in the direction of Tai Tam Gap. After about a mile the group of soldiers escorting Banfill turned around and retraced their steps until they reached the point where they had started. They then followed the route taken by the main body of the 3rd Battalion to Mount Parker Road and Sanatorium Gap, eventually arriving at Stanley Gap where both Tanaka's battalions reassembled during the afternoon on 19 December. The Japanese had captured the whole of the north shore from North Point to Lye Mun. The possession of Tai Koo Docks facilitated the supply of troops, equipment and ammunition. The road track from Tai Koo and Quarry Bay, through Sanatorium Gap, to WNC Gap became the main supply route for the Japanese Army on the Island. During the early hours on Friday 19 December, the six infantry battalions and their supporting artillery all converged on WNC Gap for what would be the crucial battle.

8

The Battle for Wong Nai Chung Gap
19 to 22 December

Wong Nai Chung Gap was a saddle through which the main road running north–south passed through the line of hills on the Island. On the north side of the gap there was a steep valley. WNC Gap is dominated by the three hill features of Jardine's Lookout, Mount Nicholson and Violet Hill. In 1941, there was a small police post on top of the knoll at the centre of the gap, and five roads led off from the gap. To the south was Repulse Bay Road, winding its way down towards the junction of Repulse Bay Road and Island Road. If you went left at this junction, it led to Repulse Bay with its beach and charming hotel set among elegant villas. The most impressive was Eucliffe, a house built in the style of a castle by the wealthy Chinese-Malayan businessman Eu Tong-sen, who died in Hong Kong in May 1941. If you turned right at the road junction, it led to Deep Water Bay with its scenic golf course and swimming beach. Deep Water Bay was sheltered on the right (west) by the promontory known as Brick Hill, better known today as the home of Ocean Park, and sheltered to the left (east) by the hilly expanse of Middle Island. During the battle, the bay formed an ideal anchorage for naval shipping. On the north side of the gap, WNC Gap Road ran in a northerly direction to the junction of Tai Hang Road and Stubbs Road.

To the east of WNC Gap was Stanley Gap Road, now known as Tai Tam Reservoir Road, which ran steeply uphill to Stanley Gap before dropping down to the reservoirs in Gauge Basin. Running westwards from WNC Gap were two road tracks. The first, known as Black's Link, led to Wan Chai Gap by way of Middle Gap. The second, Deep Water Bay Road, ran south-west towards Shouson Hill, and the

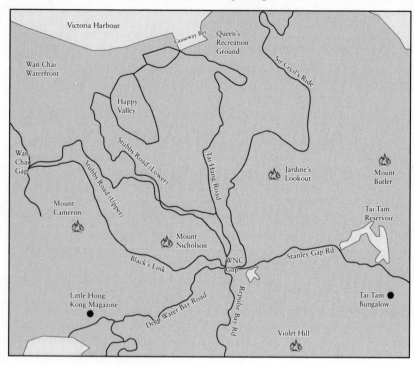

Road system around WNC Gap.

ammunition magazines near the village of Little Hong Kong. In 1941, Blue Pool Road led up from Happy Valley, crossing Tai Hang Road, and continuing in a southerly direction to merge with WNC Gap Road, at a point approximately 200 metres from the gap. The police post on the knoll has long gone; in its place there is a villa with impressive gates marked No. 1 Repulse Bay Road, which is the home of the business tycoon Stanley Ho. The pre-war reservoir on Stanley Gap Road is still there and is now used as a boating lake. Some artillery shells landed in the reservoir during the fighting, and are no doubt still languishing there today.

During the early hours of Friday 19 December, Japanese forces which had landed on the Island during the night were on the advance, and all three Japanese infantry regiments were converging on WNC Gap. The plan was that from WNC Gap, the 230th Regiment, under Colonel Shoji, would drive westwards along the north shore towards Victoria, forming the right flank of the Japanese advance. The 228th Regiment, under Colonel Doi, would proceed westwards along the line of gaps seizing

Middle Gap, Wan Chai Gap and Magazine Gap and forming the centre of the Japanese advance. The 229th Regiment, under Colonel Tanaka, would proceed south to Deep Water Bay, and then turn westwards to form the left flank of the Japanese attack.

Shoji's troops were the first to arrive in the WNC Gap area. His two battalions had followed a track known as Sir Cecil's Ride ('the Ride') from their RV situated on the west side of Braemar Reservoir. The Ride led south towards Jardine's Lookout and then continued around Jardine's Lookout in an anti-clockwise direction to WNC Gap. Tanaka deployed his 2nd Bn to seize Lye Mun Barracks, Pak Sha Wan Battery and Sai Wan AA Fort, after which they moved from their RV at Lye Mun Gap to Boa Vista and Tai Tam Gap. Having achieved these objectives, and having established a garrison at Tai Tam Gap, the main body of the 2nd Bn proceeded to their RV with the 3rd Bn at Stanley Gap. Since WNC Gap was still being contested, the Tanaka *butai* (unit) moved south by following the water catchment from WNC Gap Reservoir towards Middle Spur and Repulse Bay. Tanaka's two battalions played no major role in the battle for WNC Gap.

Doi's troops were held up overcoming resistance from the 5/7 Rajputs in Tai Koo before proceeding inland. The two battalions were split up and were out of radio communication. The 2nd Battalion was the first to land, and after overcoming resistance on the north shore proceeded south onto the high ground around Braemar Hill. There is some confusion about the exact route taken by this battalion, but it is likely that they continued upwards in a southerly direction ascending Siu Ma Shan, which would lead them onto the ridge path between Mount Butler and Jardine's Lookout. They then moved south-west towards the slopes of Jardine's Lookout, where they joined the attack on 'A' Coy, WG. 'A' Coy had already been pushed off the ridge, east of the summit of Jardine's Lookout, by units from Shoji's 230th Regiment which had been ordered up the north face of Jardine's Lookout from their positions on the Ride. Colonel Doi accompanied the 1st Battalion, which, after clearing resistance in Tai Koo, proceeded up Mount Parker Road and passed through Sanatorium Gap before turning east towards Stanley Gap and WNC Gap.

Jardine's Lookout, Stanley Gap and WNC Gap were primarily defended by No. 3 Coy, HKVDC, whose Coy HQ was located at Stanley Gap; and 'D' Coy, WG, whose Coy HQ was located between WNC Gap Road and Blue Pool Road, directly opposite West Brigade HQ. These two companies were supported by two mobile platoons from 'HQ' Coy, WG, based at Wan Chai Gap, and by 'A' Coy, WG, based at Shouson Hill. No. 3 Coy, HKVDC, was commanded by forty-nine-year-old Major Evan Stewart, who in civilian life had been headmaster of St Paul's School. Major Stewart's company was made up of men principally drawn from the Eurasian community in Hong Kong. 'D' Coy, WG, was commanded by thirty-five-year-old Captain Alan Bowman, who had also been a school teacher in civilian life. His battalion commander was Lt-Col John Sutcliffe, whose Bn HQ was located at Wan Chai Gap.

West Brigade HQ was situated on the hillside above WNC Gap Road some 200 metres north of the gap. A semi-circular path, protected by a blast wall, gave access to the shelters. To the north of this cluster of shelters there was a car park for brigade vehicles, and beyond that was a cluster of two further splinter-proof shelters. Major Stewart estimated that there were less than 250 soldiers from the Canadian infantry and the HKVDC defending this area. These numbers were bolstered by the deployment of the two mobile platoons from Wan Chai Gap, and the deployment of 'A' Coy from Shouson Hill. After this reinforcement, there were 400 to 500 Canadian and British troops at Jardine's Lookout, Stanley Gap and WNC Gap but they were facing four Japanese front-line infantry battalions, each battalion numbering approximately one thousand men.

When the war started the bulk of No. 3 Coy, HKVDC, had been deployed on Stonecutters Island. Following the evacuation of British troops from the Mainland, and the subsequent evacuation of Stonecutters, No. 3 Coy was ordered to report to West Brigade HQ for deployment around WNC Gap. In his neat handwriting, Major Stewart describes in the company war diary their arrival at Jardine's Lookout in the early hours of Friday 12 December.

> Reported to West Brigade, who knew nothing about us, but indicated Jardine's Lookout in general as our area. At 0230 hours made a recce with Lt Field and located PBs 1 and 2, occupied by Winnipeg Grenadiers, also JLO 2 where Sgt Winch was placed with a section. Failed to find any place to act as Coy HQ or rest shelters for men. Shelters all occupied by AA gunners. At 0730 hours reported to West Brigade and suggested taking over the PBs. At 0815 hours got in touch by telephone with Major Forsyth, HKVDC, and so was able to locate JLO 1 and 3 and Coy HQ. Found Coy HQ shelter occupied by AA gunners. Some slight friction.[1]

Twenty men from No. 9 Platoon, No. 3 Coy, were deployed in the two pillboxes, PB 1 and PB 2, located on the western slopes of Jardine's Lookout above Sir Cecil's Ride. Each PB had a crew of ten men, and each PB was armed with four Vickers MMGs. The PBs were about 75 metres apart and connected by telephone. The platoon was commanded by Lt Bevan Field supported by Sgt George White. Field occupied PB 1, the upper pillbox, which faced south-west towards WNC Gap, and White occupied the lower PB, PB2, which faced north-west. The remainder of the platoon, under L/Cpl Roylance, was deployed at a roadblock on Blue Pool Road situated immediately below 'D' Coy, WG shelters.

No. 7 Platoon, commanded by Captain Leslie Holmes supported by Sgt Ernie Zimmern, manned the three Forward Defended Localities (FDLs), known as JLO 1, JLO 2 and JLO 3 located astride the Ride north of Jardine's Lookout. These section posts consisted of machine gun emplacements, weapons pits and barbed wire entanglements. Captain Holmes and Sgt Zimmern established their Platoon HQ at JLO 2.

No. 8 Platoon, commanded by Lt Donald Anderson supported by Sgt George Winch, manned four section posts around WNC Gap, Stanley Gap and Sir Cecil's Ride. No. 3 Coy used the large sunken bunker which today can be seen beside a small car park on Tai Tam Reservoir Road as their QM Stores, and as Platoon HQ for Lt Anderson's No. 8 Platoon. On top of the QM Stores bunker, there was a wooden shed which was used as a mess hut by the gunners from the Stanley Gap AA Section. The mess hut was accessed from the gun road leading uphill and providing vehicular access to the 3.7-inch AA position. Major Stewart's Coy HQ was located in a splinter-proof shelter built into the hillside directly below the Stanley Gap AA Section. The only access to Coy HQ was by a flight of steps leading down from the AA gun position. On the summit of Jardine's Lookout there was an AOP, but the hilltop was otherwise undefended. A few days before the Japanese landings took place, Stewart had recommended that either a section or a platoon be deployed to the crest of Jardine's Lookout, but this was rejected by West Brigade HQ on the grounds of insufficient troops.

At approximately 2230 hours on Thursday 18 December, Stewart received a message from West Brigade HQ advising him that a landing at North Point was expected, and to watch out for infiltration by small parties of the enemy. Fifteen minutes later, Stewart received a further message from West Brigade HQ stating that the landing was believed to have been a false rumour and to stand down. Major Stewart took no action and kept his troops stood-to. It seems extraordinary that some three hours after the landings had commenced, West Brigade was not aware that Japanese troops had landed on the Island in considerable strength. This was compounded by the breakdown in telephone communication, and the resultant confusion as to what was happening on the north shore. The so-called 'fog of war' was working overtime. West Brigade HQ must have been notified by Fortress HQ that this was not a false alarm, and that landings had occurred, because a short time later West Brigade HQ started deploying reinforcements from 'A', 'D' and 'HQ' Coy, Winnipeg Grenadiers. However, Fortress HQ continually underestimated the numbers of Japanese troops that had landed on the Island.

At 2350 hours, No. 18 Platoon, 'D' Coy, WG, commanded by Lt McCarthy, reported to No. 3 Coy, HKVDC, HQ, at Stanley Gap for deployment. Pte Hall, No. 3 Coy, was assigned to act as guide to conduct the Canadian platoon to their deployment position on the Ride with their right flank extending up to the two PBs, and their left flank extending downhill to the valley bottom. Lt George Birkett, 'HQ' Coy, WG, was ordered to deploy his mobile platoon to the summit of Jardine's Lookout. His platoon sergeant was twenty-six-year-old Tom Marsh, who described in his memoirs of the battle their deployment from Wan Chai Gap that night.

> Two trucks were sent to enable our speedy delivery. Hurriedly we put on our equipment, loaded ourselves with hand-grenades and ammunition, filled our water bottles, and with our machine guns, were ready. The two trucks hurtled down the winding road in pitch darkness. There were now twenty-nine of us. Lt Birkett rode in the front seat of the forward truck. I rode in the front seat of the one following. ... Ahead of us, we could see the red sky and the fires in the city. We careened and bumped over and around obstacles in the road and crashed through roadblocks. ... Before leaving we had been told that the Japanese were already on the Island. The air was bright with sparks and acrid with the smell of smoke. Guns thundered. Shells shrieked and exploded. The deadly rattle of machine guns and the whine of snipers' bullets added to the bedlam.[2]

Pte Trick and Pte Smelts were the drivers assigned to take the platoon from Bn HQ at Wan Chai Gap to Stanley Gap. The trucks first stopped at West Brigade HQ to report their arrival and for any further orders. They then drove up the steep incline of Stanley Gap Road. Major Stewart recalled Lt Birkett's platoon arriving just after midnight in the early hours of Friday 19 December. Sgt Winch, No. 3 Coy HKVDC, was assigned to guide Lt Birkett's platoon to the PBs from where they would make their own way up to the summit of Jardine's Lookout.

> With Lt Birkett, who had a map, and the Volunteers in the lead, the men picked up their loads and followed. We were strung over some distance and had difficulty keeping in touch, as it was very dark. I brought up the rear to encourage the stragglers. The men cursed

and sweated under their heavy loads as we left the main road and took a side path that wound over and along the foothills.[3]

They reached the PBs, but because of the darkness, rain and thick undergrowth, they had difficulty in finding the back-path that led up from the PBs to the summit of Jardine's Lookout. Birkett telephoned Stewart, who ordered him to remain at PB 1 until dawn and then to deploy to the summit at first light.

Lt Charles French, 'HQ' Coy, WG, was ordered to take his mobile platoon from Wan Chai Gap to the col between Jardine's Lookout and Mount Butler. His trucks arrived at Stanley Gap shortly after Birkett's platoon. They were provided with an HKVDC guide and proceeded down Stanley Gap Road in the direction of Gauge Basin. After passing the Stanley Gap 3.7-inch Howitzer Section, they turned left on Reservoir Path, a thin trail that led uphill from Stanley Gap Road to the ridge that linked Jardine's Lookout and Mount Butler. The platoon deployed in the saddle between the two hills at the eastern end of a disused water catchment. Their position was close to JLO 1, which was located on Sir Cecil's Ride below them. Lt Eric Mitchell, in command of No. 16 Platoon, 'D' Coy, WG, moved up to his assigned area on a ridge

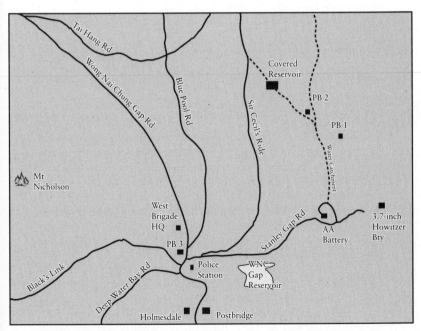

WNC Gap and Stanley Gap.

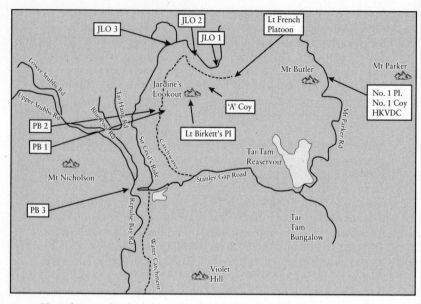

PBs and Forward Defended Localities (FDLs) at Jardine's Lookout.

north-west of Stanley Gap in a position to defend both Stanley Gap and to be able to fire downhill towards WNC Gap. 'A' Coy, WG, commanded by Major Albert Gresham, was ordered to deploy to Jardine's Lookout from their positions at Shouson Hill.

Colonel Shoji's two battalions proceeded along the Ride in two files. They marched quietly, their footfalls softened by their canvas boots known as *jika-tabi*. In the early hours of Friday 19 December, probably around 0300 hours, Shoji's forward troops bumped up against JLO 1. The section post opened fire, causing many casualties to the leading Japanese troops. The column came to a halt, and the troops took cover. The Japanese commander ordered one squad forward to draw fire, while another squad was sent up the hillside to outflank the British position. After having been outflanked and attacked from the hillside to the right, L/Cpl Hung, the section commander, fell back with what was left of his section to JLO 2. The Japanese then continued along the Ride until they bumped up against JLO 2. The Japanese used the same tactics, outflanking the position by going up the hillside and then lobbing grenades down from the higher ground. Captain Holmes, the platoon commander, and Cpl Hing, the section commander, were both killed at JLO 2. Platoon Sgt Ernie Zimmern gave the order to fall back to JLO 3, but was killed while providing covering fire for the withdrawal. After having overrun JLO 2, Shoji ordered the 3rd Battalion to continue along the Ride towards WNC Gap, while the 2nd Battalion was ordered to deploy up the north face of Jardine's Lookout and then proceed to WNC Gap in a pincer-type movement. The 2nd Battalion advanced up the hillside on a broad front and reached the ridge path where they came up against 'A' Coy, WG, on their front, Lt French's platoon to their left, and Lt Birkett's platoon to their right.

JLO 3, the next defensive position on the Ride, was situated by a small hutment above and to the east of Tai Hang Road. Pte Cheung Siu-ling was deployed at JLO 3, and he recalled in a deposition that Pte MacKechnie came from JLO 2 with a message from Captain Holmes that they should report to Coy HQ at Stanley Gap. A runner, Pte Lock, from JLO 3 was sent to Brigade HQ by way of Blue Pool Road, where he telephoned Coy HQ and reported that the FDLs were being heavily attacked. The number of enemy troops was indicated as being around three hundred. There was no fighting at JLO 3 because the rest of the section fell back to their HQ area where they participated in the defence of Stanley Gap. Between JLO 3 and WNC Gap, there were still two more defended positions on the Ride. There was Lt McCarthy's platoon, located below the PBs, and further along the Ride, near the head of the valley, there was a section post commanded by Cpl Ma.

McCarthy had moved his platoon just before dawn from their position on the Ride back to their day positions at 'D' Coy shelters, and as a result, the Japanese were able to pass through this position without interference. A small group of soldiers from this platoon, including Cpl Derek Rix and L/Cpl Ronald Atkinson, made their way up to PB 2 and became trapped there when the battle commenced. Shoji's lead troops next encountered Cpl Ma's section post, which was located 100–200 metres from the end of the Ride at WNC Gap. Ma's section was ready for the advancing Japanese. This section stood their ground and inflicted heavy casualties on the Japanese. Out of the nine men in Ma's section, five were killed and four were wounded. Eventually, the Japanese outflanked the position and overran it with a bayonet charge. Ma was wounded in the face and was left for dead. He eventually reached Saint Albert's Hospital at Rosary Hill after crawling through the undergrowth in Japanese-held territory for two nights. The firefight at Ma's position had caused a bunching-up of Japanese troops at the end of the Ride. Dawn was just breaking, and in the early light, the Japanese troops were now visible from PB 1. At approximately 0630 hours on Friday 19 December, PB 1 opened fire. It was a perfect target, with Japanese troops spread out left and right at the head of the valley. Very heavy casualties were inflicted on the Japanese by the concentrated fire from the Vickers guns. The number of Japanese troops at the head of the valley was estimated to be from 250 to 400, with more following behind.

The AOP on Jardine's Lookout

Just before first light, Lt Birkett left PB 1 and led his platoon up the back-path to Jardine's Lookout. They went past the remains of a 3-foot-thick wall, which was part of a ruined lookout building which dated back to the late 1840s and was located on the flat area behind the PBs. They passed through the outer wire, and up a thin trail leading to the summit. As they approached the crest in the early-morning darkness, they came under machine gun and rifle fire. Sgt Marsh recalled that they incurred several casualties, three being killed before they reached the AOP. When they arrived at the AOP, they encountered a large body of Japanese infantry coming up the north face and fanning out to attack the ridge. Marsh described their arrival on the summit under fire.

> There was a shout up ahead. They had found Jardine's Lookout. It was a pillbox [AOP] built into the side of the hill near the top. One side stuck out, and from it, a short tunnel led into the pillbox, which contained a room about 10 feet by 10 feet in area. In the front was an iron door with a machine gun slot but we never used it. It was evident that this position was under, or soon to be under attack. Possibly the former garrison had just left ... and we walked right into a battle.[4]

The AOP is still there today, but it has been converted into a viewing platform. If one looks closely, there is still a deep trench which leads to a doorway which gives access to the main compartment of the AOP. Inside the main compartment, the walls are damaged by shrapnel, and one can see the shell-blasted embrasure, which took a direct hit from a Japanese mountain gun.

> The day was just breaking. A number of our platoon never actually entered the pillbox for Lt Birkett assigned the men to positions below the fort as soon as they had struggled that far up the hill. They immediately set up their machine guns and opened up on the enemy. While climbing over the top of the hill, at the back of the pillbox, I came upon an English Artillery Observer studying the enemy's position through his binoculars. ... He hurried away, as I supposed to his battery, but we never received any artillery support in the vicinity. When I joined Lt Birkett, he was lying behind a rock on the slopes in front of the pillbox. On our right, we could see small figures moving slowly backwards. This, we were told by Lt W. V. Mitchell who made his way over to us in passing, was 'A' Coy of the Grenadiers. He wanted to know what unit we were. He also said he thought we had fired at 'A' Coy. This was possible in the confusion when we first took

our position, but as Lt Birkett pointed out, it was much more likely that the fire came from the enemy who was attacking our own position and who now, nearly surrounded us. Lt Mitchell was able to re-join 'A' Coy.[5]

This eyewitness account by Tom Marsh is helpful because it pinpoints the whereabouts of 'A' Coy, WG, and confirms that they were on Jardine's Lookout and that they were under attack and already withdrawing back towards Stanley Gap at or around dawn on Friday 19 December. Birkett hurriedly deployed his men on the north-facing slope below the AOP. There was no time to dig in, so the troops used the boulders and rocks as cover. The Japanese to their immediate front were in at least company strength, outnumbering the Canadian defenders by three or four to one. The Japanese were attacking uphill from Sir Cecil's Ride but had artillery and mortar support. Birkett later ordered the platoon to move back to the crest of the hill and to concentrate their strength around the AOP. As they withdrew back up the slope, Birkett was wounded in the leg but managed to take up a position with a Bren gun on the roof of the AOP. Marsh was shot in the leg and in the face, with a bullet passing through his right cheek and exiting through his left cheek, but he managed to drag himself back up the slope to the AOP.

Here the situation was indeed desperate. All but the seriously wounded were up top along the parapet manning the machine guns or supporting them with rifle fire. The Japanese had brought their mortars to bear on the emplacement and shells were exploding all around us. Being weak and dizzy, and not being able to see properly, I was of little or no use. I almost passed out again, so I took cover inside the tunnel that ran to the partly underground chamber of the pillbox. Several of the platoon, dead or desperately wounded, were lying in this inner chamber. The place was also being used to store ammunition and spare arms. At intervals, men came in to get ammunition or to dress their wounds. The enemy had, by this time brought up field artillery and were shelling us. Suddenly there came a terrific explosion. They had scored a direct hit on the pillbox. I was blown into the connecting tunnel … and I lost consciousness. I awoke later in the afternoon to find Cpl Britton lying across me. He was badly wounded, and when I tried to move, he motioned for me to lie quietly. The Japanese had wiped out all resistance by mortar and artillery fire, and their infantry was now storming the position and bayoneting the wounded. I again passed out and remembered no more until I awoke to a fine drizzle of rain in the darkness. There was no movement from the pillbox. All was quiet. Only the dead remained.[6]

This gallant platoon of Winnipeg Grenadiers led by Lt Birkett and Sgt Marsh had fought on until they were literally blasted off the hilltop, and until they were all killed or wounded, with only a few managing to escape back down the hillside to the PBs. Marsh's left arm had been broken in the explosion. He was probably saved from being bayoneted with the other wounded because he was unconscious, and with the bullet wound to his face and leg he must have looked convincingly dead. After nightfall on Friday he limped back down the hill to the PBs, which had previously been manned by the HKVDC, but by then they were occupied by the Japanese. He was taken prisoner and held overnight at PB 1. The area was being shelled by British 6-inch howitzers located near the Jockey Club Stables. The Japanese must have wondered whether to kill him, but instead, and perhaps realising that this was an opportunity to get out of the area that was being shelled, they kept him overnight and early the next morning they took him down to the collection point for prisoners of war at the mess hut at Stanley Gap.

The Mess Hut

The wooden shed which had been used as a mess hut for the gunners at the AA position was approximately 36 feet by 15 feet. It had a cement floor and wooden walls and roof. A trestle table ran down the centre. At the far end of the hut there was a large square-shaped military oven and cooking range. The hut was built on top of the sunken bunker that had been used as a store for No. 3 Coy, HKVDC. The concrete floor and oven are all that remains of the mess hut today. Marsh was put in the hut on Saturday morning. Most of the other occupants had been captured during Friday and had been there overnight. Marsh described the appalling conditions in which the prisoners were held.

> The building ...was now crammed with prisoners. Many, like myself, were wounded and some appeared to be dead. The floor literally ran with blood. There was not enough room in which to lie down. Most sat huddled in attitudes of despair with their knees drawn up. The only clear space was around the guard by the door, and he kept it this way by the swing of his rifle butt. Here was gathered all the misery of military defeat.[7]

The prisoners had their hands tightly bound behind their backs. The Japanese provided no food, no water, and no medical help for the wounded. There was no sanitation, and the prisoners were left to bleed, urinate, defecate, vomit and in some cases die where they lay. The Japanese showed no sympathy and no humanity. They wanted to inflict maximum suffering and degradation on their prisoners. It has been described as Hong Kong's *black hole*.

The Japanese had a field gun mounted near the hut which attracted British counter-bombardment. On Saturday morning, the building was bracketed and then hit by friendly fire. The explosion killed and wounded a large number of the prisoners, many of whom were already wounded. The Japanese sentry positioned by the door was killed. The prisoners in the mess hut included the two drivers Richard Trick and Ed Smelts. There were a number of Winnipeg Grenadiers from 'A' Coy, 'D' Coy and 'HQ' Coy, including Lt William Mitchell from 'A' Coy and his brother Lt Eric Mitchell from 'D' Coy. There were a large number of HKVDC and members of many other units including Royal Engineers, Royal Artillery and Royal Navy. Survivors accounts and depositions vary as to the number of prisoners crammed into this structure. The estimates range from 100 to 200. The number kept increasing as new prisoners were brought in, but was probably in the region of 120 by the time they were marched off on Saturday morning.

The Japanese ordered all those who could walk to go out and assemble on the road. This left only the dead and the seriously wounded lying on the bloodied and soiled floor. Lt William Mitchell had been seriously injured when the hut was hit by friendly fire. His brother Lt Eric Mitchell, although not badly wounded, insisted that he remain with his brother. They were both put to death with all the remaining non-walking wounded. The Japanese, according to their practice, simply bayoneted or clubbed them to death. It was a case of march or die. Marsh forced himself to his feet and staggered out to join the death march.

As the prisoners left the mess hut, their hands were re-tied tightly with wire, and then they were tied again in clusters of several men. They were marched down Stanley Gap Road to the reservoirs, and then up Mount Parker Road, through Sanatorium Gap and down to the north shore. Mount Parker Road is a steep ascent in normal conditions, but for these tightly bound, wounded, thirsty and exhausted men it was a harrowing ordeal. Many were tied together in such a way that they had to walk sideways or even backwards. Those who dropped were prodded by bayonets or beaten with rifle butts back to their feet, and those who could go no further were cut loose, bayoneted and their bodies thrown over the roadside. The surrendered prisoners had to run the gauntlet of Japanese troops coming the other way towards the front line, who frequently beat the prisoners with helmets and rifle butts as they passed.

'A' Coy Winnipeg Grenadiers

In the early hours of Friday 19 December, Major Albert Gresham, commanding 'A' Coy, WG, was ordered to move his company up to Jardine's Lookout. The company left their positions at Shouson Hill at approximately 0200 hours. Gresham's company, less one platoon, were driven up to West Brigade HQ for orders. His orders were to deploy to Jardine's Lookout and then work his way eastwards to Mount Butler. During that Friday, the company was completely destroyed, with a large number killed and wounded. Those who were captured were taken to the mess hut. Survivors' statements, made after the war, give different accounts of where they were. The Canadians, having only just arrived in Hong Kong, were unfamiliar with the topography of the Island. Some thought they were on Violet Hill, and others thought they were on Mount Butler. Even the citation for CSM Osborn's Victoria Cross states, incorrectly, that they were fighting on Mount Butler.

The other Canadian reinforcement platoons under Birkett, McCarthy and French, had started their deployment by proceeding from West Brigade HQ to No. 3 Coy HQ at Stanley Gap where HKVDC guides were assigned to conduct them to their deployment areas. At 0200 hours, Major Stewart was advised by West Brigade HQ that a company under Gresham was on its way to WNC Gap from Shouson Hill. However, there is no record of Gresham's company arriving at Stewart's HQ. Stewart provided this explanation in the company war diary.

> Major Gresham's company never arrived. Survivors of the unit state that after advancing over difficult country, Gresham halted and waited for daylight. At dawn, they met the enemy and fought it out. Gresham was killed, and his company was badly cut up. It was suggested they must have crossed Violet Hill and got into Tai Tam Valley.[8]

However, references to their being in the Tai Tam Valley, on Violet Hill or on Mount Butler cannot be correct as we know from Sgt Tom Marsh's eyewitness account that 'A' Coy was seen on the right flank of Birkett's platoon at dawn on Friday. Marsh made direct contact with Lt Mitchell from 'A' Coy, and at that time 'A' Coy was already in action and retreating from the ridgeline back down the hillside towards Stanley Gap, where they had started their deployment. They were driven up to Stanley Gap from West Brigade HQ in the same transport that brought them from Shouson Hill. They probably started their deployment at around 0300 hours and took up positions on Jardine's Lookout some 200–300 metres east of the AOP on the summit. They were positioned between Birkett's platoon on Jardine's Lookout and French's platoon in the col between Jardine's Lookout and Mount Butler. French's platoon was in dead ground, and not visible to either Birkett's platoon or to Gresham's company. As dawn broke, they were attacked by a large body of Japanese troops advancing up the north face of Jardine's Lookout from the Ride.

In the area where Marsh saw 'A' Coy being pushed back, a number of spent Japanese 6.5mm Arisaka rounds and loading clips have been found. South of the ridge path, in the direction of Stanley Gap, some spent Canadian rounds and Japanese grenade parts were found. This and the description of events provided by Tom Marsh suggests that the Canadian company had got up to the ridge before dawn, and then found themselves facing a large body of Japanese troops who forced them back down the hill towards Stanley Gap. In the retreat down the hillside, they were split into different groups, and Gresham was killed during the withdrawal. The fighting withdrawal took place throughout the morning and continued into the early afternoon. The terrain between the ridgeline and Stanley Gap is very difficult, with low but thick undergrowth, boulders and steep ravines. Cpl Hall from 'A' Coy was one of those who thought they were on Mount Butler.

> Our company had been fighting on Mount Butler under Major Gresham. Although I do not know the size of the Japanese forces with which we were engaged, I believe it was at least a regiment. We had been fighting since dawn and were completely cut off from the other units when at about 1600 hours Lt McKillop, who was the senior officer left alive, ordered our surrender, as our ammunition was practically exhausted and the large proportion of our company had been killed or badly wounded. About two platoons of Japanese disarmed us; our numbers having been reduced to twenty all-ranks. We remained in the position where we had surrendered for about fifteen or twenty minutes and were then marched down to a shack [the mess hut], about half a mile below.[9]

Cpl Hall recalled that there were around ninety prisoners held in the mess hut at Stanley Gap during the night of 19/20 December, but more were added the next day. Reports from other survivors describe how the Japanese troops, on higher ground, were able to lob grenades down on to the Canadian positions. Many of these grenades were flung back before they could explode. It was during one of these grenade exchanges that forty-two-year-old CSM John Osborn, a veteran of the First World War, threw himself on a grenade that he was unable to reach in time to throw back. He did this to protect a group of his men, some of whom were wounded. Sgt Pugsley was with CSM Osborn when he was killed.

CSM Osborn took charge of the two Bren guns of my platoon and directed covering fire for the withdrawal. He was cool and steady at all times and greatly helped the spirit of the men. All this time we were under fire from the right flank. The Japanese opened up on our right Bren gun, killing the crew and knocking out the gun. We still continued resistance with the one gun and rifle fire, under the direction of CSM Osborn and Major Gresham, trying to get back to Wong Nai Chung, but discovered that numbers of Japanese had worked around behind us [most likely from the Doi *butai*] and that we were cut off. At about 1515 hours, Major Gresham decided to surrender, stepped out of the depression with his hands up, and was immediately shot down and killed. By this time the Japanese had got close enough to throw grenades into our positions, and CSM Osborn and myself were discussing what was best to be done when a grenade dropped beside him. He yelled at me and gave me a shove, and I rolled down the hill, and he rolled over on to the grenade and was killed. I firmly believe he did this on purpose, and by his action saved the lives of myself and at least six other men who were in our group. This happened at about 1530 hours. Within the next ten minutes, the Japanese rushed our positions and took the remnant of the company prisoners.[10]

CSM Osborn was awarded the Victoria Cross, not just for his act of self-sacrifice, but for his leadership and gallant conduct during the fighting that day. This was the only Victoria Cross that was awarded during the Battle for Hong Kong. L/Cpl Bradbury recalled surrendering with some thirty-six remaining survivors of 'A' Coy.

I was taken prisoner on 19 December. 'A' Coy had been engaged in fighting a rear-guard action and had been forced back to Jardine's Lookout. It was at Jardine's Lookout that I, together with approximately thirty-six other members of 'A' Coy, was taken prisoner. One group of Grenadiers consisting of Pte Land, Pte Osadchuk, Pte Stodgell and Pte Whalen was thirty yards from my position. I personally saw Pte Land remove a grenade from his pocket, draw the pin, and throw it towards where a group of seven Japanese soldiers were visible. The grenade exploded killing at least four Japanese soldiers. The three surviving Japanese together with about eight or ten others who were nearby rushed to the spot and killed all four Grenadiers using their bayonets. The remaining Grenadiers were then ordered by a Japanese officer to be marched to a nearby hut.[11]

Other depositions refer to the killing of these four grenadiers but do not mention the cause, which may not have been seen by all. After the surrender, the non-walking wounded were put to death where they lay on the hillside, while those who could walk were led down to the mess hut. Given that 'A' Coy's orders were to proceed to Jardine's Lookout and then work their way to Mount Butler, they were not lost, they were in the right place. Although opinions vary, I believe that they were initially attacked by units from Shoji's 2nd Battalion 230th Regiment advancing up from the Ride. Later that morning they were attacked on their right flank by Doi's 2nd Battalion 228th Regiment, and then attacked from their rear by Doi's 3rd Battalion.

Pillboxes 1 and 2 on Jardine's Lookout

At 0630 hours on Friday morning, Lt Field opened fire from PB 1 on the lead troops from Shoji's 3rd Battalion bunched-up at the head of the Ride. In the early light, the flags carried by some Japanese soldiers and the white gloves worn by officers helped give away their positions, and as the light improved very heavy casualties were inflicted on the Japanese troops on and around Sir Cecil's Ride.

> It was now light enough to observe and identify a concentration of enemy troops on the southern end of Sir Cecil's Ride. The Ride was covered with troops for some hundred yards from the southern end. There appeared to be about 250 men there, while more were coming up to their rear and others had already deployed towards the AA position at Stanley Gap and towards Wong Nai Chung Gap.[12]

Initially, one Vickers gun was used which was handled by Field himself to avoid any accidental fire on British and Canadian positions. As the light improved all three machine guns that could bear were brought into action. PB 2, lower down the hillside, was facing a north-westerly direction and therefore unable to fire in the direction of WNC Gap, although some of the crew fired from the roof of their PB.

The Stanley Gap AA Section was attacked shortly before dawn, the section commander reported to RA, HQ that they were under attack from the west and north-west. RA, HQ first ordered an AOP party consisting of one officer and four ORs to assist the AA gunners. The officer in charge may have been twenty-five-year-old 2/Lt Baron Platts, who, according to the Royal Artillery war diary, had been manning an AOP in the area of Jardine's Lookout. It was probably 2/Lt Platts that Sgt Marsh had seen at the AOP on Jardine's Lookout earlier that morning. 2/Lt Platts was killed that morning, presumably while trying to assist the AA section with the AOP party from the command post higher up the hill.

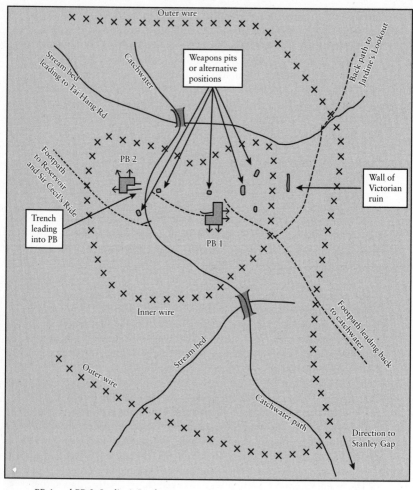

PB 1 and PB 2, Jardine's Lookout.

RA, HQ then ordered the commander of the nearby Stanley Gap Howitzer Section, consisting of three 3.7-inch howitzers, to send a party of gunners to assist the AA position. The Indian officer in command tried to get through with his men, but they were intercepted by Japanese troops at Stanley Gap. After an exchange of fire in which many casualties were incurred, the gunners withdrew down Stanley Gap Road. The AA position was overrun by 0800 hours, and the two

3.7-inch AA guns were captured before they could be put out of action. Major Stewart, CSM White, Sgt Winch and four ORs were trapped in No. 3 Coy HQ in a concrete bunker below the AA position.

Having captured the AA position, the police station knoll, and the ADS at the top of Blue Pool Road, the Japanese turned their attention to the two pillboxes which had caused so many casualties among their ranks that morning. They made two attempts to advance along the shallow water catchment which ran from the AA position passing between the two PBs and emerging at the col between Mount Butler and Jardine's Lookout. The first attack was driven off when Lt Field came out from PB 1 and lobbed grenades at Japanese troops infiltrating along the catchment. The second attempt was beaten off by L/Cpl Broadbridge, Pte Jitts and Pte Leonard from PB 2.

The Japanese used machine guns and mortars to blast the pillboxes. PB 1, the higher of the two pillboxes, bore the brunt of the attack. Japanese snipers were able to use dead ground to infiltrate close enough to PB 1 that they could fire through the loopholes. Pte Young was killed by shrapnel coming through the apertures at PB 1. By the late morning, almost every member of the crew of PB 1 had been wounded, and three of the four Vickers guns were damaged and no longer serviceable. At one stage, the crew of PB 1 heard Japanese soldiers on the roof of their pillbox. The Japanese tried to insert grenades down the commander's observation tower and the ventilation shaft. They were unable to do this because the observation tower had steel shutters around the viewing aperture which were tightly closed. The ventilation shaft made a right-angle turn into a series of horizontal air ducts, and as a result, the grenades exploded harmlessly in the roof cavity at the bottom of the shaft. The Japanese then proceeded to throw grenades through the open loopholes. Lt Field shot one of the Japanese soldiers as he passed a loophole.

When the grenades were thrown through the loopholes, the crew assembled in the passageway by the main entry door which was screened from the gun compartment by an inner wall. The passageway is a small area, and the crew were only just able to squeeze into this confined space. Today one can enter PB 1 through one loophole which has not been sealed up. Inside the PB you immediately notice that the walls and ceiling are peppered with fragmentation damage from these grenade explosions. The noise of the explosions would have been deafening, the smoke would have made it difficult to breathe and hard to see, and the shrapnel from the grenades would have been flying around inside the main compartment, ricocheting off the walls, ceiling and floor. Lt Field telephoned Sgt White at PB 2 to ask if they could help drive the enemy off their pillbox.

PB 2 organised a first attempt to drive off the enemy, approaching up the main path. This attempt failed with the loss of one man mortally wounded, Pte Fisher who was leading. A second attempt, by three Canadian soldiers and three Volunteers, under Corporal Rix, took the enemy by surprise and killed them all, losing one killed and one wounded.[13]

After the grenade assault, the crew moved into their outside weapons pits with their rifles and their one serviceable Vickers gun. At about 1400 hours five Canadians came down from Jardine's Lookout, the remnants of Birkett's platoon. They had an LMG with them and joined the defence of the PBs. By early afternoon, ammunition was running low, and Field did not think the position could be held much longer. Telephone communication lines had been cut, and since there was no sign of a British counterattack coming to relieve them, Lt Field ordered the evacuation of the PBs. Sgt White sent the crew of PB 2, including the walking wounded, under L/Cpl Broadbridge, down a gulley towards Blue Pool Road. They then started evacuating the crew from PB 1. The evacuation of the pillboxes was completed at around 1630 hours, and the remaining defenders gathered at PB 2. Lt Field had been wounded on four different occasions during the day. He had been injured in the face and chest by shell blast through a loophole, then he was wounded in his left arm by shrapnel, then a bullet wound to his neck that grazed his jugular vein, and finally a bullet wound in his already injured left arm.

In the early evening, Pte Stephen Hall, who had been captured at Stanley Gap, was sent down to the PBs under a flag of truce with a message from a Japanese officer that if they surrendered, and came out unarmed, their lives would be spared. By this time there were only a few survivors left, including Lt Field, Sgt White, L/Cpl Hung and two Canadian soldiers including Cpl Rix. They were down to their last rounds of ammunition, and all of them were wounded to some extent. They decided to surrender, and came out from PB 2, in single file, up the path towards PB 1 led by Lt Field and with Sgt White bringing up the rear. While going up the path to PB 1 L/Cpl Hung was shot by a sniper and had to be left wounded in one of the PBs. They proceeded to the flat area behind PB 1, near the ruined wall, where the Japanese officer was waiting. The Japanese officer spoke to them through an interpreter saying, 'Now we are no more enemies, we are friends', and offered them cigarettes. The survivors were taken to the mess hut. Pte Hall, the flag bearer, died the next morning when the mess hut was hit by friendly fire. The wounded left in the pillboxes were put to death.

The Loss of Stanley Gap

The Shoji *butai* were the first Japanese troops to reach WNC Gap. They had rushed the gap and captured the police station knoll before dawn. The AA gun position was heavily mortared before Japanese troops started working their way up the hillside, and up Stanley Gap Road to overrun the position. The section commander, Lt Robert ('Buck') Plummer, and a number of the gunners held out at the command post until later in the day when they ran out of ammunition and had to surrender. Those who could walk, including Plummer, were taken down to the mess hut. Major Stewart, trapped in his Coy HQ shelter, heard the mortar bombs exploding around the gun position above his concrete shelter. At 0710 hours, during a lull in the firing, Stewart went up the steps to the AA position. Stewart described in the war diary the chaos at the gun site.

> Enemy dropping mortar shells with uncanny accuracy on AA gunners position. Went up there with CSM White and two men. Could not find an officer; was told both killed; BSM dead, the men were restless as there was no cover from the mortar fire; local defence positions to the north not manned; the enemy had already reached the upper shelters; close quarter sniping.[14]

Thirty minutes later, Sgt Winch made his way through the bombardment to Coy HQ and reported that the surviving AA gunners were withdrawing down Stanley Gap Road towards Gauge Basin. Seventeen of the AA gunners had been killed and many more wounded. One of the injured gunners, L/Bdr Alan Wood, had been hit by shrapnel during the mortar barrage, but he managed to escape before the Japanese overran the position. He jumped down from the roof of the magazine to the gun road below and then escaped down Stanley Gap Road to the 6-inch howitzer position located between Stanley Gap and Tai Tam Hill. The Indian section commander, on being asked to fire on the Stanley Gap AA position, would not do so without orders from a senior British officer. Wood continued along Stanley Gap Road to Gauge Basin and from there to Stanley where he was admitted to St Stephen's College Hospital.

Later in the day, British artillery fire was put down on the AA position from two 6-inch howitzers located at the Jockey Club Stables. Colonel Doi described the Stanley Gap AA position as being very difficult to occupy because of the intensity of artillery fire. He also related how two British gunners at the AA position locked themselves in an ammunition locker, refusing to come out. The next day, when

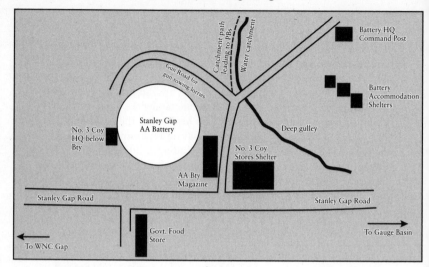

Stanley Gap.

the steel doors were forced open, it was found they had taken their own lives with their revolvers. The Japanese gave them a decent burial because this would have appealed to the Japanese psyche; they would have seen it as death before dishonour, and for the Japanese soldier this was the way of the warrior.

Lt Anderson, commanding No. 8 Platoon, was killed in the fighting at Stanley Gap. By the afternoon large numbers of Japanese troops had closed in on Stanley Gap, and the defenders found themselves completely surrounded and withdrew to the relative safety of the QM Stores bunker. The occupants in the bunker had hoped they could escape at dusk and re-join British lines, but later that afternoon the Japanese surrounded the bunker and started throwing grenades down the ventilation shafts which caused injuries to many of those in the bunker. The Japanese then addressed them in English, calling on them to lay down their arms and come out in return for their lives. CQMS Fincher, No. 3 Coy, in charge of the QM Stores, was the senior rank and he decided that the position was no longer tenable and took the decision to surrender. The occupants laid down their weapons and came out of the bunker in single file. They were lined up in three rows on the roadside in front of the bunker and made to kneel. Shortly afterwards they were subjected to a vicious attack in which at least three were killed and others severely wounded. Fincher described the incident in a deposition made for war crimes trials.

eventually able to get back to British lines. Today a memorial close to the knoll commemorates the many SJAB personnel who were killed during the Battle for Hong Kong, including the ten Chinese orderlies who were slaughtered at the ADS at WNC Gap.

West Infantry Brigade HQ

The Brigade HQ shelters were located on the hillside of Mount Nicholson overlooking Blue Pool Valley and facing the western slopes of Jardine's Lookout. WNC Gap Road was immediately in front of the Brigade HQ, and across the road there was a cluster of shelters on the hillside between WNC Gap Road and Blue Pool Road which were occupied by 'D' Coy, WG, commanded by Captain Alan Bowman.

During the morning of 19 December, West Brigade HQ found itself in the front line with the Japanese able to fire directly into the shelters from the other side of the valley. It was difficult to get away as the road in front was covered by Japanese machine guns. Japanese troops around the ADS were only 200 metres away. 'A' Coy, 2/RS, was ordered to relieve the besieged HQ but they had been unable to fight their way up Blue Pool Road and WNC Gap Road. They incurred heavy casualties and only a few, all wounded, managed to reach Lawson's bunker. Maltby received a telephone call from Lawson at around 1000 hours on Friday 19 December, at which time Lawson said that he was going to try and fight his way out. After ordering the destruction of the telephone exchange, he left the shelters with a small group of brigade staff, but they were hit by machine gun fire in front of the shelters. Lawson was shot in the thigh, the bullet fracturing his femur, and he bled to death from his wound. Captain Uriah Laite, padre of the Winnipeg Grenadiers, found Lawson's body after the garrison at 'D' Coy shelters had surrendered on 22 December. He was allowed to take Lawson's identification bracelet, which he kept throughout internment, and after the war he returned it to Augusta, Lawson's widow.

S/Sgt Thomas Barton, Corps of Military Staff Clerks, was in charge of a team of clerks and orderlies at Brigade HQ. He wrote an unpublished report, dated 3 December 1945, describing the situation at both Brigade HQ and 'D' Coy shelters during the battle. The personnel at Brigade HQ had been on continual stand-to from the time that reports came in of the Japanese landings on Thursday night to the following day when Japanese troops were seen on Sir Cecil's Ride opposite Brigade HQ. Barton described how they were pinned down by enemy fire.

Just after dawn on the morning of 19 December a large body of Japanese was engaged coming along Sir Cecil's Ride. …We were given

I was captured with about twenty others in the late afternoon of 19 December. We were assembled on the roadside, and an officer was going through my pockets at the time. Japanese troops were moving up the other side of the road. One Japanese, with a camouflage net over him, caught sight of us and in English accused us of killing too many Japanese. He came across the road with his rifle lowered and made for some fellows at the back of me. I heard slight groans but did not see the actual bayoneting. We were later bound and led past these three lads lying in a pool of blood (Pte Gosling, Pte Lim and Pte MacKechnie). We were then taken up to a small mess hut.[15]

Cheung Siu-ling described how, apart from those bayoneted to death, many of the group were beaten with helmets, pick-axe handles, entrenching tools and rifle butts.

I saw Pte Gosling being hit first, and as he fell down he was bayoneted, and Pte MacKechnie also suffered the same fate. L/Cpl Lim was first hit with rifle butts, and later he was trampled to death. Pte Shaw's head was also hit with a pickaxe. I was hit in the head with the butt of a rifle. After that, I was pretty dazed and the next thing I knew I was tied up in the mess hut.[16]

Major Stewart with six men decided to remain in the Coy HQ shelter in the expectation that a counterattack would be launched. The trapped occupants bolted the heavy steel door and jammed the steel window shutters. They blocked up the ventilation shaft with a greatcoat and blankets to prevent grenades being thrown in. There was no food, and little water and the air was musty without ventilation. They could hear the enemy around them, but the Japanese made no effort to force an entry. They remained in their shelter for four days until the night of Monday 22 December by which time it had become evident that there was no prospect of relief, and without food, and with the water running out, they decided to try and escape. They planned to leave in pairs, with each pair leaving at fifteen-minute intervals. The first pair to go was CSM White and Cpl Knox at 2315 hours. The next pair to leave at 2330 hours was Pte Brown and Gunner Finley. Finley had been wounded in the face when the AA battery was attacked and was weak from loss of blood. Sgt Winch and Pte Allen left at 2345 hours. Major Stewart was the last to leave at 2355 hours, but for some reason he decided to go up the steps to the AA gun position. He was fired upon and then withdrew back down the steps, joining up with Sgt Winch and Pte Allen. Although they ran into enemy patrols, all of the Coy HQ occupants made it safely back to British lines.

The Advanced Dressing Station at WNC Gap

The ADS was situated at the junction of Blue Pool Road and WNC Gap Road. It was about midway between the police station knoll and West Brigade HQ. The ADS was comprised of three adjoining splinter-proof shelters. The role of the ADS was to act as a collection point for battlefield wounded. The ADS would provide early medical treatment, which included the cleaning and dressing of wounds, after which casualties would be either sent to a military hospital or released for duty depending on the seriousness of their injuries. The ADS was under the command of Captain Beauchamp Barclay, RAMC. His staff included Sgt Cunningham, Pte Evans and Pte Jones, all from RAMC, and Pte Mapp, RASC, who was acting as Captain Barclay's driver. L/Cpl Linton, 1/Mx, an intelligence clerk from West Brigade HQ, was billeted at the ADS because of the lack of accommodation space at Brigade HQ. There was also an Indian policeman, from the police post on the knoll, who had sustained facial injuries from shrapnel during Thursday evening. There was a group of ten Chinese St John Ambulance Brigade (SJAB) personnel at the ADS who acted as stretcher-bearers and orderlies.

Although the shelling around the gap had been heavy on Thursday, Captain Barclay decided to remain at the ADS where they had telephone communication with Brigade HQ, Field Ambulance HQ, and with St Albert's Relief Hospital. He had been asked to remain on standby with his vehicle, which was parked outside the ADS, to help Brigadier Lawson go around the posts. The vehicles in the Brigade HQ car park had all been damaged by shell fire. L/Cpl Linton described what happened at the ADS when the position first came under attack in the early hours of Friday morning.

At 0200 hours 19 December, I was awakened by Sgt Cunningham and told to vacate the stretcher upon which I had been sleeping as it might be needed for casualties. A warning had been received that Japanese troops had landed on the Island. At about 0400 hours Captain Barclay left the ADS to go to the latrine. Shortly afterwards several shots were fired in the valley below the ADS, and Captain Barclay re-entered and remarked that the shots appeared to be from a revolver. Within three minutes an automatic with a very high rate of fire opened up, and rifle fire became general. Captain Barclay ordered the door closed, and jamming handles hammered into position. ... An attempt was made to open the door from the outside. ... Shortly afterwards a grenade was dropped down the ventilator but did no damage due to the steel cover underneath it.[17]

Cunningham recalled hearing a group of Japanese soldiers on the roof daybreak trying to force the ventilators open. They then heard the sou of explosions from one of the other medical shelters. The Japanese h managed to insert grenades into the shelter where the SJAB person were accommodated and shortly after this Cunningham saw the SJ orderlies and the Indian policeman, most of whom were injured, com out to surrender. They were all put to death by the Japanese.

By this time the telephone line was no longer functioning. The A occupants remained in the shelter all day Friday, and throughout morning on Saturday. The Japanese made several attempts to open steel door and window apertures, but they held firm. With food and wa running low, the occupants made an effort to show an improvised I Cross flag through the steel window shutters. However, as soon as t opened the shutters the Japanese outside opened fire and then rene their efforts to force the door open. Captain Barclay took the decis to surrender the position and led the occupants out. The Japanese their hands behind their backs, tore off their Red Cross armbands, beat them with boots and fists. They were then taken down into valley below the ADS, which the Japanese were using as a camp. T were blindfolded and tied to trees together with an Indian soldier, could speak no English. Linton described how they managed to esc that night.

About 1800 on 21 December, rain commenced to fall, and the Japane retired to their bivouacs leaving no sentry to guard us, but havin sentries patrolling at short intervals around the camp. I managed t work the blindfold down so that I could observe my surrounding At dusk, the Indian started to work on his bonds and within an hou had freed himself and disappeared without making any attempt t aid us. I freed myself, Pte Evans, and Sgt Cunningham. When abou to release Captain Barclay he declined because there were too mar sentries around the camp and therefore no chance of escape. I pointe out that the Indian had already gone with no alarm raised, after whic he doubled away in a southerly direction.[18]

Pte Mapp and Pte Jones had been taken away as part of a work pa Captain Barclay must have been captured a few days later, beca Linton stated that Mapp told him, whilst they were in POW camp, he had seen Barclay in Japanese hands on 23 December after he had recaptured. He was not seen again, and it is assumed he was put to d for escaping. Linton, Evans, and Cunningham headed north, tow: Tai Hang Road, but separated and scattered after being fired uj Evans was killed during the escape, but Linton and Cunningham w

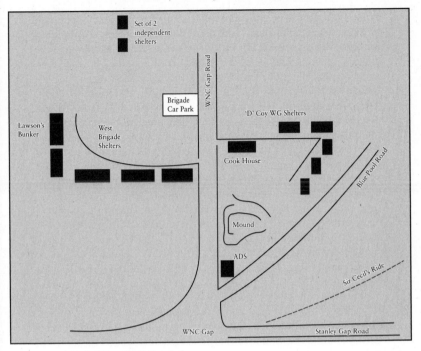

West Brigade HQ and 'D' Coy shelters.

artillery support that morning by the Hong Kong Singapore Royal Artillery. With this support and the fire from our Bren guns and rifles, many casualties were inflicted upon the enemy. By about ten o'clock Major Lyndon and a Captain in the Royal Artillery decided to see if they could find a way that was not covered by the Japanese so that the HQ could get out. Previous to this Captain Bush had gone across the road to where the remnants of 'D' Coy were. ... Soon after Major Lyndon and Captain Fox made their way up the hill above the Brigade HQ, a volley of fire was heard and the only indication they got it was the squealing of Captain Fox's springer spaniel that accompanied them. It was about this time when we were completely cut off from all avenues of retreat, and the situation was hopeless that Brigadier Lawson gave orders for us to try and make a break for it and told us we could choose whatever way we liked as all were under fire from the Japanese.[19]

On the hillside above the shelters, Captain Fox, RA, had been killed, but Major Lyndon had escaped injury. He lay still because any movement brought down Japanese fire. He remained there all of

Friday and Saturday until nightfall on Sunday 21 December when he came down from the hillside and joined the troops still holding out at 'D' Coy shelters. On being advised by the brigadier to make a break for it, a number of the brigade staff including S/Sgt Barton and Captain Billings, Brigade Signals Officer, decided to go up the hill behind the shelters but this time taking a more northerly direction. They were fired on, resulting in one of their party being killed and several being wounded. The survivors remained where they were on the hillside until nightfall when, under cover of darkness, they made their way back to Brigade HQ. By then, the shelters were occupied only by the dead and the wounded. Barton helped make the wounded as comfortable as possible and dressed their wounds. In his report, he recalled that there were two Royal Scots each with an arm almost severed, and one member of the RAF with shrapnel injuries to his back. After doing what they could for the wounded, the survivors from the hillside sprinted across the road to 'D' Coy shelters, some being shot as they crossed.

Later in the siege, Japanese troops were on the hillside above Brigade HQ, but they made no attempt to come down and occupy the HQ bunkers while the troops at 'D' Coy shelters were still holding out. The HQ bunkers had little food, and no water supply, but the splinter-proof shelters were solidly built military structures, protected by a semi-circular blast wall, and the wounded that remained at Brigade HQ survived. If Lawson had remained in his HQ, he most probably would have survived, and it would have given him the opportunity to try and melt away after dark rather than trying to escape in broad daylight. Lawson was the most senior officer to be killed in the Battle for Hong Kong. On Monday 22 December, after the Japanese captured the position, they gave Lawson a respectful burial in admiration of such a senior officer being killed in action.

'D' Coy Winnipeg Grenadiers Shelters

When 'D' Coy shelters came under attack on 19 December, two of their three platoons had been deployed. One platoon had been assigned to 'A' Coy and had been ordered up to Jardine's Lookout, while another platoon, under Lt Mitchell, had been deployed to defend Stanley Gap. The personnel left at 'D' Coy shelters included the company commander, Captain Bowman, his HQ personnel, and the bulk of Lt McCarthy's platoon which had just returned to the company shelters from their night position on Sir Cecil's Ride. During the siege of 'D' Coy's position they were joined by additional personnel from Brigade HQ, 'HQ' Coy, and by members of other units who had been cut off, or wounded, during the various counterattacks that were made to recapture the gap. These included men from a variety of different units including the Royal Engineers, the Royal Artillery and the Royal Scots. There were between forty and fifty personnel occupying the shelters, many of whom were wounded and incapacitated by the time they were forced to surrender on Monday 22 December.

On Friday morning, Lt Thomas Blackwood, 'HQ' Coy, WG, was ordered with some twenty ORs to man a pillbox at WNC Gap. This must have been PB 3, which still survives today on the hillside above Black's Link. The twenty men referred to in this context presumably included two sections of ten men to provide an alternating shift of ten men to man the PB. Blackwood's party came under fire as they neared the gap. Japanese troops had by then occupied the head of the valley, the area around the ADS, the mound north of the ADS, and the police station knoll. Lt Blackwood withdrew his men down the road and joined Captain Bowman at 'D' Coy shelters. This explains why PB 3 did not open fire – it was unoccupied at the time. Later that morning, Lt Blackwood and Pte Morris, 'D' Coy, showed great courage by volunteering to bring in Lt-Col Walker, HKVDC, who had been wounded earlier that morning while leading a counterattack on the gap. He was lying on the road near Brigade HQ and within range of Japanese machine guns and grenades. Walker, although badly wounded in the legs and unable to walk, became the most senior officer at 'D' Coy shelters.

Bowman was killed on Friday while single-handedly going out, armed with a Tommy gun, to dislodge a Japanese sniper who was firing very effectively on 'D' Coy shelters from a location close to their position. Lt Philip assumed command of the company but was injured later that day by a grenade blast, resulting in his being blinded in one eye and sustaining shrapnel injuries to his legs and chest. Lt Blackwood then assumed day-to-day command. Captain Bush, staff captain, and Captain Billings, brigade signals officer, had both managed to get across the road from Brigade HQ earlier on Friday morning. Bush was slightly injured by the same grenade blast that had wounded Lt Philip. The fact that grenades could be lobbed at their positions demonstrates how close the Japanese were to 'D' Coy shelters.

The wounded men at 'D' Coy shelters were placed in the cookhouse shelter, which was the shelter closest to Brigade HQ. Padre Laite did his best to apply dressings and to make the wounded comfortable in the absence of any medics. The occupants were initially able to maintain telephone contact with Lt-Col Sutcliffe at Wan Chai Gap, but on Saturday 20 December the telephone line was cut, and there was no further external communication. On Saturday, a Royal Artillery officer had managed to drive up WNC Gap Road to ascertain the situation and see what artillery support could be provided. He stopped his car quite close to 'D' Coy shelters and on stepping out of his vehicle was promptly shot in the shoulder. Despite his wound, he was able to escape through the undergrowth in the valley below the road and made his back towards Tai Hang Road. Later, and presumably following his report, an artillery barrage was laid down in the vicinity of WNC Gap. After nightfall, the two staff officers Bush and Billings, with Cpl McArthur acting as a driver, used the Royal Artillery officer's abandoned vehicle to escape from the shelters. They had mentioned their intention to escape to Padre Laite and invited him to join them. Padre Laite declined because he felt that it was his duty to stay with the wounded. Barton was critical of these two staff officers for escaping a position which was still in action and still holding out.

Major Lyndon made his way down from the hillside above West Brigade to 'D' Coy shelters on Saturday night. As senior officer after the wounded Lt-Col Walker, he assumed command from Lt Tamworth, HKVDC, who had taken command from Lt Blackwood who had been injured that evening. Lyndon, Tamworth and Barton went back to Brigade HQ late on Saturday night to try and fix the telephone which had been put out of action when Lawson left the position. They were unable to repair the telephone exchange, and the position remained out of communication. At that time, there were still a dozen wounded lying in the Brigade HQ shelters.

The Japanese were sniping from the roof of the ADS shelters, from the nearby mound, and from the hillside above Brigade HQ. Cpl Meirion Price and Pte Gordon Williamson, both from 'D' Coy, were involved in several raids against Japanese snipers, machine gun positions and grenade throwers. They were both awarded the Military Medal for their gallant actions during the siege. By Sunday 21 December, the garrison at 'D' Coy shelters was running short of food, water and ammunition, and casualties were still mounting. During the early hours on Monday 22 December, the Japanese launched a more determined attack starting with a barrage of grenades. It was during this attack that Major Lyndon, who had left the position to carry out a recce, was killed by friendly fire while returning through the undergrowth. Tamworth recalled that just before dawn he heard soldiers in the medical shelter shouting out to the Japanese that they were willing to surrender. Barton's report corroborates this.

> Someone near the Cook House shouted: 'Japanese we surrender'. ...
> We shouted back for him to keep quiet, and that we would fight on. ...
> He stated that Colonel Walker had ordered it. That was different.[20]

A white flag was shown, and the firing died down as the Japanese realised that the garrison was attempting to surrender. After the decision to surrender had been communicated to the remaining effectives, they were told that anybody who wished to escape could do so before the Japanese arrived. Several men decided to try and get away in two groups. One group, which included S/Sgt Barton, went down WNC Gap Road, and the other group went down the valley. Both groups were able to get back to British lines. Tamworth described the subsequent surrender of the position.

> At about 0900 hours I saw a captured Indian soldier with his hands tied behind his back, and at the end of a long rope tied to his waist, standing on the rising ground to our front. He made me understand we were to follow him out; he was then pulled back to Blue Pool Road. I followed him calling on our remaining effectives to come with me. As I reached Blue Pool Road, I was seized by two Japanese soldiers, and my hands were tied behind my back. The Japanese officer standing by came forward and struck me in the face and motioned me to walk up Blue Pool Road. I was joined by other men from the shelters; we were tied together and told to sit down on the side of the road facing Blue Pool Valley where we remained until 1700 hours.[21]

Padre Laite does not mention Tamworth in his diary, and nor does Tamworth mention Laite. Laite was in the medical shelter, which was furthest from the Japanese. Laite recalled the decision to surrender and stated that Lt Philip, although wounded, went out from the medical shelter to surrender the position.

> Altogether, including three British soldiers and four Chinese, we had thirty wounded men in that shelter. Shortly after dawn, we were told that our ammunition was exhausted. Lt Philip consulted Lt-Col Walker, who gave us no hope of being allowed to live even though we surrendered, but it was the only thing left for us to do. Lt Philip, wounded, bandaged, and weak though he was, stepped out of the shelter to surrender.[22]

The Japanese gave Laite water for the wounded, and they were surprised to see that he gave the water to the wounded first and drank last himself. Laite tried to persuade anybody that could possibly walk to do so, realising that those who could not walk would be killed. Three Canadian soldiers and two British soldiers who were unable to walk were killed at 'D' Coy shelters, as were the non-walking wounded at Brigade HQ. Only Lt-Col Walker, due to his rank, was provided with a stretcher and carried out. The surrender seems to have been more piecemeal than described by Tamworth, as Laite was taken by the Japanese along the trenches, and at each shelter he was told to call the men out with their hands above their heads. Perhaps because of Laite's help during the surrender, and because he was a padre, the Japanese released him. He was escorted down the road and pointed in the direction of Happy Valley, from where he was able to get back to British positions. The rest of the prisoners were marched in two groups, one moving fast and the other, with the more seriously wounded, moving slowly. They were taken up Stanley Gap Road, up Mount Parker Road and down to North Point.

The mixed group of Winnipeg Grenadiers and other troops at 'D' Coy shelters were the last to surrender at WNC Gap. They held out against a much larger force from Friday 19 December until Monday 22 December. By the time they surrendered they had run out of food, water and ammunition and three-quarters of the garrison were wounded. They had taken a heavy toll on the Japanese, and they had so far prevented Colonel Shoji's 230th Regiment from advancing towards Happy Valley and Wan Chai. Throughout this period, British, Indian and Canadian troops had made a series of counterattacks, and despite great gallantry in the prosecution of these counterattacks, all attempts to dislodge the Japanese from their positions at WNC Gap were unsuccessful. With the loss of WNC Gap, the Battle for Hong Kong was over. The Hong Kong garrison surrendered three days later.

1. Japanese troops landing on North Shore of Hong Kong Island. (Courtesy of the Imperial War Museum).

2. Japanese troops fighting in King's Road, North Point.

Above: 3. Salesian Mission Building.

Left: 4. Japanese artillery firing at North Point Power Station.

Below left: 5. HMS *Tamar* alongside the west wall in RN Dockyard.

I was captured with about twenty others in the late afternoon of 19 December. We were assembled on the roadside, and an officer was going through my pockets at the time. Japanese troops were moving up the other side of the road. One Japanese, with a camouflage net over him, caught sight of us and in English accused us of killing too many Japanese. He came across the road with his rifle lowered and made for some fellows at the back of me. I heard slight groans but did not see the actual bayoneting. We were later bound and led past these three lads lying in a pool of blood (Pte Gosling, Pte Lim and Pte MacKechnie). We were then taken up to a small mess hut.[15]

Cheung Siu-ling described how, apart from those bayoneted to death, many of the group were beaten with helmets, pick-axe handles, entrenching tools and rifle butts.

I saw Pte Gosling being hit first, and as he fell down he was bayoneted, and Pte MacKechnie also suffered the same fate. L/Cpl Lim was first hit with rifle butts, and later he was trampled to death. Pte Shaw's head was also hit with a pickaxe. I was hit in the head with the butt of a rifle. After that, I was pretty dazed and the next thing I knew I was tied up in the mess hut.[16]

Major Stewart with six men decided to remain in the Coy HQ shelter in the expectation that a counterattack would be launched. The trapped occupants bolted the heavy steel door and jammed the steel window shutters. They blocked up the ventilation shaft with a greatcoat and blankets to prevent grenades being thrown in. There was no food, and little water and the air was musty without ventilation. They could hear the enemy around them, but the Japanese made no effort to force an entry. They remained in their shelter for four days until the night of Monday 22 December by which time it had become evident that there was no prospect of relief, and without food, and with the water running out, they decided to try and escape. They planned to leave in pairs, with each pair leaving at fifteen-minute intervals. The first pair to go was CSM White and Cpl Knox at 2315 hours. The next pair to leave at 2330 hours was Pte Brown and Gunner Finley. Finley had been wounded in the face when the AA battery was attacked and was weak from loss of blood. Sgt Winch and Pte Allen left at 2345 hours. Major Stewart was the last to leave at 2355 hours, but for some reason he decided to go up the steps to the AA gun position. He was fired upon and then withdrew back down the steps, joining up with Sgt Winch and Pte Allen. Although they ran into enemy patrols, all of the Coy HQ occupants made it safely back to British lines.

The Advanced Dressing Station at WNC Gap

The ADS was situated at the junction of Blue Pool Road and WNC Gap Road. It was about midway between the police station knoll and West Brigade HQ. The ADS was comprised of three adjoining splinter-proof shelters. The role of the ADS was to act as a collection point for battlefield wounded. The ADS would provide early medical treatment, which included the cleaning and dressing of wounds, after which casualties would be either sent to a military hospital or released for duty depending on the seriousness of their injuries. The ADS was under the command of Captain Beauchamp Barclay, RAMC. His staff included Sgt Cunningham, Pte Evans and Pte Jones, all from RAMC, and Pte Mapp, RASC, who was acting as Captain Barclay's driver. L/Cpl Linton, 1/Mx, an intelligence clerk from West Brigade HQ, was billeted at the ADS because of the lack of accommodation space at Brigade HQ. There was also an Indian policeman, from the police post on the knoll, who had sustained facial injuries from shrapnel during Thursday evening. There was a group of ten Chinese St John Ambulance Brigade (SJAB) personnel at the ADS who acted as stretcher-bearers and orderlies.

Although the shelling around the gap had been heavy on Thursday, Captain Barclay decided to remain at the ADS where they had telephone communication with Brigade HQ, Field Ambulance HQ, and with St Albert's Relief Hospital. He had been asked to remain on standby with his vehicle, which was parked outside the ADS, to help Brigadier Lawson go around the posts. The vehicles in the Brigade HQ car park had all been damaged by shell fire. L/Cpl Linton described what happened at the ADS when the position first came under attack in the early hours of Friday morning.

At 0200 hours 19 December, I was awakened by Sgt Cunningham and told to vacate the stretcher upon which I had been sleeping as it might be needed for casualties. A warning had been received that Japanese troops had landed on the Island. At about 0400 hours Captain Barclay left the ADS to go to the latrine. Shortly afterwards several shots were fired in the valley below the ADS, and Captain Barclay re-entered and remarked that the shots appeared to be from a revolver. Within three minutes an automatic with a very high rate of fire opened up, and rifle fire became general. Captain Barclay ordered the door closed, and jamming handles hammered into position. ... An attempt was made to open the door from the outside. ... Shortly afterwards a grenade was dropped down the ventilator but did no damage due to the steel cover underneath it.[17]

Cunningham recalled hearing a group of Japanese soldiers on the roof at daybreak trying to force the ventilators open. They then heard the sound of explosions from one of the other medical shelters. The Japanese had managed to insert grenades into the shelter where the SJAB personnel were accommodated and shortly after this Cunningham saw the SJAB orderlies and the Indian policeman, most of whom were injured, coming out to surrender. They were all put to death by the Japanese.

By this time the telephone line was no longer functioning. The ADS occupants remained in the shelter all day Friday, and throughout the morning on Saturday. The Japanese made several attempts to open the steel door and window apertures, but they held firm. With food and water running low, the occupants made an effort to show an improvised Red Cross flag through the steel window shutters. However, as soon as they opened the shutters the Japanese outside opened fire and then renewed their efforts to force the door open. Captain Barclay took the decision to surrender the position and led the occupants out. The Japanese tied their hands behind their backs, tore off their Red Cross armbands, and beat them with boots and fists. They were then taken down into the valley below the ADS, which the Japanese were using as a camp. They were blindfolded and tied to trees together with an Indian soldier, who could speak no English. Linton described how they managed to escape that night.

> About 1800 on 21 December, rain commenced to fall, and the Japanese retired to their bivouacs leaving no sentry to guard us, but having sentries patrolling at short intervals around the camp. I managed to work the blindfold down so that I could observe my surroundings. At dusk, the Indian started to work on his bonds and within an hour had freed himself and disappeared without making any attempt to aid us. I freed myself, Pte Evans, and Sgt Cunningham. When about to release Captain Barclay he declined because there were too many sentries around the camp and therefore no chance of escape. I pointed out that the Indian had already gone with no alarm raised, after which he doubled away in a southerly direction.[18]

Pte Mapp and Pte Jones had been taken away as part of a work party. Captain Barclay must have been captured a few days later, because Linton stated that Mapp told him, whilst they were in POW camp, that he had seen Barclay in Japanese hands on 23 December after he had been recaptured. He was not seen again, and it is assumed he was put to death for escaping. Linton, Evans, and Cunningham headed north, towards Tai Hang Road, but separated and scattered after being fired upon. Evans was killed during the escape, but Linton and Cunningham were eventually able to get back to British lines. Today a memorial close to the knoll commemorates the many SJAB personnel who were killed during the Battle for Hong Kong, including the ten Chinese orderlies who were slaughtered at the ADS at WNC Gap.

West Infantry Brigade HQ

The Brigade HQ shelters were located on the hillside of Mount Nicholson overlooking Blue Pool Valley and facing the western slopes of Jardine's Lookout. WNC Gap Road was immediately in front of the Brigade HQ, and across the road there was a cluster of shelters on the hillside between WNC Gap Road and Blue Pool Road which were occupied by 'D' Coy, WG, commanded by Captain Alan Bowman.

During the morning of 19 December, West Brigade HQ found itself in the front line with the Japanese able to fire directly into the shelters from the other side of the valley. It was difficult to get away as the road in front was covered by Japanese machine guns. Japanese troops around the ADS were only 200 metres away. 'A' Coy, 2/RS, was ordered to relieve the besieged HQ but they had been unable to fight their way up Blue Pool Road and WNC Gap Road. They incurred heavy casualties and only a few, all wounded, managed to reach Lawson's bunker. Maltby received a telephone call from Lawson at around 1000 hours on Friday 19 December, at which time Lawson said that he was going to try and fight his way out. After ordering the destruction of the telephone exchange, he left the shelters with a small group of brigade staff, but they were hit by machine gun fire in front of the shelters. Lawson was shot in the thigh, the bullet fracturing his femur, and he bled to death from his wound. Captain Uriah Laite, padre of the Winnipeg Grenadiers, found Lawson's body after the garrison at 'D' Coy shelters had surrendered on 22 December. He was allowed to take Lawson's identification bracelet, which he kept throughout internment, and after the war he returned it to Augusta, Lawson's widow.

S/Sgt Thomas Barton, Corps of Military Staff Clerks, was in charge of a team of clerks and orderlies at Brigade HQ. He wrote an unpublished report, dated 3 December 1945, describing the situation at both Brigade HQ and 'D' Coy shelters during the battle. The personnel at Brigade HQ had been on continual stand-to from the time that reports came in of the Japanese landings on Thursday night to the following day when Japanese troops were seen on Sir Cecil's Ride opposite Brigade HQ. Barton described how they were pinned down by enemy fire.

> Just after dawn on the morning of 19 December a large body of Japanese was engaged coming along Sir Cecil's Ride. …We were given

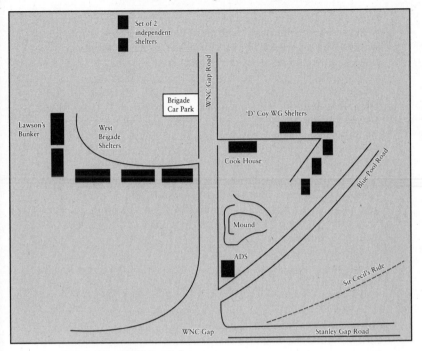

West Brigade HQ and 'D' Coy shelters.

artillery support that morning by the Hong Kong Singapore Royal Artillery. With this support and the fire from our Bren guns and rifles, many casualties were inflicted upon the enemy. By about ten o'clock Major Lyndon and a Captain in the Royal Artillery decided to see if they could find a way that was not covered by the Japanese so that the HQ could get out. Previous to this Captain Bush had gone across the road to where the remnants of 'D' Coy were. … Soon after Major Lyndon and Captain Fox made their way up the hill above the Brigade HQ, a volley of fire was heard and the only indication they got it was the squealing of Captain Fox's springer spaniel that accompanied them. It was about this time when we were completely cut off from all avenues of retreat, and the situation was hopeless that Brigadier Lawson gave orders for us to try and make a break for it and told us we could choose whatever way we liked as all were under fire from the Japanese.[19]

On the hillside above the shelters, Captain Fox, RA, had been killed, but Major Lyndon had escaped injury. He lay still because any movement brought down Japanese fire. He remained there all of

Friday and Saturday until nightfall on Sunday 21 December when he came down from the hillside and joined the troops still holding out at 'D' Coy shelters. On being advised by the brigadier to make a break for it, a number of the brigade staff including S/Sgt Barton and Captain Billings, Brigade Signals Officer, decided to go up the hill behind the shelters but this time taking a more northerly direction. They were fired on, resulting in one of their party being killed and several being wounded. The survivors remained where they were on the hillside until nightfall when, under cover of darkness, they made their way back to Brigade HQ. By then, the shelters were occupied only by the dead and the wounded. Barton helped make the wounded as comfortable as possible and dressed their wounds. In his report, he recalled that there were two Royal Scots each with an arm almost severed, and one member of the RAF with shrapnel injuries to his back. After doing what they could for the wounded, the survivors from the hillside sprinted across the road to 'D' Coy shelters, some being shot as they crossed.

Later in the siege, Japanese troops were on the hillside above Brigade HQ, but they made no attempt to come down and occupy the HQ bunkers while the troops at 'D' Coy shelters were still holding out. The HQ bunkers had little food, and no water supply, but the splinter-proof shelters were solidly built military structures, protected by a semi-circular blast wall, and the wounded that remained at Brigade HQ survived. If Lawson had remained in his HQ, he most probably would have survived, and it would have given him the opportunity to try and melt away after dark rather than trying to escape in broad daylight. Lawson was the most senior officer to be killed in the Battle for Hong Kong. On Monday 22 December, after the Japanese captured the position, they gave Lawson a respectful burial in admiration of such a senior officer being killed in action.

'D' Coy Winnipeg Grenadiers Shelters

When 'D' Coy shelters came under attack on 19 December, two of their three platoons had been deployed. One platoon had been assigned to 'A' Coy and had been ordered up to Jardine's Lookout, while another platoon, under Lt Mitchell, had been deployed to defend Stanley Gap. The personnel left at 'D' Coy shelters included the company commander, Captain Bowman, his HQ personnel, and the bulk of Lt McCarthy's platoon which had just returned to the company shelters from their night position on Sir Cecil's Ride. During the siege of 'D' Coy's position they were joined by additional personnel from Brigade HQ, 'HQ' Coy, and by members of other units who had been cut off, or wounded, during the various counterattacks that were made to recapture the gap. These included men from a variety of different units including the Royal Engineers, the Royal Artillery and the Royal Scots. There were between forty and fifty personnel occupying the shelters, many of whom were wounded and incapacitated by the time they were forced to surrender on Monday 22 December.

On Friday morning, Lt Thomas Blackwood, 'HQ' Coy, WG, was ordered with some twenty ORs to man a pillbox at WNC Gap. This must have been PB 3, which still survives today on the hillside above Black's Link. The twenty men referred to in this context presumably included two sections of ten men to provide an alternating shift of ten men to man the PB. Blackwood's party came under fire as they neared the gap. Japanese troops had by then occupied the head of the valley, the area around the ADS, the mound north of the ADS, and the police station knoll. Lt Blackwood withdrew his men down the road and joined Captain Bowman at 'D' Coy shelters. This explains why PB 3 did not open fire – it was unoccupied at the time. Later that morning, Lt Blackwood and Pte Morris, 'D' Coy, showed great courage by volunteering to bring in Lt-Col Walker, HKVDC, who had been wounded earlier that morning while leading a counterattack on the gap. He was lying on the road near Brigade HQ and within range of Japanese machine guns and grenades. Walker, although badly wounded in the legs and unable to walk, became the most senior officer at 'D' Coy shelters.

Bowman was killed on Friday while single-handedly going out, armed with a Tommy gun, to dislodge a Japanese sniper who was firing very effectively on 'D' Coy shelters from a location close to their position. Lt Philip assumed command of the company but was injured later that day by a grenade blast, resulting in his being blinded in one eye and sustaining shrapnel injuries to his legs and chest. Lt Blackwood then assumed day-to-day command. Captain Bush, staff captain, and Captain Billings, brigade signals officer, had both managed to get across the road from Brigade HQ earlier on Friday morning. Bush was slightly injured by the same grenade blast that had wounded Lt Philip. The fact that grenades could be lobbed at their positions demonstrates how close the Japanese were to 'D' Coy shelters.

The wounded men at 'D' Coy shelters were placed in the cookhouse shelter, which was the shelter closest to Brigade HQ. Padre Laite did his best to apply dressings and to make the wounded comfortable in the absence of any medics. The occupants were initially able to maintain telephone contact with Lt-Col Sutcliffe at Wan Chai Gap, but on Saturday 20 December the telephone line was cut, and there was no further external communication. On Saturday, a Royal Artillery officer had managed to drive up WNC Gap Road to ascertain the situation and see what artillery support could be provided. He stopped his car quite close to 'D' Coy shelters and on stepping out of his vehicle was promptly shot in the shoulder. Despite his wound, he was able to escape through the undergrowth in the valley below the road and made his back towards Tai Hang Road. Later, and presumably following his report, an artillery barrage was laid down in the vicinity of WNC Gap. After nightfall, the two staff officers Bush and Billings, with Cpl McArthur acting as a driver, used the Royal Artillery officer's abandoned vehicle to escape from the shelters. They had mentioned their intention to escape to Padre Laite and invited him to join them. Padre Laite declined because he felt that it was his duty to stay with the wounded. Barton was critical of these two staff officers for escaping a position which was still in action and still holding out.

Major Lyndon made his way down from the hillside above West Brigade to 'D' Coy shelters on Saturday night. As senior officer after the wounded Lt-Col Walker, he assumed command from Lt Tamworth, HKVDC, who had taken command from Lt Blackwood who had been injured that evening. Lyndon, Tamworth and Barton went back to Brigade HQ late on Saturday night to try and fix the telephone which had been put out of action when Lawson left the position. They were unable to repair the telephone exchange, and the position remained out of communication. At that time, there were still a dozen wounded lying in the Brigade HQ shelters.

The Japanese were sniping from the roof of the ADS shelters, from the nearby mound, and from the hillside above Brigade HQ. Cpl Meirion Price and Pte Gordon Williamson, both from 'D' Coy, were involved in several raids against Japanese snipers, machine gun positions and grenade throwers. They were both awarded the Military Medal for their gallant actions during the siege. By Sunday 21 December, the garrison at 'D' Coy shelters was running short of food, water and ammunition, and casualties were still mounting. During the early hours on Monday 22 December, the Japanese launched a more determined attack starting with a barrage of grenades. It was during this attack that Major Lyndon, who had left the position to carry out a recce, was killed by friendly fire while returning through the undergrowth. Tamworth recalled that just before dawn he heard soldiers in the medical shelter shouting out to the Japanese that they were willing to surrender. Barton's report corroborates this.

Someone near the Cook House shouted: 'Japanese we surrender'. ... We shouted back for him to keep quiet, and that we would fight on. ... He stated that Colonel Walker had ordered it. That was different.[20]

A white flag was shown, and the firing died down as the Japanese realised that the garrison was attempting to surrender. After the decision to surrender had been communicated to the remaining effectives, they were told that anybody who wished to escape could do so before the Japanese arrived. Several men decided to try and get away in two groups. One group, which included S/Sgt Barton, went down WNC Gap Road, and the other group went down the valley. Both groups were able to get back to British lines. Tamworth described the subsequent surrender of the position.

> At about 0900 hours I saw a captured Indian soldier with his hands tied behind his back, and at the end of a long rope tied to his waist, standing on the rising ground to our front. He made me understand we were to follow him out; he was then pulled back to Blue Pool Road. I followed him calling on our remaining effectives to come with me. As I reached Blue Pool Road, I was seized by two Japanese soldiers, and my hands were tied behind my back. The Japanese officer standing by came forward and struck me in the face and motioned me to walk up Blue Pool Road. I was joined by other men from the shelters; we were tied together and told to sit down on the side of the road facing Blue Pool Valley where we remained until 1700 hours.[21]

Padre Laite does not mention Tamworth in his diary, and nor does Tamworth mention Laite. Laite was in the medical shelter, which was furthest from the Japanese. Laite recalled the decision to surrender and stated that Lt Philip, although wounded, went out from the medical shelter to surrender the position.

> Altogether, including three British soldiers and four Chinese, we had thirty wounded men in that shelter. Shortly after dawn, we were told that our ammunition was exhausted. Lt Philip consulted Lt-Col Walker, who gave us no hope of being allowed to live even though we surrendered, but it was the only thing left for us to do. Lt Philip, wounded, bandaged, and weak though he was, stepped out of the shelter to surrender.[22]

The Japanese gave Laite water for the wounded, and they were surprised to see that he gave the water to the wounded first and drank last himself. Laite tried to persuade anybody that could possibly walk to do so, realising that those who could not walk would be killed. Three Canadian soldiers and two British soldiers who were unable to walk were killed at 'D' Coy shelters, as were the non-walking wounded at Brigade HQ. Only Lt-Col Walker, due to his rank, was provided with a stretcher and carried out. The surrender seems to have been more piecemeal than described by Tamworth, as Laite was taken by the Japanese along the trenches, and at each shelter he was told to call the men out with their hands above their heads. Perhaps because of Laite's help during the surrender, and because he was a padre, the Japanese released him. He was escorted down the road and pointed in the direction of Happy Valley, from where he was able to get back to British positions. The rest of the prisoners were marched in two groups, one moving fast and the other, with the more seriously wounded, moving slowly. They were taken up Stanley Gap Road, up Mount Parker Road and down to North Point.

The mixed group of Winnipeg Grenadiers and other troops at 'D' Coy shelters were the last to surrender at WNC Gap. They held out against a much larger force from Friday 19 December until Monday 22 December. By the time they surrendered they had run out of food, water and ammunition and three-quarters of the garrison were wounded. They had taken a heavy toll on the Japanese, and they had so far prevented Colonel Shoji's 230th Regiment from advancing towards Happy Valley and Wan Chai. Throughout this period, British, Indian and Canadian troops had made a series of counterattacks, and despite great gallantry in the prosecution of these counterattacks, all attempts to dislodge the Japanese from their positions at WNC Gap were unsuccessful. With the loss of WNC Gap, the Battle for Hong Kong was over. The Hong Kong garrison surrendered three days later.

Above: 6. Captured British armoured cars at WNC Gap.

Right: 7. British prisoners from the Shing Mun Redoubt led by Captain Cyril Jones.

Below right: 8. One of three 9.2-inch guns at Fort Davis.

9. Military HQ, known as China Command. (Courtesy of the Imperial War Museum)

10. Brigadier Cedric Wallis.

1. Japanese troops landing on North Shore of Hong Kong Island. (Courtesy of the Imperial War Museum).

2. Japanese troops fighting in King's Road, North Point.

Above: 3. Salesian
Mission Building.

Left: 4. Japanese artillery
firing at North Point
Power Station.

Below left: 5. HMS
Tamar alongside the west
wall in RN Dockyard.

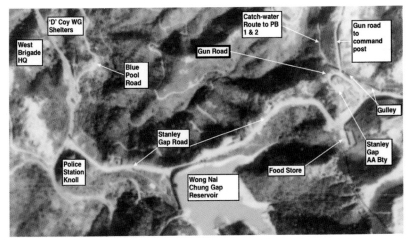

11. Aerial photograph of WNC Gap and Stanley Gap. (Author's collection)

12. Southside of Hong Kong Island. (Author's collection)

Above: 13. Surrender formality at the Peninsula Hotel. Sir Mark Young out of view to left. Lt-Col Stewart, Major-General Maltby, and Wing Commander Alf Bennett sitting at the back.

Left: 14. Lt Douglas Baird, Royal Scots. (Courtesy Catherine Baird Williams)

15. The gunboat HMS *Cicala*.

16. Grenade-damaged interior of PB 1. (Author's collection)

17. PB 2 at Jardine's Lookout. (Author's collection)

18. Bungalow 'C', St Stephen's College, Stanley. (Author's collection)

Right: 19. Wartime map and war relics found on the hills. (Author's collection)

Below: 20. West Brigade HQ shelters. (Author's collection)

Above left: 21. The AOP at Shing Mun Redoubt. (Author's collection)

Left: 22. Tunnel entrance at Shing Mun Redoubt. (Author's collection)

Below: 23. The stores shelter at Stanley Gap. (Author's collection)

24. The arrival of Canadian reinforcements in November 1941. (Courtesy of the Imperial War Museum)

25. 3.7-inch AA gun. (Courtesy of the Imperial War Museum)

Above: 26. Motor Torpedo Boats. (Courtesy of the Imperial War Museum)

Below: 27. Victoria, Hong Kong, before the war. (Courtesy of the Imperial War Museum)

28. Canadian troops training on Hong Kong Island. (Courtesy of the Imperial War Museum)

29. Major-General Maltby (with Japanese sword) after liberation, 1945. (Courtesy of the Imperial War Museum)

30. The Maryknoll Mission House, Stanley.

31. The observation tower at PB 1, Jardine's Lookout. (Author's collection)

Above: 32. Wartime sailor's identity bracelet found in the hills on Hong Kong Island. (Courtesy of Dave Willott)

Right: 33. AB Jack Siddans. (Courtesy of Arthur Faux)

Below: 34. Military structures at Stanley Gap (1947).

Command Post

AA Gun position

Gun Road

Battery Accommodation

Magazine

Mess hut floor

Stores shelter

Above left: 35. Pre-war photo showing Postbridge (centre) and Holmesdale (left) at WNC Gap. (Courtesy of Tony Banham)

Above right: 36. Captain Kenneth Allanson, RA. (Courtesy of Christopher Allanson)

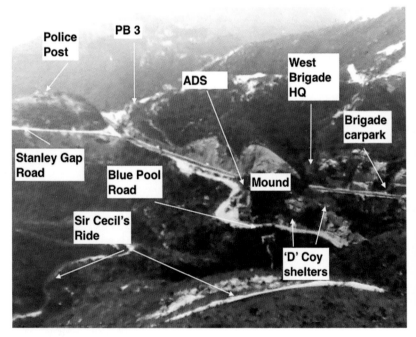

37. WNC Gap.

9

The Navy Counterattacks
19 December

In the early hours of Friday 19 December, Commander Richard Vernall, commanding officer of the HKRNVR, received an urgent telephone call from Captain Leveson Campbell, the Extended Defence Officer (XDO), based at the Battle Box. Campbell informed him that the Japanese had made a landing on the Island. Later that morning, at approximately 0430 hours, Vernall took a call from Major Henry Marsh, Commanding Officer, 'C' Coy, 1/Mx, based at nearby Shouson Hill, asking whether Vernall could send a naval patrol to investigate reports of suspected signalling by fifth columnists from a house at the top of Repulse Bay Road. The house in question was a large white villa known as Postbridge. It was the home of fifty-five-year-old George Tinson and his wife Eileen. George Tinson was a partner in the law firm Johnson, Stokes & Master. He was a veteran of the First World War and had seen action at Gallipoli, where he had been awarded the Military Cross.

At approximately 0500 hours, the HKRNVR party set off in a truck from their shore base, a large house in Deep Water Bay overlooking Middle Island. There had been no shortage of volunteers as they all wanted to be doing something useful. The party was made up of eleven out of the thirteen HKRNVR officers at the shore base and included one of the three senior ratings. The naval party was led by Lt-Cdr Dulley. They took two Bren guns with one magazine for each gun, one Lee–Enfield rifle with fifty rounds, one revolver with six rounds in the chamber and two hand grenades. They expected to be back in time for breakfast. The truck, driven by Paymaster Lt Sommerfelt, drove past the golf course at Deep Water Bay and then through the roadblock at the junction of Island Road and Repulse Bay Road. They drove up Repulse Bay Road to WNC Gap with lights extinguished in the early-morning darkness. At 0520 hours, they pulled up by the entrance of

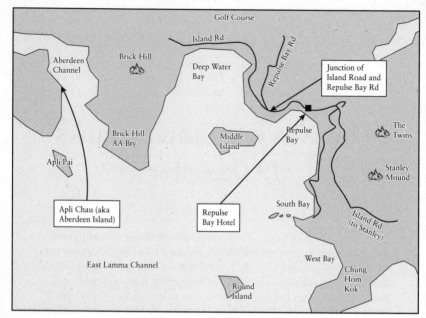

Deep Water Bay and Repulse Bay.

the narrow driveway leading to Postbridge. They debussed and made their way on foot along the drive. As they approached the house, they were stopped and challenged by an Indian sentry. There was a shouted exchange in which the naval party tried to explain who they were and why they were there. During this commotion, Captain Avery, HKSRA, came out from the house and explained that the house was being used as an Administrative HQ for West Group, Royal Artillery. He told them that they had been based at the villa for several days and that they had not observed any suspicious lights or signalling in the vicinity.

Dulley, assuming that they had come to the wrong house, decided to check the house immediately across the road called Holmesdale. This house still remains today, although now simply known as No. 4 Repulse Bay Road. The site once occupied by Postbridge is now a high-rise apartment block known as Celestial Gardens. As they went back down the driveway, to where their truck was parked, they noticed figures and heard voices on the hillside around the small police station on the knoll in the middle of WNC Gap. A hand grenade was thrown towards their party, exploding too far away to cause any casualties. At first, Dulley thought that it might have come from the Indian police on the knoll, or

Canadian troops who were in the vicinity. He shouted out who they were, but this resulted in a burst of machine gun fire being directed at them.

The naval party scattered, with most of them taking cover in a rocky gulley close to the driveway. On hearing the machine gun fire, Captain Avery came out and conducted the patrol back to the house. Dulley and Avery carried out a reconnaissance and established that Japanese troops were in possession of the hillside around the police station. These were part of the lead troops from Colonel Shoji's 3rd Battalion who had just rushed the gap. By 0630 hours, with the visibility improving, the garrison at Postbridge could see Japanese troops digging in on slopes of the knoll. They could see more Japanese troops coming down Stanley Gap Road towards the knoll. The senior Army officer at Postbridge was Major Crowe, HKSRA. His staff included Captain Avery, Captain Atkinson and two subalterns. There were twenty-five IORs, of whom twenty were relatively new and untrained recruits. The HKRNVR group consisted of eleven officers and one Seaman Gunner.

Lt-Cdr Grenham tried using the house telephone to report to Commander Vernall at Deep Water Bay, Lt-Cdr Chattock at XDO office, and Commander Montague at AIS. He was unable to get through to any of them, but earlier he did manage to get through to the Central Exchange, who put him through to No. 2 police station, which connected him to WNC Gap Police Station. They heard the bell ring, but perhaps predictably it was not answered. The Japanese had already taken the station. The Indian police constable from the small police post was at the ADS overnight after being treated for injuries incurred during shelling the previous day. Postbridge remained out of communication throughout the siege.

The garrison at Postbridge exchanged fire throughout the day with Japanese troops on and around the knoll. Some of the defenders took up positions beside a low wall surrounding the front of the property. The wall was some 20 metres in front of the main door, and from the wall they could fire at the Japanese on the knoll only 300 metres away. The Japanese replied with machine gun fire and mortar fire. The Indian recruits and those members of the garrison not at a firing position, either on the wall or at the windows, helped by filling sandbags and fortifying the house. Dulley, Grenham and Morahan from the naval party were at sniping positions at the windows on the upper floor with Crowe and Atkinson acting as spotters. Ammunition was limited as neither group had expected to end up in a full-scale battle, but Postbridge was now on the front line. During the morning, Captain Avery, who had been shooting from the front wall, was shot in the head. Grenham dragged him from the wall back into the house while still under fire. Avery never recovered and died from his wounds later that morning.

While fighting raged at Postbridge, the senior naval officer (SNO) at the Aberdeen Industrial School (AIS) naval base was ordered at 0700 hours to arrange a naval contingent to take over the positions vacated by 'A' Coy, Winnipeg Grenadiers at Shouson Hill. An hour later that order was cancelled, and instead they were ordered to proceed with utmost dispatch to WNC Gap with all available naval personnel to reinforce West Brigade HQ. The RN party had not been fully briefed. They were not made aware of the Japanese presence at WNC Gap, nor had they been notified of British or Canadian positions in the area, for example the presence of a naval party at Postbridge. Commander Montague, the SNO at Aberdeen, had asked for the naval contingent to be met by guides from West Brigade who would be able to conduct them to their deployment positions.

The RN contingent left the naval base at AIS in four trucks containing some sixty-five officers and men. The majority of the contingent was made up from the ship's company of the destroyer HMS *Thracian*, which had been damaged beyond repair and beached at Round Island. The contingent also included a number of men from HMS *Tamar*, the former base ship, which had been scuttled during the first week of the war. The RN contingent was under the command of Lt Dines, RNR, formerly First Lieutenant of HMS *Thracian*. The naval party must have looked conspicuous in their blue uniforms with webbing, rifles and steel helmets. The lorries departed from Aberdeen at 0815 hours. They drove eastwards along Island Road, passing the HKRNVR base at Deep Water Bay, before turning left on Repulse Bay Road. WNC Gap had been in Japanese hands since before dawn, and it would have been impossible for guides from West Brigade HQ to get from their position, which was already coming under fire, and to pass through the gap from north to south in order to intercept the RN contingent. As a result, the trucks drove right up to the gap, where they were ambushed one after the other.

As the first truck passed Twin Brook, a villa halfway up Repulse Bay Road, they were fired on from the hillside above the road, wounding Lt Merry, HKRNVR, and one naval rating. Merry, who was armed with a shotgun, was lightly wounded in one arm. It was still early in the morning, and the Japanese had only just seized the gap, and they had not ventured further. The Japanese did not reach this locality until much later in the day when the Tanaka *butai* followed the water catchment above Repulse Bay Road to Middle Spur. The shots must have come from either fifth columnists, or more likely, friendly fire from jittery guards at Twin Brook which was being used as a NAAFI store. The trucks carried on up the road and went past the entrance drive to The Ridge, which consisted of a row of five houses built on a spur of Violet Hill above Repulse Bay Road. The houses on The Ridge were being used as a depot for the Royal

Army Ordnance Corps (RAOC). Sentries positioned there waved the RN trucks onward and upwards. The HKRNVR party at Postbridge saw the first truck coming up the road at 0845 hours. At first, they thought the trucks carried reinforcements coming to relieve them at Postbridge, and that they would stop below the house, where they would be out of range of the Japanese machine guns. To their astonishment, the convoy carried on up the road to the gap. They tried to signal the trucks to stop, realising that they were running straight into a Japanese ambush.

The Japanese withheld their fire. The first truck rounded the last bend, drove past Holmesdale, and got to a point on the road where a bridge crosses a gulley just below the gap and close to the driveway for Postbridge. The truck slowed down, drawing up near an Army lorry parked at the roadside where a soldier was taking cover underneath his vehicle. The soldier shouted out a warning about the proximity of Japanese troops on the hillside. The soldier may have been BQMS Thomson, HKVDC, who later joined the garrison at Postbridge. Lt Dines ordered his men to debus and take cover, but as they did this the Japanese opened fire with machine guns, rifles and hand grenades. In this opening fire, one of the party was killed and seven were wounded, Lt Dines among them. Those who could take cover underneath the truck did so; there was no other cover available on the road. Some of the wounded were unable to move and remained exposed on the back of the open truck.

During a lull in the firing, Lt Dines ordered all those who were not severely wounded, and who were still able to move, to make a dash for the left-hand side of the road where the hillside dropped away steeply towards Deep Water Bay Golf Course. Dines remained with the wounded at the truck, and Lt Merry led some twelve ratings across the road. As they ran for the low stone wall beside the road, the Japanese machine guns opened up on them. They jumped over the wall into the shrub and thick vegetation some ten feet below the road. Merry and one rating were hit as they ran across the road and were left behind. Merry subsequently died from his wounds. Those that had got across the road made their way down the hillside, emerging from the trees and shrubbery at the far end of the golf course. The golf course was being used as a depot for the RASC and Staff Sgt Patrick Sheridan, RASC, recalled the crew of the first truck limping to the clubhouse where they were given first aid. The naval party made their way back to AIS, arriving there at around 1130 hours.

The second truck, under the authority of Tom Quilliam, a commissioned gunner from HMS *Thracian*, was close behind the first truck. As the first truck stopped, they pulled up behind and were fired on at the same time. The crew of the second truck were able to debus with only one casualty. The driver then managed to back the truck down the road, with the crew taking cover as best they could from behind the reversing truck. Quilliam and Petty Officer Cullum went forward to undertake a recce and determine the position and strength of the Japanese at the gap. They were pinned down by enemy fire, and remained by the roadside until nightfall when they withdrew down Repulse Bay Road, and joined the garrison at Repulse Bay Hotel. From his position at the roadside, Quilliam witnessed Petty Officer Ayles, from HMS *Thracian*, making a dash with a party of four sailors at the hillside around the police station. Ayles was armed with a hand grenade and had tried to rush one of the Japanese machine gun positions, but he was killed in the process. Regulating Petty Officer Lilley, who was wounded when the crew of the second truck debussed, took charge after Quilliam and Callum went forward and failed to return. RPO Lilley took the remainder of the party, consisting of twelve ratings, up the rocky gulley that led from the road near Holmesdale towards Postbridge. They joined the garrison at Postbridge at approximately 0915 hours.

The third truck, with Sub-Lt Dobson in charge, had been the first to leave AIS but had broken down on the way. Having effected repairs, they drove up Repulse Bay Road and passed the second truck, which had been reversed down the road. Dobson's vehicle then came under fire this time from both the knoll and from the area to the west of the gap near Black's Link. Several of the crew were injured and were left on the truck, but Dobson and ten ratings were able to get off the vehicle and took cover under the hillside below Postbridge. They later made their way up the gulley and established contact with the garrison in Postbridge who advised them to remain where they were until nightfall. Dobson and his party reached Postbridge at approximately 1915 hours. The fourth truck, with Sub-Lt Kempton in charge, arrived some thirty minutes after the first truck and pulled up a little further down Repulse Bay Road, but it was still close enough to the gap to be within the range of the Japanese machine guns positioned around the entrance to Black's Link. They were fired on, with a number of ratings killed and wounded. Kempton, who was sitting beside the driver, was killed instantly by machine gun fire. Those who escaped injury and most of the walking wounded from the fourth truck took cover in Holmesdale.

The wounded in the back of the first truck were told to lie still so that the Japanese would assume they were dead. However, at around noon, movement by one or more of the injured was observed by the Japanese who fired into the back of the truck causing further injuries. The wounded remained where they were until dark when at approximately 2000 hours, they started to make their way slowly down Repulse Bay Road to a point where they met with Surgeon-Lt Whitfield and an ambulance party from AIS at about 2230 hours. The crew from the second truck had made their way to Postbridge. The third truck still had wounded in the back, and those who had managed to get off the truck had reached Postbridge after dark. The crew from the fourth truck had taken refuge in Holmesdale but also had wounded lying in the back of their truck.

A fifth and sixth truck carrying some eighty ORs from the Dockyard Defence Corp (DDC), under the command of Major Campbell and Captain Rossini, had been sent from AIS. This party left Aberdeen after the RN contingent. Lt-Cdr Pears, the commanding officer of HMS *Thracian*, had set off by car ahead of the DDC party. On discovering that the RN trucks had been ambushed he halted the DDC lorries and instructed them to proceed to the RASC Depot at Deep Water Bay and to remain there as a reserve pending further orders. The DDC contingent returned to AIS later that morning after the RASC Depot was evacuated.

At Postbridge the defenders were running short of ammunition. At 1045 hours, Captain Atkinson ran a field telephone line from Postbridge to the RAOC Depot at The Ridge. The line ran down the steep slope at the back of the house to Repulse Bay Road, and then down the road for some 500 metres to The Ridge. At The Ridge, he reported on the situation at Postbridge and asked the senior ordnance officers to provide machine guns and ammunition to be dispatched to Postbridge as quickly as possible. During the afternoon two Bren guns and three Lewis guns arrived from The Ridge, and 15,000 rounds of .303 ammunition were sent up from the Little Hong Kong Magazine. The machine guns came still packed in heavy-duty grease, but BQMS Thomson, who had arrived at Postbridge at noon, and two of the military personnel were able to free them from the protective grease, clean them up, and get them into workable condition. Major Crowe called for artillery fire to be brought down on the police station knoll. A barrage of 6-inch and 4.5-inch howitzer shells were laid down but landed north and northeast of the knoll. Accurate fire was difficult because of the proximity of the surrounding hills.

The defenders at the wall were ordered to return to the house because Japanese troops had started to work their way along the water catchment, on the hillside above the house, which allowed them to outflank the wall party. During the afternoon George Tinson, the homeowner, was shot and fatally wounded. During the evening, a small group of Japanese troops infiltrated down from the water catchment to the house. Two members of the garrison who had gone out to repair the field telephone line to The Ridge reported that they had seen Japanese troops in the undergrowth near the house. A Japanese soldier was shot dead by Lt McDouall, HKRNVR, while passing one of the ground-floor windows. He had probably been part of the small group that had infiltrated up to the house and planted explosives on the north-east side of the villa.

There was a tremendous explosion which blew out all the windows frames, demolished the staircase and started fires. Three of the defenders were blown over the sandbag parapet on the veranda at the back of the house. After the explosion, the Japanese opened fire with machine guns and grenades. The house was partly on fire, and the flames were illuminating the defenders. Lt-Cdr Dulley was killed, and Captain Atkinson was seriously injured. The position was no longer tenable, and Major Crowe gave the order to evacuate. The wounded were helped down the slope at the back of the house. They were followed by the IORs with the naval group taking up the rear.

During the day, the wounded naval personnel at the first truck could hear Japanese voices on the hillside around the police station, but the Japanese had not yet come down to the road. This allowed those who could walk to get away once night fell. The walking wounded started to hobble back down Repulse Bay Road, led by Sub-Lt Owen. Owen was a member of the HKRNVR but had been assigned to HMS *Thracian*. His fifty-three-year-old widowed mother Phyllis Owen was living in Hong Kong and was later incarcerated at Stanley Camp. Owen survived his wounds and was subsequently imprisoned at Sham Shui Po Camp. He was a Japanese speaker and acted as an interpreter in the POW camps. In the evening two ambulances sent from AIS cautiously made their way up Repulse Bay Road. As they got closer to WNC Gap, Surgeon-Lt Whitfield and Surgeon-Lt Dawson-Grove got out and proceeded up the road on foot with the ambulances following slowly behind them, not knowing whether the Japanese were around the next corner.

Staff Sergeant Sheridan together with other members of the RASC and men from a variety of other units had been formed into a composite company and placed under the command of Lt-Col Frederick, RASC. They had initially been ordered to form a line on Bennet's Hill to defend Aberdeen. Then, in the evening, they had been ordered to counterattack WNC Gap. They were taken by truck up Repulse Bay Road. The trucks halted some 500 metres from The Ridge, and the troops were ordered to proceed quietly on foot to The Ridge and to be alert for any Japanese patrols. As Sheridan's group reached the driveway leading up to The Ridge, a naval officer asked for their help with the wounded further up the road.

> We set off up the road in the company of the naval man. We find the naval men lying in a typhoon nullah by the side of the road, calling for water. We stop and give them some. They are all badly wounded, and we discover they have been there since about 0800 hours and it now 2200 hours. It seems no ambulance could get up this road during

daylight. ... We made them as comfortable as possible and left them a full water bottle. We continued up the road towards the gap and found several lorries. ... Some dead naval men are in the cabs; others lie on the road or in the back of the lorries.[1]

They continued up the road, and out of the darkness a voice challenged them. It turned out to be a Canadian officer armed with a Tommy gun. He had become separated from his men and was trying to get back to his unit. The Canadian officer warned them not to make any noise as the Japanese were dug in above the road. Sheridan then reached Holmesdale, which he referred to as the 'white house'. In his memoir, he relates how they found some fifteen wounded naval personnel in the house. There were also two women, a Chinese woman who had been shot through the chest and a European lady who was dead. The wounded were all in need of urgent medical attention. Two of Sheridan's group went back to The Ridge to see if any transport could be arranged to get the wounded to hospital. Sheridan was waiting outside the house when the Canadian officer came back and asked for their help with a wounded sailor lying in the middle of the road. Sheridan crawled up the road as quietly as possible to retrieve the wounded sailor and brought him back to Holmesdale.

Although I was carrying a Lee–Enfield .303 rifle and about 300 rounds of ammunition slung in bandolier fashion, I thought it best to get down and crawl towards the wounded man. It was about 50 yards, and I found he had a smashed hip and was unable to move. He had been in the first lorry. He had been lying there all day and had feigned death when he heard the Japs talking during the day.[2]

After bringing the wounded sailor to Holmesdale, Sheridan and his group then returned towards The Ridge to re-join their unit.

We set off down the road, and meet an armoured vehicle trying to manoeuvre between the [lorries] ... accompanied by a British officer and some Indian troops all in their bare feet. They are about to stage a raid on the Japanese positions near Wong Nai Chung Gap. Further on we meet a naval surgeon and two RN ambulances. He enquires how far to the white house and how many wounded. We give him all the information and ask if he requires any help. He said he had sufficient in each ambulance and continued up the road. We also find he had attended all the wounded men on the roadside near the entrance to The Ridge and would pick them up on the way back.[3]

The vehicles which Sheridan referred to were two HKVDC armoured cars, and the Indian troops were gunners from HKSRA. This group to their great credit succeeded in retaking the police station, if only temporarily. They incurred a very high casualty rate, and their three British officers were all killed. The armoured cars were put out of action at the gap and later captured by the Japanese.

One of the ambulance men, with HMS *Thracian*'s coxswain, CPO Bill Corpse, carried on up Repulse Bay Road towards Holmesdale to collect the wounded. They soon found that one ambulance was insufficient. The ambulance left for AIS, and CPO Corpse with two RN ratings remained with the wounded at Holmesdale to await the return of the ambulance. However, before the ambulance returned, Japanese troops, perhaps hearing the wounded or seeing their movement at Holmesdale, came down the road, entered the property and killed everyone inside. Two men were said to have survived their injuries and managed to escape. I have not seen a deposition or any other report on what occurred at Holmesdale, nor have I found any information as to the identity of the two women. The 1941 jurors list has a listing for Frank Groves, general manager of American Express, with an address of Homesdale, Repulse Bay, missing the 'l', perhaps in error. Frank Groves appears to have left Hong Kong before the outbreak of war. The list of civilian internees at Stanley Camp shows a Norwegian national, John Stenersen, who was manager of American Express. He had a pre-war address of No. 4 Bungalow, Repulse Bay. The property is known today as No. 4 Repulse Bay Road. It was perhaps owned or leased by American Express to accommodate their general managers. John Stenersen and his wife Edna both survived the battle and subsequent incarceration at Stanley Camp. The identity of the two women and the identity of the two survivors of the killing at Holmesdale remains a mystery, at least for the time being. The attempt by the Royal Navy to reinforce West Brigade HQ had been disastrous. The RN incurred a 50 per cent casualty rate as a result of the operations at and around WNC Gap.

A Royal Navy ID Bracelet Found in the Hills near WNC Gap

In January 2015, local history enthusiast Dave Willott was using a metal detector to look for war relics in a gulley just off Stanley Gap Road and close to the luxury housing development known as Parkview. The gulley had several dugouts and trenches on either side. It was situated close to where a roadblock may have operated on Stanley Gap Road, and the gulley may have been used as a section position, providing cover for the unit manning the roadblock. The site is close to the current road barrier at the entrance to the Tai Tam Country Park. It was probably a British or Canadian position that was subsequently used by the Japanese.

Dave found some interesting items including shoulder flashes, buttons, webbing buckles, spent ammunition and even what was left of a military boot. Shotgun cartridges were also found, which at first I thought must be post-war until I read that some of the RN personnel like Lt Merry and Sub-Lt Owen were armed with shotguns. However, the most exciting find was an ID bracelet belonging to a British naval rating. It bore the name J. Siddans followed by the initials Q. O. and then his naval service number, and the abbreviation 'C of E' denoting his religion. A quick check showed that John ('Jack') Siddans was listed as an able seaman serving with HMS *Tamar*. The initials Q. O. indicated that he was qualified in ordnance, suggesting that Jack Siddans was in the gunnery branch of the Royal Navy. After conducting some research, we were able to establish that Siddans came from Alderley Edge in Cheshire. A story was published in the local newspaper, following which Arthur Faux, a member of Siddans's family, contacted me. Arthur filled in some of the gaps in my knowledge and kindly sent me photographs of Siddans in his naval uniform.

Finding an ID bracelet or disc would normally indicate that the owner had died. However, Siddans survived the fighting and his initial incarceration at Sham Shui Po Camp. In September 1942, he was detailed to be transported to Japan with other POWs to work as slave labourers at docks, mines and factories. They boarded the *Lisbon Maru*, an armed Japanese freighter. In early October, the freighter was sunk by an American submarine. The submarine commander had no way of knowing that the vessel was carrying some 1,800 British prisoners of war. Siddans survived the sinking, and the initial machine-gunning of survivors in the water, and was eventually picked up by a Japanese escort vessel. Military historian Tony Banham was able to confirm from naval records that Siddans died off Shanghai. The POWs who were picked up by the Japanese escort vessels were kept on the open deck and given no blankets, and little food or water. Those who died from exposure were thrown over the side. This was the likely fate of Siddans. He left a wife, Florence, in England who remarried some years after the war. There were no children.

How did Jack Siddans's ID bracelet end up in that spot, in a gulley, on a hillside, situated in the middle of Hong Kong Island? I believe that Siddans was part of the RN contingent that was sent up to WNC Gap to reinforce West Brigade HQ. Naval records and war diaries show the names of some but not all of the RN contingent. The contingent consisted of some sixty to seventy men. Most of the personnel were made up from the crew of HMS *Thracian*, which had been beached two days earlier, as they were available for operations ashore. The naval documents show that some personnel from HMS *Tamar* also took part. When the war began, Jack Siddans was a forty-one-year-old three-badge able seaman serving on HMS *Tamar*. During the first week of the war, the *Tamar* personnel were moved to the China Fleet Club and later to AIS in Aberdeen. Siddans was an older, more experienced sailor serving with the gunnery branch, all of which would have made him a suitable candidate for inclusion in the naval force sent to WNC Gap.

If these assumptions are correct, he must have been captured and possibly wounded around WNC Gap and then held at the mess hut on Stanley Gap Road before being marched to North Point on Saturday 20 December. There may have been a roadblock near the gulley, and the prisoners may have been searched by Japanese troops at the roadblock. Anything of value that had not been taken already would have been kept by the Japanese soldiers manning the roadblock. Other items like buttons, insignia and shoulder flashes may have been ripped off their uniforms and thrown to one side, and I think this may have included Jack Siddans's ID bracelet. It lay there undisturbed from 20 December 1941 until January 2015 when it was unearthed, and the story unfolded.

The Motor Torpedo Boats

At about the same time that the RN contingent was sent up to reinforce the Army at WNC Gap, the MTB flotilla was ordered to attack Japanese landing craft and other vessels that were ferrying men and equipment across the harbour in broad daylight. The MTBs were ordered to secure alongside HMS *Robin*, at Aberdeen, to take on ammunition in preparation for the attack. The attack was to be made in pairs. The first MTBs to be sent into the harbour were MTB 07, commanded by Lt Ashby, and MTB 09, commanded by Lt Kennedy. These two boats had been off duty the previous night, and their crews were well rested. Their orders were to enter the harbour, and to shoot at anything in sight until all their ammunition was expended.

At 0845 hours, the two MTBs headed through the western entrance to Victoria Harbour at a speed of 30 knots. MTB 07 led the way with MTB 09 one or two cables astern. They raced past the anti-boat boom, and as they neared the RN Dockyard they were strafed by Japanese aircraft, the bullets spitting up the water around the boats. They kept close to the Hong Kong side of the harbour, but as they reached North Point they were fired on by Japanese troops already on the Island. Since they were being fired at from both sides of the harbour, they moved into midstream. By this time, they had sighted the landing craft, and other vessels, transporting Japanese troops and equipment across the harbour. Many of the Japanese landing craft were towing other vessels, with one powered craft towing two or more boats. Ashby, in MTB 07, signalled to 09 to attack independently. He throttled up to the top speed of 37 knots and swung into the attack.

> I opened fire on the landing craft with all five Lewis guns at a range of one hundred yards with excellent effect and passed down the leading string at about a distance of five yards firing continuously. I dropped two depth charges, which failed to explode due to insufficient depth of water. However, this made no difference as the landing craft capsized in my wash and there appeared to be no survivors. I now came under machine gun fire from both shores and from wrecks in the harbour, howitzer and light artillery fire from both shores, and machine gun and cannon fire from aircraft.[4]

The boat had been peppered by bullets and shell fragments, but the worst damage occurred when a Japanese cannon shell exploded in the engine compartment, putting the starboard engine out of action and wounding the leading stoker, Reginald Barker. He later died from his wounds. The boat's speed was reduced to 22 knots, but Ashby continued the attack.

> I turned and attacked a second bunch of landing craft with machine gun fire at point-blank range. ... all remaining landing craft turned back and beat a hasty retreat to Kowloon. Another cannon shell now put my port engine out of action, and my Telegraphist was killed by machine gun fire. My speed was reduced to 12 knots, and I was making water in the engine room, so I had no alternative but to extricate. I headed for the Naval Yard under intense machine gun and howitzer fire and attacks by three aircraft.[5]

MTB 09 followed 07 into the attack with all her Lewis guns blazing and her first lieutenant, Sub-Lt Brewer, firing a Bren gun from the conning tower. Lt Kennedy described the attack by 09.

> After shooting up a group of three landing craft, two of this group had capsized, but the motor craft was still under way heading back towards the shelter of the many junks and boats which had been collected in Kowloon Bay. Speed was reduced, and the motor craft was put out of action by Lewis guns. ... I carried on further up the bay to within two cables of the junks moored there, firing at a single landing craft and a sampan making back for shelter. The course was then altered to starboard towards Channel Rock and opened fire from close range on two small boats aground on the rocks behind which a few Japanese took cover.[6]

MTB 09, having used up most of her ammunition, and with no further targets, withdrew westwards at full speed. Japanese gunfire from both sides of the harbour followed them until they got close to the RN Dockyard at which point the Japanese guns were no longer able to follow. MTB 09 had sustained multiple hits, but she had been lucky as there were no casualties among her crew. She soon caught up with MTB 07, which was heading slowly out of the harbour on one engine. After passing through Sulphur Channel, her last engine came to a stop, and she was taken in tow by MTB 09.

The next two boats to attack were MTB 11, commanded by Lt Collingwood, and MTB 12, commanded by Lt Colls. They sped past the first two MTBs returning from their mission, but by now the Japanese were on full alert, and heavy fire was directed at the two MTBs as they drove towards Kowloon Bay. The landing craft had all withdrawn after the first attack. There were no obvious targets for them to attack other than the Japanese machine gun posts on semi-sunken ships in the harbour. MTB 11 was hit several times. The coxswain was wounded in the throat, and stoker PO Stonell took over the wheel. MTB 12 received a direct hit to the fuel tank and blew up with only two survivors. Able Seaman Bartlett managed to jump overboard and swam ashore on Hong Kong Island and was later admitted to Queen Mary Hospital. Telegraphist Hunt, although wounded, was able to swim ashore, but landed on the Kowloon side where he was immediately taken prisoner. MTB 11, with no targets to fire at, sped out of the harbour, zigzagging at full speed to avoid the fire from both sides of the harbour and from enemy aircraft. After exiting the harbour and rounding Mount Davis, Collingwood signalled the Port War Signal Station on Mount Davis that MTB 12 had been lost and that there were no more landing craft in the harbour. The two Thorneycroft boats, Lt Wagstaff's MTB 26, and Lt Parsons's MTB 27, were the next boats to join the attack. They were preparing to enter the harbour, but as they reached Green Island, a signal was received from the Port War Signal Station with orders to hold back and not to attack. Whether MTB 26 saw the signal or not, she did not wait but proceeded straight into the harbour, where she was hit and put out of action with no survivors.

Although little was achieved militarily, the Royal Navy had at least struck back. It was a gallant attack, undertaken in broad daylight, by lightly armed wooden boats, whose only advantage was speed and surprise. It has sometimes been compared to the charge of the Light Brigade for its audaciousness and for the courage of the boat crews.

10

Chaos and Confusion
19 December

By noon on Friday 19 December, the Japanese had control of all the high ground to the south of their landing area, consisting of Mount Parker, Mount Butler and Jardine's Lookout. The AA section at Stanley Gap had been overrun, the police station at WNC Gap had been captured, and Brigadier Lawson lay dead outside his bunker at West Brigade HQ. The Brigade HQ was no longer functioning, and the brigade staff were either dead, wounded, or pinned down at Brigade shelters, or on the hillside above. Major Webb ('Tim') Temple, commanding officer of West Group, RA, and Major Geoffrey Proes, commanding officer of the newly established Counterbattery Group, had both been killed at West Brigade HQ. Captain John ('Jack') Fox, West Group RA, had been killed with his pet spaniel while trying to escape by way of the hillside above Brigade HQ. Major John Monro, RA, recalled telephoning both Major Tim Temple and Captain Jack Fox that morning before the exchange was put out of action.

> I rang up to ask Jack Fox what the position was at Wong Nai Chung. I could hear the machine gun fire down the phone. He had been manning one himself. … A quarter of an hour later I rang up again, this time I got Tim. He said they were surrounded and fighting a tremendous battle with small arms.[1]

2/Lt John Trapman, based at Wan Chai Gap AOP, spoke to Major Proes during the morning, at which time Proes was already wounded. He also talked to Captain Fox, who was shooting a battery at the time. Captain Fox's wife, Patricia, had remained in Hong Kong and was working as an ANS nurse at the War Memorial Hospital on the Peak. A new West Group HQ was established at Wan Chai Gap, initially under Trapman and later under Major Duncan and Lt Allanson. Major-General Maltby had to take direct command of West Infantry Brigade until a new brigade commander, Colonel H. B. Rose, was appointed on 20 December. Rose was a veteran of the First World War, in which he had been awarded the MC. He had previously commanded the HKVDC. His orders were to clear the enemy from both WNC Gap and Stanley Gap.

The Japanese had moved inland from their bridgehead on the north shore with surprising speed, and there was a grave danger that British troops and guns would be cut off in the eastern sector of the Island. Having occupied Mount Parker, the Japanese overlooked East Brigade HQ at Tai Tam Gap, which started coming under small arms fire during the morning. 'C' Coy, RRC, was defending the road approach to Tai Tam Gap, supported by two armoured cars. Brigadier Wallis decided that morning to withdraw East Brigade to the Stanley Peninsula. At that time, he expected to be able to withdraw the howitzers at Gauge Basin (two 3.7-inch), Tai Tam Fork (one 3.7-inch) and Red Hill (two 4.5-inch). Major-General Maltby agreed to the plan, and Wallis issued orders for the withdrawal of East Infantry Brigade to commence at around 1100 hours. East Group Royal Artillery issued orders for the howitzer sections to be withdrawn to Stanley, but this was hampered by the lack of lorries to tow the 4.5-inch guns at Red Hill and the lack of mules to move the 3.7-inch howitzers at Gauge Basin and Tai Tam Fork.

Lt-Col Cadogan-Rawlinson reached Bridge Hill shelters at 1000 hours after withdrawing from the north shore where his battalion had been decimated. Brigadier Wallis ordered him to hold the Tai Tam X-Roads at all costs until 1400 hours, by which time Wallis expected to have got the bulk of his troops over the dam, through the X-Roads, and back to the Stanley vicinity. Cadogan-Rawlinson set about defending the X-Roads and deploying his group, which consisted of four British officers and ten Indian ORs. Wallis established his new Brigade HQ at Stone Hill shelters on Island Road. He planned to set up a defensive perimeter stretching from Bridge Hill at the Tai Tam X-Roads to Stanley View and linking Notting Hill, Sugar Loaf, Stone Hill and Stanley Mound.

Brigadier Macleod, Commander Royal Artillery (CRA), ordered the destruction of the coastal defence batteries in the eastern sector. These included Fort Bokhara (two 9.2-inch), Fort D'Aguilar (two 4-inch), Fort Collinson (two 6-inch) and Chung Hom Kok (two 6-inch). The Chung Hom Kok artillery fort, also referred to as Chung Hom Kok, should not have been included as it was not in the eastern sector of the Island and was under no immediate threat. At Fort Bokhara, Major Templer, the commanding officer, received his orders at 1100 hours to destroy the battery and evacuate the personnel to Stanley. He recalled in his diary that the two 9.2-inch guns were put out of action in the time-honoured way of placing one round in the muzzle and then firing another round from the breach.

If the Japanese had captured the Tai Tam X-Roads, they would have been able to cut off the extrication route to Stanley. There were two critical hold points to prevent the Japanese from reaching the X-Roads that morning. These were Tai Tam Gap, which was strongly defended, and Gauge Basin, which was weakly defended. The Gauge

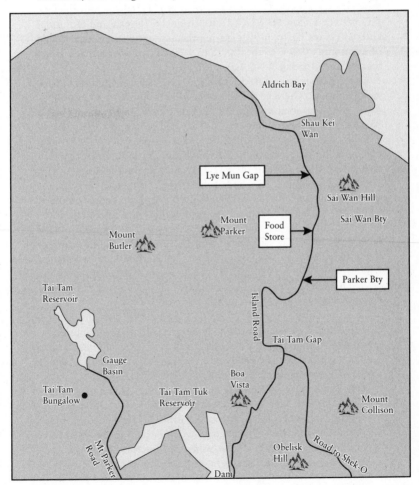

Tai Tam Gap.

Basin area is like a vast amphitheatre surrounded by hills, with Boa Vista to the east, Mount Parker and Mount Butler to the north, and Jardine's Lookout to the north-west. Mount Parker Road ran down from Sanatorium Gap to the Tai Tam upper reservoir. At that point there was an intersection of roads: Stanley Gap Road led westwards to WNC Gap, and Mount Parker Road continued southwards to the lower reservoir and emerged on Island Road at the Tai Tam X-Roads. During the morning on 19 December, all that stood in the way of the Japanese Army at Gauge Basin were the two HKSRA 3.7-inch howitzer sections and what was left of No. 1 Platoon and the Coy HQ of No. 1 Coy, HKVDC. Units from the Tanaka and Doi *butai* entered Gauge Basin, mostly during the early afternoon, but instead of continuing down to the Tai Tam X-Roads, they proceeded along Stanley Gap Road to WNC Gap.

Captain Penn arrived back at his Coy HQ at the Tai Tam Bungalow at 0530 hours. There he found the CSM and the Coy HQ personnel. There were also some stragglers from other units, including some from No. 3 Coy and some Indian troops. They had been pressed into service with No. 1 Coy by the CSM. Penn made a telephone call to 2/Lt Redman commanding No. 2 Platoon at Repulse Bay View. Redman reported that it had been quiet in their sector, and they had had no contact with Japanese troops. Penn had around thirty men which included the stragglers. In consultation with Captain Bompas, the senior officer at Gauge Basin 3.7-inch Section, Penn deployed his men around the knoll on which the howitzer section was positioned. The troops provided local defence for the guns and formed a line facing the direction of the anticipated Japanese advance from Sanatorium Gap and Mount Parker. At 0700 hours Penn finally got through to Brigadier Wallis and briefed him on the loss of Sanatorium Gap and their current situation at Gauge Basin.

> He instructed me that we were to hold our Gauge Basin positions ... and that a counterattack was being staged in the early morning from WNC Gap which would sweep the enemy out of the Tai Tam area and that two platoons from 'D' Battalion [Royal Rifles of Canada] were being sent up to us to reinforce our defences. They would join us by way of the road from Tai Tam X-Roads. I enquired when we might expect them, and he instructed me to wait, and I heard him turn and ask someone else when these platoons would be moving off. I hung on for some minutes, but finally, we were disconnected, and though we tried repeatedly, we were unable to get through to Brigade or even 'D' Battalion again. We never saw any sign of the two promised platoons from 'D' Bn.[2]

From his Coy HQ, Penn could see Japanese troops moving along the ridgeline from Sanatorium Gap towards Jardine's Lookout. At one stage, he saw Canadian troops on the ridge between Mount Butler and Jardine's Lookout withdrawing towards the west pursued by Japanese troops. This may have been 'A' Coy, WG, fighting their way back to Stanley Gap. The Tai Tam Bungalow was situated on a mound a few hundred metres from Gauge Basin 3.7-inch Section. At about 0930 hours Penn's position at the Tai Tam Bungalow and the Gauge Basin 3.7-inch Section started coming under small arms fire from a higher knoll situated about 400 metres to the east. The 3.7-inch section position was also hit by light mortar fire. The mortar fire was probably from knee-mortars used by the Japanese infantry. On a site visit to the knoll, I found a British war-time splinter-proof shelter near the crest. I also found several spent Japanese casings around the hilltop. There is no record of this knoll having been defended, even though it provides a clear line of fire onto the howitzer position.

Penn estimated that the Japanese troops on the knoll numbered around twenty-five to thirty. He had an LMG brought up to the Tai Tam Bungalow to lay down fire on the knoll. The gunners at the 3.7-inch howitzer section were incurring casualties from this close-range flank fire. Captain Bompas and 2/Lt Eddison at the section position arranged for one of the guns to be manhandled and turned around to face the knoll. They fired their gun over open sights at the Japanese on the knoll. On visiting the howitzer site, I found a large number of spent 0.45-inch TSMG casings at and around the gun pits. This demonstrates that the battery personnel were having to use Tommy guns to defend themselves in relatively close-range fighting. Japanese fire from the knoll died down and ceased altogether by about 1030 hours.

By this time large numbers of mostly Indian gunners from the three HKSRA howitzer sections on Stanley Gap Road were seen withdrawing towards the Tai Tam X-Roads. The sections on Stanley Gap Road included three 3.7-inch, two 4.5-inch and two 6-inch howitzers. At 1100 hours, the howitzers at Gauge Basin Section were firing off rounds rapidly in preparation for a withdrawal. At about this time a runner, L/Cpl Edward Gaubert, arrived at Coy HQ having been sent from the CSM with a message that all troops were ordered to withdraw to Stanley. 2/Lt Carter also confirmed to Captain Penn that Captain Bompas had relayed the same instructions. Captain Penn destroyed the telephone exchange and then gave the orders for the withdrawal.

I ordered all weapons and equipment to be loaded into our transport, together with as many boxes of small arms ammunition (SSA) as could be taken. Our transport of two Chevrolet vans, one Morris truck, and four private cars were able to accommodate all ranks, weapons, and about twenty to thirty boxes of SAA and between 1130 and 1145 hours we left for Stanley. Progress down the narrow road to the Tai Tam X-Roads was very slow owing to the large number of Indian troops we overtook proceeding down the road.[3]

The two 3.7-inch howitzers at Gauge Basin were disabled and abandoned. The two 4.5-inch howitzers at Red Hill Battery were inadvertently put out of action. The Indian commissioned officer commanding the Red Hill Section had disabled his guns following a miscommunication. It had been intended that he withdraw the guns to Stanley. The section commander was apparently ordered 'to get out of action', but the officer interpreted this somewhat ambiguous order as 'put the guns out of action'. Even if the order had been correctly given and correctly understood, it would have been impossible to move the guns without towing trucks. The only gun that was successfully withdrawn to Stanley was the 3.7-inch howitzer at Tai Tam Fork Section; the other howitzer from this section had been lost at Lye Mun Barracks.

On this single day, East Group lost four 6-inch, four 4.5-inch, and three 3.7-inch howitzers. West Group lost two 6-inch and three 3.7-inch howitzers on Stanley Gap Road. Altogether sixteen howitzers were lost. East Group lost all their howitzers except for the one gun brought back to Stanley. The loss of so much of the mobile artillery on Friday 19 December was a devastating blow for the British and Canadian infantry who later had to mount counterattacks with inadequate artillery against well-entrenched Japanese positions.

The road to Stanley was jammed with vehicles and men. Wallis was worried that the bunching of men and vehicles would make them vulnerable to attacks from the air, but low cloud helped keep aircraft at bay during the withdrawal. A platoon headed by Lt James Ross from 'B' Coy, Royal Rifles of Canada, was the last to leave Tai Tam Gap. They had been sniped at from Mount Parker and Boa Vista on their left flank. By 1600 hours, the platoon was exchanging fire with Japanese troops trying to outflank the Canadians by working their way in a clockwise direction around Tai Tam Gap towards the cemeteries. At 1645 hours, Lt Ross and his platoon withdrew in the nick of time. By late afternoon the withdrawal from the eastern part of the Island had been completed, and the infantry was reforming and reorganising in new positions on the hills around Stanley.

For the Navy, things were equally chaotic. At 0930 hours on Friday 19 December, HMS *Cicala* intercepted a signal from the Commodore to Commander Montague, SNO (Aberdeen), with the order to scuttle all ships except the MTBs. *Cicala* sent a signal to SNO (A) asking whether the Commodore's signal applied to *Cicala*. It probably did, but Montague replied that they were not to scuttle. Montague ordered Lt Hazlehurst on HMS *Robin* to disregard the order and keep the gunboat in action. HMS *Robin* was armed with a 3.7-inch gun which was subsequently used very effectively for landward firing in support of the Army.

That morning HMS *Cornflower* and all the auxiliary patrol vessels (APVs) were scuttled in Deep Water Bay. The HKRNVR shore base was evacuated, and all ships companies reported to the naval base at AIS where they were deployed in the hills to fight as infantry. In addition to the APVs, the following RN ships were scuttled that morning: RFA *Ebonol*, an oiler; HMS *Redstart*, a minelayer; HMS *Tern*, a gunboat; HMS *Barlight*, a boom defence vessel; HMS *Aldgate* and HMS *Watergate*, boom gate vessels; and HMT *Alliance*, a naval tug. The scuttling of ships had a demoralising effect on those who witnessed it. The Commodore's decision to scuttle so many ships was criticised later as being too hasty. The decision was taken based on information passed to the Commodore about the proximity of Japanese troops to Aberdeen Harbour and to the naval anchorage at Deep Water Bay.

The remote-controlled minefields were blown up, and the shore-based mine control stations at Chung Hom Kok and Shek-O were destroyed to prevent the new technology from coming into Japanese hands. Sub-Lt William Haslett was serving at Mine Control Station-Tathong, located at Shek-O. He had moved out of his flat in Prince Edward Road, Kowloon and taken up residence in a small Chinese village house on the beach at Shek-O. When the station was evacuated, the commander gave orders that all personnel were to proceed immediately to Stanley in the five available private cars. Haslett disobeyed orders and instead went to his home in the village to collect some of his personal effects. When he returned to the mine control station, it had been abandoned, and the villagers were looting the premises. He went up the road to the exclusive Shek-O Country Club, surrounded by expensive European bungalows. The club and the surrounding bungalows had all been evacuated – all, that is, except for No. 13 Shek-O, home to sixty-four-year-old Herman Dawson-Grove and his fifty-five-year-old wife Ethel. They had not been informed of the evacuation and had remained in their bungalow.

The Dawson-Groves had two adult sons, one of whom was a student at Hong Kong University, the other a doctor serving as a naval surgeon in the HKRNVR. Haslett joined the Dawson-Groves at their bungalow, where they remained overnight until Saturday 20 December, when a

Japanese infantry detachment arrived at the property. The soldiers commandeered the two private cars belonging to the family and ordered Herman Dawson-Grove to drive one, and his wife the other. They were ordered to drive towards Big Wave Bay, which was only a short distance away. At this point, Ethel was ordered to return to her home. Haslett and Dawson-Grove were put to work and made to carry equipment up the hillside. This was difficult, both for the elderly retiree and for forty-seven-year-old Haslett who had recently recovered from a heart attack. When they flagged, they were beaten and kicked. The Japanese contingent, with their two European prisoners, proceeded uphill to Fort Collinson, which had been evacuated the previous day. They then made their way along Island Road to Tai Tam Gap where they spent the night lying in the open without food or water. On Monday 22 December, they watched a large mass of Japanese infantry, which they estimated at 1,500 to 2,000 men, pass through the gap towards Tai Tam and Stanley. These troops were followed by horse-drawn artillery. The two prisoners were then released and made their way back to No. 13 Shek-O where they remained until the capitulation. All three were later incarcerated at Stanley Camp.

After the order to scuttle ships, the Royal Navy was left with HMS *Cicala*, the five remaining MTBs, and HMS *Robin* moored in Staunton Creek at Aberdeen. HMS *Tern* with her two 3-inch guns would have been usefully retained as she provided a very effective anti-aircraft platform. The APVs were slow and cumbersome, and many of them were undermanned because their Chinese crews had absconded. They were mostly converted tugs and launches, but they were armed with 12-pdr (3-inch) or 6-pdr (2.25-inch) naval guns, which could have supported military operations. The naval base at AIS was not evacuated as ordered, initially because it contained a hospital facility, which could not be evacuated so quickly, and later because it was realised that the Japanese were not as close to Aberdeen as had been thought. AIS continued to operate as a naval base up until the surrender on Christmas Day.

Friday 19 December was a desperate day, and chaos and confusion reigned. Orders were given and then countermanded. There were a series of poorly coordinated counterattacks launched against much stronger Japanese positions at WNC Gap. Ships were scuttled and remote-controlled minefields detonated. The mobile artillery lost sixteen howitzers, which were either abandoned or overrun. The Rajput battalion on the north shore had been almost wiped out, leaving East Brigade with only one complete infantry battalion. East Group had lost all their guns, except the one howitzer brought back to Stanley, leaving East Brigade with inadequate artillery support. Four of the coastal defence batteries were abandoned and their guns disabled. Half of the Island was given up. The command structure for West Infantry Brigade and West Group Royal Artillery was destroyed. Brigadier Wallis, at his new HQ in a ravine at the base of Stone Hill, made plans for a counterattack on WNC Gap which would commence early the next morning. Major-General Maltby in the Battle Box knew that if anybody could break through, it would be Wallis.

11

The Army Counterattacks
19 to 21 December

During the early hours on Friday 19 December, Major-General Maltby asked Colonel Clifford, chief engineer, to provide a party of Royal Engineers, acting in the role of infantry, to reinforce the troops at WNC Gap. They were to report to Brigadier Lawson at West Brigade HQ. A party was formed consisting of seventy British and Chinese sappers led by forty-nine-year-old Lt-Col Reginald Walker, HKVDC. Walker had served in the First World War and had been awarded the Military Cross for conspicuous gallantry in March 1918. In civilian life, he was chief engineer of the Kowloon–Canton Railway Company. The sappers proceeded from their positions at Shouson Hill by route march, up Deep Water Bay Road to WNC Gap, with the ammunition sent up by truck. The sappers arrived at the gap at 0630 hours, but by that time the Japanese had seized the police station and were picketing the ADS on the north side of the gap. The sappers were unable to pass through the gap because of the intensity of Japanese mortar and machine gun fire covering the approaches to West Brigade HQ. Walker, leading from the front, made a dash for it and managed to get through the gap, but as he neared Brigade HQ he was shot and wounded in both legs.

The Japanese had got to the gap first, and they were there in strength. The effort to get through the gap to Brigade HQ was called off, and two sections, one from 40th Fortress Coy under Major Murray and one from 22nd Fortress Coy under Lt Robson, were deployed on the south-west side of the gap to cover the entrance to Black's Link and Deep Water Bay Road. The remainder of the sappers withdrew along Black's Link to reform and reorganise for a further counterattack which was made later in the day with the Winnipeg Grenadiers. Those killed included Major Murray and Lt Holliday. Lt Holliday had only recently got engaged to Brenda Morgan, an Army nurse, who was killed during shelling at

St Albert's Hospital five days earlier. Holliday's body was identified after the war by the hospital badge that his fiancée had given him as a keepsake.

At about the same time that the sappers were deploying at WNC Gap, Lt James Sutcliffe, RAOC, was being driven from the magazines at Shouson Hill to Queens Road Ordnance Depot. Cpl Ryan was driving, and Pte Stopforth was following in an ammunition lorry. Ryan, perhaps with a sense of premonition, had loaded a Bren gun and a box of ammunition in the boot of the car. In his personal war diary, Sutcliffe recalls dozing off as they drove up Deep Water Bay Road towards the gap. As they reached the gap, he was woken by the sound of machine gun and rifle fire. They found themselves in the middle of a full-scale battle.

> I joined the Winnipeg Grenadiers and Fortress Coy Royal Engineers in forming a line across the entrance of the track off the main road. My first impression as I lay down on the bank with my revolver pointed down the main road to the left was that everybody was blasting away in every direction. Cpl Ryan and Pte Stopforth placed their Bren gun on my left and Stopforth started bursting away at the hill in front [the knoll]. They then suggested I should move with them to a higher and better position to the left. Seeing no object in doing so I refused but told them to go to it. Their place was taken by Captain Cartwright-Taylor [RE] with a Bren gun. I was wounded by machine gun fire twice.[1]

Ryan, the twenty-five-year-old son of a retired colonel in the Royal Artillery, was killed by machine gun fire. Stopforth had seen his body caught on the barbed wire entanglement around a pillbox. The pillbox must have been PB 3, which fits the description of his moving to the left for higher ground. Ryan was awarded a posthumous Mention in Despatches (MiD). Sutcliffe was taken in a military ambulance to the RN Hospital in Wan Chai, the ambulance managing to pass through the gap.

Later that morning, Captain Otway, RE, arrived at the gap having made his way across country from a searchlight position situated on the shoreline at Lye Mun. His detachment of six sappers had been surrounded by Japanese troops trying to capture the searchlight and put it out of action. The sappers had fought the Japanese off with their rifles and a Bren gun and had kept the beam exposed, illuminating Japanese landing craft crossing the Lye Mun channel. Their position was eventually overrun, and all of the crew were killed, except Otway who fought his way out of Pak Sha Wan Battery, and Cpl Pelham who escaped by entering the water and swimming along the shore. When Otway reached WNC Gap at 0945 hours, he immediately set about organising a counterattack on the police station knoll. He collected some nine men, including some of Lt-Col Walker's sappers, and two or three from the RN contingent which had been ambushed earlier. The naval personnel may have included Jack Siddans. Captain Otway's group made several attempts to recapture the police station knoll from the south side, but the Japanese were too well entrenched. Otway was awarded the MC for this and other actions during the battle.

Captain Kenneth Campbell had replaced Captain Jones as commander of 'A' Coy, 2/RS. The company, which was acting as a reserve company, received orders that morning to move to Wan Chai Gap in preparation for a possible counterattack on WNC Gap. From Wan Chai Gap, they could attack either in an anti-clockwise direction by way of Black's Link, or in a clockwise direction by way of Stubbs Road and WNC Gap Road. 'A' Coy set off from their Garden Road Barracks at 0615 hours. They were instructed to take the back route along Coombe Road, rather than Stubbs Road, to avoid their deployment to Wan Chai Gap being observed by the Japanese. At 0700 hours, Lt-Col Simon White, 2/RS, received a phone call from Brigadier Lawson asking that 'A' Coy be sent up to WNC Gap as quickly as possible because the Japanese were by then in close proximity to his HQ. Their orders were to break through to West Brigade HQ and to extricate the brigadier and his staff. Major-General Maltby telephoned Lt-Col White and stressed the importance of 'A' Coy's mission. White replied that his men would go 'like the hammers of hell'. Campbell set off at approximately 0730 hours in trucks provided by the Winnipeg Grenadiers. They drove down Stubbs Road and debussed at the petrol station located at the intersection of Stubbs Road and WNC Gap Road. From the road junction, they proceeded on foot, with No. 8 Platoon turning right and moving up WNC Gap Road, and No. 7 Platoon continuing along Tai Hang Road before turning right and going up Blue Pool Road.

At 0815 hours, Lt-Col Sutcliffe, WG, telephoned through to Lt-Col White to say that Lawson had reported that 'A' Coy had not yet arrived. At 2/RS Bn HQ there had been no report from 'A' Coy. 2/Lt Swettenham, a newly commissioned officer from the HKVDC, volunteered to take out a patrol consisting of himself and three ORs to contact 'A' Coy and report back on the situation. The four men squeezed into a small car and departed from Wan Chai Gap at around 0900 hours. They were unable to make direct contact with 'A' Coy, but they managed to get close to West Brigade HQ. They reported back that there were no Japanese on the road to the north of West Brigade shelters, although there was heavy fire from Jardine's Lookout across the valley, and that vehicles were ablaze in the Brigade HQ car park.

At approximately 1330 hours, a runner from 'A' Coy reported to Bn HQ that they had got to within 200 yards of West Brigade shelters, but they were pinned down by concentrated fire and had sustained heavy casualties. 2/Lt Fenwick had been killed, and 2/Lt Hart had been wounded. The troops going up WNC Gap Road were more exposed than those in the valley to the fire from Jardine's Lookout, and had moved off the road and joined those in the valley trying to work their way up Blue Pool Valley towards the gap. The runner was sent back with orders for 'A' Coy to stay where they were, and if possible to get a patrol into Brigade HQ. Lt-Col White spoke to Lt-Col Sutcliffe, relaying the situation report from 'A' Coy. He suggested that if Sutcliffe's battalion could reinforce 'A' Coy, they should be able to get to the shelters and retrieve the brigadier and his staff. Sutcliffe agreed to this but was unable to get his troops through to WNC Gap. While 'A' Coy, 2/RS were fighting their way to relieve West Brigade HQ, what was not known at that point was that Brigadier Lawson was already dead. Some half a dozen personnel from 'A' Coy under Sgt Arnott, although all wounded, had been able to reach West Brigade shelters, which, however, had been put out of action by that time. The wounded Royal Scots were unable to relay the situation to their Bn HQ as the telephone exchange had been destroyed before Lawson left his HQ.

In the early afternoon, Captain Campbell was wounded and evacuated. The company had been reduced from seventy-six ORs to less than twenty effectives – those still able to fight. With Campbell wounded, 2/Lt Fenwick killed and 2/Lt Hart wounded, Sgt Whippey took command of the depleted company. When it became clear that no further advance could be made because of the intensity of fire, the remaining men were withdrawn to Bn HQ, which during the afternoon had moved from Wan Chai Gap to a position on Stubbs Road near the junction with Tai Hang Road.

After the failure of the counterattacks during the morning, Fortress HQ ordered a general advance to commence at 1500 hours. This would entail an attack by the Winnipeg Grenadiers and the Royal Scots. The Winnipeg Grenadiers were ordered to deploy along Black's Link from their positions at Wan Chai Gap, and to counterattack WNC Gap from the west. The Grenadiers would be comprised of 'HQ' Coy, and one platoon from 'C' Coy, which was to be sent up from their positions at Aberdeen Reservoir. In addition, a small party of Royal Scots from 'A' Coy and a detachment of Royal Engineers were available to support the Grenadiers.

Lt-Col Sutcliffe's battalion had suffered significant depletion during the day. The two mobile platoons from 'HQ' Coy under Lt Birkett and Lt French had been wiped out, 'A' Coy had been destroyed, and the remnants of 'D' Coy were pinned down at their Coy HQ shelters at the gap. This left only 'B' Coy, based at Pok Fu Lam Reservoir, and 'C' Coy, based at Aberdeen Reservoir, at full strength. Lt-Col Sutcliffe ordered Major Ernest Hodkinson to lead the counterattack by 'HQ' Coy. His first objective was to seize WNC Gap, and relieve both Brigade HQ and 'D' Coy; then, as a second objective, they were to press on to Mount Parker.

The main force for the counterattack was to be provided by the Royal Scots, who were to attack in battalion strength. Their objective was to seize WNC Gap and occupy Jardine's Lookout. Captain David Pinkerton's 'D' Coy, supported by the Bren gun carrier platoon, was to attack by proceeding straight up WNC Gap Road. They would rush WNC Gap and then counterattack Jardine's Lookout. 'C' Coy, under Lt Frank ('Pip') Stancer, were to attack up Blue Pool Road on Pinkerton's left flank. A composite company, consisting of personnel from 'B' Coy and 'HQ' Coy, under Captain Douglas Ford would counterattack from the west by way of Black's Link. The plan was that the three companies would converge at the gap. Lt-Col White had been told that WNC Gap was lightly held. Whereas, in fact, the Japanese had four infantry battalions in the vicinity of the gap and supporting artillery. 'D' Coy and three Bren gun carriers proceeded to their start line near the petrol station at the junction of Stubbs Road and Tai Hang Road.

The attempt by the Royal Scots to break through on WNC Gap Road stalled; the troops were pinned down by heavy fire and were waiting until nightfall before restarting their advance. The Winnipeg Grenadiers led by Major Hodkinson proceeded independently along Black's Link. Their one Bren gun carrier, provided by 2/RS, led the way with the infantry following behind. The attack was made in broad daylight. There was no communication with Bn HQ other than by runner, as no field telephone line accompanied the advance.

Professor David Macri, writing in *Canadian Military History*,[2] relates how the US Army had a small role, not generally known, in the Battle for Hong Kong. Major Reynolds Condon, assistant military attaché to the US Embassy in Chungking, had been in Hong Kong since October 1941. He was accompanied by the military attaché for air, Major Richard Grussendorf, and Captain William Clarkson, adjutant of the American Military Mission to China. They were in Hong Kong for medical treatment. The three American officers were meant to be acting in an advisory capacity, but they took up arms and were often involved in the action on the front line. Major Condon, for example, accompanied Major Hodkinson's troops during the counterattack along Black's Link. Condon recalled that at 1530 hours only two Canadian platoons with one Bren gun carrier were at the forming up point, plus ten sappers and twenty Royal Scots. He found that apart from the single Bren gun mounted on the carrier, there was only one Bren gun for each platoon. On reaching Middle Gap, they came under fire from a Japanese field gun.

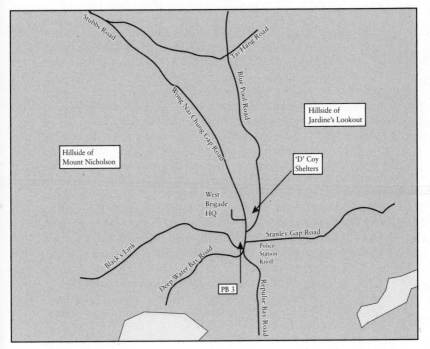

Wong Nai Chung Gap.

Middle Gap is about halfway along Black's Link. It is the gap between Mount Cameron on the right and Mount Nicholson on the left. After passing Middle Gap, the right-hand side of the track opens up while the left-hand side is protected by the slopes of Mount Nicholson. At Middle Gap, Major Hodkinson ordered Lt Corrigan and his platoon to deploy up Mount Nicholson. Their orders were to flush out any Japanese on the high ground to the left of the track and to establish a position on the east-facing slope of Mount Nicholson from which they could provide harassing fire on Japanese positions at WNC Gap. Major Condon described the advance along Black's Link.

> At a gap about halfway, we ran into interdiction fire at the rate of a shell every fifteen seconds. By timing and dispatching his men in groups, the Major traversed this spot with only one man wounded. ... The Major, with the other platoon, followed the path around the mountain. With the Bren gun carrier in the lead, we proceeded cautiously around each nose, reconnoitring the next stretch of road, through which we ran.[3]

In the late afternoon, a large concentration of Japanese troops, most likely from Colonel Tanaka's 229th Regiment, were observed resting at the food store on Stanley Gap Road opposite the AA position. This was the RV for Colonel Tanaka's two infantry battalions. The Winnipeg Grenadiers, without telephone communication, were unable to call in and direct an artillery strike. Condon had suggested sending back the carrier to report the target and request artillery fire based on a grid reference, but instead a decision was made to engage the Japanese troop concentration with machine gun fire. The Japanese quickly dispersed after taking minimal casualties. As Hodkinson's force proceeded along Black's Link, the lead troops came under machine gun fire from their right flank. The fire was thought to be coming from the water catchment on the slopes of Violet Hill above Postbridge. The garrison at Postbridge was still holding out, and garrison members recall seeing the Canadian troops counterattacking from Black's Link and Mount Nicholson in the early evening. Condon, who was generally very critical of the way the British and Canadian forces conducted the battle, praised the defenders at Postbridge.

> Whenever the Japanese tried to cross the concrete road through the gap, they got a burst of fire in the flank. It was probably that one group of brave men that had prevented the Japanese from advancing all the way to Wan Chai Gap.[4]

Hodkinson's troops continued their advance by rushes supported by covering fire, but for the most part the advance had stalled, and the troops were pinned down on this exposed section of Black's Link, some 500 metres from the gap, waiting for darkness before resuming the advance.

Lt Corrigan's platoon had struggled up the hill, each man carrying 250 rounds of ammunition, in addition to their rifles, water canteens and other equipment. After having reached the summit, they had to descend almost to the bottom, down a long and steep gradient, which was open and in clear view of Japanese troops positioned across the valley. They did this by running and diving for cover until they reached a shallow depression where they set up the Bren gun in a position where they could fire on the Japanese below. After nightfall, Corrigan's platoon withdrew, having to ascend the mountain before coming down onto Black's Link. They arrived back at WG Battalion HQ in Wan Chai Gap in the early hours of Saturday 20 December.

At around 2000 hours, a section of two armoured cars under the command of Sgt Walker, HKVDC, made their way through the gap from the south by way of Repulse Bay Road. However, both vehicles were put out of action at the gap when grenades exploded underneath the vehicles, causing damage to the oil sumps and axles. Lt Tamworth, RE, had taken part in the Royal Scots advance up WNC Gap Road earlier that day. The advance had ground to a halt because of the intensity of fire from Jardine's Lookout. Tamworth recalled meeting Sgt Walker coming down WNC Gap Road.

> At about 2030 hours I saw Sgt Walker, HKVDC, Armoured Car Platoon, walking down the road from WNC Gap. He said he had just gone through the gap where he had abandoned his armoured car, and that the gap was only lightly held by the Japanese, and that it would only require a few men to retake it.[5]

At dusk, Hodkinson took a reconnaissance patrol of four men, equipped with a 2-inch mortar, over a spur of Mount Nicholson at the bottom of Black's Link. Having crossed the spur, they emerged on the north side of the gap close to West Brigade shelters. Hodkinson crossed the road to 'D' Coy's shelters, where he used the telephone to brief Fortress HQ. He was ordered to attack the police station knoll. After conducting a reconnaissance of the area around the police station knoll, his patrol attacked and overran a Japanese roadblock. Hodkinson then organised a frontal assault on the police station, during which he was seriously wounded by a grenade blast, and all members of the patrol became casualties. The attack had to be called off. Hodkinson was evacuated to hospital and two of the patrol, Sgt Charles Watson and Cpl William McAuley, both wounded, took refuge at 'D' Coy shelters. Hodkinson was awarded the DSO, and Sgt Watson was awarded a MiD.

Condon had remained at the command post on Black's Link. At 2100 hours, he recalled the arrival of some 150 Royal Scots. This was the composite company consisting of men from 'B' Coy under Lt Glasgow, and 'HQ' Coy under 2/Lt Hamilton, a newly commissioned officer from No. 1 Coy, HKVDC. The company was commanded by Captain Douglas Ford. His orders were to link up with Captain Pinkerton at WNC Gap and then capture Jardine's Lookout. Condon also described the arrival of what he thought was a large platoon of Canadian troops which had advanced up Repulse Bay Road. To Condon's surprise this platoon then quickly proceeded to attack the knoll and captured the police station.

> Another platoon of Canadians had arrived, with four officers, including a Major. They decided to storm the police station at once. If there were any orders given, I didn't hear them. The officers simply walked off, followed by as many of the men as felt the urge, and took the station with grenades and rifle fire. The Major and two other officers were killed in the attack.[6]

The troops that Condon saw arriving at the gap and seizing the police station were, in fact, the gunners from the Hong Kong Singapore Royal Artillery (HKSRA). The detachment consisted of one hundred Indian gunners led by British officers, including Lt-Col Yale, Major de Vere Hunt and Captain Feilden. Fortress HQ had been pressing Brigadier Wallis, and Lt-Col Shaw, Eastern Fire Command, RA, for reinforcements to be sent to WNC Gap, but Wallis had spent most of the day moving his troops back towards Stanley, and reorganising and redeploying his brigade. The only troops immediately available were the East Group, RA gunners who had lost most of their mobile howitzers during the withdrawal that morning. They were assigned to fight as infantry under the command of Major Edward de Vere Hunt and to recapture WNC Gap. This they commendably did, and seized the police station, albeit briefly. Wallis saw them passing his Brigade HQ at Stone Hill on the evening of Friday 19 December.

> A Royal Artillery party under the command of Major de V. Hunt with Captain Feilden and some one hundred Indian gunners were sent off in vehicles. They left Stone Hill HQ about 1900 hours and were accompanied by Lt-Col Yale, RA, who had been sent to Stanley Fort to rest, as he was unfit after the Mainland withdrawal. This good officer said he insisted on accompanying his men.[7]

The gunners were ordered to clear Repulse Bay Road of disabled vehicles, which were preventing the armoured cars from getting up the road to the gap. During the attack, Captain Feilden was killed, and Lt-Col Yale was wounded and later reported as missing in action. Major de Vere Hunt, who led the assault, survived. He must have gone through the gap, like Sgt Walker, because he later reported in person at Fortress HQ. Major Monro recalled his dishevelled arrival, armed with a Tommy gun, at the Battle Box. The RA war diary states that after leaving Fortress HQ, Major de Vere Hunt returned to WNC Gap at first light on Saturday 20 December and was killed in action. The gunners incurred a large number of casualties: three officers and thirty ORs were killed, and only thirteen made it back to Stanley; the rest were wounded or captured. Maltby wrote in his Report on Operations that at or around 0135 hours on Saturday 20 December he was informed that the enemy had been cleared from WNC Gap Police Station. However, the Japanese were able to rush reinforcements from Stanley Gap Road, and they recaptured the police station in the early hours of Saturday.

The Royal Scots' counterattack up WNC Gap Road and Blue Pool Valley was made in broad daylight and commenced at 1530 hours. The overall plan called for 'C' and 'D' Coy to retrace the route taken by 'A' Coy earlier that day, exposing them to the same flank fire from Jardine's Lookout. The composite company made up from 'B' and 'HQ' Coy would simultaneously attack from Black's Link. The pincer movement would close at WNC Gap. The battalion's three remaining Bren gun carriers, under Captain Slater-Brown, led the advance up WNC Gap Road with 'D' Coy following behind. The road was difficult to drive up because of the number of wrecked vehicles. The Japanese withheld their fire until they had sufficient targets and then opened fire with mortars and machine guns from the slopes of Jardine's Lookout across the valley. The leading Bren gun carrier received a direct hit from a mortar bomb, killing Captain Slater-Brown and all the other occupants. Further casualties were incurred in the infantry column following behind. The troops took cover as best they could, but all efforts to move forward were prevented by the heavy and accurate fire from across the valley. The attack was called off with the intention of resuming it later that night.

2/Lt Douglas Baird, 2/RS, led his platoon up Blue Pool Road while Lt Pip Stancer led the other two 'C' Coy platoons along WNC Gap Road. Baird reached a point where he was close to WNC Gap Road.

> I halted the platoon and crept forward with a corporal to inspect the road more closely. Stancer's group had been held up further down by machine gun fire. In front of me was one of the Bren gun carriers. I told the corporal to wait for me while I crawled behind the Bren gun carrier. I mounted it from the back and got inside. There were three bodies on the floor. One was that of Captain Slater-Brown, a sergeant and a lance corporal. I took each of their identity discs. Darkness had set in by the time I got out of the carrier and returned to the corporal and platoon.[8]

Douglas Baird went back to liaise with Pip Stancer. They decided to remain in their positions overnight and for Baird to send a recce patrol from his platoon that night to get as close as they could to the gap. Cpl Daniel Garrie led the three-man patrol. He returned quite quickly to brief his platoon commander that they had been right up to the gap, reached the police station, and found nobody there. It must have been during that brief interlude after the police station was captured, and about the time that Sgt Walker was able to walk through the gap unimpeded before Japanese reinforcements reoccupied the knoll.

At around midnight, 'D' Coy resumed their advance, going past West Brigade shelters on the right, and 'D' Coy shelters on the left, and then up to the gap. Captain Pinkerton ordered 2/Lt Fairbairn to lead a platoon attack on the police station knoll. However, the knoll was strongly defended by Japanese troops who had once again reoccupied the police station. As Fairbairn's platoon approached the steps leading up to the police station, they were met by a volley of grenades, machine gun fire, and rifle fire, and the platoon was forced to withdraw. 2/Lt Ford, Captain Douglas Ford's brother, led a second platoon attack from the rear of the knoll, while at the same time Captain Pinkerton led a frontal assault up the steps leading to the police station. Pinkerton was wounded in this attack, and Ford was unable to make progress up the steep slope and through the wire entanglements. With casualties increasing, the attack was withdrawn.

At about this time Captain Ford's composite company arrived. With Pinkerton incapacitated, Captain Ford assumed command of the Royal Scots at the gap. A further effort was made to seize the police station. 2/Lt Mackenzie, a newly commissioned officer from No. 2 Coy, HKVDC, managed to reach the police station, but was shot in the head and blinded. 2/Lt Gordon, another subaltern who had been commissioned from the HKVDC, was seriously injured during the attack on the police station, and he subsequently died from his wounds.

With daylight approaching and the police station still in Japanese hands, Ford withdrew what was left of his force to a spur of Mount Nicholson where they could fire down on the gap and deny the Japanese access to Black's Link and the slopes of Mount Nicholson. However, in this open position they were under fire and casualties started to mount. Runners were sent to Bn HQ to ask for food, water and ammunition to be sent forward, but the runners never made it back to Bn HQ, presumably shot by Japanese snipers. The Royal Scots remained in their exposed position throughout the day, withdrawing after dusk on Saturday night.

On Saturday morning, 'C' Coy, 2/RS was still bogged down in Blue Pool Valley. They formed a loose line extending back toward Tai Hang Road. There was a gap of around 400 metres between 'C' Coy's positions and those of Captain Kampta Prasad's 'B' Coy, 2/14 Punjabs, on a knoll north-west of Jardine's Lookout. Lt Stancer was wounded in the head by shrapnel during a Japanese mortar barrage on Saturday morning. He was helped down to Tai Hang Road and evacuated to hospital. 'B' Coy, 2/RS, was sent to fill the gap between the Punjabi Coy and 'C' Coy. The Royal Scots and Captain Prasad's Punjabi company held on for a few more days in the area of Blue Pool Valley and Tai Hang Road but were eventually pushed back to Stubbs Road and Wan Chai Gap.

At dawn on Saturday 20 December, Condon hitched a ride on the Bren gun carrier back to WG Bn HQ at Wan Chai Gap. He wanted to report directly to Sutcliffe on the situation at the gap, and he hoped to obtain rations for the troops, and morphine and medical assistance for the many wounded. He was astounded by the lack of urgency at Wan Chai Gap.

The CO had not previously had a single report of this action. He instructed me to bring all the Canadians back for a rest, he did not agree that they could get rest where they were while remaining in a position to support the Scots if needed. My request for medical assistance could apparently not be complied with, nor could I be provided with morphine. Laying a telephone wire was for some reason not considered feasible. At the cookhouse, the NCO in charge refused to issue rations until I threatened him.[9]

The Royal Scots and Winnipeg Grenadiers incurred a large number of casualties during the counterattacks that took place on Friday 19 December. Lt-Col Sutcliffe had insufficient troops at Wan Chai Gap to make further counterattacks and therefore decided to move 'B' Coy, WG, from Pok Fu Lam Reservoir to Wan Chai Gap to participate in a further counterattack along Black's Link. Sgt Ken Porter, 'B' Coy, WG, recalls their deployment during the morning of Saturday 20 December.

Left Pok Fu Lam around 1030 hours, had 150 rounds SAA, 100 rounds in pouches and 50 rounds in a bandolier plus two Mills bombs. ... Arrived at Battalion HQ at Wan Chai Gap around 1330 hours.[10]

At around 1730 hours, 'B' Coy proceeded in single file to Middle Gap by way of Black's Link. Major Hook, the company commander, was leading, followed by CSM Fryatt and Sgt Porter. At Middle Gap, Major Hook deployed No. 11 Platoon, commanded by Lt Hooper, with the 3-inch mortar detachment around the north side of Mount Nicholson. No. 10 Platoon, commanded by Lt MacKechnie, and part of No. 12 Platoon, commanded by Lt Young, together with Coy HQ, continued along Black's Link. The plan was that once the company reached the forming-up point on Black's Link, they would remain there during the night with the attack due to commence at dawn on Sunday 21 December.

During the evening, while 'B' Coy, WG, was moving to their start line, they were attacked by a Japanese patrol. The Japanese were driven off by machine gun fire, but most of the company had by then fallen back to Middle Gap. It rained heavily during the night, and the troops were wet and cold by dawn. At first light, the company continued along Black's Link towards WNC Gap. Sgt Woods, armed with a Tommy gun, was acting as point. He was shot and killed by Japanese troops manning a dugout at a junction of paths on the brow of a rise near the main path leading up to Mount Nicholson. The Japanese had by this time mined the track to prevent further use of the Bren gun carrier. The Grenadiers returned fire using a 2-inch mortar. This was followed by an infantry assault from both the left flank, above the track, and from the right flank, below the track. The Japanese were dispersed, withdrawing up the slopes of Mount Nicholson. They then started to infiltrate behind the Grenadiers, who were coming under increasing fire from the hillside on their left. The Canadian troops lined the bank, and with the hillside providing some protection, they returned fire uphill. Some Japanese troops managed to work their way behind the Canadian troops and opened fire with a machine gun, killing both Lt Hugh Young and CSM Walter Fryatt.

No. 11 Platoon which had been sent up Nicholson had also run into Japanese troops and had been heavily engaged. The attack stalled and both the flank party on Nicholson and the road party on Black's Link sustained heavy casualties. All the officers had been either killed or wounded, and out of the ninety-eight men involved in the initial counterattack, twenty-nine were casualties. The Grenadiers withdrew to Middle Gap to regroup but found themselves under artillery and mortar fire. The attack was called off, and the company withdrew to Wan Chai Gap. This was the last counterattack made by West Brigade troops. The Japanese retained WNC Gap and had full possession of Mount Nicholson. Their next target was Mount Cameron, which would open the way to Wan Chai Gap.

Maltby had ordered a series of counterattacks throughout Friday and Saturday in a desperate effort to recapture WNC Gap. These counterattacks were put in courageously, but they were not well coordinated. Some of the counterattacks were made in broad daylight with inadequate mortar and artillery support. All the counterattacks were made on well-defended and strongly entrenched positions. The Japanese, with four infantry battalions concentrated in the vicinity of WNC Gap, could not be dislodged. The strategy now turned from attack to defence. It was now just a matter of holding out for as long as possible.

12

East Brigade Strikes Back
20 to 21 December

On Friday 19 December, Wallis issued a warning order at 2200 hours from his newly established Brigade HQ at Stone Hill, providing details of the counterattack which was to commence at 0730 hours on Saturday 20 December. The start line would be Stanley View, located at the junction of Island Road and Chung Hom Kok Road. The counterattack would follow two routes. The main advance would take place along Island Road to Repulse Bay, then up Repulse Bay Road to WNC Gap. A separate advance would be made, by one infantry company, from Repulse Bay, through Repulse Bay View, and then along the water catchment to Gauge Basin and from there to WNC Gap. The plan was that these two prongs would meet at WNC Gap from the south and from the east. It was a battalion-level infantry attack involving the Royal Rifles of Canada, No. 2 Coy HKVDC and units from 1/Mx.

Wallis left the overall command of the attack to Lt-Col Home commanding the Royal Rifles of Canada since the attacking force was mainly made up by his battalion. Wallis decided to go with the troops to give what support he could from the front. Wallis, under pressure from Fortress HQ, had wanted a start time at 0500 hours, but Home said the earliest he could commence the counterattack was 0800 hours because his infantry companies were widely dispersed in new positions on the line of hills around Stanley.

The Advance Guard passed through Stanley View, on time at 0800 hours, and proceeded down the road towards Repulse Bay. Wallis had expected to drive straight through Repulse Bay and was unaware that the Japanese were already there. During the night two Japanese infantry battalions, commanded by Colonel Tanaka, had occupied Middle Spur and Violet Hill, both of which overlooked Repulse Bay. Just before dawn, Japanese troops had proceeded downhill from

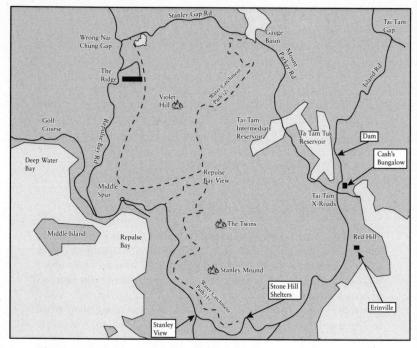

The vicinity of the East Brigade counterattacks.

Middle Spur and seized the roadblock at the intersection of Island Road and Repulse Bay Road. A Japanese platoon had occupied the Repulse Bay Hotel garage block and was exchanging fire with British troops at the hotel. With their arrival in Repulse Bay, the Japanese had established a continuous line extending from the north shore, through Sanatorium Gap, down to Gauge Basin, along Stanley Gap Road to WNC Gap, and along the water catchment to Middle Spur, and then down to the junction of Repulse Bay Road and Island Road. This had split the Island defence in two and placed the Japanese between West Brigade and East Brigade.

The Advance Guard consisted primarily of 'A' Coy, RRC. The main body that followed consisted of Advanced Brigade HQ, a signals detachment, 'HQ' Coy of RRC, and two 1/Mx machine gun platoons drawn from 'B' and 'D' Coy, 1/Mx. On the right flank of the advance, 'B' Coy, RRC, was positioned on Stanley Mound, while No. 2 Coy, HKVDC, was to provide additional support on the right flank at a lower level by following the water catchment from Stanley View towards Repulse Bay View. Artillery support was limited due to the loss of most of East Group's howitzers the previous day. There was one 18-pdr field gun, commanded by 2/Lt Phillips, 965 Defence Battery, RA. The gun, which was positioned at Stanley View, could fire a 3.3-inch calibre 18-pound shell up to 3.5 miles. The 18-pdrs and 2-pdrs of 965 Defence Battery were initially deployed to beach defence. There were two 3.7-inch howitzers at Stanley which could support the first part of the advance. The two howitzers would utilise the AOP on Stanley Mound. One of the guns was the howitzer brought back from Tai Tam Fork Section, and the other had been put together from spare parts in Stanley.

Lt-Col Home established his Advance HQ in a house, which Wallis described as belonging to Lt-Col Frederick, RASC, at a grid reference which on wartime maps would place it on the eastern side of Repulse Bay. The advance stalled at Repulse Bay because of the presence of Japanese troops at the hotel garage block, and the presence of Japanese machine gun and mortar positions on the hillside known as Middle Spur. The hotel garage block was a long building opposite the West Wing of the hotel. It still exists today, but it is now used as a Ferrari showroom. Home asked for artillery support to clear the garage block, which was under small arms fire from troops and naval personnel at the hotel. Brigadier Wallis described how he went back to Stanley View by motorbike to arrange the artillery support.

> The brigade commander doubted whether it was wise to fire on this building as battalion communications were so slow that the garage might well change hands before firing could be brought down. The battalion commander still pressed for artillery support, accordingly, the brigade commander went back to Stanley View on the pillion of a 1/Mx motorcycle and moved the 18-pdr under 2/Lt Phillips to a road bend from which effective fire was opened on the garage, only to be called off, as its capture by 'D' Battalion was reported. The road from Stanley View towards Repulse Bay was now under steady machine gun and occasional mortar fire. The brigade commander returned and directed the battalion commander to attack and capture Middle Spur and at the same time to push a second company through Repulse Bay View.[1]

The attack through Repulse Bay View was to be led by 'D' Coy, RRC, commanded by Major Maurice Parker. 'D' Coy had spent an uncomfortable night on top of Stanley Mound. It had rained during the night, and there were no concrete shelters on the hilltop, just shallow weapons pits and trenches. Major Parker utilised the nearby AOP with its telephone exchange as his Coy HQ. Early the next morning, his company was ordered down to Stanley View to participate in the counterattack.

At 0800 hours, I was ordered to bring my officers forward to meet Lt-Col Home. We went to the bend in the road near Repulse Bay Hotel. RRC Battalion HQ was strung out along the road near this bend. Brigadier Wallis, Lt-Col Home and I went forward to make a reconnaissance with the object in mind of putting 'D' Coy through with 'A' Coy to Wong Nai Chung Gap. … Whilst making our reconnaissance, enemy troops holding Repulse Bay Hotel garage and vicinity opened up with machine gun fire making reconnaissance impossible. A decision was reached to have my company try to contact West Infantry Brigade at Wong Nai Chung Gap by going there via Violet Hill. This country was entirely unknown to any of us. Brigadier Wallis's information about enemy strength was negligible. A map route was decided upon, and at 1100 hours the Coy moved forward. A section of mortars under Lt Ross and Lt Languedoc were attached to my command.[2]

Major Parker and his platoon commanders returned to their company positions near Stanley View. Major John Price, 'HQ' Coy, and Flight-Lt Fred Thompson, Brigade Intelligence Officer, were ordered to accompany Major Parker during the counterattack. The company clambered up the hillside to reach the water catchment that runs from the base of Stanley Mound to Repulse Bay View. They walked inside the catchment, which provided some protection and concealment. Parker described their route along the first water catchment leading to Repulse Bay View as being approximately a mile. At Repulse Bay View, shown on current maps as Tsin Shui Wan Au, literally meaning Repulse Bay Gap, there is a junction of paths. One leads up to Violet Hill, one leads very steeply up to the Twins, and one leads downhill to Tai Tam Tuk Reservoir. At this junction of paths, 'D' Coy would have left the water catchment and taken the uphill path leading towards Violet Hill. This required them to cross an open area, which Parker described as 200 to 300 metres, running between the two water catchments. This path led to another intersection of paths. One path continued straight up the hillside to the summit of Violet Hill, the path to the left led towards Middle Spur and WNC Gap. The path on the right led towards Gauge Basin. They followed this path, beside a shallow water catchment, that took them around Violet Hill in an anti-clockwise direction towards the reservoirs at Gauge Basin. Concealment was provided by the hillside to their left.

They passed two splinter-proof shelters at Repulse Bay View which Parker thought showed signs of a hurried departure. The concrete war shelters remain today, although now largely hidden by the undergrowth. One is situated at the lower junction of paths, and the other one is closer to the upper junction of paths. These shelters had initially been occupied by a platoon from the Winnipeg Grenadiers. They were later replaced by 2/Lt Redman's platoon from No. 1 Coy, HKVDC. Redman had withdrawn his platoon to Stanley the previous evening, but before withdrawing he had observed Japanese troops already on top of Violet Hill, which posed a threat to his position, and no doubt explained the look of hurried departure. 'D' Coy continued along the second water catchment in a north-east direction until they came out at Gauge Basin. The path took them past the Tai Tam Bungalow, which until the previous day had been used by Captain Penn, HKVDC, as his Coy HQ. The ruins of this building still remain today, and interestingly a 1941-type field telephone exchange was found on the slopes below the bungalow and was most likely the one that Penn destroyed before he withdrew to Stanley.

While 'D' Coy was advancing along the two catchments, Captain Penn had been ordered to stand by and await further orders at Brigade HQ at Stone Hill. His company at that stage consisted of Coy HQ, the remnants of No. 1 Platoon under 2/Lt Carter, and No. 2 Platoon under 2/Lt Redman. The Bren gun carrier platoon was operating under brigade orders and was located close to the Tai Tam X-Roads. At around midday, while Wallis was still pinned down at Repulse Bay, he received a telephone call from Lt-Col Willcocks at Stanley advising that Royal Artillery OPs had reported a large group of Japanese troops, numbering around three hundred, and a mobile battery, proceeding south from Tai Tam Gap towards the Tai Tam Tuk Reservoir. It was thought that this enemy force might be launching an attack on Stanley. Wallis ordered Penn to occupy a position across Island Road at Palm Villa to defend the approaches to Stanley, and to destroy the battery should it approach. Penn deployed his company in the gardens at Palm Villa on his right, and on the hillside across the road to the left. Palm Villa was a large house situated on Island Road, between Stanley and Red Hill. It was located where the tennis courts of the present-day American Club are now situated. At that time, it was the home of Lo Man-kam, a prominent lawyer and LEGCO member. 'C' Coy, RRC, commanded by Major Bishop, was also redeployed during the day from Stanley View to Palm Villa to help protect the right flank of the Stanley Perimeter. The RRC war diary describes an exchange of fire with the Japanese mobile battery as it approached the reservoir and dam.

> A patrol under Major Bishop with 2/Lt Edwards [commanding the HKVDC Bren gun carrier platoon] on a motorcycle and two carriers engaged enemy at Tai Tam Reservoir. Tracks show that a horse-drawn battery had gone along the road towards Wong Nai Chung.[3]

The Bren gun carriers had engaged the mobile battery as it approached the Tai Tam Tuk Reservoir. The battery then returned fire, and shelled a private residence known as Cash's Bungalow, having assumed the gunfire was coming from that location. Cash's Bungalow was a large villa situated on a mound just north of the Tai Tam X-Roads. The Bren gun carriers withdrew following the bombardment of the area around the X-Roads and were unable to prevent the horse-drawn battery from crossing the dam and reaching the X-Roads, where they turned right towards Gauge Basin. The battery then deployed near the track leading to Stanley Gap Road. At that location, they were right in the path of Major Parker's 'D' Coy advancing from Repulse Bay View. Lt Simons, commanding No. 18 Platoon, was in point position when they came across the Japanese battery, which by then was already in action. Lt Simons and Platoon Sgt MacDonell deployed their platoon along the shallow water catchment, and just as the platoon opened fire a Japanese staff car containing senior officers drew up at the battery. The Canadian troops caught the Japanese by surprise, causing considerable damage to the battery and a large number of casualties.

No. 17 Platoon, commanded by Lt Power, had been sent up a higher path, and they spotted Japanese troops at or around the abandoned 3.7-inch howitzer battery at Gauge Basin. They engaged the Japanese with a Bren gun. The Japanese replied with 75mm mountain guns. The two Canadian platoons then withdrew under fire, returning to the main body. Parker realised his company was in a precarious position, low on ammunition, out of communication with Battalion HQ, and with the enemy in strength at Gauge Basin and above them on Violet Hill. He ordered a withdrawal back to Stanley View. As the company withdrew, they came under increasing fire from Japanese troops on Violet Hill. The steep hillside to their right offered some protection until they reached the point where they had to cross the open area between the two water catchments. No. 18 Platoon went across first and set up a machine gun in the 6-foot-deep lower catchment to cover the rest of the company's withdrawal.

The company arrived back at Stanley View after nightfall and in heavy rain. The Japanese forces were far too strong on Violet Hill and at Gauge Basin for one infantry company without artillery to have any chance of getting through to WNC Gap. The mortar platoon which had been attached to 'D' Coy jettisoned their 3-inch mortar and ammunition during the withdrawal. This was unfortunate given the shortage of 3-inch mortars and mortar bombs. Perhaps one day a metal detector may discover the rusted remains of the mortar on the hillside below the water catchment, and perhaps the twenty-four mortar bombs that were also discarded. As for 'D' Coy, they had at least struck back, destroying a battery and inflicting heavy casualties on the enemy.

After having dispatched 'D' Coy to work their way, in an anti-clockwise direction, around Violet Hill, Wallis ordered an attack by units of 1/Mx in a clockwise direction around the same hill feature towards Middle Spur and WNC Gap. A platoon, under the command of Lt Witham, was despatched from 1/Mx Detachment HQ at Stanley. On arrival in the Repulse Bay area, this unit was split into two sections, one under Lt Falconar, and the other under 2/Lt Witham. Their orders were to advance towards Middle Spur supported by covering fire provided by machine guns from No. 2 Coy, HKVDC. However, by this time Tanaka had two battalions deployed at Middle Spur and on Violet Hill. As the two Middlesex sections got closer to Middle Spur, they came under intense fire from Japanese machine gun positions on Violet Hill. The start line for this attack was on the east side of Repulse Bay, where an uphill trail intersects with Violet Hill Path. On the path leading down from the summit of Violet Hill towards Middle Spur, a large number of spent Japanese 7.7mm machine gun rounds were found in a position from which it would have been possible to fire on anyone approaching Middle Spur from the east along Violet Hill Path. Lt Falconar and three ORs were killed, and a number of casualties incurred. The attack faltered, was broken off, and both sections were withdrawn. There was no chance of success, it was two sections against two battalions.

Once the hotel garage had been recaptured, 'A' Coy, WG, continued the advance along Island Road through Repulse Bay towards the road junction with Repulse Bay Road. However, the advance stalled again because of heavy machine gun fire from Japanese positions on the hillside around Middle Spur. A large number of casualties were incurred as Canadian troops worked their way towards the western side of Repulse Bay. Some of the troops took cover at the hotel and at Eucliffe, others on the right-hand side of the road under the hillside. With the advance faltering, some troops were sent along the shoreline, but they were also unable to progress further and could not get through the road junction. The 9.2-inch and 6-inch coastal defence guns at Stanley could not be brought to bear, and likewise, the 3.7-inch howitzers at Stanley were unable to fire on the Repulse Bay area. 2/Lt Phillips, in command of the 18-pdr positioned at Stanley View, knocked out several Japanese mortar positions on the hillside beside the hotel, earning praise – not lightly given – from Brigadier Wallis.

> Enemy mortars entrenched on Violet Hill were engaged over open sights by 2/Lt Phillips who handled his gun well. He was only able to fire from an exposed position on the road where he was himself under fire. He put four mortars out of action and inflicted heavy casualties.[4]

By late afternoon no progress had been made. 'A' Coy was pinned down at Repulse Bay, and 'D' Coy was out of touch. There were indications that

Japanese troops were working their way towards the Twins and Stanley Mound, which if achieved would have threatened the road link between Repulse Bay and Stanley. In the late afternoon orders were issued from Fortress HQ to East Brigade to 'hold what you have, including Repulse Bay Hotel, and do what you can to get through via Gauge Basin'. 'A' Coy was ordered to remain at Repulse Bay to augment the small garrison in the hotel. The attack was withdrawn. Little had been achieved other than positioning 'A' Coy at Repulse Bay Hotel, in a very exposed position with the Japanese on the high ground around the hotel. A Japanese battery had been destroyed by 'D' Coy, but other than that the counterattack had failed to achieve anything significant. It rained heavily during the evening on Saturday 20 December, and the troops that had been involved in the counterattack were soaked and exhausted. There was little respite; orders were issued for an eastward counterattack to commence early the next morning.

The counterattack that commenced on Sunday 21 December was a second attempt by East Brigade to link up with West Brigade, but this time by going through Gauge Basin, where it was thought there may be less resistance. The first objective was to seize the Tai Tam X-Roads. Once that was achieved, the column would turn left at the X-Roads, and drive along the side of Tai Tam Tuk Reservoir, and up to Gauge Basin. At Gauge Basin, they would turn left on a dirt track that led to the metal road section of Stanley Gap Road. They would follow Stanley Gap Road to WNC Gap, the second objective, and join hands with West Brigade.

An orders group was called at 0700 hours at Brigade HQ at Stone Hill shelters. The meeting included the RRC Coy Commanders ('B', 'C', 'D' and 'HQ' Coy) and the commanders of HKVDC, No. 1 Coy (Captain Penn) and No. 2 Coy (Major Forsyth). At the orders meeting, Penn suggested that a company should be sent up from Palm Villa to occupy the ridgeline from Notting Hill to Bridge Hill to protect the left flank of the advance along Island Road towards the X-Roads. An objection was raised due to the difficult nature of the country, consisting of steep hillsides covered by thick but low vegetation. The proposal was adopted, although it was decided that the flank party would be in platoon strength rather than company strength. The Advance Guard was commanded by Major Macaulay, commanding officer of 'HQ' Coy, RRC. The Advance Guard consisted of No. 1 Coy, HKVDC, the Bren gun carrier platoon, and platoons drawn from 'HQ' Coy and 'B' Coy, RRC, and a 3-inch mortar detachment. The main body, following the Advance Guard, consisted of RRC Bn HQ, Advanced Brigade HQ, No. 2 Coy HKVDC, 'D' and 'C' Coy, RRC, and a 3-inch mortar detachment. The start point was Palm Villa.

The Royal Artillery was ordered to be on standby to provide fire support in the vicinity of Red Hill and Bridge Hill. The signals section was instructed to run out a field cable behind Brigade and Battalion HQ to ensure effective communications were maintained. Wallis assigned Major Templer, RA, Captain Bompas, HKSRA, and Flight-Lt Thompson, RAF, to the Advance Guard to provide additional support for Major Macaulay under whose command they would be operating. At approximately 0930 hours the Bren gun carriers departed from Palm Villa. They were closely followed by a platoon from 'HQ' Coy, RRC, with one section proceeding along the water catchment on the left flank which was above and parallel to the road. No. 1 Coy, HKVDC, formed the rear of the Advance Guard. However, Japanese troops had occupied the Tai Tam X-Roads and the high ground on both flanks, consisting of the Notting Hill–Bridge Hill ridgeline on the left, and Red Hill on the right.

The Flank Guard was made up of a platoon of RRC under the command of Captain Clarke. 2/Lt Carter, HKVDC, who knew the surrounding countryside, was chosen to act as guide for the Canadians. Carter took with him ten riflemen from No. 1 Coy, HKVDC.

> We proceeded with Captain Clarke's party until about halfway up, when as my party was making better time and the remainder of the path was obvious, it was decided that my ten men would push on making for the Notting Hill shoulder of Bridge Hill. We pressed on and made the crest shortly afterwards, arriving there probably about 1000 hours. No opposition was met on the way up except sniping fire as we neared the crest, but on reaching the top, we came under rather heavier fire which we located after some time as coming from the rear crest of Bridge Hill to our half left. ... Below us, to our right, we could see that our main body was held up at Red Hill and enemy positions were observed on Red Hill itself and these we subsequently saw reinforced from the direction of the Tai Tam X-Roads. We endeavoured to harass this enemy position with rifle fire at about eight hundred yards, but we badly missed light automatics, the Canadians not yet having put in an appearance. Captain Clarke with a small number of his party eventually arrived behind a small knoll short of and rather below Bridge Hill, but it was some two hours after we had arrived before Captain Clarke's main party arrived with the Bren guns. They were shortly afterwards reinforced by a still larger party under Major Parker.[5]

On Notting Hill, at the location described by Carter, a large number of British rifle-fired spent .303 casings were found in a position to fire at the crest of Bridge Hill, and down to Red Hill. These were the rounds fired by 2/Lt Carter's section. In a nearby saddle, two screw-on caps for

2-inch mortar bombs were found. This evidenced the position of the 2-inch mortar which was brought up by Captain Clarke's platoon in the late afternoon. The 2-inch mortar is referred to in No. 1 Coy war diary as being used to bomb Red Hill, but the diary states that only six mortar bombs were carried up the hill, which was insufficient to deal with the Japanese forces on Red Hill, and they were soon out of ammunition. Bridge Hill was cleared of Japanese by 1400 hours and once the crest was cleared Lt Bryden, No. 2 Coy, HKVDC, positioned his MMG section on the summit. These two hills and the ridge between them are still littered with hundreds of spent rounds, Japanese, Canadian and British, evidencing the scale of the battle to secure these hilltops on the left flank of the advance.

As the Advance Guard approached the driveway to Erinville, the villa owned by Benny Proulx's parents-in-law, located at Turtle Cove, the Bren gun carriers came under fire from Red Hill on the right flank. The carriers ground to a halt, one of the crew from the leading carrier was killed, and the troops that were following the carriers took cover. The Japanese fire was coming from the abandoned 4.5-inch howitzer position on Red Hill, and from Cash's Bungalow at the Tai Tam X-Roads. The bungalow had been the home of Albert Cash, an inspector with the Public Works Department from 1938 to 1940. A Japanese machine gun position had been established at the bungalow and was used to fire at Canadian troops going up Notting Hill and Bridge Hill. The mound today is very overgrown, but the ruins of the bungalow and its garden wall can still be seen. In a location by the low garden wall, dozens of spent Japanese machine gun rounds were found. The garden wall provided cover, and from this position one could see that the machine gun positioned there could be fired at the approaches to the Tai Tam X-Roads and on the hills on the left flank of the brigade advance.

Several casualties were incurred near the driveway to Erinville. These included Flight Lt Thompson, an RAF Volunteer Reserve officer who had been posted to Hong Kong as adjutant of the RAF station at Kai Tak. He was severely wounded in the neck while riding in one of the Bren gun carriers. He was taken to St Stephen's College Hospital at Stanley, where he was injured again when the hospital was hit by mortar fire. He survived the infamous events of Christmas Day 1941 there, and after the capitulation he was transferred to Bowen Road Military Hospital where he remained for three years before eventually making a full recovery.

After the carriers came under fire, the infantry deployed a fighting patrol under Captain Bompas, HKSRA, and Lt Fry, RRC, to try and secure the hills on the right flank. The patrol deployed down the hillside towards Erinville, and then passing to the left of the villa, proceeded uphill to clear enemy troops from the crest of Red Hill. Penn deployed his machine gun sections in a position to provide covering fire for the troops moving up Red Hill. He positioned one machine gun at what he described as the 'new house'. The new house was situated further back towards Stanley on the cliff edge and out of range of the X-Roads. It was here that Lt-Col Home had established his Bn HQ. Macaulay and the Advance Guard were positioned further up the road near the driveway leading to Erinville. Penn deployed his remaining two LMG sections with the Advance Guard and volunteered to take these two LMG sections up the path to Red Hill to secure a position where they could lay down effective fire on Cash's Bungalow and the X-Roads.

> We opened up on Cash's Bungalow with a few bursts, which appeared to cause a certain amount of commotion in that vicinity and shortly afterwards an enemy party was observed apparently coming from Cash's Bungalow, running down the path from the X-Roads towards the pumping station. We were able to engage this target before they disappeared, I think with effect, and we continued to maintain bursts of fire on the X-Roads.[6]

The abandoned Red Hill 4.5-inch howitzer position was some 150 metres from Penn's LMG position. Penn's group suspected that there were still Japanese concealed in the splinter-proof shelters at the howitzer position. Seven men were detailed to go forward and investigate, but as they drew near, they were fired on from the crest of Red Hill on their right rear. They withdrew back to the LMG position. The Japanese on the crest of the hill edged forward and were able to bring fire down on Penn's party while remaining mostly out of view. Penn's section then came under fire from Japanese troops hidden in the concrete shelters at the howitzer position. As a result of being fired on from the front and the right flank, they started to take casualties. Sgt Stephens was killed, 2/Lt Redman was shot in the groin, and Captain Penn was shot in the face. They withdrew back to the main road and took up firing positions at the roadside facing Red Hill.

Fry and Bompas had both been killed as they neared the top of Red Hill. Captain Penn was evacuated to St Stephen's College Hospital. The injury turned out to be less severe than it may have looked – a bullet had entered one cheek and exited through the other without hitting any of his teeth. He discharged himself to re-join his company on 24 December. 2/Lt Edwards, commanding the carrier platoon, took command of No. 1 Coy, until later in the day when a replacement machine gun officer, Lt Blackaby, 'D' Coy, 1/Mx, was sent out from Stanley.

At around 1300 hours, fire from both the flanks died down, and Major Macaulay ordered the Advance Guard to press forward to the X-Roads.

As the leading carrier approached and came in sight of the X-Roads, they saw a group of Japanese officers looking at a map which they had spread out in the middle of the road. The carrier opened fire, but then came under fire from a machine gun positioned at the X-Roads. The carrier withdrew, and a halt was called while the 3-inch mortars were brought forward by truck. Lt Ross then proceeded to lay down a barrage of mortar fire on Cash's Bungalow and the vicinity of the X-Roads. After the mortar barrage, the Bren gun carriers, and the troops forming the Advance Guard, consisting of around thirty from RRC and HKVDC, rushed the X-Roads.

Japanese troops on the lower slopes of Bridge Hill, on the left-hand side of the road, lobbed grenades and fired down on the carriers and their supporting infantry. 2/Lt Edwards then ordered the carriers to withdraw a short distance, and went forward with a section of infantry and succeeded in dispersing the Japanese from the X-Roads. At this point, Cpl Houghton, No. 1 Coy, HKVDC, who in civilian life had been an employee of the Chartered Bank, was shot in the head and died from his wounds. 2/Lt Edwards went to assist Houghton and tried to drag him clear of the road. However, in doing so, he was shot and killed. Macaulay had also been wounded, suffering a compound fracture to one arm. The Advance Guard withdrew to a less exposed position, but one that still commanded the X-Roads. Although they had reached and briefly held the X-Roads, the Japanese were still on Red Hill, and on the lower slopes of Bridge Hill. In order to reinforce the X-Roads, the Japanese sent three light tanks forward from Tai Tam Gap. They were observed coming down the road towards the dam. The light tanks were fired on by Lt Bryden's MMG position on the crest of Bridge Hill, and by the Advance Guard from their position close to the X-Roads. The light tanks withdrew after an exchange of fire. By late afternoon it was clear that the counterattack was faltering. There was now a shortage of officers, there were insufficient troops, the 3-inch mortars were out of ammunition, and the Bren gun carriers were called away to Repulse Bay to mount a second counterattack westwards through Repulse Bay. The attack on the X-Roads had run out of steam, and Wallis reluctantly called off the attack and gave the order to withdraw back towards Stanley.

During the afternoon, Wallis had briefed Maltby on the situation at Red Hill and the X-Roads. He reported that it was unlikely that his force would be able to get through Gauge Basin and reach WNC Gap that day. The GOC then gave orders that all available men, and the Bren gun carriers, were to proceed to Repulse Bay, and from there to try and break through to WNC Gap by way of Repulse Bay Road. The GOC stated that he considered this as being very important and urgent. Maltby took the decision to withdraw the Bren gun carrier platoon from an ongoing counterattack, realising that Wallis would not break through that way within the day. He wanted to coordinate a counterattack that had been launched by 'B' Coy, WG, that was proceeding along Black's Link, with an attack by East Brigade from the south. Wallis ordered Major Templer to take command of this third counterattack by East Brigade. Templer's orders were to reorganise the defences at Repulse Bay Hotel, and then proceed up Repulse Bay Road and retake WNC Gap. At 1530 hours, Templer left Palm Villa heading for Repulse Bay with two HKVDC carriers, commanded by Sgt Lemay. He was accompanied by some thirty to forty troops which had been assembled from 'HQ' Coy, RRC, and from HKVDC personnel at Palm Villa.

In anticipation of the counterattack, Major Young, commanding 'A' Coy, RRC, at Repulse Bay Hotel, was ordered to send a fighting patrol up Repulse Bay Road to The Ridge, and to clear the road of enemy troops, and then to remain at The Ridge until further orders. Somewhat surprisingly, given the number of Japanese troops on the hillside around Middle Spur, this small force consisting of two platoons from 'A' Coy was able to pass through the road junction and proceed up Repulse Bay Road to Altamira and The Ridge. Templer arrived at Repulse Bay Hotel at approximately 1700 hours. He reorganised the defences at the hotel, and then immediately set off in a car with the two lorries and the two Bren gun carriers. Shortly after leaving the hotel, Templer's car was hit by a burst of machine gun fire from Middle Spur. The car was disabled, and Templer boarded one of the lorries. In this exchange of fire one carrier was put out of action, and the other ditched while trying to turn. The loss of the two carriers was a major setback which would make the counterattack all the more difficult.

Templer's force also went unimpeded through the road junction that had proved so dangerous the previous day. They drove past the entrance to The Ridge and reached the gap. Templer established his HQ on the road just south of the gap and organised his force into two platoons, each consisting of thirty to forty men. One of the platoons was equipped with two Bren guns and was ordered to take up a position on the high ground above Postbridge near the reservoir and in a position to be able to provide covering fire for the attacking platoon. The attacking platoon, under the command of Major Young, was to attack the police station knoll from the direction of Postbridge. The attack was to start when the LMGs opened fire. The attack never materialised because after about twenty minutes the first platoon reported that both their LMGs had jammed. Without the covering fire from the Bren guns, and with darkness closing in, Templer realised there was little chance of success against the well-entrenched Japanese positions. The attack was called off, and 'A' Coy took up positions in Altamira and at House No. 5 at

The Ridge. Templer got hold of an abandoned bicycle and cycled back to Repulse Bay Hotel, once again managing to pass through the road junction without being shot.

Despite every effort, the counterattacks put in by East Brigade had failed to achieve the objective of recapturing WNC Gap and linking up with West Brigade. They had incurred further depletion of men and equipment, and nothing significant had been gained. The troops were exhausted from having been in continual action, and Brigadier Wallis was running out of options. The next day, Monday 22 December, he would deploy the Canadian troops from 'A' Coy, and the assorted troops under Lt-Col Frederick at The Ridge, to try and recapture the road junction and to intercept the main Japanese supply route along the water catchment running from WNC Gap to Middle Spur. If these two objectives were achieved, a further counterattack could be made on WNC Gap.

13

Escape from The Ridge
19 to 22 December

The feature known as The Ridge is a spur jutting out from the western slopes of Violet Hill. It is located a kilometre down Repulse Bay Road to the south of WNC Gap. In 1941, there were five houses on The Ridge. If you looked north from The Ridge, towards WNC Gap, you could see the knoll with the small stone-built police station on its crest. In front of it, you could see two large white villas, one being Postbridge and the other, just across the road, being Holmesdale. At the top of the track leading from Shouson Hill to WNC Gap, now known as Deep Water Bay Road, there was another large villa known as Lynx Hall, or simply as Danby's House. Immediately west of The Ridge, and across Repulse Bay Road, was the Spanish-style villa known as Altamira.

Further down Repulse Bay Road were other villas like Twin Brook, Monte Verde, and Overbays. Most of these villas have long gone, but a few survive like Altamira and Holmesdale. High-rise apartment blocks were built on the sites of many of these former villas, and some still bear the name of the original villa. To the east of The Ridge was the steep hillside of Violet Hill, and on the hillside, some 30 metres above The Ridge, there was a water catchment running from the direction of Repulse Bay to WNC Gap Reservoir. The path which runs beside the water catchment is marked on maps as Tsz Lo Lan Shan Path, which translates as Violet Hill Path.

The five private houses on The Ridge had been commandeered by the Army and were being used by the Royal Army Ordnance Corps (RAOC) as a depot for stores and equipment. During the first week of the war, the RAOC stores and workshops in Queen's Road were moved to less exposed locations at The Ridge and Shouson Hill. This was done in accordance with pre-arranged war plans and was supervised by forty-year-old Captain Victor Ebbage, RAOC. During the first week,

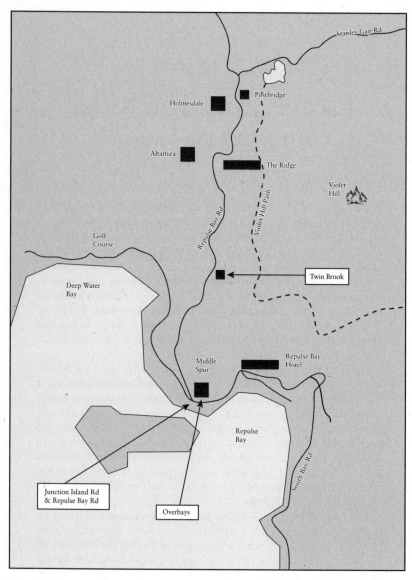

Repulse Bay Road.

it had been relatively quiet at The Ridge until 13 December when a bomb landed just below House No. 5, causing light damage and knocking out window panes. On 14 December, Lt-Col Robert McPherson, RAOC, moved to The Ridge, and as senior officer assumed command of the depot from Captain Ebbage. After the Japanese landings, Postbridge, Holmesdale, Altamira and The Ridge all found themselves on the front line.

To the south, The Ridge overlooked the golf course in the valley below, and beyond the golf course was the broad expanse of Deep Water Bay. The golf course and the clubhouse were used by the Royal Army Service Corps (RASC) as a depot. Forty-eight-year-old Lt-Col Ernest Frederick, RASC, was commanding officer of the RASC Depot at Deep Water Bay (DWB) and the RASC workshops at Shouson Hill. During the morning on Friday 19 December, the depot was being hit by over-shots from the battle raging at WNC Gap. Lt-Col Frederick was ordered to relocate the RASC personnel to the Dairy Farm in Pok Fu Lam, and there to await further orders. Shortly after the RASC had left the depot, Captain Potts, HKVDC, attached to the RASC, arrived at the depot in the Studebaker car in which he and his companions had escaped from the Lye Mun Magazines earlier that morning. In his diary, he described the clubhouse as being full of tinned provisions, while other stores were stacked in piles around the golf course. They helped themselves to some of the tinned rations and freshly baked bread. While there, they heard the sound of gunfire from WNC Gap and decided to drive up there to see what was happening.

> We proceeded up Repulse Bay Road till we reached a corner just short of the gap where a lorry driver stopped us and advised us not to proceed any further as the Japanese had already got possession of the police station and we should be under fire. There is a ridge slightly further down the road, which commands a clear view of the gap; on this ridge Eu Tong-sen, a multi-millionaire from Singapore where he had made his money in tin mines had built five houses. ... These five houses stand some fifty feet above the road and are reached by an approach road. The first house is a smallish one, then come two large semi-detached houses next to a large house and finally a smaller single house. There is a good deal of space between the houses in the shape of tennis courts and gardens.[1]

On The Ridge, House No. 1, nearest to the hillside, was used as RAOC HQ. Houses 2, 3 and 4 were used for stores and equipment and House No. 5, which was the house nearest to Repulse Bay Road and to Altamira, was used as accommodation for ORs. The tennis courts were used to stack stores. Potts was surprised to find that no one at The Ridge was firing at the Japanese who could be clearly seen at the gap.

> On our arrival, I noticed there were a few men lying down with rifles behind the stone parapet of the approach road leading past the houses, but no one was firing. Looking across to WNC Gap I could see the police station was in the hands of the Japanese and that they were engaged in attacking Tinson's house, a beautiful home belonging to a solicitor who was a great friend of mine. ... The Japanese were also attacking the pillbox [PB 3] at the foot of the bridle pass [Black's Link] leading from the gap up Mount Nicholson. ... The police station, Tinson's house, and the pillbox were all approximately the same range (about 1,000 yards), so I was surprised that no effort was being made to assist them.[2]

The semi-detached houses were full of stores. Captain Potts and Sgt Gow took out two Lewis guns, cleaned them up, got some troops to help load up the drums and started firing away at the Japanese around WNC Gap. After a short period of time, one of the Ordnance officers from the depot came along and ordered them to stop firing, on the basis that there were British and Canadian troops near the gap, and there was a risk of hitting these positions. He added that Potts had no authority to open fire from The Ridge without the permission of Lt-Col Macpherson, his commanding officer. Potts then left The Ridge and joined up with the rest of the RASC at Sassoon Road near the Dairy Farm.

At approximately 1300 hours, Lt-Col Frederick was ordered to take the RASC contingent from the Dairy Farm and collect any unattached units that were available at Aberdeen Industrial School (AIS), and then proceed to Bennet's Hill. They were to defend a line running from Bennet's Hill along the water catchment towards WNC Gap. The water catchment emerges on Deep Water Bay Road a kilometre south-west of the gap. Lt-Col Frederick formed a composite company made up from the RASC contingent and the military personnel available at AIS.

> I collected approximately fifty officers and ORs comprised of RAOC, RE, RN, HK Police and RAF and then awaited the arrival of the RASC. A position was taken on Bennet's Hill (catch-water and ground above) by about 1600 hours. At approximately 1800 hours message received to abandon Bennet's Hill and capture Wong Nai Chung Gap. No details as to the route to be taken, so transport was ordered to take troops as far a possible up Repulse Bay Road. It was completely dark with rain

by the time movement commenced (approximately 2000 hours), and as vehicles were driving with no lights, numerous delays occurred owing to lorries colliding and becoming entangled in wire. The first lorries halted near The Ridge where I went forward to reconnoitre. Two cars were returning from the gap, and I was told that they had been heavily machine-gunned on trying to get through which was also my experience when I went forward to verify. As I knew Lt-Col Macpherson and a party of RAOC were at The Ridge, I proceeded there with my advance party and had the main party further down the road proceed on foot to The Ridge.[3]

Having arrived at The Ridge, Frederick called up Colonel Andrews-Levinge, Commander RASC (CRASC), and advised him that the composite company had arrived at The Ridge and would attack WNC Gap the next morning. At 2300 hours, the CRASC telephoned Frederick with new orders for him to return to Shouson Hill and reoccupy the RASC workshops. It was decided that this move should take place the following morning.

At first light, on 20 December Frederick's group prepared to set off for Shouson Hill by way of Repulse Bay Road and Island Road. However, during the early hours before dawn, Japanese troops had infiltrated down from Middle Spur to Repulse Bay Road and had already captured the all-important roadblock at the junction with Island Road. The first to leave The Ridge that morning was forty-five-year-old Captain Robert Bonney, RAOC. He had also been ordered to reopen the RAOC workshops at Shouson Hill. He took with him Staff Sgt James O'Toole and a small party of ordnance men. They left in Bonney's car with some inside and some standing on the running board. As they approached the junction in the half-light of dawn, they slowed down, expecting the roadblock to be manned by Canadian troops. Instead, they found themselves being shouted at and prodded by Japanese soldiers who had taken over the position a short while earlier. The RAOC group were taken prisoner, tied up, relieved of their valuables, and marched around the corner to Island Road. A short while later the unsuspecting RASC party arrived in trucks and were ambushed at the road junction. Frederick described the ambush in the RASC war diary.

At about 0100 hours, orders were received from CRASC that my party would proceed to Shouson Hill by road and I was told the DWB/Repulse Bay Road junction was held by Canadian troops. This information was confirmed by CRASC on my enquiring some five hours later. My party left The Ridge just before dawn, although the advance party were allowed through, very heavy machine gun and rifle fire was opened up on the main body as they reached the road junction. The firing was maintained, and as it was impossible to locate the enemy and my casualties were heavy, I ordered the party back to The Ridge.[4]

Some of Frederick's party managed to make their way to Shouson Hill by going down the hillside on the west side of the road and reaching Deep Water Bay. Others took refuge in nearby villas along the lower part of Repulse Bay Road including Twin Brook and Monte Verde, but the majority made their way back up Repulse Bay Road to The Ridge. L/Cpl Colebrook was a member of the RAOC workshop section. He had left The Ridge by car and must have reached the road junction just after Captain Bonney. Colebrook was in a car with Frank Haynes, a retired RSM who was working as a civilian employee, and two Chinese cooks. Colebrook stopped at the roadblock and got out from the driving seat only to find that he was surrounded by Japanese soldiers. He noticed that Haynes got out on the other side. It was a two-door car, and the two Chinese cooks remained in the back seat. At that moment, the RASC lorries arrived, and firing commenced. Colebrook ran for cover on one side and Haynes on the other. The car went up in flames, killing the two Chinese cooks. Colebrook was hit in the foot by a bullet, but he managed to make his way up the road and took refuge at Twin Brook. The house was empty; it was being used as a NAAFI store and was full of supplies including chocolate and cigarettes. The house telephone was in working order, so Colebrook called through to RAOC HQ at The Ridge. He spoke with Macpherson who asked him to try and make his way back to The Ridge after nightfall.

Frederick reported the ambush to Colonel Andrews-Levinge in the Battle Box. The information was passed to Brigadier Peffers, the chief staff officer, and 'G' Branch, who suggested that it was probably Canadian soldiers manning the roadblock that had mistakenly fired on Frederick's party and not the Japanese. The military commanders had no idea, nor could they readily accept, that the Japanese had already penetrated as far as Repulse Bay on the south side of the Island. Captain Potts had returned to The Ridge with Lt-Col Frederick's party on Friday night, but he had remained at The Ridge on Saturday morning and had not been part of the group going to Shouson Hill to reopen the workshops. From The Ridge, he could see that the Japanese held the police station, the pillbox, and Postbridge. Potts and several others once again manned the parapet wall along the driveway in front of the houses and commenced firing with Lewis guns and rifles at Japanese troops near the gap. The party at the wall then started to come under fire from Japanese snipers infiltrating along the water catchment towards The Ridge. The wall party took some casualties from this flank fire before moving into the houses. Machine guns were installed at the front and rear windows of the houses and sandbags and bales of uniforms were used to make parapets at the windows.

Potts was in the large semi-detached house when he got a call from HQ in House No. 1 ordering him to cease fire until further orders. During the afternoon, they had the frustrating experience of having to watch Japanese troops coming along the water-catchment unimpeded. At one point during the afternoon, he opened fire from the back window at Japanese troops moving along the water catchment from Repulse Bay towards WNC Gap, but again he was telephoned from RAOC HQ and told to hold fire.

The numbers of personnel at The Ridge had increased as a result of the arrival of units like the Hong Kong Chinese Regiment, under Major Mayer, who arrived on 18 December, and then by the addition of Frederick's composite force on 19 December, and by stragglers from various other units operating nearby. In the late morning on Saturday 20 December, The Ridge came under heavy machine gun and mortar fire. Frederick described the intensity of gunfire directed at The Ridge and the mounting casualties.

> Two Japanese machine guns commenced an almost continuous fire on us from the police station and snipers were most active and accurate from the catch-water. Two RAOC personnel were killed, and Lt-Col Macpherson, Captain Hickey, RCASC, and myself were wounded, and several ORs were hit. A few hours later a trench mortar was also brought up against us, and some damage to buildings and further casualties were caused, several men being killed.[5]

Mortar bombs hit Houses No. 4 and No. 5, killing Pte Taylor at House No. 5 and wounding Macpherson in the arm while he was moving between houses. An ambulance was called to evacuate the wounded. The ambulance and a lorry with Red Cross markings arrived at dusk. The vehicles were initially machine-gunned from WNC Gap, but after a few minutes the firing ceased, and the wounded were quickly loaded and evacuated. These included Captain Walter Scotcher, RASC, and Captain Overton Hickey, RCASC. They were both lightly wounded and were taken with the other casualties to St Stephen's College Hospital in Stanley. Hickey lost his life in the massacre at St Stephen's, of which more later. Scotcher survived. Frederick was disparaging about Scotcher in the RASC war diary: 'As Scotcher had proved to be completely useless and was complaining of a sore foot, I sent him away with the wounded.' Scotcher's daughter, Peggie, was a military nurse serving with the Nursing Detachment of the HKVDC. She married Lt Drummond Hunter, 2/RS, on 25 December while he was a patient in Bowen Road Military Hospital. Lt Hunter had been wounded in the arm and shoulder by machine gun fire while fighting on Golden Hill. On 24 December, he incurred an injury to the spine when an ambulance that was transferring him to the Hong Kong Hotel Relief Hospital for convalescence crashed during an air raid. He was brought back to Bowen Road Military Hospital where he remained until December 1942. Peggie and her mother, Bertha, a history graduate from Oxford University, were incarcerated in Stanley Camp.

Those who had been captured at the road junction on Saturday morning 20 December, including Captain Bonney and S/Sgt O'Toole, spent the whole day tied up sitting by the roadside between the road junction and the golf course. Later another Japanese unit took charge of the prisoners and escorted them back to WNC Gap. They were taken up a nullah from Island Road to Repulse Bay Road, and then across the road and up another nullah that brought them onto the hillside of Middle Spur, from where they continued uphill until they intercepted the water catchment that runs along the side of Violet Hill. At this point, Bonney was taken away by his captors and was not seen again. One can speculate that he may have tried to escape and then been shot, or he may have refused to divulge information to his captors and then been shot. The Japanese did not need a reason to shoot surrendered prisoners. The rest of the group were taken back along the water catchment, past The Ridge, still under siege, to WNC Gap.

Charlie Colebrook, hiding out at the NAAFI store in Twin Brook, waited until dark on Saturday night and then made his way back to The Ridge through the undergrowth on the hillside. He arrived safely at The Ridge, tripping over the body of Pte Taylor, as he rushed through the door. On Sunday 21 December, Colebrook was asked to man a Bren gun on one of the upper-floor windows facing the water catchment. A wounded RASC sergeant helped him by filling the magazines. Like most soldiers, they were eager to shoot back, but Colebrook recalled in an interview after the war that Macpherson was still giving orders to restrain fire. Captain Potts observed large numbers of Japanese moving along the water catchment that day, but he was still under orders to hold fire.

The Japanese troops by this time were using the catch-water like a highway; they had erected a tent just below the pillbox, and they had their flags spread out on the slopes of Mount Nicholson to indicate their positions to their airmen who were flying around all day as they wished. They also had a light field gun firing from the gap at a gunboat

[HMS *Cicala*] in Deep Water Bay. All this we watched patiently. I rang up the HQ House as I thought it possible they could not observe what was taking place but found I was mistaken. They had seen everything, but we were still to hold fire![6]

During the afternoon on Sunday 21 December, Brigadier Wallis spoke to Lt-Col Frederick and asked him if he could organise an attack on the road junction and the water catchment through which the Japanese were moving troops and equipment from WNC Gap to the Middle Spur and Repulse Bay area. Frederick told Wallis that he would try to do this with his composite force, but that he would prefer to augment his collection of non-combatants with properly trained infantry first. The brigadier promised to provide additional troops. It was at this time that Major Templer was ordered to counterattack WNC Gap with predominantly Canadian troops from the garrison at Repulse Bay Hotel and Palm Villa. Frederick recalled the Canadian troops arriving at The Ridge in two groups during the evening of 21 December.

> About 1900 hours a party of thirty Canadians under Lt Johnston arrived, and at approximately 2200 hours a further party under Lt Blaver arrived. ... Lt Blaver informed me they had reached nearby Altamira at about 1600 hours and had sat there until receiving orders at 2145 hours to report to me.[7]

The attack on the road junction and Middle Spur was planned to commence the same night, which would be during the early hours of Monday 22 December. Frederick divided the personnel at The Ridge into three groups. Group A, consisting of some sixty troops, was to remain at The Ridge under Lt-Col Macpherson. Group B, consisting of one hundred troops, was under the command of Major Mayer, HKCR, and included Lt Blaver, RRC, and thirty riflemen from 'A' Coy, RRC. Group B's objective was to seize the road junction at the bottom of Repulse Bay Road. Group C, consisting of approximately one hundred troops, was commanded by Lt Johnston, RRC. This group was made up from 'A' Coy, RRC, and assorted troops from The Ridge. Their objective was the water catchment on Middle Spur.

Frederick, with a small group including Major Mould and Lt Joyce, would go with Group B. Once the road junction had been cleared, they would pass through to Repulse Bay Hotel. At the hotel, they were to lead a party with Major Templer back up Repulse Bay Road to join up with Group A and B, the former at The Ridge and the latter at the road junction, and then mount a further attack on WNC Gap. The troops were issued with thick woollen socks to cover their boots and muffle the sound of boots on the road. The advance party was due to move off at 0300 hours on Monday 22 December, with the main body leaving shortly afterwards.

Captain Potts was asked to attend an orders group at House No. 1 at around midnight on Sunday 21 December. He was allocated to Group B, whose orders were to seize the junction and occupy Overbays, a private house overlooking the road junction. Potts recalled that Group B was made up of some thirty troops from RRC, some forty Chinese troops from the HK Chinese Regiment (HKCR) and some thirty men drawn from the RASC and the RAOC. Each man had a rifle and was issued with 150 rounds of ammunition. There were a handful of Bren guns, and some men had been issued with hand grenades. It was a large composite force, mostly populated by non-combatants other than the Canadian riflemen. Although socks had been issued and used to cover boots, it was difficult to move a large body of men down a metal road in complete silence. The Japanese must have heard them coming and were waiting to ambush them. The Japanese withheld their fire as the advance party passed through the road junction. Then, as the main body approached, they opened fire with devastating effect. Frederick described the ambush.

> At the bottom of Overbays drive, three derelict lorries were at the side of the road. The advance party went through to the road junction with no signs of the enemy, and the main party was about one-third past Overbays drive-way when very heavy machine gun fire and grenades were opened on them from the lorries and the spur dividing Repulse Bay Road and Deep Water Bay Road [Island Road]. Our party split, a portion scattering in the Deep Water Bay Road [Island Road] area and the remainder taking cover at the bottom of Overbays drive. ... We opened fire on the enemy and after about ten minutes appeared to have silenced them. A patrol of myself, Lt Blaver and six Canadians went out and after finding a few dead on the spur and more dead on the lorries, were nearly as far as the road junction corner when the 'dead' commenced to machine-gun us from the spur and the lorries. As we doubled back, hand grenades and what appeared to be dynamite speeded us on. ... Lt Johnston suggested we move into Overbays until dawn, as the element of surprise for getting up to catchment had gone.[8]

Captain Potts survived the initial ambush at the road junction and was part of the group that took refuge in Overbays. He recalled Lt Piggott, 1/Mx, taking charge and organising return fire at the Japanese positions on the bank across the road. Piggott, who had been assigned to the HKCR, was killed in action that morning near the road junction. The spur between Island Road and Repulse Bay Road is now built over.

Where Overbays once stood, there is an expensive-looking low-rise apartment complex bearing the same name. Potts wrote in his diary that the house was owned by Mr Sun Fo, son of Dr Sun Yat-sen. The house had a large reception room on the ground floor. The front door opened directly into this large room, which was surrounded by windows. Opposite the front door was a set of French windows opening onto a veranda above the road junction. Another set of French windows gave access to a lawn at the side of the house. A low flight of steps near the front door led to a raised landing running along one side of the house with a further flight of steps leading to the upper floor. The landing had windows all along it facing the hillside. The house was surrounded by the Japanese, and unsuitable for defence because of the array of windows.

As dawn broke on Monday 22 December, just a few hours after they had reached the house, they could see Japanese troops moving around on the hillside of Middle Spur directly behind the property. There were approximately 120 British and Canadian troops in Overbays, many of whom had been wounded during the ambush. During the morning, the Japanese directed machine gun and sniper fire at the house and casualties started to increase. At around 1000 hours Lt Johnston asked Lt-Col Frederick for permission to lead a small fighting patrol to clear up some of the snipers who had infiltrated close to the house. He called for volunteers, and a sergeant and two riflemen joined him. They went out the French windows, across the lawn, and followed a path leading up the hillside. Johnston managed to reach Repulse Bay Hotel after dusk, arriving before the garrison evacuated the hotel. Captain Potts and Lt Andrews, RA, also asked Frederick for permission to follow Lt Johnston up the hill and try to reach the hotel.

> About 1030 hours Captain Potts and Lt Andrews asked permission to make a dash for it, and as our position looked almost hopeless, I agreed and told the remainder of my party that anyone could go who cared to. All elected to remain. About noon I telephoned Major Templer telling him our position and asked if he could give any assistance or send an ambulance for our wounded, some of whom were in a very bad way. I was told nothing could be done for us.[9]

The two officers crossed the lawn and reached the path that led up to Middle Spur. They could see that the path would take them through an area of exposed hillside, so they moved to the right and took shelter in a ravine in which there was thick undergrowth. They remained there all day until nightfall and then crept down the ravine. The gully came to an end where the hillside overhung the road, and a concrete drain dropped down to the road. They slid down the drain and found themselves on

Repulse Bay Road, with Overbays some 200 or 300 metres to their right, and Repulse Bay Hotel some 300 or 400 metres to their left. They were opposite Eucliffe, which was some five metres below the road level. Instead of turning left towards the hotel they turned right and went up the road towards Overbays and the road junction, but with the idea of heading to Deep Water Bay and Aberdeen. They heard a shout in the darkness and the sound of a group of men running down the road from the junction. Thinking it might be a Japanese patrol, they crossed the low retaining wall and dropped down onto the hillside just outside the grounds of Eucliffe. They then made their way down the hillside to the shoreline below.

Andrews decided to swim across Deep Water Bay, which he thought was the safest way to avoid Japanese patrols, while Potts preferred to try and work his way along the shoreline, not feeling able to swim that distance. There were several houses below Island Road with gardens running down to the rocky shore. The road junction was just above the first house and Potts could see the Japanese sentries as he passed. He noticed that they had barricaded the road with lorries. He carried on along the shoreline until he reached the last house which was just around the corner from Deep Water Bay. He tried to access the road, but a dog started barking, and he noticed there was another Japanese roadblock at the bottom of the hill. Potts decided to take to the water and swam towards the beach at Deep Water Bay. He tried to come ashore, but the wiring on the beach was too thick to get through. He went back into the water reluctantly, as the sea was cold and it was covered in a film of oil from the scuttled naval vessels in the bay. It was just as well that he had not come ashore at the beach, because the sappers had laid 800 anti-personnel mines and 200 anti-tank mines along the beach. Potts came ashore at the western end of the bay close to Brick Hill. He had to climb a steep rock-face to reach Island Road. He hauled himself over the road parapet and walked along the road in the direction of Aberdeen, his body covered in oil and his feet lacerated from the rocks and barnacles. Eventually, he reached a British roadblock where a sentry told him that Andrews had passed through earlier.

The garrison at Overbays continued to hold out and was taking a toll on the Japanese. Sgt John Adams, RAOC, was described as indefatigable throughout the day and was responsible for killing a number of Japanese snipers until he was shot dead by a sniper at 1500 hours. Frederick put in a second call to Templer at Repulse Bay Hotel, but Templer told him the garrison at the hotel were also under siege and repeated they could do nothing to assist. Later in the afternoon, a captured Indian soldier, dressed in civilian clothes, appeared at the house with a demand from a

Japanese officer that they surrender. The Indian was detained and placed under guard. At 1800 hours Frederick received a telephone message in French from Templer instructing him to evacuate the house and make his way to Repulse Bay Hotel that evening. He was to avoid the main road and the crown of Middle Spur and try to get to the hotel before midnight so as to join the military evacuation of the hotel scheduled for that night. At around 1900 hours Frederick commenced dispatching groups of men from Overbays to try and make it through to the hotel.

> It took about an hour to get all the troops away. ... When all troops had left the house, I went and repeated my promise to QMS Singleton, who had volunteered to remain with the seriously wounded, that I would get an ambulance to him at the first opportunity. I collected my party and arrived at Repulse Bay Hotel at about 2030 hours where I reported to Major Templer. Major Mould and Lt Markey arrived with their parties shortly afterwards, and we were told to prepare for an immediate march to Stanley. All requests for an ambulance to be sent to Overbays were turned down.[10]

The wounded remained at Overbays together with a few who volunteered to stay and help, including QMS Singleton, RASC, who was left in charge and had himself been wounded by grenade fragments. Singleton had assisted the wounded throughout the day as best he could without bandages or medical equipment. When the garrison at Overbays left the house to try and withdraw to Repulse Bay Hotel, around thirty-five men in one of the rooms on the upper floor were unintentionally left behind. These included L/Cpl Line, RAOC, and Pte Canivet, RCOC. Having received no orders, L/Cpl Line shouted down to Singleton on the ground floor to ask if any help could be given for their wounded. Singleton was surprised that there was anybody left upstairs. He had received orders to surrender the house to the Japanese in the hope that the wounded would be spared. Among Singleton's group, there was a Portuguese member of the HKVDC who could speak Japanese. The plan was that he would communicate their intent to surrender.

However, the party upstairs had no wish to surrender and were in favour of following the others and trying to reach the hotel. The telephone in the house was still working so they put a call through to the hotel to ask if any of the earlier parties had got through. At that stage, they had not, and they were told that it was impossible to get through and that they may be better off by surrendering if only to save the wounded. This was confirmed when Sgt Andrew Jack, RAOC, and a Canadian soldier returned to the house having been ambushed and unable to reach the hotel.

The Portuguese interpreter shouted out to the Japanese, in their own language, that the garrison was willing to surrender. The Japanese did not respond. It is likely that they had already decided that they were going to kill all the troops holding out, perhaps because they had not surrendered earlier when they had the opportunity, perhaps because they had detained the Indian intermediary, and perhaps because of the casualties that they had inflicted on the Japanese. Pte Canivet on the upper floor recalled the Japanese storming the house early the next morning, on Tuesday 23 December.

The Japanese stormed the house using hand grenades and a small portable machine gun. The wounded men downstairs were literally murdered in cold blood. Our white flag was torn down, and our interpreter was bayoneted and pinned to a door to die. The Japanese came upstairs and kicked open the door of the room we were in. First, they sprayed the room with machine gun fire and followed it up with a barrage of grenades. These were very slow in going off, and we were all busy tossing them out the windows as fast as we could. It was during the grenade barrage that I received a piece of shrapnel in the jaw. Many of the men were seriously wounded and many killed. Two of us opened fire on the Japanese with our rifles and managed to get three of them before they got away. The next thing they did was to try and pour kerosene on the ground floor and set fire to the house. We got as many of the wounded out of the windows as possible and then jumped ourselves. Many headed down Repulse Bay Road but were immediately met with heavy machine gun fire, so we headed for the sea. Eight of us started to swim, with the Japanese firing at us. Four of us reached the other side of Repulse Bay.[11]

In his deposition, Canivet mentions that they went to a civilian house owned by a Mr Ritchie who provided them with beer, bully beef and clothes. This was probably the home of sixty-two-year-old William Ritchie, a retired officer from the China Postal Service, and his wife, Isabella. They lived in a villa on South Bay Road near where Canivet and his group struggled ashore after their 2-mile swim. William Ritchie and his wife were later incarcerated in Stanley Camp. They survived internment and settled in Canada after the war. After leaving what I assume must have been William Ritchie's home, Canivet and his small group were later captured by a Japanese patrol while trying to reach Stanley.

A party of six Japanese captured us. They tied us together, and when eventually we were made to crawl into a ditch, we knew the end had arrived for us. Then the shooting started. I was hit four times, and I lay very quietly, waiting, hoping that the next shot would be a clean one and have it finished. I heard my comrades die miserable deaths. They didn't bother to investigate the job they had done, just left us for dead. I was hit in the left shoulder, left elbow, left hip and right hand. .... The three others were dead. They were a staff sergeant in the HKVDC, a corporal in the RAOC, and a sapper in the Royal Engineers. I never knew any of their names.[12]

CQMS Fred Hamlen, RASC, had been shot in the thigh by a Japanese sniper while at Overbays. He was still able to walk despite his injury and joined the escape groups which left Overbays during the night of 22/23 December. His group was ambushed before they could get to the hotel. After being fired on, they split up in the darkness and Hamlen joined up with three Canadian soldiers in the grounds of Eucliffe.

We took refuge in a gardener's outhouse. There we stayed all night. Looking through the windows at daybreak we saw that the Japanese were in complete control of the house and appeared to be using it as a headquarters. It was impossible to escape during the daytime, so we decided to wait until nightfall. Later in the morning, the Japanese started [throwing grenades] in the vacant rooms and locked outhouses and very soon the door of our outhouse was broken down, and we were taken prisoner. After stripping us of all arms and equipment, the Japanese proceeded to beat us up badly with rifle butts.[13]

The Japanese guards found ammunition clips on the three Canadians and threw the clips at their faces, causing them to bleed from the cuts. The four captives had their hands tied behind their backs. They were brutally prodded by bayonets and led from the outhouses, at the rear of the house, to the grass terrace overlooking Repulse Bay Beach.

We were taken to a grass bank just outside of the main building of Eucliffe and facing the water. We knew then we were going to be shot because on top of the bank were pools of blood and at the bottom of the bank near the sea were dozens of dead bodies. ... The Japanese made us sit with our feet over the bank facing the sea. A firing squad was then brought from the house, and in a few minutes, we were all shot. Owing to the fact that I turned my head to the left as I was being fired at, the bullet passed through my neck above the left shoulder and came out at my right cheek. I did not lose consciousness, and the force of the bullet knocked me free from the others, and I rolled down the bank. I then lay on a concrete path with my hands tied behind my back, and the bodies of the three Canadians rolled down on top of me.[14]

His deposition states that one of the Canadians had been killed instantly, inferring the others died slowly from their wounds. Hamlen had been shot in the thigh, bayoneted in the legs, and shot through the neck and face, but he survived. He made his way along the shoreline and joined up with other British and Canadian troops hiding out below the cliffs.

During the morning of 23 December, Colonel Tanaka was at Eucliffe while the Japanese were rounding up and killing British and Canadian soldiers who had tried to escape from The Ridge and Overbays. Tanaka later addressed a group of captured civilians who had been marched to the entrance drive of Eucliffe from the hotel. These included Joseph Baud, a French national, who had been staying at the hotel.

> I saw about half a dozen or more British and Indian soldiers kneeling down in front of Eucliffe. About this time two others were captured on the road and joined the others. Then a small motorcar came down and passed in front of me. I recognised my friend Mr Delcourt dressed in HKVDC uniform. The interpreter made him kneel down, and I heard Delcourt saying to the interpreter, 'I am not English I am Belgian.' The interpreter replied, 'Well you are Belgian, but you are helping the English, in that case, you deserve to be shot.'[15]

Forty-two-year-old Armande Delcourt, a Belgian national, had been serving in the ASC section of the HKVDC and had been at The Ridge with other members of the ASC unit. He had been wounded by a bayonet but had managed to find a small car in which he was driving towards Repulse Bay Hotel, not realising that the whole of Repulse Bay was now in Japanese hands. Delcourt was one of those executed at Eucliffe.

The civilians were then taken back to the hotel. Baud testified after the war that he saw British and Canadian soldiers being executed on the lawn at Eucliffe. He saw Japanese soldiers stand behind the captured soldiers and shoot them in the back of the head, one after the other. Madame Ohl, a French national by marriage, was staying at the Repulse Bay Hotel with her husband. She also saw the killing of surrendered soldiers at Eucliffe. She remained at the hotel with other third-nationals after the British and American civilians had been marched off to North Point on 24 December. She recalled that a few days after the surrender she saw the bodies collected and burnt. One of the dead must have had a grenade in his pocket because Madame Ohl recalled that the grenade exploded and injured two or three of the Japanese soldiers, who were taken away on stretchers.

Following Lt-Col Frederick's departure from The Ridge in the early hours of 22 December, around sixty personnel were left at the depot under the command of Lt-Col Macpherson including Major Flippance, commanding officer of the ASC Coy, HKVDC, Captain Strellett, ASC Coy, Captain Ebbage and L/Cpl Colebrook, RAOC. Colebrook recalls the Japanese closing in on The Ridge during the morning of 22 December, but this time Macpherson, who had been so reticent before, allowed them to fire back and they killed a large number of the Japanese at close range. The Japanese attack was beaten off, but The Ridge then came under increasingly heavy fire from machine guns, mortar and light artillery. Japanese troops at the water catchment were infiltrating down the steep slope to The Ridge near House No. 1. As a consequence, at some stage during the afternoon of 22 December, Macpherson decided to surrender the position. He ordered the garrison to cease fire and gave instructions to display a white flag. Either the Japanese could not see the flag, or they were in no mood to accept a surrender, for they continued to fire on The Ridge, perhaps because they had lost so many of their own men on the water catchment and the approaches to The Ridge earlier that day. Macpherson then opened the door and tried to display the flag more overtly, but this was met by a burst of fire resulting in Macpherson being seriously wounded in the leg.

In the late afternoon, Major Templer telephoned Macpherson at The Ridge. He spoke in French in case of Japanese eavesdropping, saying that if the remaining garrison were able to withdraw after dark and reach Repulse Bay Hotel by midnight, they could join the military evacuation of the hotel. Macpherson then ordered those who were physically able to try to reach the hotel after nightfall. He and the other wounded who were unable to walk would have to remain at the mercy of the Japanese. Flippance went to all five houses and told the men in each house of the escape plan. There was little time left to try and reach the hotel by midnight, which would involve passing through Japanese lines. As dusk descended, they started to make their way down the nullah at the back of The Ridge which led down to Repulse Bay Road. Colebrook left in a group which included Major Flippance and Captain Strellett. Colebrook's group must have got close to the hotel because early the next morning on 23 December, they could see a Japanese flag flying over the hotel. Colebrook's group were tired, hungry and no doubt demoralised by seeing the hotel in Japanese hands. Colebrook led them back to Twin Brook, where he knew there were rations and provisions. In the morning, a group of Japanese soldiers came up the drive, surrounded the house, and demanded their surrender in exchange for their lives. They complied, were tied up, and marched up to WNC Gap, but their lives were spared, whereas so many others were killed when captured or put to death on the lawns of Eucliffe.

Captain Ebbage and the garrison at House No. 1 had been unable to make good their escape at dusk because of heavy machine gun fire being directed at their HQ. They eventually left The Ridge at 1940 hours with Ebbage leading a party of senior NCOs including Sergeant-Major Neale and QMS Cooper. They went down Repulse Bay Road, moving up to the hills some 500 metres before the road junction. They tried to reach the hotel but found it impossible to get through. They came across many of their own wounded and dead as they tried to get past Middle Spur. Neale was killed that night, but Ebbage and Cooper continued to evade the enemy by hiding in a ravine near The Ridge. They eventually gave themselves up on 28 December, not realising that the colony had surrendered three days earlier.

Major Charles Young led the remnants of his company and other assorted troops from Altamira and House No. 5 towards Repulse Bay. The men removed their boots and proceeded cautiously down Repulse Bay Road, but they were unable to get through to the hotel. They went down the hillside to the shoreline where they hid out among the rocks during daylight hours on 23 December. They then split into four parties, each under an officer. The bodies of two of these officers, Lt Lyster and Lt Scott, were later found at Stanley View, each with bayonet wounds and their hands tied behind their backs. Remarkably, some of their group had managed to get through to Stanley. Major Young's party found an old motorboat anchored offshore, probably somewhere near Middle Island. His party paddled the boat out to sea using improvised oars. They boarded the beached destroyer HMS *Thracian*, and after spending a night on the vessel they used the ship's Carley floats to paddle to Lamma Island. They later crossed back to Hong Kong Island, landing at Telegraph Bay, by which time Hong Kong had capitulated, and they were taken prisoner.

The wounded men who had been left at The Ridge were put to death by the Japanese with bayonets and rifle butts. Lt-Col Lindsay Ride, commanding the Hong Kong Field Ambulance, was given permission on 29 December to take an ambulance towards Stanley to look for British and Canadian wounded. He recalled seeing many bodies of British dead still lying on the road from WNC Gap southwards towards Repulse Bay. He also discovered some of the bodies of those who were executed at The Ridge.

> On approaching the houses on The Ridge there were a number of British dead, and some of them were lying on their faces with their hands behind their backs, but untied. These bodies had bayonet marks on the back, and some of them had the side of the skull knocked in. At the base of the retaining wall between two of these houses were over a dozen bodies with their hands and ankles tied and blood marks on top of the retaining wall.[16]

Major John Crawford, WG, who was with Lt-Col Ride, estimated the number of bodies thrown over the parapet wall as being around twenty. He also stated in a deposition that he found a dozen bodies at the base of the cliff near House No. 1 in a position that suggested they had been lined up against the cliff and shot or bayoneted. This group of bodies included that of Lt-Col Macpherson.

Lt-Col Frederick made it to Stanley Village early in the morning on 23 December, having escaped from The Ridge, Overbays and Repulse Bay Hotel all within the space of twenty-four hours. Many of the soldiers at The Ridge were non-combatants who found themselves on the front line. The Japanese Army had decided that they would not take prisoners from The Ridge or Overbays. There were some extraordinary escapes by men who cheated death, like Pte Canivet and CQMS Hamlen, who both lived to tell their shocking story.

14

The Siege of Repulse Bay Hotel

20 to 23 December

The Repulse Bay Hotel opened for business in January 1920. It was a charming hotel set among beautiful gardens with a long veranda giving splendid views over the beach and bay. The original hotel was demolished in 1982 in order to build the high-rise apartment blocks that we see today. A replica of part of the original iconic hotel was constructed in its place, offering an air of artificial charm. The hotel was surrounded by the greenery of the mountains. The low hillside to the west is Middle Spur, and the steep hillside at the back is Violet Hill. In December 1941, the beach was still lined with bathing huts, but it was mined, and covered with wire entanglements and other beach defences including two pillboxes and their Lyon light structures. PB 17 was located at the back of the beach and close to the hotel garage block. The garage was a long building with an entrance for vehicles at either end. The second pillbox, PB 18, was located near the Lido. The Lido was a long white concrete beachside complex that was opened in 1935 and had been popular for tea dances, sunbathing and swimming parties.

During the night of 19 December, Colonel Tanaka, commanding the 229th Infantry Regiment, took two battalions of infantry along Violet Hill Path, which follows the water catchment from the reservoir at WNC Gap towards Repulse Bay. The 3rd Battalion acted as point, followed by the Regimental HQ, with the 2nd Battalion acting as rear-guard. Tanaka also sent troops up to the crest of Violet Hill. The main body of his troops would have passed above Postbridge, which was still under siege by units of Colonel Shoji's 230th Regiment, and a little later they passed the five houses on The Ridge. It is likely that Tanaka knew there was an AOP at

Middle Spur close to the small service reservoir. He may have known that this spur would provide the only suitable access down to Repulse Bay Road. We know that the bulk of his troops turned right on Violet Hill Path and went down a steep trail leading to the reservoir at Middle Spur. There is no detailed description of what happened at Middle Spur, but there was clearly an exchange of fire, as a large number of spent British and Canadian casings were found in the area. Some of these casings were found in trenches close to the reservoir, in a position to fire at Japanese troops coming down the hillside from Violet Hill Path.

The underground service reservoir, the AOP and a nearby splinter-proof shelter remain today. The splinter proof shelter may have been used as accommodation for a section of troops who guarded the reservoir, or it may have provided accommodation for the gunners manning the AOP. There are several weapons pits and trenches around the reservoir. At least one of the weapons pits was used by the Japanese as a machine gun position because a large number of spent Japanese 7.7mm machine gun rounds were found in the pit. It was in a position to be able to fire on Repulse Bay Hotel and the road in front. When I first visited this site in April 2011, I found a British steel helmet lying beside a trench. It was badly rusted, having lain there exposed to the elements for almost seventy years. On the hillside between Violet Hill Path and the reservoir, there are still a large number of fox-holes that were hastily dug by Japanese troops to take cover from British artillery fire directed at the concentration of Japanese troops on and around Middle Spur. Some spent Japanese rounds were found on the steps leading up to the AOP.

A note in the Royal Artillery war diary states that at 1045 hours on Saturday 20 December the AOP was reported as having been surrounded. I assume that after an initial exchange of fire from the trench, the defending troops locked themselves in the AOP. Japanese troops must have picketed the AOP, and later forced an entry, while others continued along a path leading downhill from Middle Spur, emerging on Repulse Bay Road near the junction with Island Road. These troops then seized the roadblock at the road junction after overcoming a section of Winnipeg Grenadiers that were manning the position. We know that by dawn on Saturday 20 December the road junction was already in Japanese hands.

A little later that morning, American news reporter Gwen Dew, a guest at the hotel, was about to go down to breakfast when she heard a British officer knocking on the doors of the rooms along her corridor warning guests that there were Japanese troops in the vicinity and instructing them to assemble in the hotel lobby. Gwen's room was in the west wing, overlooking the hotel garage block. She looked out of her window and noticed a group of Japanese soldiers looking up at the hotel. Benny Proulx, together with some of his naval colleagues, had moved to the hotel after their mine control station at Chung Hom Kok had been evacuated. He had arranged for his family to leave their home, Erinville at Turtle Cove, and move into the hotel because of the proximity of Japanese troops. Proulx was also staying in the west wing, and he recalled being woken by his eldest son Michael who told him there were Japanese soldiers outside. Proulx went to the window, which overlooked the road, and saw for himself the group of some thirty Japanese soldiers, outside the hotel garage, no more than a stone's throw from his room.

A short time later four unsuspecting naval personnel from the hotel garrison, together with a soldier from the nearby pillbox on the beach, were captured by the Japanese. They had no idea that there were Japanese troops in the area. Proulx and a group of soldiers and naval personnel had taken up a position behind a balustrade on the west wing lawn which overlooked the road and the garage block. They could see the captured soldier being slapped across the face and berated by a Japanese officer, while a Japanese soldier stood behind with his bayonet pointed at the prisoner's back. On a pre-arranged signal, the soldiers opened fire, one aiming at the Japanese officer while the others fired on the rest of the group, trying to avoid hitting the five British prisoners. The startled Japanese and their captives dashed for the cover of the garage, leaving four or five dead or injured behind them. The siege of Repulse Bay Hotel had begun.

The hotel was full of civilians of every nationality, some of whom had been staying there before the war began while others had sought refuge at the hotel after hostilities had commenced. One of the guests was thirty-eight-year-old Henry Woulfe-Flanagan, who had been based in Tientsin working for China Maritime Customs (CMC). In late November, he had received instructions to proceed to Shanghai and to take up the post of acting deputy commissioner of CMC. He embarked with his wife, Dorothea, and three-year-old daughter, Susan, in early December on the SS *Fausang*. However, while en route the captain received instructions to sail direct to Hong Kong and not to stop at Shanghai, in anticipation of war breaking out. They arrived in Hong Kong on Sunday 7 December. The following morning, still aboard the *Fausang*, Woulfe-Flanagan witnessed the attack on Kai Tak.

One bomb dropped within fifty yards of the *Fausang*. Subsequently, at 2 pm a larger raid was made, and our ship became a direct target with bombs falling all around us with many near misses, but without the SS *Fausang* sustaining a direct hit. The decks, however, were machine-gunned. In the course of the day, first the women and children, and subsequently the men were put ashore.[1]

Three days later, on 11 December, the *Fausang* was scuttled in Hong Kong harbour along with other merchant ships. (In 1942 she was salvaged by the Japanese, put back into service, and renamed the *Fusei Maru*. Her new career was cut short in September 1943 when she was torpedoed and sunk by the US submarine *Seawolf*.) On 12 December, Woulfe-Flanagan moved with his wife and daughter to Repulse Bay Hotel. The hotel was already full, and guests had to share rooms. The hotel manager was thirty-eight-year-old Miss Marjorie Matheson. Hotel guests praised her for her calm efficiency throughout the siege. On Sunday 7 December, her sub-manager Kiri Kaluzhny and night-manager Boris Gellman, both members of the HKVDC, were mobilised and had to report for duty. Other staff had also been called up to serve in the ARP and other essential services. This left the hotel very short-staffed, but many of the guests pitched in to help once the siege commenced.

Jan Marsman and George Dankwerth, both of Marsman & Co., and Richard Wilson of United Press, Manila, had joined forces after the Clipper was destroyed and they had become stranded in Hong Kong. They decided to move to Repulse Bay Hotel, thinking it would be a safer location than the hotels in Victoria. Hotel guest Hugo Mladinich, manager of Standard Brands, Manila, had been in Hong Kong on a business trip, and he had also been at the airfield on Monday 8 December expecting to take the Clipper back to the Philippines. He was incarcerated in Stanley Internment Camp, but as a US national he was repatriated in June 1942. His wife, at their home in the Philippines, was interned at Santo Tomas Camp in Manila and was not freed until American troops fought their way into the camp in February 1945.

The oldest hotel guest was eighty-one-year-old Dr Lewis Arlington, a writer and Sinologist. There were diplomats like Baron Jules Guillaume, the Belgian Ambassador to China, and a number of European residents of Shanghai who had been visiting Hong Kong. There were wealthy Chinese families and the European owners of villas in the Repulse Bay area who had moved to the hotel for safety. Ethel Wilmer was one of several guests whose husbands were serving with the HKVDC. Her sixty-one-year-old husband Harry, an employee of Jardine Matheson, was a veteran of the First World War. After the battle ended, they were both interned at Stanley Camp. Ethel died in May 1944 aged sixty-three. Harry survived the period of incarceration and was first repatriated to New Zealand on a hospital ship, and then in January 1946 he was repatriated to Britain. He died later that year aged sixty-five. Two more lives cut short by the privations of internment.

A committee was formed to represent and organise the civilians during the siege. The committee was comprised of Major Charles Manners, a veteran of the First World War and a well-known businessman in Hong

Kong; Andrew Shields, a member of LEGCO and a director of HSBC; and Jan Marsman, the proprietor of Marsman & Co. After the battle, Marsman was able to avoid internment by claiming to be a resident of the Philippines, and he later escaped from Hong Kong to Free China. Manners and Shields both died while interned at Stanley Camp.

The Japanese troops besieged in the garage block tried to signal to their comrades on the hillside by pushing Japanese flags on bamboo poles through the windows, but the flags were shot away each time they appeared. Grenades were thrown into the garage through the open doorway at the west end of the building, and it was during this exchange of fire that the advance troops from East Infantry Brigade began arriving in Repulse Bay. The lead troops were fired on from the eastern end of the garage block as they approached the hotel. Artillery fire from an 18-pdr positioned at Stanley View was brought to bear on the garage, and the garage was retaken shortly after this. A small number of Japanese troops managed to escape by dropping from the rear windows, but the rest had been killed. The British captives had all survived. 2/Lt Peter Grounds, 1/Mx, who had been in charge of the pillboxes along this section of the shoreline and had helped organise the attack on the garage, was killed during the firefight. Sub-Lt Edward Slay, HKRNVR, was killed while firing from the window in one of the rooms in the hotel's west wing.

As a result of heavy fire from Middle Spur, the counterattack by East Infantry Brigade had stalled at Repulse Bay. 'A' Coy, RRC, commanded by Major Young, was ordered to remain at Repulse Bay and to hold the hotel, while the rest of the attacking force withdrew to the defensive perimeter around Stanley. From this time on the hotel was under constant fire. Any movement resulted in fire from Japanese snipers concealed on the hillside around the hotel. Many of the civilians took shelter during the day in a large drainage tunnel that ran under the hotel and emerged on the beach. It was damp and dark, lit only by a few kerosene lamps, but it provided protection from bullets and mortar bombs. During the daylight hours, members of the garrison armed with a rifle and assisted by a spotter with binoculars were posted at every rear window. They would scour the hillside for movement or a muzzle flash to reveal the snipers' positions. At times the hotel came under mortar fire; the noise and blast of the mortar bombs shaking the building would have been terrifying for the civilians huddled either in the drainage tunnel or in the lobby for safety.

Major Templer arrived at the hotel at around 1700 hours on Sunday 21 December with orders to take command of all the troops in the Repulse Bay area. Conditions at the hotel were rapidly deteriorating. There was no running water, no electricity and the toilets were overflowing. Several members of the garrison had been killed. There was a growing number of wounded men, who were given first aid by Elizabeth Mosey, the sixty-four-year-old hotel nurse. She had taken the job expecting it to be a semi-retirement type role with only the light nursing requirements of a resort hotel. Instead, she found herself in a full-scale battle, dealing with serious battlefield injuries. She used the hotel's Bamboo Lounge as a hospital and was assisted by some of the hotel guests. Later in the siege, an ambulance with a doctor was sent out from Stanley. The ambulance was shot up at the road bridge just to the east of the hotel, but the doctor made it through to the hotel on foot.

It became clear that something had to be done urgently about the civilians in the hotel – either they had to leave, or the military had to leave. Discussions were held about the possibility of evacuating the civilians either by barge from the beach or by lorry to Stanley after nightfall on Monday 22 December. However, both options for evacuating civilians were considered too dangerous, and in the end, it was decided to evacuate the military personnel from the hotel overnight on Monday, so that the civilians could surrender the hotel to the Japanese on the morning of Tuesday 23 December. To avoid any panic, the civilians, other than the senior representatives, were not told of the planned military evacuation. After nightfall on 22 December, Templer addressed the troops in the lobby, speaking in both English and Urdu. He told them they were to take off their boots and march in their socks to Stanley by way of Stanley View. The plan was that the troops would follow Benny Proulx through the drainage tunnel to the beach, and he would then lead the way along the beach and up the hillside to Stanley View.

At approximately 0200 hours in the early morning of Tuesday 23 December, Proulx exited one of the rear windows, crossed the exposed terrace, and entered the greenhouse where a manhole gave access by way of metal rungs to the drainage tunnel. Proulx clambered down while Templer remained at the top of the ladder supervising the troops who followed Proulx into the tunnel. However, the clatter of steel helmets and rifles made such a lot of noise, and the progress was so slow, that Templer decided that the rest should go out through a side exit of the hotel rather than through the drain. When Proulx reached Beach Road, he only counted some thirty men emerging from the tunnel behind him whereas the garrison consisted of over two hundred troops. He went back through the tunnel only to discover that the rest of the military had left through another exit. He re-joined his group, and they proceeded along Beach Road, walking in single file with the hillside on their left and the beach on their right. They carried on past the Lido and then started looking for the path that led uphill to Stanley View. They could hear the sound of shooting and shouting as other parties ran into Japanese patrols, but their group made it through the barbed wire entanglements and up to Stanley View, which was still held by Canadian troops. They reached Stanley at around 0600 hours on Tuesday 23 December.

Evacuation of the Pillboxes

Major Marsh, commanding 'C' Coy, 1/Mx, based at Shouson Hill, was responsible for the pillboxes along the shoreline from the west side of Brick Hill (PB 12) to South Bay (PB 20). The pillboxes in the vicinity of Repulse Bay Hotel included PB 17 on the beach near the hotel garage block, PB 17 (A) east of the hotel, PB 18 near the Lido, PB 19 at Middle Bay and PB 20 at South Bay. PB 17 (A) was not a beach defence pillbox and was not manned by the Middlesex Regiment. It was at one time utilised by the Winnipeg Grenadiers, but it was unoccupied during the siege of the hotel. 2/Lt Cheesewright, 1/Mx, commanded PB 15 at Deep Water Bay, PB 16 opposite Middle Island, and PB 17 at Repulse Bay. 2/Lt Grounds, 1/Mx, commanded PB 18, PB 19 and PB 20. The pillboxes from PB 12 to PB 16 had been evacuated with the exception of PB 14, situated at the western end of Deep Water Bay near the current location of the Country Club. This pillbox became cut off, and its crew were all killed. After Grounds was killed in the exchange of fire with the Japanese in the hotel garage, command of all 'C' Coy pillboxes in the Repulse Bay area passed to 2/Lt Cheesewright.

The crew of PB 17 had been augmented by several Winnipeg Grenadiers who been separated from their units, some of them possibly from the roadblock at the junction of Repulse Bay Road and Island Road. During the night of 20 December, Pte Hogan, 'C' Coy, 1/Mx, and Pte Rutherford, 'C' Coy, WG, were taken by surprise and killed while on sentry duty outside PB 17. The PBs along the shoreline at Repulse Bay were in touch with their Coy HQ at Shouson Hill by telephone but had become isolated from the rest of the company because the Japanese occupied the road between Repulse Bay and Shouson Hill. On Monday 22 December, Cheesewright was called to a meeting at Repulse Bay Hotel and ordered by Templer to evacuate his pillboxes that night.

At about 1700 hours 22 December, I was called to Repulse Bay Hotel by Major Templer, RA, who informed me that he was taking over command of the area and that I was to evacuate my PBs after 2400 hours. I protested that although I was cut off from my Coy HQ, I was still in telephone communication with my Coy Commander. Major Templer repeated that I was to take orders from him and that I was to take all my men through to Stanley by route march and that on no account must there be any sound, as it would jeopardise the whole withdrawal scheme. No boots were to be worn on the march. I issued these orders to PB commanders on returning to PB No. 17, which I used as my HQ. I found more Canadians had arrived making the strength of the PB personnel up to seventeen. Three men were posted as sentries, and a meal prepared.[2]

Cheesewright ordered the crews of the four PBs to be out of their pillboxes by midnight and ready to join the other crews as they marched through. Cpl Munchenbach, commander of PB 20 at South Bay, was instructed to act as guide as he knew the trail up to Stanley View. At around 2000 hours the men in PB 17 heard shouts and a commotion outside their pillbox. They opened the door to let in Pte Dodson and Pte Matthews. Pte Claude Dodson was the soldier who had been taken prisoner by the Japanese on 20 December at the hotel garages. The two soldiers informed Cheesewright that the Japanese were all around the PB and that the third sentry, Pte White, WG, had been bayoneted. Cheesewright then telephoned Sgt Manning at PB 19, at Middle Bay, and ordered him to fire on PB 17, which drove the Japanese off, at least temporarily.

As we could not move until 2400 hours, we had the unpleasant task of waiting in the PB with the enemy in the immediate vicinity. The crew remained calm and orderly. Soon the Japanese returned, and we saw flashes and heard explosions, presumably grenades thrown at the door and loopholes, also on the roof. At 2345 hours, Pte Matthews and myself opened the door and cleared the way with grenades. We succeeded in getting all our men out on the road. We reached PB 18 and found it was empty. Sniping commenced from the beach, and a firefight started behind the Dairy Farm Kiosk. We remained there for about thirty minutes and eventually started again and reached PB19. We found Sgt Manning was still in the PB waiting on the telephone and his crew assembled on the road ready to move as instructed. There was still a certain amount of shooting so I sent a man down to get Sgt Manning and took my party on to PB 20. There I found the crew of PB 18 quite safe. Sgt Manning arrived, checked his kit and found one gun missing. He called for volunteers to return to the PB to get the gun and L/Cpl Edmunds and Pte Evans volunteered. Cpl Caslake, Pte Jenkins and myself armed with Tommy guns accompanied them. We found the MG on the road and got safely back to PB 20. The whole party, fifty-seven strong, of which thirty-five were Middlesex now moved off, but the guide went too quickly, and we lost touch as it was very dark.[3]

One of the Canadian soldiers knew the way up to Stanley View by way of a trail beside the pipelines. They went up this trail where they met up with the original guide. They passed through Stanley View and reached Stanley Prison at 0515 hours. It was a remarkable achievement to fight their way out of the PBs, to link up with the other PBs, and to escape with all their weapons to Stanley.

Surrender of the Hotel

The last of the troops left the hotel just before dawn, and a white flag was hoisted, but nobody was sure whether it had been seen by the Japanese in the pre-dawn light. As the Japanese carefully approached the hotel from the rear, Shields, who spoke some Japanese, was calling out in their language that there were no soldiers in the hotel, and that they were civilians. The Japanese entered early that morning with fixed bayonets. The hotel guests were ordered to come down and assemble in the hotel lobby. They were then lined up in front of the hotel. The Japanese relieved them of anything of value, like rings and necklaces. Some of the guests had remained in their rooms, including Gwen Dew and Beatrice Ohl, but most had come down and joined the line-up and were then marched the short distance up to Eucliffe, which the Japanese were using as an HQ. The group consisted of elderly guests, like Dr Arlington, and mothers with young children. On the way, they had to pass the bodies of British soldiers still lying where they fell. They gathered outside the entrance gates to Eucliffe and were then addressed by a senior Japanese officer, who it later transpired was Colonel Tanaka. They were made to remove their hats and bow while Tanaka berated them through an interpreter. He chastised the men for not fighting for their country as Japanese men would, and he chastised the women for not staying at home, like Japanese women.

Beatrice Ohl had been staying with her husband and children at the hotel. She was a French national, married to Rene Ohl, who was the manager of Messageries Maritimes. She had chosen to stay in her room that morning, but from the hotel she had seen the killing of British soldiers held captive in the grounds of Eucliffe. She testified at war crimes trials conducted after the war.

> I remember Miss Matheson, the Manageress, coming in at 7:30 in the morning and she told us we had surrendered the hotel. Then the Japanese came in and took everybody over to Eucliffe. I did not go as I stayed in my room with my husband. After that, we were called down into the dining room and given a lecture. We were told to clean up the hotel, and as I stood in the hotel, I heard some shots. They came

from the direction of Eucliffe, and when I looked out of the window in the direction of Eucliffe, I saw what appeared to be European soldiers kneeling down, their bodies on the grassy slopes. After that, we went back to our rooms and then looking out the window I saw a Chinese civilian bayoneted by the Japanese. He had come to the hotel. We had lunch, and we were left alone. The next morning all the British civilian prisoners were taken away and I with my husband and children and about sixteen or seventeen other people, all foreigners, remained in the hotel. We stayed there until 3 January 1942.[4]

During the day, they were ordered to tidy up the hotel and to collect all military equipment including helmets, gas masks, weapons and other kit that had been discarded by the soldiers. They were told to make a complete list of all civilian residents of the hotel with names and room numbers. Lunch was served, which for those who were marched off the following day would be their last meal for some forty-eight hours. They were told to be in their rooms by 2100 hours for roll call. The Japanese took over some of the rooms for billeting their troops. The next morning, 24 December, the residents were required to assemble early in the morning. A roll call was conducted, and one of the hotel guests, Victor Needa, a Eurasian jockey who could speak Japanese, acted as interpreter. They were then segregated, with the third nationals like Beatrice Ohl, and some infirm like Albert Compton, remaining at the hotel. Elizabeth Mosey insisted on remaining in the hotel to look after her wounded patients. The Chinese men were separated from their wives and children and then marched off with the British, Dutch and American civilians. The civilians in the marching group numbered some 150. They were given a few minutes to pack a suitcase, and then marched out of the hotel to begin their incarceration, which for most would last three and a half years, ending with the Japanese capitulation in August 1945.

The Long March to North Point

They were marched from the hotel to North Point. This involved a long climb up Repulse Bay Road to WNC Gap, and then down Blue Pool Road to Causeway Bay and North Point. The line lengthened as the elderly, and mothers with young children, fell further behind. Henry Woulfe-Flanagan stated that several abandoned cars were commandeered by the Japanese sentries and used to run the women and children in relays to the gap. Later a lorry was obtained in which they were able to place their baggage. As they went up Repulse Bay Road, the group had to pass many of the British dead. Henry Woulfe-Flanagan testified that a number of the bodies they passed had their hands tied behind their backs.

During many hours of this walk we were passing through what had been a battlefield, and here again, I came across evidence of the most savage butchery. In fact, in many cases where it was necessary to move bodies in order to clear the road, I saw Japanese soldiers step forward with a knife and stoop down and cut the bonds, which tied their hands. A young Canadian soldier was brought from a house during our march and joined our ranks. He was wounded in the chest, but nevertheless, his hands were bound, and he told me he had been given neither food nor water since his capture some twenty-four hours previously. My wife and I managed to get him to swallow a little water. I helped him along as best I could, but later he was separated from us. Later we saw a starving Indian soldier surrender. He was systematically kicked and beaten by the Japanese, and when he was lying on the ground, he was ordered to stand up, and on doing so, he was promptly tripped and knocked down again. This game was continued for a good ten minutes and was undoubtedly staged for our special benefit. We saw Chinese who had been accused of looting strung up to railings as if for crucifixion tied by wire and continually being assaulted by the Japanese.[5]

At around 1500 hours they reached North Point, by now completely exhausted, where they sat on the pavement outside a temporary Gendarmerie HQ for several hours while the Japanese arranged for two senior members of the group, Charles Manners and Andrew Shields, to pass through the front line and relay to the Governor and GOC the futility of further resistance. Japanese newspaper reporters took photographs of the dishevelled group of civilians, some of whom were interviewed by Japanese reporters curious to see the captured foreigners. Some of the men in the group were interrogated by the Gendarmes. Hank Marsman related how sixty-three-year-old John Seth was punched and kicked and thrown to the ground when his answers failed to satisfy the interrogators. Sixty-year-old Alfred Humphries was beaten with the flat of a sword and with fists.

Manners and Shields left the group in the evening, although it was not until the following morning that they crossed the front line. They were instructed to return by noon on 25 December. At dusk on 24 December, the remainder of the group was moved into the looted and badly damaged Duro Paint factory at North Point. British guns were still periodically shelling the North Point area, and shells were exploding close to the paint factory. Shields and Manners returned at noon on Christmas Day as they had been ordered, but the Japanese were angry that they were late. The Japanese were using Tokyo time, which was one hour ahead of Hong Kong time. During the afternoon on Thursday 25 December, the civilian group were taken by lorry from the paint factory to Tai Koo Sugar Refinery from where they were taken by lighter to Kowloon and incarcerated in the Kowloon Hotel, which was serving as a temporary civilian internment centre.

In the late afternoon, on Christmas Day, the sound of gunfire died down, and an eerie silence prevailed. Hong Kong had surrendered.

15

The Japanese Advance
20 to 25 December

The Japanese advance was held up at WNC Gap by the persistence of the garrison holding out at 'D' Coy, WG shelters, and by the Royal Scots and 2/14 Punjabs doggedly holding on to Tai Hang Road and the lower part of the Blue Pool Valley. This prevented the Japanese from moving down WNC Gap Road and Blue Pool Road towards Happy Valley and Wan Chai. Likewise, the presence of British troops holding out at The Ridge curtailed Japanese vehicular access and troop movement down Repulse Bay Road. Consequently, the Japanese were forced to use the water catchment on Violet Hill as the main supply route for their troops at and around Middle Spur, who were laying siege to another holdout position at Repulse Bay Hotel. These holdout positions at WNC Gap, The Ridge and Repulse Bay were surrendered during the period 22–23 December, allowing the Japanese to accelerate their advance westwards.

The Japanese Advance along the South Shore

Colonel Tanaka's two battalions arrived at Stanley Gap during the late afternoon on Friday 19 December. Their RV was the food store building opposite the Stanley Gap AA position. One company had remained in the rear to garrison the Tai Tam Gap and Boa Vista locality. Tanaka's original plan had been to move south-west from WNC Gap to Shouson Hill, but WNC Gap was still being contested, and instead he decided to move south by way of the water catchment running from WNC Gap Reservoir towards Repulse Bay. He ordered one detachment to proceed directly to Shouson Hill. Tanaka, when questioned at war crimes trials held after the war, stated that he was unaware of the route this detachment took. They may have followed a path from WNC Gap down to Deep Water Bay Golf Course, cutting their way through the wire entanglements that covered those slopes, and then ascended the hillside from or near the golf course. They may have followed Deep Water Bay Road under cover of darkness towards Shouson Hill. The RASC Depot at the golf course and the workshops at Shouson Hill had been evacuated. 'A' Coy, Winnipeg Grenadiers, had been headquartered at Shouson Hill, but most of the company had been deployed and destroyed the previous night. 'C' Coy, 1/Mx, were headquartered at Shouson Hill, and those troops that were not manning beach defence pillboxes guarded the area around Little Hong Kong Magazines.

The Shouson Hill area was lightly held, and the Japanese detachment managed to avoid British patrols and occupy a dominant hill feature at Shouson Hill, referred to as Hill 143. At the top of this dome-shaped hill, there was a disused pre-war AA fort. The concrete gun emplacements and the retaining walls provided good cover for the Japanese to fire down onto Island Road and Deep Water Bay. Having established themselves at

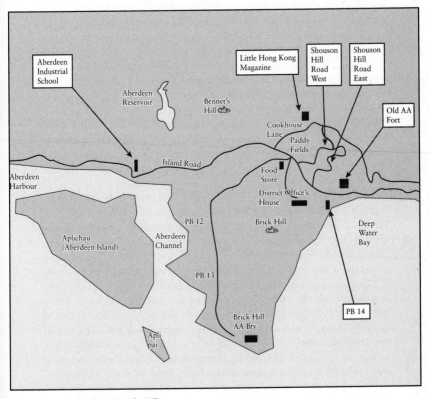

Shouson Hill and Brick Hill.

the old AA fort, troops from this unit infiltrated down to Island Road and the paddy fields and hutments either side of Island Road, north of Brick Hill. One section of Japanese troops occupied a culvert running underneath Island Road and held it with great determination despite every effort to dislodge them.

By the morning of 20 December, the Tanaka *butai* were in possession of Violet Hill and Middle Spur, both of which overlooked Repulse Bay. They had possession of the critical road junction between Deep Water Bay and Repulse Bay and by occupying the old AA fort they had secured a foothold on Shouson Hill. Later in the day Japanese troops started moving westwards along Island Road towards Deep Water Bay Golf Club and may have linked up with the detachment sent to Shouson Hill. The presence of Japanese troops at the old AA fort, at the culvert and at the road junction had closed off the vehicular route from Aberdeen to Repulse Bay and Stanley. Any further encroachment westward by the Japanese posed a threat to the Little Hong Kong Magazines, the 1/Mx positions on Shouson Hill, the Brick Hill AA Section and ultimately the naval base situated at the Aberdeen Industrial School. It was important to dislodge the Japanese at Shouson Hill in order to clear the road for a counterattack on the road junction which if recaptured would open the way to Repulse Bay and Stanley. During the morning on 20 December, in the absence of immediately available Army units, the senior naval officer at AIS was ordered to send a naval patrol acting as infantry to stop the Japanese from advancing further west towards Aberdeen. At about the same time, 'A' Coy, 2/14 Punjabs, commanded by Captain Thomson, was ordered to proceed to Aberdeen, to liaise with the Navy and then to clear the area of enemy troops. 'A' Coy was understrength and consisted of only thirty to forty personnel.

Earlier that morning, a Royal Scots detachment based at AIS, under CSM Robert Milne, had been sent out to conduct a recce of the area. The Royal Scots had exchanged fire with Japanese troops who were located east of the government food store building on Island Road. They reported that a section of Japanese troops had occupied a drainage culvert running under the road. A party from 'C' Coy, 1/Mx, under 2/Lt Mace, tried to break through and clear the Japanese from the culvert using a Bren gun carrier. The carrier was shot up and overturned. One soldier was wounded and was taken to nearby PB 14, situated on the shoreline under Brick Hill. The rest of the 1/Mx detachment withdrew under fire. Later that morning the RN patrol arrived from AIS, led by Commander Millett and comprising six HKRNVR officers and thirty-five naval ratings. The patrol deployed around the government food store building at the junction of Cookhouse Lane and Island Road.

Captain Thomson, 'A' Coy, 2/14 Punjabs, arrived at 1030 hours. His orders were to clear the enemy from Island Road, and then to proceed eastwards in the direction of Repulse Bay. He immediately set out along the road with two 15-cwt trucks, but as they rounded the bend east of the food stores, they were fired on by the Japanese at the culvert some 200 metres from the food store building. The driver of the first lorry was killed instantly, and the second lorry was disabled. These two vehicles, together with the overturned Bren gun carrier, blocked the road and made it difficult for other vehicles to break through. Thomson was forced to withdraw his troops to the food store. An attempt was made to destroy the Japanese section holding out at the culvert by mortar fire from Bennet's Hill, but the Japanese were too well entrenched and were able to take cover in the culvert which ran under the road, and protected them from the mortar barrage

The RN contingent was split into two parties. One, under Lt-Commander Collingwood-Selby, was deployed to the south of Island Road, while the other, under Lt-Commander Binney, was deployed north of the road close to the junction with Cookhouse Lane. The remainder, consisting of 2/14 Punjabs, the 2/RS detail and some twelve naval ratings, were deployed near the food store. A stand-off developed, and skirmishes were fought against small parties of Japanese troops who had infiltrated into the hutments and paddy fields either side of Island Road. During the afternoon, Major Gordon Neve, GSO-2, and Captain Godfrey Bird, GSO-3, both staff officers from Fortress HQ, visited the naval base at AIS and then proceeded to the food store at Brick Hill to assess the situation. Major Neve assumed command of the military forces in the area around the food store. At approximately 1530 hours, Major Neve led a fighting patrol in an attack on the enemy section in the culvert. The patrol consisted of Captain Bird, Sub-Lt Knox, HKRNVR, and CQMS Benson, 2/RS, with six ORs. They occupied a forward trench east of the food store with line-of-sight on the culvert and opened fire. The Japanese returned fire both from the culvert and also from huts situated south of Island Road. The Japanese in the hutment to the half-right were between the culvert and Major Neve's trench, and close enough to be within grenade range. Grenades were exchanged, but Major Neve's group only had three Mills bombs. One or more of the Japanese grenades exploded in their trench, severely wounding Major Neve, Captain Bird and several others. The casualties were evacuated to AIS. Major Neve died from his wounds at Queen Mary Hospital in January 1942.

During the same afternoon 2/Lt Wood, 'C' Coy, 1/Mx, led two successive assaults against the Japanese in the culvert. In the first attack, which used machine guns, his unit failed to dislodge the Japanese, but a second attack with grenades destroyed the enemy position. Wood then drove through the vehicle wreckage in an 8-cwt truck. He must have had to abandon the vehicle because Major Marsh wrote that Wood later returned on foot to Coy HQ. At 1800 hours, Major Charles Boxer arrived by car from Fortress HQ with Wing Commander Alf Bennett. They were both Japanese linguists, and before the war had been responsible for listening to Japanese communications. The two staff officers decided to go and find out what was happening at Brick Hill and why the road was not yet opened up. Major Boxer went forward on foot between the food store and the hutments on a reconnaissance patrol. He was accompanied by Lt Price and Sub-Lt Forster both HKRNVR. They came under fire, and grenades were thrown at them from the hutment. Boxer was wounded in this exchange and was later carried back to the food stores by Price and Forster. Lt Price was killed near the food store by sniper fire. The road remained blocked.

The next morning, HMS *Cicala* received a signal ordering her to proceed to Deep Water Bay to assist PB 14, which was reported as being surrounded by Japanese troops. As *Cicala* sailed into Deep Water Bay, Lt Beattie was on the compass platform searching for the pillbox with his binoculars. He was sniped at from the hillside of Brick Hill while standing on the exposed compass platform. The ship was then engaged by Japanese artillery located at WNC Gap. *Cicala* was straddled by shells and immediately withdrew stern-first while engaging the enemy artillery with her 3-inch HA gun. Once she was out in the open water of the Lamma Channel, she deployed her 6-inch forward gun to return fire at the Japanese artillery. She fired fifteen HE rounds and five anti-personnel rounds at a range of approximately 5,000 metres.

At 0900 hours, while in the Lamma Channel, *Cicala* was attacked by a squadron of six Japanese aircraft. She quickly adopted the AA configuration, with Lt Davies in charge of the 3-inch HA gun and Lt Beattie at the pom-pom gun. The aircraft attacked the ship individually, dropping sticks of bombs, which *Cicala* managed to avoid. However, on the third and fourth attacks, *Cicala*'s luck ran out and she received a series of direct hits. One bomb exploded on the upper deck, one went through the mess decks, and another passed right through the bottom of the ship. One man was killed, and three were severely injured. The ship lost way and started sinking by the stern. Lt-Commander Gandy brought MTB 10 alongside *Cicala* and took off the crew. Lt Kennedy, in MTB 09, was ordered to ensure that *Cicala* sank to prevent her from falling into Japanese hands. MTB 09 fired off three depth charges alongside the stricken ship. After surviving some sixty-three dive-bombing attacks, *Cicala* finally gave up the ghost and sank slowly in the East Lamma Channel.

Sgt Jack Rich and his crew at PB 14 may have seen *Cicala* sailing close inshore that morning, and then withdrawing under fire. They had previously reported by telephone to Major Marsh, at Coy HQ, that they were under close-range enemy fire, and that during the previous night they had heard Japanese troops on top of their pillbox. They also reported that they were running very short of food and water, but it was difficult to assist them as by that time they were behind enemy lines.

Maltby, impatient that 'A' Coy, 2/14 Punjabs, had made such little progress in freeing up the road, ordered Lt-Col Gerald Kidd, the battalion commander, to dispatch a senior officer to the location and take command. Kidd decided to go himself. His orders were to open the road between Aberdeen and Repulse Bay, and in so doing dislodge the enemy from the Shouson Hill area. It had rained heavily during the night, but Sunday 21st was a bright and clear morning. The RN party, under Lt-Commander Binney, with several officers and twenty-five ratings, left AIS and reported to Lt-Col Kidd at the junction of Island Road and Cook House Lane. The Punjabs had remained on Island Road throughout the night. The company had by then been depleted to less than platoon strength and consisted of Captain Thomson, Lt Forsyth and about twenty IORs. Kidd's first objective was to seize the old AA fort. Once the enemy had been cleared from the old AA fort hill and the road, two Bren gun carriers were standing by to force their way along Island Road and through to Repulse Bay.

The combined force proceeded up Cookhouse Lane, with Lt-Col Kidd leading the way. Thomson and Forsyth with some twenty IORs followed, and behind them came the RN contingent. They proceeded up the sunken lane in a north-easterly direction to the junction with Shouson Hill Road West. They then moved in an easterly direction and passed House No. 11, which was being used as Major Marsh's Coy HQ. They passed the Advanced Dressing Station and came within sight of the red-roofed bungalow immediately below Hill 143. The bungalow, which was occupied by Japanese troops, had to be stormed before the Punjabs could scale the hillside to clear the AA fort. The Punjabs were split into two sections, one under Thomson and the other under Forsyth. One section was to attack from the north-west and the other section from the south. Kidd, with four IORs, was to attack the rear of the bungalow using grenades, and the naval party was to attack the front of the house. It was while attacking the bungalow that Lt-Col Kidd was shot in the head and killed instantly.

The hillside was steep, and it was slippery because of the overnight rain. There was no mortar or artillery support, and the Japanese were able to fire down on the two assault teams as they struggled up the hill. With casualties mounting, the attack had to be called off.

There were only eight IORs and two British officers left. The remnants of the two Punjabi sections withdrew back to the ADS without being aware that the naval party was still at the bungalow. Lt-Commander Binney had lost eight men killed or wounded in attacking the bungalow. Once he realised that the attack by the Punjabs had been unsuccessful, he ordered the RN contingent to withdraw back to Island Road. The road down to the ADS was by then covered by Japanese machine guns, and they were forced to take shelter under a road bridge before withdrawing to the food store after dark. Two naval officers, Lt Mitchell and Sub-Lt Rose, became separated from the rest of the naval party. They reached House No. 23 some forty-eight hours later on 23 December, having spent two days evading Japanese patrols. No. 23 was being utilised by a naval contingent commanded by Major Dewar, RASC, and Lt Horey, RNVR.

Major Dewar had been at The Ridge, and on 20 December had been part of the group under Lt-Col Frederick which had left The Ridge with orders to reoccupy the RASC workshops and facilities at Shouson Hill. The group, some of whom were in lorries and others marching, were ambushed at the road junction with Island Road. Most of the survivors withdrew back up Repulse Bay Road to The Ridge. Dewar, who had left The Ridge after the main party, continued down the road, passing those returning to The Ridge from the ambush, and waited to see if any stragglers had been left behind. He came across Sgt Sheil, RASC, who thought there were no other British troops in front of his position. While at the roadside they spotted a group of Japanese soldiers working their way up the road towards them. They let the Japanese approach and then opened fire at close range, killing at least four, with another four to eight killed or wounded. The Japanese then started reinforcing their troops on the road while trying to outflank Dewar and Sheil's position by moving up the hillside. Dewar and Sheil managed to escape entrapment by going down the steep hillside on the right-hand side of the road, which led down to the golf course at Deep Water Bay. They followed the perimeter of the golf course towards Shouson Hill, staying under cover of the trees. They noticed the Japanese flag flying from the old AA fort.

They reached the food store building at Brick Hill before the Japanese had started to infiltrate into that area. Near the food store, they came across a naval party made up from HMS *Tern*'s crew and commanded by Lt Horey. Horey's party consisted of some twenty naval personnel. Dewar and Sheil decided to join up with Horey's group. Dewar, as the senior officer, assumed command. Dewar and Horey reported to Major Marsh at his Coy HQ and were asked to garrison House No. 23. The aim was to help protect Marsh's exposed flank, prevent snipers getting into houses that overlooked Marsh's Coy HQ and to assist in keeping the road clear from Aberdeen to the Little Hong Kong Magazines. Dewar reported to his commanding officer, Lt-Col Andrews-Levinge, that he had reached Shouson Hill, and was assisting in the defence of the area. As it happened, No. 23 was Andrews-Levinge's home. His wife Ida was a VAD nurse working at St Stephen's College Hospital at Stanley. She survived the massacre there and was interned at Stanley Camp after the capitulation. The house provided line-of-sight to the old AA fort and sniper fire was exchanged periodically. Marsh issued the naval party with khaki uniforms to replace their conspicuous blue uniforms and provided them with LMGs and a Vickers gun, and he allocated two 1/Mx machine gunners to their group.

By the end of the day on Sunday 21 December, nothing much had been achieved in the Shouson Hill area. The attack on the old AA fort had failed, and there had been a large number of casualties. The Japanese were still in control of the former AA fort, and they had a foothold on Brick Hill. They had occupied the district officer's house, which was built on a spur of Brick Hill directly above PB 14. Marsh called for an artillery barrage to be laid down on the district officer's house to try and assist the beleaguered crew of PB 14, who were still holding out although completely surrounded. Some thirty howitzer rounds were fired. One shell struck the area south of the house, but the other rounds went wide. It was a difficult target because the house was situated on a narrow ridge with little depth or breadth. During the morning on 22 December, an ambulance from Aberdeen managed to get through to the brick-and-tile works close to PB 14 without being shot up. The one serious casualty, Pte Bridge, who had been wounded on 20 December, was evacuated. At the same time, food and water were passed to the PB crew. Marsh described how this gallant crew continued to hold out until 24 December, when they were all killed.

During the day on Tuesday 23 December, several appeals for help came from PB 14 by telephone to which I was powerless to respond. It appears that during the previous night ... some of the PB crew had manned the Lyon Light shelter with a Bren gun to cover the PB and prevent the enemy from getting on to it. However, the Japanese had thrown grenades through the shutters, and the occupants were all wounded. I finally tried to get an ambulance through to them again, after all efforts by Royal Navy MTBs, and the gunboat had failed to relieve them. I had hoped to obtain an armoured car to relieve them, but none was available. ... Early in the morning of 24 December PB 14 again rang up but after a few whispered words about the enemy being on top of their PB the telephone went dead, and I heard no more.[1]

Major Dewar was instrumental in observing and directing artillery fire at Japanese troop movements on Mount Nicholson and on the east side of Mount Cameron. He directed fire several times with the 9.2-inch guns at Stanley on Japanese troop concentrations on Nicholson. There are still numerous foxholes on Nicholson where Japanese troops dug in to seek cover from this artillery fire. Major Marsh took part in firing one of the Vickers guns installed at House No. 23.

Throughout the day [22 December] all movement on Nicholson was engaged by effective MMG fire at a range of 1,700 yards. The MMG was concealed in a sandbagged position well inside a window of No. 23, whilst I was firing the gun with the naval ratings busy re-filling belts, and with a naval officer spotting through field glasses beside me, we hit several Japs who were climbing the hills.[2]

On Thursday 24 December, there was a very heavy mortar barrage directed at the 1/Mx positions on Shouson Hill, which was thought to be preliminary to an attack. Marsh ordered Lt Hanlon, RAOC, and his ordnance group to evacuate the magazines with the intention of concentrating his troops on the high ground around House No. 23. On reporting this to Fortress HQ, Marsh was told that another ammunition convoy was expected to pick up ordnance from the magazine that night (24/25 December). Marsh then instructed Lt Hanlon to reopen the magazines, and Dewar and his contingent of Army and Navy personnel were ordered to reinforce the RAOC detail at the magazines. The ammunition convoy came through at around 2200 hours, using Cookhouse Lane, which was screened by thick undergrowth on either side.

At 0400 hours on 25 December, the Japanese attacked the Brick Hill AA fort located at the southern end of the promontory. The AA position was under the command of twenty-two-year-old Lt Gordon Fairclough, RA. With him was Captain Bob Bartram, RA, who was in command of some fifty Chinese recruits for the 5th AA Regiment. The gunners used one of the 3.7-inch AA guns as an infantry weapon by lowering the gun to the horizontal position, and setting the fuses so that the shells would explode shortly after leaving the barrel. The positioning of one gun, behind the other, meant that only one of the guns could be utilised, but this one gun took a heavy toll on the attacking Japanese infantry. Captain Bartram was last seen engaging the Japanese with a sub-machine gun before he was shot through the neck and killed. The Japanese, attacking from the high ground to the north of the promontory, eventually overran the guns. Fairclough was shot through the chest. The impact of the bullet knocked him down the steep hillside, and he lost consciousness. After nightfall, he escaped down the cliff to the shoreline, not realising that by this time the colony had surrendered. He was incarcerated at Sham Shui Po Camp, from where he escaped in February 1942, and made his way to Free China and re-joined British forces. The RA war diary reports that one BOR from this AA section also managed to escape by getting down to the shoreline and swimming to Aberdeen.

'C' Coy, WG, commanded by Major Baillie, was responsible for the defence of Aberdeen Reservoir and Bennet's Hill. Bennet's Hill was situated between the reservoir and Aberdeen. A number of troops from other units, including RAF and RN personnel, had been assigned to this sector to augment the Winnipeg Grenadiers. The troops defending the hill and the reservoir were subjected to a heavy mortar barrage on 24 December, and during the evening the Japanese attacked the reservoir and the northern end of the bridge where 'C' Coy shelters were located. By the afternoon on 25 December, Aberdeen Reservoir and Bennet's Hill were at best thinly held.

At around 1030 hours on Christmas Day, Marsh was informed that a temporary ceasefire was in progress. This had been implemented to allow Charles Manners and Andrew Shields to cross the front line on parole from their Japanese captors to meet with the Governor and GOC. An hour later, while the ceasefire was still in progress, several Japanese soldiers came up Cookhouse Lane with a group of Chinese in front acting as a shield. Marsh went out to meet them, but none of them spoke English, and after a while they withdrew back down the sunken lane. At around 1600 hours another party of Japanese approached, again with a group of Chinese in front. Marsh had got the impression from calls he had made to other senior officers that the garrison was on the point of capitulation. In fact, by 1600 hours the garrison had already surrendered. Marsh, although not aware of this, decided to surrender the position.

> My act of surrender to their officer in the normal manner without arms did not prevent one of them from emptying his automatic pistol at me at close range, but the bullets passed through the inside of my trouser legs and only grazed one leg. My company clerk was less fortunate, as he turned around he was promptly shot in the side and had one arm hit by a bullet, and in this state, he was forced to march with the remainder of us, we were all tied up in bundles of four, to Repulse Bay Hotel.[3]

At about the same time as Marsh surrendered his HQ, the Aberdeen naval base received a signal informing them of the official surrender. Lt Lewis Bush, HKRNVR, being a Japanese linguist, was ordered to assist in conducting the surrender of the naval base and liaising with the Japanese.

I stayed at the main gate with the senior naval officer, a destroyer captain named Pears, to await the arrival of the victors. It was almost dark when they did appear, a corporal and a first-class private. They seemed doubtful about the wisdom of approaching too close, and so I went to meet them and spoke in Japanese. The corporal smiled as if greatly relieved and pointing to his bandaged neck said he'd been wounded by one of our bullets, and that his company commander would arrive shortly. … About half an hour later a lieutenant arrived who said his name was Suzuki, whom I conducted to my senior officer.[4]

The next day, 26 December, the AIS personnel were taken by truck and route march to Murray Barracks where British POWs were being assembled prior to incarceration. Bush was required to remain at AIS with a party of some ten officers and men. He was asked to act as an interpreter for the Japanese, and in this capacity, he was ordered to go to Government House with Lt Suzuki and a Japanese colonel who wished to interview Maltby. The Governor was being held at the Peninsula Hotel in Kowloon. Maltby, Collinson and other senior officers from Fortress HQ had collected in the lounge at Government House. Maltby asked the Japanese colonel whether it was the normal Japanese Army practice to rape and kill nurses and to bayonet wounded patients in their hospital beds. The Japanese colonel replied that if this had occurred, the culprits would be identified and punished. Maltby also asked about a group of British soldiers and sailors who had been manning the magazines at Little Hong Kong as there had been no word of them. Suzuki replied that the garrison at the magazine was still holding out, had fired at Japanese soldiers when they approached the magazines and had rigged the magazines with explosives. It was agreed that Bush would accompany Suzuki to the magazines and try to persuade the garrison to surrender. Bush and Suzuki arrived at Shouson Hill at around 0100 hours on 28 December, and after a discussion, the defenders at the magazines agreed to surrender. They were then taken to Aberdeen, and given a slap-up meal by their Japanese captors who admired their willingness to blow themselves up together with the magazines rather than surrender. The next day they were moved to Murray Barracks as prisoners of war, but they earned the distinction of being the last to surrender.

The Japanese Advance along the Line of Gaps

After the failure of the various counterattacks, the British and Canadians had adopted a defensive strategy, and by holding Mount Cameron they prevented the Japanese from proceeding along Black's Link to Wan Chai Gap. Wan Chai Gap was an important military position which included the reconstituted West Brigade HQ and West Group HQ. It accommodated both the Winnipeg Grenadiers and Royal Scots Battalion HQs. The Army occupied many of the residential houses on two parallel roads on the west side of Mount Cameron. The higher of the two roads was Middle Gap Road, and the lower was Mount Cameron Road. The houses were to some extent protected from shelling and bombing by the hillside of Mount Cameron above them. The Army also commandeered a number of the houses on Coombe Road, on the western side of the gap, which led uphill to Magazine Gap. Some of the houses were still occupied by civilians, but most had been taken over by the Army and were being used for billeting, and for storing supplies including ammunition.

On 21 December, Major Trist, WG, second-in-command of the battalion, was ordered to gather all available men and to hold Mount Cameron against an anticipated Japanese attack. During the afternoon, some one hundred men, under Trist, occupied weapons pits and trenches along the line of the ridge facing Mount Nicholson. On 22 December, a detachment of twenty Royal Engineers was dispatched to join Trist's positions on Cameron. The defence was organised into two companies. The right-hand company was under the command of Captain White, WG, and consisted of the RE detachment and two WG platoons. The left-hand company was commanded by Captain Bardal, WG, and consisted of three WG platoons. Difficulties were encountered in supplying water, food and ammunition to the troops on Cameron. It was a steep climb, and everything had to be manhandled up the hill, very often under fire. As a result, the troops manning the hilltop positions were insufficiently rationed and supplied. The lack of hot food, water and other supplies, combined with constant sniping, aerial bombing, artillery and mortar fire, and lack of sleep, did much to undermine the morale of the troops defending Mount Cameron.

On the night of 22/23 December, a Japanese patrol infiltrated onto the crest of Cameron and was able to work its way towards the rear and then bring LMG and light mortar fire on to the British and Canadian positions. This outflanking move by the Japanese led to a precipitous withdrawal by both the left-hand and right-hand companies from their positions on Cameron. With Cameron thought to be in Japanese hands, Wan Chai Gap was compromised, and the bulk of the infantry withdrew up Coombe Road to Magazine Gap, and along to Mount Gough. Sgt Ken Porter, 'B' Coy, WG, was on Middle Gap Road that evening when a truck stopped and Major Pirie and a staff sergeant, both from 2/RS, asked for some men to help them evacuate a group of civilians from two houses at the end of the road. The Japanese must have been in close proximity because just after this Sgt Porter and his group were ambushed by a Japanese patrol which had infiltrated down the slopes of

Mount Cameron. Porter and the Royal Scots used grenades to destroy and disperse the Japanese patrol. Porter described the withdrawal from Cameron as being chaotic, with houses set on fire, and vehicles and troops crowding the three narrow roads. The Royal Artillery was ordered to lay down a barrage on the crest of Cameron. Sgt Porter helped bring down a wounded officer from the rocky path leading up to Mount Cameron, with some of the artillery shells landing uncomfortably close. He then got on the truck, thinking they were returning to Wan Chai Gap.

> Piled on the truck and I sat right on the back with my rifle cocked and a mills [grenade] nestling in my lap. By this time someone had set fire to the ammo in No. 555 and it was going off with a helluva bang. As we went further along the road, just below No. 551, someone had fired the other magazine, and this sure as hell was blazing. All this time I figured that we were going to Wan Chai Gap, but when we got to the gap, we kept going along the upper road [Coombe Road leading to Magazine Gap].[5]

Had the Japanese been aware of the extent of the withdrawal and chaos, they could have walked right in and taken possession of both Mount Cameron and Wan Chai Gap. It is not clear who ordered the withdrawal from Wan Chai Gap, if anybody, but presumably it was Lt-Col Sutcliffe with the assent of Colonel Rose, commanding West Infantry Brigade. Sgt Porter described a conversation he overheard at Wan Chai Gap during the afternoon before the withdrawal took place.

> When at Wan Chai Gap, heard Colonel Rose and Lt-Col Sutcliffe talking to the GOC and telling him that we couldn't stand much more and asking for an armistice. This was the first definite inkling I had of how badly disorganised things really were up above.[6]

Having evacuated Wan Chai Gap and moved up Coombe Road to Mount Gough, the Winnipeg Grenadiers started to regroup and get the men organised into their respective companies and under shelter before the daylight arrival of Japanese aircraft. West Group, RA, under Major Crowe evacuated their HQ at Wan Chai Gap and established a new HQ at Victoria Gap. During the late afternoon on 22 December, before the withdrawal took place, Lt Corrigan, WG, had been ordered to take a patrol out along Black's Link and set up a listening post as close to Middle Gap as they could get. The patrol departed Wan Chai Gap at dusk and got to within 200 metres of Middle Gap. Just before daylight, they moved back along Black's Link to Wan Chai Gap only to find the whole place deserted. They found West Brigade HQ and their Battalion

HQ shelters empty. Corrigan took his patrol up Coombe Road and reported to Lt-Col Frederick Field, RA, who was in charge of troops at Magazine Gap.

Major-General Maltby was informed of the loss of Mount Cameron and Wan Chai Gap in the early hours of 23 December, at which time Colonel Rose advised him that troops were withdrawing in disorder and that efforts were being made to rally them at Magazine Gap and Mount Gough. A detachment of forty Royal Marines was sent up from the RN Dockyard to Magazine Gap to report to Lt-Col Field, and to help repossess Wan Chai Gap. Lt Corrigan was asked to guide the Royal Marine patrol. The Marines proceeded along Black's Link with Corrigan's unit acting as point. They established a section post on the road to defend the approaches to Wan Chai Gap from Black's Link. The Royal Scots had established themselves on the left flank of the summit of Mount Cameron and the Royal Marines subsequently occupied the right flank. During the afternoon of 23 December, the Winnipeg Grenadiers were ordered to reoccupy their positions at Wan Chai Gap and Mount Cameron.

On 23 December, during close-quarters fighting with a Japanese patrol on Mount Cameron, Corrigan was attacked by a Japanese officer wielding a sword. Corrigan grabbed the sword and struggled with his opponent in a fight to the death that knocked them both down the hillside. Corrigan then remembered his sidearm on a lanyard around his neck, but his right hand was badly cut from the sword, making it difficult to squeeze the trigger. Eventually, he was able to shoot his opponent and was left with a severely cut hand and a Japanese sword that had been earned the hard way. Corrigan, always in the thick of action, became known as the 'fighting lieutenant'.

During the afternoon of 25 December, when Corrigan returned to Wan Chai Gap from patrolling on the south side of Mount Cameron, he found the Battalion HQ deserted for the second time. Then he saw that the white flag was flying and discovered that the colony had surrendered. At 1700 hours, Lt-Col White and Captain Ford, 2/RS, together with an orderly, proceeded under a white flag to the Japanese HQ in Stubbs Road to convey the surrender of the military forces in that area.

The Japanese Advance along the North Shore

After the troops holding out at 'D' Coy shelters, opposite West Brigade HQ, had surrendered on Monday 22 December, the way was clear for Colonel Shoji's 230th Regiment to start moving down Blue Pool Road into Happy Valley. After the war, Shoji was acquitted of war crimes, and although his regiment generally behaved more humanely with captured soldiers than the other two infantry regiments, it is likely that it was units from Shoji's *butai* who killed a large number of Chinese civilians taking refuge at No. 42 Blue Pool Road. A group of Japanese soldiers, coming down Blue Pool Road from WNC Gap, entered the property at dusk on 22 December. The Chinese men were ordered out of the house and into the backyard, where they were all slaughtered with bayonets.

Japanese troops, under divisional command, infiltrating westwards towards Causeway Bay came up against the Middlesex Regiment, who had established a strong defensive position on Leighton Hill, a ridge overlooking the racecourse and the surrounding area. The defence of Leighton Hill and the pillboxes, PBs 53, 54, and 55, located around the waterfront of Causeway Bay, were the responsibility of 'Z' Coy, a composite company commanded by Captain Christopher Mann. To the north of Leighton Hill, the ridge extended onto what was known as Chinese Cemetery Ridge, which ran north-east towards Tai Hang Road, and the north-west slopes of Jardine's Lookout. On 19 December, Captain Course, commanding 'B' Coy, 5/7 Rajputs, was positioned on Chinese Cemetery Ridge and to his immediate south was 'B' Coy, 2/14 Punjabs, commanded by Captain Kampta Prasad. Prasad's Coy was deployed to this position at dawn on 19 December. The company had to fight their way to the area designated to them astride Tai Hang Road.

> Owing to the darkness and thick country, it was difficult to clear the enemy out of this area. No 11 Platoon was sent up Blue Pool Road and was not seen again for two days. The area was cleared with hand grenades. No 10 Platoon took the feature on Tai Hang Road at about 1000 hours, and No 12 Platoon occupied a hill on its left. 2/Lt Gillmore was wounded in the head, and both platoons had around twelve casualties. The enemy was engaged at close quarters for about half an hour and was beaten off. It was found impossible to move from this position.[7]

Thirty-four-year-old Walter Gillmore had been commissioned from the Armoured Car Platoon of HKVDC. He died from his wounds in April 1942. 'B' Coy, 2/14 Punjabs, remained in this location, but they were pinned down by Japanese sniper fire from the slopes of Jardine's Lookout above them. On 21 December, they were subjected to an artillery barrage and then attacked from three sides forcing them to withdraw. The company withdrew along Tai Hang Road to the Royal Scots Bn HQ on Stubbs Road, by which time the company had been reduced to less than thirty-five men.

On 19 December, the day following the Japanese landings, Lt-Col Gerald Kidd, 2/14 Punjabs, had been ordered by Fortress HQ to relieve

Captain Newton's, 'D' Coy, 5/7 Rajputs, who were reported to have been surrounded near Braemar Reservoir. In fact, Newton's Coy had been overrun during the previous night, and Newton had been killed in action close to the power station at North Point. Colonel Shoji had established his HQ at Braemar Reservoir during the night. The bulk of his force had already set out along Sir Cecil's Ride to WNC Gap, where they were in action at dawn. Lt-Col Kidd assembled a force consisting of 'A' Coy under Captain Thomson and 'D' Coy under Captain Mathers. The force first advanced up Caroline Hill but found no Japanese troops in the area between Leighton Hill and Caroline Hill. From Caroline Hill, they could see Japanese troops moving along the ridgeline towards Jardine's Lookout, but they were out of range. In the late afternoon, the Punjabs descended the eastern slopes of Caroline Hill and then started up the western slopes of the ridge above Tai Hang village to attack Japanese troops on the ridge path.

> When the two companies were halfway up the western slopes of the main feature, they were fired upon by the enemy who had been lying up in the catch-water. It was evident that a large force of the enemy was moving along the catch-water and on observing the advance of our troops a proportion of the enemy had remained hidden in order to deal with them. The attack was pressed home with great force but owing to overwhelming light automatic and mortar fire only a few men managed to reach the col. They were beaten off again but managed to stay long enough to ensure that Captain Newton was not in the area of the reservoir.[8]

The Punjabs then descended in an orderly withdrawal, but incurred further casualties as they withdrew to Caroline Hill, and from there to Happy Valley. The attack had been well executed but had achieved nothing militarily and resulted in thirty casualties. Captain Course, commanding 'B' Coy, 5/7 Rajputs, was killed in action on 19 December. A British officer who could speak Urdu was needed to take over command of 'B' Coy. Lt-Col Cadogan-Rawlinson asked Fortress HQ to send an MTB to bring him and his party, consisting of Captain Offer and seven IORs from Stanley. An MTB was dispatched and brought them to Aberdeen, where they obtained transport on a police lorry to Leighton Hill. Cadogan-Rawlinson established his HQ jointly with the Middlesex Regiment. He commanded what was left of his battalion in coordination with Lt-Col Henry ('Monkey') Stewart, 1/Mx, the battalion commander. Captain Offer took command of a composite company consisting of the remnants of 'B' and 'D' Coy, 5/7 Rajputs.

By 22 December, 1/Mx Bn HQ at Ventris Road, near Happy Valley racecourse, was increasingly in the front line and a new Bn HQ was opened at Gilman's Garage on Hennessy Road. 'Z' Coy maintained their forward positions on Leighton Hill. The 5/7 Rajput Coy on Chinese Cemetery Ridge was forced to withdraw. By 23 December, 'Z' Coy was still holding out on Leighton Hill. The company consisted of some forty personnel and six Vickers machine guns. 'Z' Coy was a composite company made up of military clerks, bandsmen and any spare soldiers that were available and not required for manning the PBs. Their numbers were bolstered by the addition of stragglers, including some HKVDC personnel who had withdrawn from Jardine's Lookout, some Indian soldiers, presumably Rajputs from the north shore, and some Canadians from Jardine's Lookout and WNC Gap. The Japanese were infiltrating through the streets below but were unable to dislodge the defenders on Leighton Hill, who were well entrenched and whose Vickers guns were taking a toll on the Japanese infantry and holding up their advance along the north shore of the Island.

The defence of Leighton Hill was legendary, a small group of men defending a prominent hill feature and stopping a much larger force from advancing toward their target. They were under constant shell and mortar barrage. The defenders took shelter during the shelling in their slit trenches, and in the ruins of houses that had once been government quarters. The slightest movement brought down Japanese fire, so they restricted movement to the hours of darkness and stayed concealed by day. The garrison stubbornly held on until Wednesday 24 December when the position became untenable as food, water and ammunition supplies dwindled. Captain Mann was ordered to withdraw after dark to Gilman's Garage and then deploy his men along the Canal Road front line. After the withdrawal from Leighton Hill, the next strong point was Morrison Hill at the north-west corner of the Happy Valley racetrack. This was a knoll which had been partially demolished before the war. Captain Flood, 1/Mx, was detailed to establish a platoon on the knoll armed with four Vickers guns. The position was occupied at 0400 hours on 24 December.

The front line in Wan Chai, stretching from the waterfront up the hillside to Mount Parish and Bowen Road, was coming under increasing pressure. If the line were breached, it would open the way for the Japanese to push forward into Victoria. Accordingly, Fortress HQ rushed in various reinforcements to help defend the frontline in this sector. These included units from the Military Police, Royal Corp of Signals, Royal Artillery and Royal Engineers. During the evening on 24 December, an AOP was established at the top of the HSBC building, the tallest building in Hong Kong, to provide observation on the

Japanese positions in North Point and the Happy Valley area. The OP had telephone communication with both Fortress HQ and West Group RA. The Royal Engineers laid anti-tank mines at road junctions. These proved to be very effective, and on Thursday 25th two Japanese lorries loaded with troops were blown up by landmines when driving up Gap Road towards Queens Road.

On Christmas morning, the line extended from Canal Road to Gilman's Garage, to Morrison Hill, to Mount Parish and up to Bowen Road. The 1/Mx Bn HQ had been moved back to the Sailors and Soldiers Institute close to the eastern end of the RN Dockyard. On the right flank, there was a company of 5/7 Rajputs located on Mount Parish, and to their right a detachment of Royal Marines. To the right of the Royal Marines was a detachment from 5th AA Regt deployed on Bowen Road. Morrison Hill was heavily shelled that morning, knocking out two of the four Vickers guns and killing several of the defenders, including 2/Lt Wynter-Blyth, 1/Mx. During the morning, the line came under considerable artillery and mortar bombardment. 'Z' Coy reported it may become difficult to hold their position along Canal Road. Accordingly, a second line was prepared further back running from O'Brien Street to Kennedy Road. Lt Graham, 1/Mx, was sent back to prepare what would be the last line of defence. At around 1045 hours, a message was received from Fortress HQ that a truce would be observed by both sides to allow the two civilians, Andrew Shields and Charles Manners, who had crossed the lines earlier that morning, to pass back through the front line. The fighting resumed sometime after 1200 hours.

In the early afternoon, the Rajput company on Mount Parish was pushed back, exposing the right flank between the Middlesex positions and the Royal Marines. There was concern that as a result of this withdrawal the Japanese may be able to enter the ARP tunnels above Stubbs Road on Mount Parish, which would give them access to Gap Road and Kennedy Road. The Royal Artillery was ordered to destroy the tunnel portals. This was achieved with an 18-pdr field gun, positioned at Wan Chai Market, originally from Belchers Battery.

At 1425 hours Lt-Col Stewart moved his Bn HQ to Murray Barracks, and 'Z' Coy took over the Sailors & Soldiers Institute as their Coy HQ. At around 1515 hours, the GOC called Stewart, explaining euphemistically that he was about to make a very grave decision, and asking for an appreciation of the situation on the Wan Chai front line. He asked how long Stewart could hold the existing line. Stewart explained that 'Z' Coy was in the process of making an orderly withdrawal to the O'Brien Street line, after which there was no organised defence line between the front line and the centre of Victoria. Stewart told the GOC that the current line from Canal Road to Morrison Hill could not be held for more than one hour and that once he occupied the O'Brien Street line he could hold on until nightfall. Stewart asked Maltby if there were further reserves that could be deployed to the Wan Chai front. The GOC replied that there were none. At 1523 hours, the GOC telephoned Stewart and told him of the decision to surrender, and that Stewart was authorised to hoist the white flag and break off the fighting. At 1605 hours, two staff officers, Lt-Col Lamb, RE, and the Japanese linguist Wing Commander Alf Bennett, RAF, came from Fortress HQ to 1/Mx Bn HQ with a message from the GOC ordering Lt-Col Stewart to accompany them to convey the surrender to the Japanese commander on the Wan Chai front. The battle was over.

16

The Battle for Stanley
22 to 25 December

On the evening of 21 December, after two days of continuous counterattacks made by the Royal Rifles of Canada, supported by units from 1/Mx and the HKVDC, Lt-Col Home told Brigadier Wallis that his men were exhausted and that he felt nothing more was to be gained from further resistance. Following the death of both Brigadier Lawson and Colonel Hennessy, Lt-Col Home, as the senior ranking Canadian officer, felt that he had a responsibility to the Canadian Government to ensure that Canadian lives were not needlessly given up. The counterattacks having failed, there could only be one outcome, yet Brigadier Wallis and the GOC clearly intended to fight on. Home told Wallis that he wanted to speak directly with the Governor on this matter, presumably by telephone as East Brigade was at that stage cut off from the rest of Hong Kong. The Army follows a procedure known as the chain of command, and Home's request to talk to the Governor would have involved going above the heads of both his commanding officer and the GOC. Had he spoken to Sir Mark Young, the Governor and Commander-in-Chief, he would have found that the Governor was the strongest proponent of continuing the fight. Churchill's orders to the Governor were unambiguous.

> There must be no thought of surrender. Every part of the island must be fought, and the enemy resisted with the utmost stubbornness. The enemy should be compelled to expend the utmost life and equipment. … Every day that you are able to maintain your resistance, you help the Allied cause all over the world, and by a prolonged resistance you and your men can win the lasting honour which we are sure will be your due.[1]

Lt-Col Sutcliffe, WG, had spoken with Lt-Col Home earlier in the day, stating that his battalion had suffered serious depletion as a result of battle casualties incurred as a result of what he saw as useless counterattacks against stronger enemy positions. The two battalion commanders were of the same opinion as to the futility of fighting on. Sir Mark Young, Major-General Maltby and Brigadier Wallis were following orders. For them it was too early to capitulate, even if the battle had effectively already been lost. Wallis writes in the brigade war diary that he tried to dissuade Home from raising this matter with the Governor, suggesting that he should at least sleep on it. Home woke up on Monday 22 December holding the same opinion regarding the futility of fighting on, but fight on he did, and

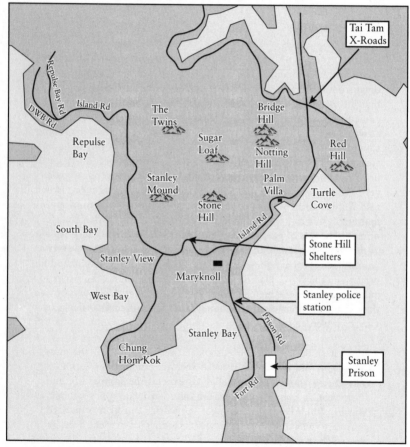

The Stanley Perimeter.

he kept his battalion in action to the very end. The working relationship between Home and Wallis, which was never good, only got worse. Wallis was very critical of Home in the brigade war diary, and suffice it to say that this has created some controversy and ill-feeling ever since the war diary, held by the UK National Archives, became publicly available. The crux of the matter was how long to hold on. The counterattacks by East Brigade had been unsuccessful, and Wallis now prepared to fight a last stand at Stanley. He organised his troops into three groups.

Forward Area

This group was under the command of Lt-Col Home, with his Battalion HQ at Stone Hill Shelters on Island Road. The troops consisted of the Royal Rifles of Canada and No 2 Coy, HKVDC. In addition, there was a 1/Mx Vickers section and a 2-pdr anti-tank gun, both guarding the eastern approaches to Palm Villa. The defensive line around Stanley, referred to as the Stanley Perimeter, stretched along the line of hills, from west to east, in an arc from Stanley View, through Stanley Mound and Stone Hill, to Palm Villa.

Support Area

This group covered the area around Stanley Village, Maryknoll House, and Stanley Prison. Lt-Col James Willcocks, HKVDC, was in command of the Support Area, which included all forces in the Stanley area other than those in Stanley Fort and those on the Stanley Perimeter. In civilian life, Willcocks served as Commissioner of Prisons, and he was commanding officer of the Stanley Platoon, HKVDC, which was made up of prison officers who were mostly ex-servicemen. The Support Area HQ was located at the Prison Officers Club. The troops included 'B' and 'D' Coy, 1/Mx, under the command of Captain Weedon, with their HQ at St Stephen's Prep School. Other troops included the Stanley Platoon, under Lt Fitzgerald, deployed around the prison, and a detachment from 'D' Coy, 1/Mx, under Lt Scantlebury, positioned at Maryknoll House. Artillery support included two 18-pdrs and two 2-pdr anti-tank guns.

Reserve Area

This group, under the command of Lt-Col Selby Shaw, RA, was responsible for Stanley Hill and Stanley Fort. The troops in this sector were mainly Royal Artillery and included the gunners from the 9.2-inch coastal defence battery and the adjacent 6-inch battery.

There were two 3.7-inch howitzers, but without pack mules, and with only fifty rounds of ammunition. MTBs and naval launches were later used to deliver ammunition.

During the morning of Monday 22 December, Wallis moved his HQ from Stone Hill shelters to the Prison Officers Club. Wallis got on well with forty-eight-year-old James Willcocks, who had been awarded the MC, DSO and MiD in the First World War. The Stone Hill shelters remain, although in a very dilapidated state. The Prison Officers Club also remains, and continues to be utilised as a club for officers of the Correctional Services Department.

The Battle for the Stanley Perimeter

At midnight on 21 December, the Royal Rifles of Canada, less 'A' Coy, were deployed on the Stanley Perimeter. 'A' Coy, commanded by Major Young, was at Altamira, The Ridge and Repulse Bay Hotel. 'B' Coy, commanded by Captain Denison, was located at Stanley View, but with one platoon on the summit of Stanley Mound and one platoon on the west side of Stone Hill. The platoon on Stanley Mound included an attached platoon from HQ Coy. 'C' Coy, commanded by Major Bishop, was located at Palm Villa, with one platoon on Sugar Loaf and one platoon on Notting Hill. 'D' Coy, commanded by Major Parker, was located at the food stores building at Chung Hom Kok.

During the night of 21/22 December, things were generally quiet on the Stanley Perimeter except for occasional sniping. The Japanese snipers were well camouflaged and were able to operate independently in the hills, infiltrating close to British or Canadian positions without being seen. In one incident, a well-concealed Japanese sniper managed to crawl down the ravine between Stanley Mound and Stone Hill above RRC Bn HQ and shot and wounded a rifleman who was unloading a lorry on the road bend in front of the Bn HQ shelters. The battalion came under attack on the Stanley Perimeter at around noon on Monday 22 December. 'C' Coy positions were attacked on Notting Hill and Sugar Loaf. The Japanese captured a Vickers gun on Sugar Loaf. A counterattack was organised by L/Sgt Goodenough, L/Sgt Roberts and Cpl Sannes. Sgt Goodenough, aged twenty, was one of the youngest sergeants in the battalion. Although twice wounded, he recaptured the gun and put it back in action against the attacking Japanese. He was posthumously awarded the Military Medal for his conduct during the battle. He died in POW Camp in 1943. Cpl Sannes was killed, and Major Bishop was wounded during the attack on 'C' Coy positions. L/Sgt Roberts showed great courage by running through a mortar barrage to assist his wounded company commander.

The 'B' Coy and 'HQ' Coy platoon position on Stanley Mound was subjected to shelling, mortar fire and machine gun fire, which continued throughout the afternoon. It was thought that this was a prelude to a major attack, and two platoons from 'D' Coy were sent up from their positions at Chung Hom Kok to reinforce the troops on Stanley Mound. The barrage was lifted in the evening, and since no attack developed, the two 'D' Coy platoons were withdrawn to Bn HQ at Stone Hill shelters, and during that night were deployed on Stone Hill.

Later that night, the Japanese attacked Stanley Mound from the Twins, which lay to the north. The defenders on the Mound repelled three separate assaults. Lt James Ross, 'B' Coy, was killed and Sgt Emile Bernard, 'HQ' Coy, was seriously injured. The two platoons put up a strong defence but were eventually forced off the hill, regrouping on the southern slopes. There was little natural protection on the summit of Stanley Mound. Today one can still see the shallow weapons pits that were hastily dug. A large number of spent Canadian, British and Japanese rounds have been found on this hilltop. One particularly interesting find was a Japanese signal device, which was used to fire a flare to denote success in capturing a position. It would have been fired that night after the Japanese captured the crest. In later years, several British and Japanese live grenades were found on the summit, close to the Wilson Trail, and reported to Hong Kong Police. The bomb disposal unit arrived by helicopter and detonated the grenades in a controlled explosion, in what must have been the first grenade explosion on that hilltop since December 1941. Climbing Stanley Mound is tough work even in light hiking gear, and one can well imagine how exhausting it must have been for the Canadian soldiers to struggle up those steep hills with their guns, ammunition, water and other equipment, all of which had to be carried up the hills. The quantity of spent rounds, shrapnel and grenade parts testifies to the fierce fight put up by the Canadian infantry on the hills that formed the Stanley Perimeter.

At midnight on the night of 22/23 December, 'B' Coy HQ, with one platoon, was at Stanley View, and two platoons were on the lower slopes of Stanley Mound and one platoon at Stone Hill. 'C' Coy was at Palm Villa. 'D' Coy was at Stone Hill positioned below the crest. By Tuesday morning, 23 December, the Japanese had control of Red Hill, Bridge Hill, Notting Hill and Sugar Loaf. The Japanese had occupied the summit of Stanley Mound and the crest of Stone Hill. Wallis was anxious to regain the latter two hill features, which directly overlooked Stanley. They represented the 'main door' to Stanley, with the 'side doors' being Stanley View in the west and Palm Villa in the east. Wallis ordered a counterattack by the RRC and HKVDC to commence at first light on 23 December, which would follow an artillery and MMG barrage. The artillery fire was provided by the two 3.7-inch howitzers at Stanley and the 6-inch naval guns at Bluff Head. The MMG barrage was provided by 1/Mx positions at Stanley Village.

> During the night 22/23 December, a request was received from the officer commanding RRC to provide MMG supporting fire at first light on the crests of Stanley Mound and Stone Hill to assist them in retaking the summits, from which they had withdrawn the previous evening. At 0700 hours, fire was opened with eight MMGs, on these two areas and continued for fifteen minutes. Shortly afterwards the Canadians were seen to reach the summits.[2]

The counterattack on the two hills was initially successful. However, later that morning, the defenders were again driven off the tops of both hills by mortar and light artillery. Home reported to Wallis that he had eighteen officers killed, wounded or missing, and only 350 men left in the battalion excluding the bulk of 'A' Coy, many of whom were still trapped in the Repulse Bay area. Some members of 'A' Coy had successfully withdrawn from The Ridge, Overbays and Repulse Bay Hotel during the early morning on 23 December. The Stanley Perimeter was being pushed back in the centre, and Home felt it was necessary to withdraw the battalion back to Stanley, to regroup and reorganise. He felt his exhausted battalion would fight better on the flatter ground around Stanley Village. Wallis asked him to remain in his current positions and to withdraw after dark. At 1800 on Tuesday 23 December, the battalion started their withdrawal from the perimeter to Stanley under fire. 'B' Coy took up new positions at the AA fort at Chung Hom Kok, with their forward positions up the road at Stanley View. The rest of the battalion fell back to Stanley. Guides were waiting at the police station in Stanley Village to conduct the Canadian companies to their new positions. Home established his Bn HQ at Bungalow 'A', one of the St Stephen's College bungalows.

Chung Hom Kok

'B' Coy, RRC, commanded by Captain Denison, moved back from their forward positions on the southern slopes of Stanley Mound and Stone Hill during the late afternoon on 23 December. Captain Denison maintained his Coy HQ at Stanley View but ordered the rest of the company to move to West Bay AA Fort, 500 metres south of Stanley View. Captain Royal, with around sixty-five ORs, took up positions at the AA fort at around 1700 hours, but two 'B' Coy platoons, No. 10 and No. 11, lost their way and moved back to Stanley Village. Lt Ray Thorn, the No. 11 platoon commander, had been killed earlier that day and was buried in the saddle between Stone Hill and the Mound. On this saddle, a very rusted .303 rifle was recently found lying on the surface. There were also numerous spent rounds and a Japanese soldier's ID tag. On Stone Hill, one of the more unusual finds was a wristwatch with an engraving on the reverse showing the name and number of Rifleman Ray Jackson of 'D' Coy, RRC. This company had two platoons positioned on Stone Hill. Jackson was killed in action on Stone Hill during the withdrawal from the Stanley Perimeter. In conjunction with the Hong Kong Veterans Commemorative Association (HKVCA), the watch was returned to an astonished member of Jackson's family, seventy-six years after his death on the hills behind Stanley.

An effort was made to conduct the two 'B' Coy platoons that had withdrawn to Stanley, to Chung Hom Kok, to re-join the rest of their company. CSM Richard Overy, with a small detachment from 1/Mx, was ordered to guide the two platoons from Stanley Police Station to Chung Hom Kok. The two platoons set out at 0600 hours on the morning of 24 December with the intention of reaching Chung Hom Kok before it got light. However, the two platoons were unable to get through an open area covered by Japanese machine guns, and consequently remained at Stanley. Captain Denison remained at his Stanley View HQ with a small force defending the left flank from any infiltration along Island Road from Repulse Bay, and from Stanley Mound on their front. Captain Royal was at the AA Fort with some twenty ORs from No. 12 Platoon and No 12 (R) Platoon. He was joined by Lt McGreevy, 'A' Coy, who had with him a composite platoon made up of around forty-five ORs from different units.

During the night of 23/24 December, Royal and McGreevy were ordered to move their combined force from West Bay AA Fort to the abandoned 6-inch coastal defence battery on Chung Hom Kok peninsula. They were ordered to occupy this headland to prevent the Japanese from establishing themselves in this locality and firing across at British and Canadian positions at Stanley. They arrived at around midnight, sentries were posted, and the troops were able to get some rest in the battery buildings. At 0445 hours on Wednesday 24 December, their positions at and around the artillery fort were attacked by a Japanese patrol that was thought to have advanced down Chung Hom Kok Road from Stanley View. This attack was beaten off, and 'B' Coy spent the rest of the day consolidating their positions.

During the morning on 24 December, it was agreed by Maltby and Wallis that the exhausted Canadian battalion, which had borne the brunt of the action thus far, would be withdrawn from the line to Stanley Fort for rest and reorganisation. The battalion would be relieved by units from 1/Mx and HKVDC. However, Royal's force at Chung Hom Kok had become separated from the rest of the battalion at Stanley. It was decided that No. 2 Coy, HKVDC, should relieve the RRC platoons at Chung Hom Kok to allow 'B' Coy to join the rest of the battalion at Stanley Fort. In the early evening, the three No. 2 Coy platoons set out from Stanley Village, consisting of No. 5 Platoon under Lt Bryden, No. 6 Platoon under Lt Prophet and No. 7 Platoon under Lt Stoker. The Coy HQ, consisting of some ten ORs, under company commander Major Henry Forsyth, remained at Stanley Police Station. The Volunteers moved off at dusk, following the shoreline towards Chung Hom Kok. However, about midway, they ran into the right flank of a Japanese assault force closing in on Stanley, probably from the direction of Stanley View or Stanley Mound. An exchange of fire took place, with close-quarters fighting. One platoon, led by 2/Lt Stoker, was cut off and fought its way back to Stanley. The other two platoons reached the Canadian positions at 2030 hours on Wednesday 24 December. Royal was duly informed

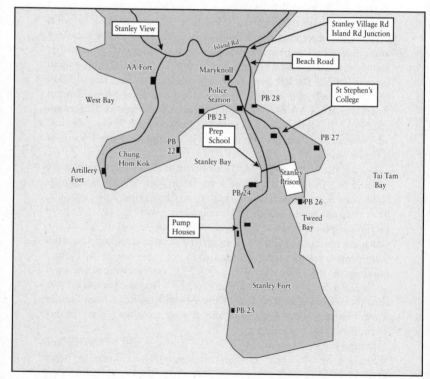

Stanley.

that his men were being relieved and that they were to return to Stanley. However, given the large force of Japanese that the Volunteers had run into, Royal decided to remain at the artillery fort with the HKVDC rather than trying to fight their way back to Stanley.

The next day, Christmas Day, at around 0530 hours, their positions were attacked. One Japanese patrol managed to get up the hill behind the artillery fort. Lt Prophet led a fighting patrol up the hill, which consisted of twelve men made up of a section from each of the HKVDC and the RRC. They were forced back by heavy fire and incurred several casualties. Pte Ian Grant, HKVDC, managed to reach the summit, but he was killed on the crest. During the afternoon, the Japanese opened fire with mortars and machine guns at the Canadian and HKVDC positions at Chung Hom Kok, more or less surrounding them. Royal gave orders to the Canadians to scatter in small groups in order to escape and evade. Lt Bryden tried to lead his men back to Stanley, but they were pinned down near Maryknoll House and were forced to surrender. Lt Prophet and some of his group avoided capture by swimming across to Stanley after dark. Royal and McGreevy evaded the Japanese overnight, and the next day, Friday 26 December, they learnt that the garrison had surrendered.

Maryknoll House

Maryknoll House was built in 1935 as a religious retreat for the Maryknoll Catholic Fathers, who were carrying out missionary work in Southern China. The retreat was also used as a language school where the Fathers were taught Cantonese, Hakka and Mandarin. It was built on a prominent hill overlooking Stanley Village and Stanley Bay. Early photographs of the house show it surrounded by thinly wooded slopes. The red-brick building with its green tiled roof remains today, but it is now surrounded by low-rise apartment blocks, and the building itself is under threat of redevelopment. Near Maryknoll house was the Carmelite Convent, situated below the hill and close to Stanley Police Station. It was built in 1937 to house Carmelite nuns. This building still survives today and serves the same purpose, offering a place for prayer and contemplation.

Maryknoll House was initially garrisoned by one platoon from 'D' Coy, 1/Mx, under 2/Lt Newman. It was later reinforced by two more 'D' Coy sections, and the enlarged garrison was commanded by Lt Victor Scantlebury. The building was also occupied by a group of Maryknoll Fathers and Catholic priests, including seminarian Bernard Tohill. The noise of battle escalated at midnight on 24 December, and wounded soldiers were brought into the house. On Christmas Day, the detachment at Maryknoll found that their position had been bypassed and that they were now cut off from the rest of the troops at Stanley. A decision was made to break out in small groups and try to re-join British forces at Stanley Fort. This plan was abandoned because of the number of Japanese troops between them and the fort, and instead they decided to try and make for the western part of the Island by heading toward Stanley View and Repulse Bay. Just before dawn on 25 December, the troops started moving off in a westerly direction in small parties. Shortly after this, they came under fire from the direction of Island Road on their right flank. Lt Scantlebury was wounded and returned to the mission house.

The Maryknoll building had been surrounded, and the attempted breakout was unsuccessful. The thirty men who made up the garrison were either killed in action or captured and then put to death. The Japanese in this vicinity, like at The Ridge, were not taking prisoners, although one soldier from the detachment had his life spared in unusual circumstances. Pte John Frelford was wounded during the attempted breakout. He then came across an injured Japanese soldier sheltering behind a boulder, and gave him water and bandaged his wounds, after which they both passed out from weakness and loss of blood.

When Frelford regained consciousness, he found that he was surrounded by Japanese soldiers who were on the point of killing him. The Japanese soldier he had helped then spoke up and told the Japanese troops what Frelford had done. The Japanese commander was astonished that a British soldier would assist an enemy in that way by providing water and bandages. As a result, they not only spared his life but took him under their charge and saw to it that he was well treated. Frelford's unit assumed he was missing in action together with the other members of his detachment.

The story only came to light when Lt Bush, a Japanese-speaking HKRNVR officer who was held by the Gendarmerie at their HQ in Happy Valley, came across Frelford in January 1942. Bush noticed that Frelford seemed to be free to walk around, and questioned a Japanese officer about him. He was told that a Japanese infantry regiment had asked the Gendarmes to look after him and ensure he received good treatment after they left Hong Kong because he had saved the life of a Japanese soldier. Frelford was later incarcerated at Stanley Camp rather than being interned at the military POW camps. In the Stanley Camp logbook, he is listed as a shop assistant, but I wonder whether his roommates or the senior camp officials knew that he was, in fact, a regular soldier in the Middlesex Regiment who had fought in the battle for Stanley.

Father Tohill heard the shattering of glass as the front door was broken open and Japanese soldiers entered the premises. The Maryknoll Fathers were made to squat in the vestibule near the front door. The soldiers, including the wounded, were rounded up and then tied tightly.

> Squatting together with us but tightly bound, were a Canadian captain and three English officers; they behaved nobly, as you would expect of a military officer. In no way would they bow to their Japanese captors, even when cruelly beaten. I cannot remember the name of the Canadian captain. The British officers were Lt Lawrence, Lt Newman and Lt Scantlebury.[3]

The Maryknoll Fathers were tied up and then led down to a path near the red-brick wall around the Carmelite Convent. The whole area was full of Japanese troops, and fighting was still in progress. Field guns were firing in the direction of Stanley Fort. One of the priests understood some Japanese, enough to realise that the soldiers guarding them were determining their fate.

> Some thought we looked like soldiers in disguise and should be liquidated, while others held that the majority of us looked too old to be military personnel. The four British officers squatting with us were grilled; someone tried to cut their shoulder straps with a sword or bayonet; an order was given for them to get up and move down to the end of the row, where they were brutally bayoneted to death, and this on Christmas morning, right outside the Carmelite Monastery! We were sickened and disgusted, but they bravely faced death.[4]

Brother Michael Hogan testified at war crimes trials held after the war that the Japanese entered the mission house at around 0700 hours and that during the early morning six British officers, rather than the four recorded by Tohill, were brought in with their hands tied behind their backs. He recalled that at around 1500 hours they were all marched down to the road.

> They marched us down to the main road and lined us up against the hillside. The six British officers were lined up in front of us. The Japanese officer phoned up somebody, and after a short conversation, he gave the command for the British officers to be marched off to the gulley only a few yards away around the corner. Shortly after I heard terrible screams of pain, and I saw a British officer running from the direction from where the screams came, to about five yards in front of me. Here was a Japanese soldier guarding us and this soldier pierced the officer with his bayonet slightly wounding the British officer who was thus forced to return to where he came from. After a time, all the screams

and cries ceased, and I presumed all the men had died. After this, we were all marched off to a building and were tied up for three days and three nights.[5]

Yim Hung, a young Chinese man, also witnessed the slaying and gave evidence through a sworn statement at war crimes trials. He saw the execution by bayonets of twelve British soldiers, which included the four to six officers referred to above. He recalled that one was a captain, four or five were lieutenants, three sergeants, two corporals and one private. It seems likely that the officers who were taken down to the Carmelite Convent with the Maryknoll Fathers were then taken to join another group of captured soldiers. The execution site was probably in the passageway at the back of the convent. It would have been out of sight to Father Tohill and the Maryknoll Fathers, who heard rather than saw the executions.

After the killing, the group of Catholic Fathers, numbering around thirty, were taken a short distance along Stanley Village Road to the garage of a nearby house. They were forced into the garage, built for one car, still tied together, and held there without food, water and sanitation for three days. At one stage the Japanese came in and collected a metal bed from the garage, which they used to cremate their battle dead. On 27 December, some two days after the surrender, the Catholic Fathers were allowed to return to Maryknoll House. The nuns in the Carmelite Convent had not been molested. There were three Belgian sisters, four Italian Canossian sisters and some twenty Chinese Carmelites. A portion of their compound wall had been destroyed by shelling, and Japanese soldiers had demanded admittance from time to time, but otherwise they were unharmed.

The Battle for Stanley Village

The battle for Stanley Village began on 24 December with the capture that morning of a building referred to as the 'white house' close to the junction of Stanley Village Road and Island Road. This building had been used as a forward observation post and had been manned by Captain West and a small detachment from 1/Mx to give early warning of any Japanese advance towards Stanley Village. At first light, Japanese troops had been observed on Stone Hill working their way down towards Island Road, and by 1100 hours a Japanese flag had been seen flying from Captain West's position.

Considerable anxiety was felt for Captain West and his section, but soon afterwards they reached Detachment HQ, after a narrow escape from their position. Finding the OP surrounded, they hid in one of the rooms of the house, whilst the enemy established a mortar section on the veranda outside. Soon afterwards, a Japanese officer discovered the party, one of whom threw a grenade, killing the Japanese officer and wounding several of the mortar section. In the subsequent confusion, the party made their escape down the stairs, and out of the front door.[6]

During the early evening on 24 December, Wallis moved his Stanley Force HQ from the Prison Officers Club to Stanley Fort, as the club building had been under fire, and communication lines were being increasingly damaged, repaired and damaged again. At 1830 hours, the Japanese mounted a heavy artillery and mortar barrage which was a prelude to the attack on the village, which started in earnest at around 2100 hours. The troops in the village area consisted of the HQ section of No. 2 Coy, HKVDC, the Stanley Platoon, and a detachment of gunners from 965 Defence Battery equipped with 2-pdr anti-tank guns under the command of Sgt Climo and Sgt Russell. In addition, a 1/Mx machine gun detachment occupied Bungalow No. 1, which was located on the high ground above the 'Y' junction. At the 'Y' junction, the Prison Road, now known as Tung Tau Wan Road, led south-east to the prison; the other, the Fort Road, now known as Wong Ma Kok Road, led south-west to Stanley Fort.

Major Forsyth, as senior officer, assumed command of all troops in the village area. The Stanley Platoon, equipped with Lewis guns, was placed on the mound opposite the police station. This low mound is where the current police station is now located. The original police station still remains, but it is now a small supermarket. The college grounds were defended by No. 1 Battery, HKVDC, acting as infantry, and by units from 'B' and 'D' Coy, 1/Mx. Sgt Thomas Russell and Bdr Harry Minshull recalled in a statement addressed to Lt Bryden, No. 2 Coy, HKVDC, Major Forsyth's leadership during the close-quarters fighting at Stanley Village.

Everything was quiet with the exception of occasional shelling and sniping. At about 2030 hours Bdr Minshull heard Major Forsyth shout down the road to get the anti-tank gun in position for action as we all could hear the distant noise of tanks approaching down Tai Tam Road. Major Forsyth was on the bank, at the side of the road with a Tommy gun from where he could give orders to all the personnel on that sector. On seeing the three tanks approaching down Beach Road, he gave orders for the anti-tank gun crew to open fire, which we obeyed and after firing about fifteen rounds of ammunition, we succeeded in setting fire to the tanks.[7]

Sgt Climo was wounded in both legs and taken to the schoolhouse near the police station. L/Bdr John Bullen, RA, who was on sentry duty, shouted out that the Japanese were attacking again and to stand-to. Major Forsyth went back to his position on the bank armed with a Tommy gun and a Webley revolver.

> Again, receiving orders from Major Forsyth to open fire with all the weapons we had, then for at least an hour things were going well under his steady orders, and all the time he was taking a toll of the enemy with his Tommy gun. As the enemy approached the positions, he gave orders to fix bayonets. Then I heard a loud burst of a grenade or mortar hit the bank near the Major who gave a groan.[8]

Forsyth was fatally wounded in the chest and legs, but he still insisted on giving his orders until too weak to do so from loss of blood. Sgt Russell took him across the road to the veranda of the police station. After Major Forsyth had been incapacitated, and without his leadership, the situation deteriorated. Sgt Henry Hopkins, No. 2 Coy, HKVDC, recalled finding Major Forsyth and CSM Swan, both wounded, at the police station.

> After withdrawing from Chung Hom Kok peninsula on the night of 24 December, to the vicinity of the HQ, I was ordered, by the platoon commander Lt Stoker, to take the platoon forward to Stanley Village and report to Major Forsyth for instructions. It would then be about 2300 hours, and I proceeded along the road as far as the garages at the north end of the football field. The white two-storeyed building [referred to as Bungalow No. 1] at the corner of the road was under fire and leaving the platoon there I went forward with seven men to find Major Forsyth. On arriving at the white house, I was informed by a member of the Stanley Platoon that Major Forsyth had been seriously wounded and was in the police station where I reported to the Major who was lying in a small hall at the south end of the station and who appeared to be severely wounded about the chest and arms.[9]

By this time casualties were mounting, and the British forces at the village were being pushed back. The Japanese had advanced past Maryknoll, and had control of the shoreline around Stanley Bay, and were able to fire at the road fork below the bungalow. The Stanley Platoon withdrew to consolidate with 1/Mx at the bungalow. The Vickers guns had been put out of action by Japanese fire and the bungalow had become untenable, with the Japanese firing directly into the building. Japanese troops were starting to outflank the bungalow on both sides by infiltrating along the two shorelines.

At 0200 hours on 25 December, the remnants of the force at Bungalow No. 1 withdrew under fire along the Fort Road going past the college playing fields to the 1/Mx Detachment HQ at St Stephen's Prep School. Some of the walking wounded made it back, but CSM Swan, himself badly wounded, chose to stay with his commanding officer. The Japanese put them to death with the other wounded when they captured the police station and the adjacent schoolhouse. In the battle for the village, a small group of men from different units had stood firm and faced a full-scale attack involving light tanks and infantry. The fighting was both fierce and up-close. Their commander, Major Forsyth, had been courageous, cool under fire, and an example to all. Wallis recommended him for the posthumous award of the Victoria Cross, but in the end, and in what seems an injustice, he received only a Mention in Dispatches (MiD).

Forty-six-year-old Sgt John William ('Bill') Hudson was serving with the Stanley Platoon during the battle for Stanley Village. His wife Margaret ('Peg') had been evacuated with their son Peter to Australia in June 1940. Rachel Hudson, his granddaughter, has compiled a family history which includes letters that Bill Hudson wrote to Peg after liberation in 1945 in which he describes, first-hand, his experiences during the battle at Stanley Village.

> First, we went to Johnnie Purves' old bungalow belonging to the college, then on 21 December, we moved to the village, just opposite the police station and the school, on the little hill. The nightmare came at 2050 hours on Xmas Eve. They attacked the village with small tanks, and thousands of troops, it was hell let loose, some of the Volunteers defended the left of the village and the Maryknoll, but the attack came direct for us from the beach and Lower Beach Road. For three-and-a-half hours we fought so, with lulls between, then they would come again screaming their heads off, just to be mowed down. By this time, we had lost McLeod, Carr, and Gowland with Foster, Cottrell and Stevens missing.[10]

George Foster survived the battle but died while interned at Stanley Camp. Cottrell and Stevens survived the battle and the subsequent incarceration. After the war ended, they resumed their careers with the Hong Kong Prison Service, but they never forgot that they owed their lives to L/Bdr John Bullen, RA. He was one of many unsung heroes, and his story of exceptional courage and self-sacrifice was revealed by chance nearly ten years after the war.

An Unsung Hero

Twenty-three-year-old L/Bdr John ('Red') Bullen was born in Crosby, Liverpool, and joined the army at the age of seventeen in 1935. He was killed in action during the night 24/25 December in the fighting around Stanley Village. The story of his bravery came to light in 1954 when Cottrell left the Hong Kong Prison Service and returned to Liverpool. He applied for a civilian role with a Territorial Army unit based at Birkenhead. On being interviewed by Major Wilson, the commanding officer, Cottrell answered questions about his military service with the Stanley Platoon during the Battle for Hong Kong, and in so doing he made reference to L/Bdr Bullen's role and conduct in the battle. A witness statement was written by Cottrell and later corroborated by a statement from Stevens.

During the fighting at the village, Cottrell and Stevens were manning Lewis guns on the mound opposite the police station. Cottrell described how at some point earlier in the evening, and before the battle began, Bullen, accompanied by a gunner, took a light truck and drove along Stanley Village Road to a position on Island Road, about 1.5 miles from Stanley Police Station, where it was known that a captured British anti-tank gun was located near a private house, which the Japanese were using as an HQ. A sentry guarded the gun, but Bullen and his accomplice were able to recapture the gun and attach it to the truck, and then tow it away under fire.

The gun was placed in an open position, opposite the school house, facing Beach Road. Cottrell described, in his statement, how the gun crew allowed the leading Japanese tank to keep advancing until it was almost at point-blank range. They fired, and the leading tank exploded and burst into flames. The Lewis gun crews then opened up on the Japanese troops that were illuminated by the flames. A second tank approached the junction and was hit and disabled. Cottrell testified that Bullen, and the other defenders, then withdrew to the schoolhouse and police station, by which time Major Forsyth had already been injured. Cottrell described how Bullen went out, and while under fire brought back six wounded men, one after the other, to the schoolhouse.

As the position became untenable, a decision was made to withdraw from the schoolhouse through the village, and to try to gain cover in some nearby woods. To reach the thicket, they had to cross an open area of the beach covered by a Japanese machine gun on Stanley Village Road. Four men made a dash and got across safely. Two more ran across and were killed by machine gun fire. Bullen told the few remaining men to stay where they were, and that he would try and take out the machine gun. He took two grenades from his pocket and ran into the centre of the gap, throwing a grenade as he ran towards the machine gun position. Private

Stevens recalled how a burst of machine gun fire hit Bullen, killing him, while he was still trying to pull the pin out of another grenade.

He never stopped fighting. Bullen was performing one heroic deed after another, recapturing the gun, helping to knock out the tanks, bringing in the wounded while under fire and then, finally, single-handedly attacking the Japanese machine gun position. Some recommended that he be awarded the Victoria Cross, but like Forsyth, who was just as much a hero, he was awarded a posthumous MiD which was gazetted in October 1955.

The Battle at St Stephen's College

The Japanese broke through the front line at Stanley Village in the early hours of Christmas Day, but it had cost them dearly, with at least two of their light tanks destroyed and many casualties among their infantry. The Japanese moved southwards toward the second line of defence, also referred to as the support line, that stretched across the grounds of St Stephen's College from the Fort Road on the west side of the peninsula, through the line of three staff bungalows and down to the Prison Road on the east side of the peninsula. The RRC had been relieved earlier that evening and had moved to Stanley Fort. Their positions on the second line of defence were taken over by No. 1 Battery, HKVDC, and 1/Mx, under the overall command of Captain West. No. 1 Battery, commanded by Captain Rees, had originally manned the 4-inch coastal defence battery at Cape D'Aguilar. Sgt Harry Millington, No. 1 Battery, was in charge of a section deployed on the east flank guarding the Prison Road. His brother Sgt Leslie Millington was positioned with a section of gunners on the centre right above the road leading to the prison. 2/Lt Jones, No. 1 Battery, was commanding a section dug in at the entrance driveway to St Stephen's College. On the west flank, 2/Lt Muir, No. 1 Battery, commanded two sections of gunners, one at Bungalow 'C' overlooking the college playing fields and the other dug in below the hillside on which the bungalow was situated, at the southern end of the playing fields. In the centre of the second defence line, on the higher ground around the college, there was a platoon of 1/Mx machine gunners with two Vickers guns positioned on centre-left, and two guns positioned on centre-right.

In the early hours of 25 December, the Japanese infiltrated between PB 28 and Bungalow No. 1. PB 28 had only one gun remaining in action. The other guns had been disabled by enemy machine gun fire through the loopholes. This PB took a heavy toll on the Japanese infantry until it was put out of action after the Japanese inserted grenades through the loopholes. The 1/Mx position at Bungalow No. 1 had both its guns knocked out, after which 2/Lt Cheesewright, 'C' Coy, 1/Mx, gave the

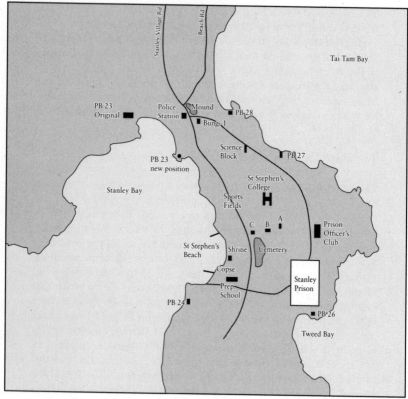

Stanley Village and St Stephen's College.

order for his two machine gun crews under Sgt Manning and Cpl Harris to withdraw and reform at 1/Mx Detachment HQ at the prep school.

Sgt Hudson, Stanley Platoon, had advised his platoon commander, Lt Fitzgerald, to fall back from the mound opposite the police station to Bungalow No. 1.

> I told him we had better fall back to the first bungalow overlooking the village, as we could hear firing and hand grenades bursting back by the prison, they had managed to break through along the beach and gone past some go-downs. It was around 0030 hours when we joined the Middlesex position in front of the bungalow; we stayed there until 0230 hours. Firing was getting intense behind us, so to save being cut off, we fell back over the college football field to the Fort Road outside the prep school.[11]

The Japanese, in overwhelming numbers, continued to attack both the left and right flanks, following the two roads, and the shoreline on each side of the peninsula. No. 1 Battery held their line despite incurring heavy casualties. Captain Rees, the commanding officer, was seriously wounded, and two officers and some thirty-five ORs were killed in action defending the second line. Sgt Harry Millington's section on the Prison Road and 2/Lt Jones's section near the entrance drive to the college were pushed back towards the prison. Millington and Jones were both killed in action.

The Middlesex platoon on the high ground in the centre of the line was attacked on each flank by flamethrowers and grenades. Their positions were overrun, and the survivors fell back. Captain West was killed at this location. On the left flank, 2/Lt Muir and the remainder of No. 1 Battery held on to their positions at Bungalow 'C'. Among the gunners at Bungalow 'C' was seventeen-year-old Tony Weller, who had joined the HKVDC by claiming he was eighteen. During the early hours, the gunners at Bungalow 'C' found that the Japanese had outflanked their position and got behind them. They took cover inside the bungalow. The Japanese then deployed a flamethrower, which killed or badly burnt most of the defenders in the bungalow. Some of the survivors rushed out and were promptly shot or bayoneted by the Japanese who had surrounded the bungalow. Weller remained in the bungalow with two other survivors. He was still there when 'D' Coy, RRC, attacked the bungalows during the early afternoon on 25 December. After the Canadian attack, the Japanese launched a counterattack, taking back the bungalow before Weller could get out and join the Canadians. They hid in the bungalow until they were found by a British burial party on 27 December. Lt Muir was killed in the vicinity of the Bungalow 'C'.

At 0745 hours on 25 December, the Middlesex Detachment was ordered to retake the bungalows and drive out the Japanese. All the available men at 1/Mx Detachment HQ were organised into two fighting patrols under CSM Overy, 'B' Coy, and CSM Tibble, 'D' Coy. The attack was unsuccessful due to the heavy fire directed from the windows of the bungalows. These two patrols were withdrawn with heavy casualties and redeployed on the high ground overlooking the cemetery, and close to the third line of defence established by Major Templer, running across the western part of the peninsula near the two pump houses on the Fort Road.

The Japanese began to work their way along the shoreline of Stanley Bay towards the prep school. They were stopped by the crew of PB 23, occupying a new position consisting of two Vickers machine gun emplacements located on a small promontory south-west of the village, and close to the college playing fields. The crew, under Cpl Goodman, had originally manned a concrete PB at the Chung Hom Kok end of Stanley Bay near where Murray House is today. The PB alternative position on the promontory came under attack with grenades. The crew held out until they ran out of ammunition and then escaped by swimming from their position on the promontory across Stanley Bay to Chung Hom Kok, where they joined up with 'B' Coy, RRC, and No. 2 Coy, HKVDC. Wallis recalled in his war diary that one survivor, 2/Lt Cole, from this PB position, made it back to the prep school with sword and bayonet wounds.

Japanese troops continued to infiltrate along the shoreline towards the prep school. Shortly before dawn on 25 December, PB 24 at St Stephen's Beach noticed Japanese troops infiltrating down paths from the roadway onto the beach near the prep school. PB 24 opened fire with its Vickers machine guns, and rifle and machine gun fire was also brought to bear from the prep school building. The Japanese troops dispersed, with most taking cover in a wooded copse at the back of the beach. Many of the Japanese took cover by withdrawing into a Chinese shrine. At 0630 hours, with improving light, a plan was made for a party from Detachment HQ commanded by Captain Weedon to flush out the Japanese from the wooded area. PB 24 would cover any attempted withdrawal by the Japanese along the beach. Captain Weedon's party threw grenades into the shine, causing many casualties among the Japanese. The remainder of the Japanese detachment tried to escape along the beach using rocks for cover. However, the combined fire from PB 24 and from Weedon's party in the thicket wiped out the Japanese detachment. Weedon was injured during this exchange of fire.

After Weedon was wounded, Lt King assumed command of the 1/Mx detachment, which by that time consisted of around fifty men from both 1/Mx and HKVDC. The HQ was now under point-blank fire, and at about 1030 hours on Christmas morning, Lt King ordered a withdrawal from the prep school back to Stanley Fort. He ordered the men to withdraw in groups of ten via PB 24 to avoid the Fort Road, which was under mortar, shell and sniper fire. The detachment was then deployed around the perimeter wire at Stanley Fort, which was the fourth and final line of defence. At this time, Wallis was commanding the Stanley Force from Major Templer's HQ, which was a weapons pit near the two pumping stations on the Fort Road. A party of gunners under 2/Lt Challinor and 2/Lt Eddison were trying to bring the two 18-pdrs and the two 3.7-inch howitzers back to Stanley Fort from the prison area. The guns had to be manhandled across the open area in front of the prison while under fire and taken to the Fort Road near the prep school where a Scammell lorry was waiting to tow the guns back to Stanley Fort. While the two subalterns were struggling with their guns, they witnessed the gallant attack by 'D' Coy, RRC, across the cemetery and through the line of staff bungalows on the high ground around the college.

'D' Company Royal Rifles of Canada

The Royal Rifles of Canada did not get the twenty-four hours of rest and recuperation that had been promised. In the early hours of 25 December, Wallis ordered Home to deploy troops to occupy the hillside immediately north of the fort overlooking Stanley Prison, the college and the village. Major Bishop's 'C' Coy were deployed to this location at 0400 hours. Bishop established his Coy HQ at the Prison Officers Club, and his company occupied the adjacent high ground. Wallis then ordered Home to mount a company counterattack on the ridge north of Stanley Military Cemetery, which included the three staff bungalows. Major Parker, in command of 'D' Coy, received orders at 0830 hours to lead the attack with the objective of recapturing the cemetery and the nearby bungalows. The Japanese had thrown everything at Stanley during the night, with fierce hand-to-hand fighting around the village and the college, and by the time day broke on Christmas morning much of the college grounds had been lost. Wallis needed to reclaim the high ground around the college to prevent further Japanese infiltration towards the fort.

The plan called for 'D' Coy to move from the fort to a forming-up point at the north-western corner of the prison, which was close to the military cemetery. Wallis, somewhat counterintuitively, ordered that the company should work their way around the prison walls in an anti-clockwise direction by going south towards Tweed Bay and then along the shoreline to the east of Tweed Bay Hospital and mount the attack from the east just to the north of the Prison Officers Club. This provided a more concealed approach. However, the majority of the company went clockwise, attacking northwards, through the military cemetery and up to the bungalows on the ridge behind the cemetery. Although artillery support had been promised, it was not available. The 9.2-inch guns and the 6-inch guns could not be brought to bear, and Challinor and Eddison were still struggling to bring the 18-pdrs and the two 3.7-inch howitzers back to the fort.

'D' Coy left the fort at 1130 hours. They reached the forming-up point at around 1300 hours, and the attack commenced at 1330 hours. The disused military cemetery, with its Victorian graves dating back to 1843, was on the higher ground to the north of the forming-up point. The Canadians formed a line abreast, fixed bayonets, and then charged through the cemetery and up the high ground towards the bungalows. They charged firing their Bren guns from the hip, catching the Japanese by surprise and driving them back toward the line of the bungalows. The company incurred heavy casualties but succeeded in ejecting the Japanese from the bungalows and capturing the high ground. Weller, wounded in Bungalow 'C', could hear the attack, but dared not come out in case he was mistaken for a Japanese soldier and shot. The Canadians consolidated their positions around the three bungalows, but the Japanese quickly counterattacked supported by artillery and mortar fire. Japanese troops moved to the east to outflank the Canadian positions.

With the bungalows being fired at by mortars and machine guns, with mounting casualties, and with ammunition running low, the order was issued to withdraw. The company reached their original starting point at 1700 hours and then returned to Stanley Fort at dusk. 'D' Coy had suffered an 84 per cent casualty rate, with twenty-six men killed and around seventy-five wounded from an original strength of 120 men. A British officer who witnessed the charge from near the cemetery, possibly 2/Lt Challinor, is often quoted describing the gallantry of the Canadian counterattack.

> We saw that last glorious charge of the Canadians, up through the graveyard and into the windows of the bungalows at the top. We saw the Japanese escaping through the back of the houses and then return with grenades, which they lobbed among the Canadians in occupation. Very few of the Canadians survived that gallant charge.[12]

Later that evening, Wallis ordered the RRC to relieve the gunners in the front line who had been fighting as infantry. The newly reorganised 'A' Coy, under Captain Price, was ordered to deploy to the third line of defence. They left the fort at around 1800 hours, but immediately incurred casualties from Japanese shelling directed at the road leading from the fort. The shelling resulted in eighteen casualties, of which six were killed. The company had not gone much further when the shelling stopped, and a car approached with headlights switched on and a white flag flying. The car carried two officers from Fortress HQ who had been sent to notify Wallis that the colony had surrendered and that he was to cease fighting.

17

The Massacre at St Stephen's College
25 December 1941

St Stephen's College was once known as the 'Eton of the East'. The college was established in 1903 to offer the same kind of education as the best public schools in England, for predominantly Chinese children in Hong Kong. The school was originally located at Sai Ying Poon and then moved to Pok Fu Lam. The school prospered, and as a result larger premises were built at Stanley. Sir Cecil Clementi, the Governor, laid the foundation stone for the main building in April 1928, and the college opened its doors at Stanley in 1929. The college and its grounds became part of the battlefield during the fierce fighting that took place at Stanley from 24 to 25 December 1941.

The main school building was being used as a temporary military hospital. The senior doctor was Lt-Col George Black, HKVDC. He was an elderly man with greying hair who had resided in Hong Kong for many years, where he was a well-known doctor in private practice. Captain Walter Scotcher, RASC, who had been taken by ambulance from The Ridge on 21 December with minor injuries, wrote a report on the events at St Stephen's College Hospital, which provides a useful record of what happened before, during and after the massacre on Christmas Day. Captain Scotcher shared a room in the hospital with Captain Overton Hickey, RCASC, who had also been lightly wounded, and evacuated from The Ridge at the same time as Scotcher. Since they were not bedbound patients, they asked if they could help around the hospital, and were given various tasks to do. Hickey was killed when Japanese troops invaded the hospital.

The hospital first came under Japanese artillery fire on Monday 22 December. The operating room was hit by one of the shells just after an operation had been conducted, and just after Lt-Col Black and the nurses had left the room. The RAMC orderly who was clearing up the room after the operation was killed by the blast. Further shells landed around the hospital, causing damage to the main ward and injuries to patients. Scotcher praised the conduct of the nurses, Mrs Ida Andrews-Levinge, Mrs Eileen Begg and Mrs Emma Fidoe, while the hospital was under fire, saying they were magnificent. After being shelled for the second time that day, Lt-Col Black asked Scotcher to go to Brigade HQ, at the Prison Officers Club, and present his compliments to Brigadier Wallis. He was to inform the brigadier of the shelling and to ask whether he may be allowed to evacuate some of the more serious cases, together with the seven European nurses, to a safer location. Lt-Col Black was referring here to either the hospital in Stanley Fort or the hospital in Stanley Prison. Captain Scotcher, with Cpl Sayer, RAMC, conveyed the message to Wallis but received a somewhat terse response.

> Informed by Brigadier that would I present his compliments to Lt-Col Black and inform him that he was not prepared to allow any transfer of patients or nurses, as in his opinion they would be as safe there as anywhere, but that he would send someone to investigate. A little while later he sent Dr Hackett, Stanley Prison Doctor, and Staff Captain Belton to see Lt-Col Black, Cpl Sayer and myself. ... The result of this visit was that eleven of the worst cases were evacuated to Stanley Prison Hospital, accompanied by Dr Ashton-Rose and Dr Balean. Fourteen near-convalescent cases were sent to Stanley Fort.[1]

There was no electricity and no running water. The relief hospital was packed to capacity, with over 200 patients, and more wounded were being brought in as the fighting drew closer to Stanley. On Tuesday 23 December, Scotcher recorded the arrival of CSM Stuart ('Tooti') Begg, who had escaped from The Ridge and from Overbays and whose wife, Eileen, was a nurse at the hospital.

> In the afternoon three men were seen to be approaching the hospital from the beach. These men turned out to be the survivors of a party of men besieged in a house called Overbays. They had escaped by swimming from Repulse Bay. ... Sgt-Major Begg, HKVDC, was in a complete state of exhaustion with a severely cut foot, Pte Hutchinson, HKVDC, was also in a very bad state, the third man was an artilleryman, name forgotten, all were admitted to hospital.[2]

On Tuesday night, 23 December, Scotcher was asked by Lt-Col Black to accompany the nurses to one of the nearby staff bungalows which the nurses were using for their accommodation. Nurse Amelia Gordon described the bungalow as being Dr Pope's house. Dr George Pope was a port health officer. He and his wife, Sarah, were interned at Stanley Camp after the British surrender. The house, better known as Bungalow A, still survives in the grounds of St Stephen's College and is now used by the college as a heritage museum. Scotcher settled down on a sofa in the large reception room, while the nurses, frightened by the sound of explosions and gunfire, occupied the bedrooms.

> I was about to settle down when there was a great hammering on the front door, I demanded to know who it was, and was informed that it was Lt-Col Home of the Canadians, and what the heck were the women and I doing in his Headquarters, explanations followed and it was eventually agreed to let the ladies stay in the rooms they were occupying while he, his staff and I settled down in the drawing room. During the general re-arrangement and settling down the telephone rang, it turned out to be Brigadier Wallis. A wordy battle took place the purport of which I gathered was that Lt-Col Home and his men were all-in and he did not spare his words on the subject.[3]

It was during that evening that the Royal Rifles of Canada had been withdrawn from the Stanley Perimeter. The next day, Wednesday 24 December, the nurses moved into the hospital, and Canadian soldiers started digging weapons pits around their new HQ. At the hospital, Black ordered all weapons, including his own revolver, to be collected and placed in a locked cupboard in the reception area. A large Red Cross flag was quickly manufactured using white bed sheets and red hospital handkerchiefs and then hoisted on the flagpole to replace the smaller one previously flown. Later that day, and during the night, the hospital found itself on the front line, with fighting raging all around the college buildings.

During the early evening on 24 December, Alberta Buxton, one of the VAD nurses, asked Scotcher if he could find out any news about her husband, Lt Henry Buxton, who was serving with No. 2 Battery, HKVDC, but had been assigned to No. 4 Battery at Pak Sha Wan. He had in fact been killed five days earlier when the Japanese landed on the Island. Scotcher knew this from Black, but nobody had yet broken the difficult news to Alberta. Scotcher told her as gently as he could that her husband had been killed in action. Alberta hardly had time to grieve, as the next morning she went through the horror of the massacre at the hospital, and she was one of three nurses raped, mutilated and killed by the Japanese.

Many wounded had been brought in during the night. Most of the patients were accommodated in the main assembly hall, including the upper galleries. This area is now used as the school library. Sgt Peasegood, RAMC, recalled in a deposition that weapons pits and machine gun positions were placed close to the hospital and that some machine guns were operated from the cover of the ground-floor veranda. This was corroborated by Sgt Anderson, RAMC.

> Numerous MG posts were set up in the grounds of the hospital. Later on, these posts actually used bales of hospital blankets and mattresses from the linen stores to build machine gun nests within six yards of the entrance to the hospital reception hall. Guns were also set up on the rising ground behind the cookhouse, and another within arm's reach of the flagpole carrying the Red Cross flag. ... Firing and grenade fire increased until nearly dawn. ... Just before dawn on 25 December British and Canadian forces dropped back without warning being given to the hospital, and the first sign of capture was the arrival of four Japanese soldiers at the entrance to the hospital.[4]

The fact that firing positions had been located around the hospital, and on the ground-floor veranda, led the Japanese to think that the building was being used as a defensive position. This and the large number of casualties incurred by the Japanese in the battle for Stanley may have been the reason for the Japanese coming so violently and so angrily into the hospital on Christmas morning. When the first four Japanese soldiers appeared at the main entrance to the hospital, Sgt Anderson and Lt-Col Black went out to meet them.

> Lt-Col Black and myself went out to meet them followed by Captain Witney. Cpl Noble and Pte Mooney, RAMC, were already outside under guard. The two officers, after their equipment had been removed, were taken around the corner of the building, the rest of us were lined up against the wall and had our armbands inspected.[5]

Lt-Col Black and Captain Witney were killed. Their bodies, when found, had wounds that indicated they had been put to death with bayonets. Lt-Col Black's sixty-one-year-old wife, Ann, and his twenty-year-old daughter-in-law, Alison, had chosen to remain in Hong Kong, and had been exempted from the compulsory evacuation order because they were both serving as volunteer nurses. They were later interned at Stanley Camp. Nurse Amelia Gordon recalled hearing howls in the early morning as the Japanese arrived at the hospital.

Just before dawn, there was a terrific howl, and shortly afterwards the Japanese arrived in large numbers at the front entrance where I was standing with the VADs. They ran into the main building whilst I remained with others in the [entrance] hall. Captain Scotcher was pulled out, and shortly afterwards he instructed me to come out and put my hands above my head. They took my steel helmet and cracked me over the head with it, searched my pockets, took off my Red Cross band and removed any valuables that I had. They shouted for everyone to come out and everyone did except Sgt Parkin, RAMC, who attempted to run past, but was shot dead instantly. They gave me the impression that they did not think that this was a hospital, and that it was more in the nature of a fortress.[6]

Peasegood was lying fully clothed on his bed trying to get some sleep when he was awakened by the sound of a rifle shot in the room at around 0600 hours. He jumped up and opened the door, where he was confronted by a Japanese soldier with a rifle and fixed bayonet about to enter. Peasegood put up his hands and was dragged out to the veranda. After about half an hour, the surrendered personnel, and those patients who had survived the killing, and who by then had been assembled outside the front of the building, were crowded into the same room from which Peasegood had emerged. Sgt Bill Parkin's body was lying on the floor in a pool of blood. His new wife, Barbara, and her eighteen-month-old son, Leslie, from a previous marriage, were in Hong Kong. They had only married on 8 October 1941. Barbara and Leslie were both interned at Stanley Camp, and it was not until much later that Barbara learnt of her husband's death.

When the Japanese entered the hospital, it was still dark outside, and the hospital's main ward was lit faintly by hurricane lamps. The Japanese troops went charging into the main hall, where most of the patients were in bed. In an orgy of unfettered rage and inhumane violence, they bayoneted patients in their beds and ripped off bandages to see if the patients were really wounded or whether they were shamming. Those who were able to get out of bed and make their way to the exit generally survived, and those who were too sick or too injured to get out of bed were generally killed. Sgt Anderson describes the mayhem in the main ward.

There were sounds of shouting and shooting as the Japanese ran down the main hall amongst the patients, and any patients who were too slow in getting out of bed, or who could not move owing to wounds were bayoneted or shot. Some of the HKVDC tried to escape, and others put up a bit of a struggle, but they were mostly bayoneted or shot.

The St John Ambulance Brigade (SJAB) men were all put in one room and systematically butchered, one only remained alive to tell us what happened. All the staff and patients were, first of all, herded into one of the storerooms, and later as all the survivors were collected by the Japanese and daylight came, they were taken upstairs and put into the small student dormitories.[7]

Stuart Begg and his wife, Eileen, survived by hiding under his hospital bed. He testified how the Japanese rushed into the main ward with blood-curdling yells, bayoneting patients in their beds, and killing anybody in their way. While hiding under the bed with his wife, he recalled that the mattress, although empty, was pierced several times by bayonets. Despite this lucky escape, Eileen Begg was one of the three nurses who were raped and killed later that day.

Pte Gisby, RAMC, witnessed the bayoneting in the main ward. The main ward had an entrance on both the south side and the north side of the building. There was a gallery and side balconies on the upper floor that were used for hospital beds. Mattresses had been placed over the windows to protect patients from shrapnel and bullets. Gisby estimated that there were around 180 British and Canadian patients and a further thirty Indian patients. During the early hours of 25 December, Gisby began dragging the most gravely wounded patients on their mattresses to the rear of the hall.

> I started to drag, on mattresses, the worst cases from the main ward into the back porch, or entrance hall of the hospital. I had almost completed the evacuation of the main ward when I saw three Japanese soldiers appear on the upstairs balcony where patients were lying. I heard a patient shouting, and then one of these three Japanese bayoneted this patient. I shouted at this Japanese who shot at me, though on account of the half-light I was not hit. I carried on taking a patient on a blanket to the back-entrance hall. When I arrived in this hall, I saw a Japanese soldier standing in the outer doorway holding a revolver and a torch. I shone my torch on my Red Cross brassard and said 'Hospital'. I was then made to lead a column of patients and staff who had congregated in the back-entrance hall into a small store.[8]

The survivors, many bleeding from fresh wounds, were led to the storerooms on the ground-floor veranda that ran along the outside of the building. They were kept in the storerooms for one or two hours before being led upstairs and crowded into the small rooms that had been used for student accommodation. They had to file up the stairs through a gauntlet of Japanese troops lashing out at them. Scotcher recalls being hit and kicked as they were bundled upstairs.

> They removed us, a few at a time, and drove us upstairs, at the top of the staircase another gang were waiting. I was sent up alone, and I was beaten and kicked, lighted cigarettes were thrust in my face; finally, they got tired of this and flung me into Room 14. The room was roughly 10 feet by 8 feet and included two single beds and a small table. On one bed was Rifleman Sweet, this lad was stabbed repeatedly while lying wounded in the main ward, on the other bed a naval man with both legs bandaged and on crutches, under each bed two more wounded one a shell shock case.[9]

Rifleman Royce Sweet had been admitted to hospital for a wound in his back. He survived the bayoneting although one arm was later amputated. The room in which Scotcher was held also included three of the nurses, Miss Gordon, Mrs Andrews-Levinge and Mrs Emma Fidoe. The three nurses were later moved to another room with the other nurses. Peasegood recalled being placed in a slightly larger room, which he described as being 10 feet by 15 feet, but into which were crowded some ninety patients and orderlies. They were so packed in that they could only stand, despite many being badly wounded. He describes how at one stage a Japanese soldier came in and started lashing out at them with a leather strap, while another threw live ammunition at them, causing head injuries to several of the men including Peasegood. Presumably, the Japanese meant to demonstrate that they had found ammunition within the hospital and that the building, whether hospital or not, was being used to fire at Japanese troops.

Every time a Japanese soldier came to the door, they were told to kneel; however, they could not do so because of the overcrowding. As a consequence, those nearest were beaten with rifles. There was no sanitation, no food, no water, no medical attention and no room to sit down. Peasegood described how the men had no choice other than to urinate and defecate on the floor, and with some of the injured still bleeding the conditions rapidly became appalling. Peasegood recalled how later that morning they heard, and those by the window saw, elements of 'D' Coy, Royal Rifles of Canada mounting their attack across the cemetery and the college grounds.

With the battle still raging outside, the Japanese started dragging people out of the rooms, one by one, to mutilate and kill them. In the late afternoon, the noise of battle diminished as by that time the colony had surrendered. The surrender had not yet been communicated to Brigadier Wallis at Stanley Fort, and desultory gunfire continued until 2100 hours.

At that time, around forty of the occupants were moved to another room, and they were all given water and cigarettes. The nightmare was over, but at what cost? The exact number killed at the hospital is not known, but most reports suggest around eighty, but with many more injured. Of the seven European nurses, five had been raped, and three of those raped had been killed. The Chinese nurses had also been raped and abused. Amelia Gordon recalled that the three nurses who were killed were taken from the room late in the afternoon on Christmas Day.

> A particularly bad lot of Japanese soldiers came in at 4:30 p.m. and removed Mrs Smith, Mrs Begg and Mrs Buxton. These three we never saw again. One of the Chinese nurses told Mrs Simmons that they had taken out the three VADs to kill them and that they would return for us shortly; moreover, they informed us that the Japanese intended killing all British if Hong Kong did not surrender that evening.[10]

Although the fighting had ended, Amelia Gordon and Emma Fidoe were repeatedly raped during the night. Miss Gordon described the terror and abuse in a deposition used at war crimes trials after the war.

> We were ordered by a Japanese soldier, speaking English, to come and bandage wounded Japanese soldiers. They took us to another room overlooking the tennis court, where there were five dead bodies of Red Cross [SJAB] personnel. We were made to sit down on these bodies. A little later two soldiers removed Mrs Fidoe, and two removed me. I was taken to another room, where there were two dead bodies, and made to take off all my clothes whilst they removed theirs. Before touching me, they apparently became afraid someone was coming and made me put my clothes on again, and I was returned to the room where Mrs Simmons and Mrs Andrews-Levinge still were. Mrs Fidoe joined us almost immediately in a weeping state and told us she had been raped. We were left in peace for a short time only, three soldiers came in and took me to a small adjacent bathroom, knocked me down and all raped me one after the other, and then let me return. Mrs Fidoe was then taken and underwent a similar experience. Both Mrs Fidoe and I were then taken out a second time and raped as before. We were all now desperate and discovering there was a Yale lock on the door we pulled it locking ourselves in. They returned several times during the night but did not force an entrance.[11]

The next morning the survivors were ordered downstairs and allocated tasks of cleaning up the hospital and removing the dead. Scotcher recalled finding one patient who had been admitted for a badly damaged index finger hacked to death at the bottom of the stairs, and several Indian patients murdered in their beds in the Indian ward. One portion of the hospital was made available to the British, while the Japanese used the main ward for their own casualties. The RAMC personnel tended the surviving patients and dressed their wounds. They were allowed access to the medical stores, but food and water were still in short supply.

The four surviving European nurses were desperate to get away from the hospital, fearful that the abuse and terror would continue the next night. Captain Stoker, HKVDC, smuggled them out in a supply truck going to Stanley Fort, together with CSM Begg who was shocked and distraught after discovering what had happened to his wife. Gisby made his way to the rear entrance hall to the spot where he had dragged patients on their mattresses the previous morning. He was surprised to find that they were still there. They had been beaten by rifle butts and had sustained broken noses and facial cuts, but they were still alive.

Anderson wrote in his deposition that the bodies of Lt-Col Black and Captain Witney were found in a staff lavatory and staff sitting room respectively, and both had been killed by sword or bayonet. He stated that the bodies of the three nurses had been cut to pieces. Anderson estimated that between sixty and seventy patients were massacred, and around twenty-five hospital staff had also been killed. The Japanese ordered that the bodies be collected and burnt. Captain Barnett, the Canadian padre, supervised the cremation pyre, which he described as being near PB 28, close to the road fork near Stanley Police Station. Civilian internees at Stanley Camp found ashes and other remains at the site of the pyre. These were collected in part and buried at Stanley Military Cemetery, with a granite slab commemorating the victims. Along with Lt-Col Black, Captain Witney and the three nurses were the many soldiers, including Chinese, Indian, Canadian and British, who died on that tragic Christmas Day at and around St Stephen's College, Stanley.

18

Surrender

25 December 1941

At 0900 hours on 25 December, two weary civilians, Major Charles Manners and Mr Andrew Shields, came through the front line in Wan Chai under a flag of truce. They had spent a sleepless night under the close watch of their captors. Theirs was a dangerous mission because British troops were unaware that two civilians would be crossing the front line. The two captives were exhausted, having endured the siege of Repulse Bay Hotel and having witnessed so much suffering, fear, horror, bloodshed, and death at the hotel and on the route from Repulse Bay to North Point. They had seen the large numbers of Japanese troops, guns and military equipment on the Island. Having crossed the front line, they met with Major-General Maltby and Sir Mark Young and reported what they had seen. The Japanese commander had sent just one message with them, which was to the effect that Japanese forces would not initiate hostilities for three hours. The two civilians were on parole with orders to return by noon. The truce was observed on much of the Island, although Japanese aircraft continued bombing, and Stanley remained under artillery fire.

The Japanese had been pressing forward on all three fronts. On the south side of the Island, they had possession of Repulse Bay, Deep Water Bay, Brick Hill and most of Shouson Hill. They were attacking Bennet's Hill, which when captured would open the way to the Aberdeen naval base. On the line of gaps, they had possession of Sanatorium Gap, Tai Tam Gap, WNC Gap, Middle Gap and were attacking Wan Chai Gap. They had full control of Mount Nicholson and most of Mount Cameron. On the north shore, there was street fighting in Wan Chai, and the British lines were being pushed back towards Victoria. It was self-evident that the colony could not hold out much longer. It had always been a matter of time, but that time could now be measured in hours rather than days.

In response to this third, more muted, entreaty to surrender, Major-General Maltby and Sir Mark Young convened a special meeting of the Defence Committee, which included the Governor, the GOC, the Commodore, the Colonial Secretary, the Attorney-General and, normally, although absent on this occasion, the Defence Secretary. The committee, somewhat surprisingly given the situation, decided that there should be no talk of surrender and that British forces would fight on. The Commodore confirmed that the Royal Navy was prepared to fight to the finish.

> On being consulted by H.E. the Governor at a Defence Council in the forenoon as regards the naval position, I reported that apart from HMS *Robin* and the five MTBs I had no ships left but was fully prepared to defend the dockyard in Hong Kong to the last. Positions were taken up along the east perimeter of the dockyard to face the enemy.[1]

By the early afternoon, the situation was rapidly deteriorating. British troops at the Canal Road line were getting ready to fall back to the O'Brien Street reserve line. This was the last line of defence on the north shore. Lt-Col Stewart, 1/Mx, had moved his Bn HQ back to Murray Barracks, and the fighting was getting close to the centre of town. Maltby described the military situation as it pertained in the early afternoon, and his subsequent decision to surrender.

> The enemy drive along the north shore was decisive. I asked Lt-Col Stewart ... how much longer in his considered opinion the men could hold the line now occupied. He replied one hour. ... At 1515 hours, I advised H.E. the Governor and C-in-C that no further useful military resistance was possible, and I then ordered all commanding officers to break off the fighting and to capitulate to the nearest Japanese commander, as and when the enemy advanced, and the opportunity offered.[2]

Sir Mark did not relish the prospect of being one of the first British colonial governors to surrender a British colony since the surrender of Yorktown by General Cornwallis in 1781. Sir Mark spoke to the Commodore to get his opinion on Maltby's view that the time had come for surrender.

> H. E. spoke to me on the telephone, informing me of the GOC's message, and asked my opinion. I told him again that I was perfectly prepared to hold on in the Dockyard, but considered that we could probably only hold out for about two hours, by which time it would

be getting dark, and that the risk of the Japanese then getting out of control and butchering the civilian population, both European and Chinese, did not warrant further resistance. Orders were then given for the fighting to cease, and I proceeded to Government House.[3]

Sir Mark and his senior military commanders had known for some time that capitulation was inevitable. It is difficult to fight a losing battle, and many criticised Sir Mark and Major-General Maltby for not capitulating earlier and thereby saving more lives, but the message from Churchill had been very clear about the need to fight on, to resist to the end. Sir Mark described his daily ambition in the closing stages of the battle as being simply to add another twenty-four hours to the period in which they were holding out. However, after hearing from Maltby in the afternoon about the worsening military situation, and after conferring with the other members of the Defence Committee, Sir Mark had little choice but to assent to the advice given by his military commander. The issue then arose as to how the surrender should be conveyed to the Japanese military commanders.

It was decided that Lt-Col Stewart, accompanied by Japanese linguist Wg Cdr Alf Bennett, would proceed through Japanese lines in Wan Chai with an orderly bearing a white flag, and attempt to relay the surrender to the Japanese commander. The sound of gunfire had subdued since white flags had been hoisted at British positions. The soldiers with the unenviable task of carrying the surrender to the enemy proceeded by walking down the middle of the road until they were stopped by Japanese troops. They were taken to a forward command post where the Japanese officer in charge had no idea what to do, so he offered them tea, and contacted his senior officers for instructions. After a period of waiting, some Japanese staff officers arrived. The British surrender party was told that the Japanese C-in-C would only discuss the surrender with the Governor and the military commander. Two members of the British delegation were sent back to pass this message to Government House. Sir Mark had asked Maltby and Collinson to join him at Government House to await the arrival of the Japanese.

After we had waited some time, a message was received from the local Japanese commander. It was brought orally by two of the officers who had been sent forward on General Maltby's instructions to communicate to the enemy the cessation of resistance. The message was that unless General Maltby and I personally went across at once to the Japanese local HQ and confirmed that the ceasefire had been ordered on our side, the Japanese commander would launch his attack at a named hour. I was most reluctant to go, but it seemed best that I should do so, and General Maltby and I accordingly went forward, and from the front line in the streets of Wan Chai we were taken in a Japanese car to the local Japanese headquarters where after considerable delay and some difficulties of interpretation we confirmed that the order to ceasefire had been given to our forces except those in Stanley, with whom it had been impossible to communicate. Thereupon arrangements were made for a message to be sent to Stanley by road, and the Japanese commanding officer then said that he would give the order countermanding the attack.[4]

The Governor and the GOC were then taken across the harbour by launch to meet with the Japanese C-in-C, Lt-General Sakai, and his staff officers at the Peninsula Hotel. In the absence of electricity, the meeting was conducted by candlelight. A Japanese photographer was in attendance, and a few grainy photographs remain, which show Major-General Maltby, Lt-Col Stewart and Wg Cdr Bennett around a table. Sir Mark was present but not visible in the photographs. He objected to the presence of the photographer, who was then sent away. They were asked whether the cessation of hostilities was unconditional, to which Sir Mark and Maltby confirmed that they had no conditions.

Sir Mark was detained at the Peninsula Hotel and kept in solitary confinement. He made repeated requests to be allowed to go back to Government House, to be able to liaise with his staff and to collect some of his personal belongings, but he was continually refused. After a while, he asked for an interview with the Japanese general, but Sir Mark must have come across as being too demanding because the interview went badly. The interpreter shouted out that he should bear in mind that he had been defeated, and that he had surrendered, and that now he had to obey Japanese orders and was in no position to make demands. In February 1942, he was transferred to Shanghai by air together with a batman, Pte Waller, 1/Mx, who was designated to assist him. They were flown first to Formosa, and then to Shanghai. They were initially held in Woosung Camp near Shanghai, and later transferred to a camp in Formosa, and finally to a camp in Manchuria.

During the afternoon, while the British commanders were conveying the surrender to the Japanese, the battle was still raging at Stanley, with artillery fire being exchanged throughout the afternoon. In the evening, two British staff officers were dispatched to Stanley by car with orders for Wallis to cease fire in compliance with the surrender that had already been communicated to the Japanese. The officers were Lt-Col Ronald Lamb, RE, and Lt James Prior, King's Own Scottish Borderers. The two staff officers arrived at around 2000 hours in a car flying a white flag and with its headlights switched on. They informed Brigadier Wallis that Major-General Maltby had issued orders for British troops to lay down their arms and surrender and that he was to comply with this order and to hand over all arms and equipment undamaged.

Wallis did not know Lt Prior and barely knew Lt-Col Lamb. He was puzzled because up until now all his communication with the GOC, as recently as that morning before the telephone line was cut, indicated that Maltby expected him to fight on and not to surrender while ammunition, food and water was still available. He was also concerned about the message that the guns should be handed over undamaged. The two officers were not carrying written orders, which was unusual for orders of this magnitude.

> After careful consideration, I decided I could not surrender without written confirmation. Accordingly, I dispatched Major Harland, 2/RS, my Brigade Major, to obtain confirmation or otherwise, with the returning white flag party. ... After a difficult journey over badly damaged roads and past numerous enemy posts, the Brigade Major returned from Japanese Headquarters situated in the Tai Tam vicinity. He confirmed that fighting had ceased. ... He carried a written message from Lt-Col Stewart, 1/Mx, saying 'the GOC authorises me to state that the white flag will be hoisted and all military operations will cease forthwith. You will consider yourselves prisoners of war. Issue orders to all concerned and cease fighting.'[5]

Stewart also sent a more personal note to Wallis, commiserating with him. At about 0230 hours on 26 December, Wallis issued orders for the Stanley Force to cease fire and for the white flag to be hoisted.

On Christmas Day, the five remaining MTBs were moored at two locations along the shoreline between Mount Davis and Aberdeen. MTBs 07 and 09 were alongside an old stone jetty at Telegraph Bay. The boats had been painted in disruptive pattern and were camouflaged with shrubbery to hide them from Japanese aircraft during daylight hours. In the afternoon, at 1515 hours, they intercepted a signal from the Commodore to Lt-Commander Gandy, the commander of the MTB Flotilla, with the one-word message 'GO'. This was the order for the MTBs to make their escape. It must have been one of the last signals sent by the Commodore before he made his way from the RN Dockyard to Government House. The Commodore had expected the MTBs to leave immediately on his pre-arranged signal, but it was still early afternoon, and Lt-Commander Gandy wanted to wait until nightfall, and go under cover of darkness. More importantly, he wanted to wait until Admiral Chan Chak, head of the Nationalist Chinese Government Liaison Office, had arrived. It had been strongly impressed on Gandy that it was imperative to get the Chinese admiral out of Hong Kong.

In addition to their naval crews, the MTBs carried three men from 'Z' Force, Mike Kendall, Colin McEwan and Monia Talan. As darkness fell, all five boats assembled on the southern side of Aberdeen Island. Four staff officers from Fortress HQ escorted Admiral Chan Chak and his entourage from Victoria to Aberdeen Harbour. These staff officers included Major Arthur Goring, Captain Freddie Guest, Captain Peter Macmillan and Squadron Leader Max Oxford. They were accompanied by Superintendent Robinson of the Indian Police Service and David MacDougall, Ministry of Information, and his assistant Ted Ross. With the help of Commander Montague, SNO (A), Admiral Chan Chak's party commandeered a launch, which had previously been used as a tender for HMS *Cornflower*. They were not sure where to find the MTBs; Commander Montague suggested they proceed to Sandy Bay or Telegraph Bay, and if they were unable to find the MTBs at these locations to proceed to Magazine Island at the western end of Aberdeen Island. Commander Montague would then rendezvous with them after dark, and after having refloated the diesel launch C-410. The launch had been used to carry ammunition to Stanley the previous night and had run aground in the Aberdeen Channel, but was expected to be refloated at high water that evening.

The *Cornflower* launch motored out across the Aberdeen Channel with her motley crew but was spotted by a Japanese machine gun post on Brick Hill. The launch came under heavy machine gun fire and was soon riddled with bullets, and its engine was incapacitated. A number of the escape party were killed or wounded, and the rest took to the water and swam ashore, including the plucky one-legged Chinese admiral, who had been wounded in the wrist by gunfire. Despite having only one leg, and having been shot in the forearm, he managed to swim ashore. He and the remnants of the escape party, having crossed to the seaward side of Aberdeen Island, were later picked up by the MTBs. Once the admiral was safely on board, the five boats sped away through the night towards Mirs Bay, on the China coast east of Hong Kong. They anchored near the small village of Nanao, where to their surprise they were joined by the naval launch C-410, which Commander Montague had used to make good his escape together with a small party of RN and Merchant Navy volunteers. Admiral Chan Chak contacted the Chinese guerrillas who were operating in that area. The boats were scuttled, and the British military party, with the aid of Chinese guerrillas, made their way across country, carrying their weapons through Japanese-occupied territory, and into Free China. It was an incredible escape in which sixty-eight servicemen and other officials made their way across southern China to freedom.

The Governor and his military commanders in Hong Kong had faced an invading force that had total control of the air. The Japanese could bomb, strafe and observe from the air with impunity. The Japanese Imperial Army had numerical superiority in men, guns and equipment. The Japanese had expected an earlier capitulation and were surprised by the stubbornness of the defenders, who rejected three entreaties to surrender. Maltby estimated his casualties as being more than 4,000, of which over 1,500 were killed in action, died of wounds or were reported as missing in action. This represented a casualty rate of 32 per cent. Maltby estimated the Japanese casualties as being 3,000 dead and 9,000 wounded, but other Japanese sources show both much higher and much lower numbers. Hong Kong held out for as long as possible. The defenders had fought against the odds, and had done their duty. Churchill always knew that Hong Kong would fall, but he wanted to cause maximum delay and maximum cost to the invader. Writing after the war, he acknowledged that this had been achieved and that the defenders had 'fought a good fight' and won 'the lasting honour'.

After the surrender, the Japanese military placed the territory under martial law. The Japanese military occupation was characterised by fear, hunger and brutality. The lack of food led to officially sanctioned deportations in which hundreds of thousands of Chinese were forced to seek refuge in villages across the border in southern China. British, American and Dutch civilians were rounded up and interned at Stanley Camp. The military personnel were placed in POW camps, initially at Sham Shui Po, North Point and Argyle Street. Many suffered from malnutrition and disease in both the civilian and the military camps. Over 5,000 POWs were shipped from Hong Kong to Japan to work as slave labourers in coal mines, factories and docks. More than 2,500 POWs died during the period of incarceration. This oppressive occupation lasted for three and a half years and finally ended with the Japanese surrender in August 1945, following the atomic bombings of Hiroshima on 6 August and Nagasaki on 9 August, and the declaration of war by Soviet Russia on 9 August and the Soviets' subsequent rapid advance through Manchuria.

On 15 August, Emperor Hirohito issued a pre-recorded radio broadcast announcing that Japan was accepting the terms of the Potsdam Declaration, which had been issued by the Western Powers and which called upon Japan to surrender unconditionally. Freedom returned slowly to Hong Kong. The Colonial Secretary and other government officials came out from Stanley Camp to re-establish British government ahead of the arrival of the British fleet on 30 August 1945. The official Japanese surrender took place at Government House on 16 September. The war was over, and peace had returned, but thousands of civilians and servicemen had died both during the battle and during the period of occupation that followed. The battle has left its mark in the neat rows of graves at the military cemeteries, the dilapidated pillboxes, batteries and bunkers that still survive, and on the battlefields where bullets, bayonets and personal effects can still be picked up to tell the story of the Battle for Hong Kong. It is a story of courage, horror and defeat, but a story that deserves to be better known.

Notes

1 Historical Prelude
1. *Narrative of a Voyage Round the World* (1843) Captain Sir Edward Belcher.

2 Hong Kong before the War
1. War Cabinet Papers. (UKNA COS (41) 28, CAB 80/25).
2. Report on Operations by Major-General Maltby. (UKNA WO 106/2401A).

3 Battle on the Mainland
1. Captain Belton's personal diary. (IWM Docs. 3671).
2. Estimates of British forces vary between 12,500 and 14,000. My figure of 12,500 is an approximate derived from Maltby's Report and adding in numbers for Royal Navy, Royal Marines, RAF and Dockyard Defence Corps.
3. Police War Diary. (UKNA CO 129/592/4).
4. Battle Progress Report of the 228th Infantry Regiment. (HKPRO HKMS 100-1-5).
5. Ibid.
6. Proceedings of court of enquiry. (UKNA CAB 106/166).
7. Ibid.
8. Ibid.
9. Ibid.
10. *Dad's Story*. Privately published memoirs of Douglas Baird edited by his daughter Catherine Williams.
11. Appendix 'C' HK Despatches. (UKNA WO 106/2401 C).
12. Ibid.
13. Progress of the 230th Infantry Regiment. (HK PRO HKMS 100-1-5).
14. Police War Diary. (UKNA CO 129/592/4).

4 Evacuation from the Mainland
1. Mainland Brigade War Diary. (UKNA WO 172/1685).
2. Colonel Clifford Royal Engineers War Diary. (UKNA CAB 106/37).
3. 2/14 Punjab Regiment War Diary. (UKNA WO 172/1691).
4. 5/7 Rajput Regiment War Diary. (UKNA WO 172/1692).

5 The Royal Navy
1. Personal diary of Major Templer. (IWM Docs. 4018).

2. Personal diary of Lt Ralph HKRNVR with permission of Sheila Peacock.
3. Operations of 2nd MTB Flotilla by Lt Gandy. (UKNA ADM 199/286).

6 The Island under Siege

1. East Brigade War Diary. (UKNA CAB 106/35).
2. Appendix B HK Despatches. (UKNA WO 106/2401 B).
3. Ibid.
4. Major John Monro private papers. (IWM Docs. 17941).
5. RSM Ford personal diary. (IWM Docs. 10841).

7 Invasion of the Island

1. Battle Report of the 228th Regiment. (HKPRO HKMS 100-1-5).
2. Ibid.
3. 5/7 Rajputs War Diary. (UKNA WO 172/1692).
4. Testimony of Martin Cho. (UKNA WO 235/1030).
5. Testimony of Chan Yam-kwong. (UKNA WO 235/1030).
6. Royal Rifles of Canada War Diary. (NA Canada DHIST 593).
7. L/Cpl Harry Long's personal diary with permission of Judy Chan.
8. Ibid.
9. Sgt Morrison statement dated 6 August 1942. (HKPRO).
10. No. 1 Coy HKVDC War Diary. (UKNA WO 172/1693).
11. Ibid.
12. Ibid
13. Ibid.
14. 5/7 Rajput war diary. (UKNA WO 172/1692).
15. Cpl Leath statement. (UKNA WO 235/1030).

16. Osler Thomas statement. (UKNA WO 235/1030).

8 The Battle for Wong Nai Chung Gap

1. No. 3 Coy HKVDC War Diary. (HKPRO HKRS 225-2-48-2).
2. War Memoirs of Sgt Tom Marsh (published on HKVCA web site) with permission Vic Marsh.
3. Ibid.
4. Ibid.
5. Ibid.
6. Ibid.
7. Ibid.
8. No. 3 Coy HKVDC War Diary. (HKPRO HKRS 225-2-48-2).
9. L/Sgt Hall, 'A' Coy, WG statement. (UKNA WO 235/1107).
10. Hong Kong Honours and Awards. (DHIST D25 Dept. of National Defence Ottawa).
11. Pte Bradbury, 'A' Coy, WG statement. (UKNA WO 235/1107).
12. Lt Field's War Diary. (HKPRO HKRS 225-2-48-2).
13. Ibid.
14. No. 3 Coy HKVDC War Diary. (HKPRO HKRS 225-2-48-2).
15. CQMS Fincher statement. (UKNA WO 361/778).
16. Pte Cheng Shi-ling statement. (UKNA WO 361/778).
17. L/Cpl Linton statement. (UKNA WO 235/1015).
18. Ibid.
19. Report by Sgt Thomas Barton with permission of Ken, Kirk and Katherine Barton.
20. Ibid.
21. Lt Tamworth statement. (UKNA WO 106/2401).
22. Padre Uriah Laite's personal diary with permission of Gray Laite.

9 The Navy Counterattacks

1. Patrick Sheridan's personal memoirs courtesy of Helen Dodd's (née Sheridan) family.
2. Ibid.
3. Ibid.
4. Lt Ashby's report in Operations of the 2nd MTB Flotilla. (UKNA ADM 199/1286).
5. Ibid.
6. Lt Kennedy's report in Operations of the 2nd MTB Flotilla (UKNA ADM 199/1286).

10 Chaos and Confusion

1. Major Monro private papers. (IWM Docs. 17941).
2. No. 1 Coy HKVDC War Diary. (UKNA WO 172/1693).
3. Ibid

11 The Army Counterattacks

1. Lt Sutcliffe, RAOC diary. (Royal Corp of Logistics Museum Archives).
2. *Canadian Military History* Vol. 20 No. 2 (2011)
3. Report by Major Reynolds Condon dated 20 August 1942. (US National Archives RG 165 Box 1738). The report is included in *The Fall of Hong Kong The Condon Report* edited by David Macri in Canadian Military History, Vol 20 No. 2 pp.65-80
4. Ibid.
5. Lt Tamworth report. (UKNA WO 106/2401).
6. Report by Major Condon. (US NARA).
7. East Brigade War Diary. (UKNA CAB 106/35).
8. *Dad's Story*. Privately published memoirs of Douglas Baird edited by his daughter Catherine Williams.
9. Report by Major Condon. (US NARA).
10. Sgt Kenneth Porter personal diary with permission of Charles Porter.

12 East Brigade Strikes Back

1. East Brigade war diary. (UKNA CAB 106/35).
2. Royal Rifles of Canada war diary. (NA Canada DHIST 593).
3. Ibid.
4. East Brigade war diary. (UKNA CAB 106/35).
5. No. 1 Coy HKVDC War Diary. (UKNA WO 172/1693).
6. Ibid.

13 Escape from The Ridge

1. Captain A.H. Potts personal diary. (HKU Library edition and internet sources)
2. Ibid.
3. Lt-Col Frederick, RASC War Diary. (UKNA WO 172/1694A).
4. Ibid.
5. Ibid.
6. Captain A.H. Potts personal diary.
7. Lt-Col Frederick. (UKNA WO 172/1694A).
8. Ibid.
9. Ibid.
10. Ibid.
11. Pte Canivet statement. (Canada NA RG 24 Vol 2899 File HQS 8959-9-4/20).
12. Pte Canivet statement. (UKNA WO 235/1030).
13. CQMS Hamlen statement. (UKNA WO 325/42).
14. Ibid.
15. Joseph Baud statement. (UKNA).
16. Lt-Colonel Ride evidence (UKNA WO 325/42).

14 The Siege of Repulse Bay Hotel

1. Deposition by Woulfe-Flanagan. (UKNA TS 26/72).

2. Lt Cheesewright 1/Mx war diary. (UKNA WO 172/1689).
3. Ibid.
4. Beatrice Ohl statement. (UKNA).
5. Woulfe-Flanagan statement. (UKNA TS 26/72).

15 The Japanese Advance

1. Major Marsh – Appendix to Hong Kong Despatches. (UKNA CAB 106/168).
2. Ibid.
3. Ibid.
4. *The Road to Inamura* (1972) Lewis Bush (p.143).
5. Sgt Kenneth Porter personal diary with permission of Charles Porter.
6. Ibid.
7. 2/14 Punjab Regiment War Diary. (UKNA WO 172/1691).
8. Ibid.

16 The Battle for Stanley

1. *The Second World War Volume III* (1950) Winston Churchill (p.563).
2. 1/Mx War Diary. (UKNA WO 172/1689).
3. *Some Notes from a Diary of the Years 1941-1942* by Bernard Tohill. Saint Louis Old Boys Association web site.
4. Ibid.
5. Statement by Brother Hogan, Maryknoll. (UKNA WO 325/42).
6. 1/Mx war diary. (UKNA WO 172/1689).
7. Statement by Sgt Russell and Bdr Minshull addressed to Lt Bryden, HKVDC (UKNA CAB 106/168).

8. Ibid.
9. Sgt Henry Hopkins No. 2 Coy statement addressed to Lt Bryden. (UKNA CAB 106/168).
10. Letter by Sgt Bill Hudson with permission of Rebecca Hudson.
11. Ibid.
12. Quote thought to have been attributed to either 2/Lt Challinor or 2/Lt Eddison.

17 The Massacre at St Stephen's College

1. Walter Scotcher's Report. (UKNA WO 311/561)
2. Ibid.
3. Ibid.
4. Sgt Anderson statement. (UKNA WO 361/778).
5. Ibid.
6. Sister Gordon statement. (UKNA WO 361/778).
7. Sgt Anderson statement. (UKNA WO 361/778).
8. Pte Gisby statement. (UKNA WO 311/561).
9. Captain Scotcher report. (UKNA WO 311/561).
10. Sister Gordon statement. (UKNA WO 361/778).
11. Ibid.

18 Surrender

1. Commodore Collinson's Report. (UKNA ADM 199/1286).
2. Maltby's Report. (London Gazette 27 January 1948).
3. Collinson's Report. (UKNA ADM 199/1286).
4. Report by Sir Mark Young. (HK Government Gazette 2 July 1948).
5. East Brigade war diary. (UKNA CAB 106/35).

Selected Bibliography

Published Books

Alderson, Gordon L. D., *History of Royal Air Force Kai Tak* (1972)

Allister, William, *Where Life and Death Hold Hands* (1989)

Anderson, William S., *Corporate Crisis NCR and the Computer Revolution* (1991)

Baird, Kenneth, *Letters to Harvelyn* (2002)

Banham, Tony, *Not the Slightest Chance – The Defence of Hong Kong, 1941* (2003)

Barman, Charles, *Resist to the End Hong Kong 1941-1945* (2009)

Baxter, George E., *Personal Experiences during the siege of Hong Kong Dec 8-25, 1941*

Bérard, Leo P., *17 Days until Christmas* (1997)

Bertram, James *Beneath the Shadow* (1947)

Birch, A & Cole, M., *Captive Christmas – The Battle of Hong Kong December 1941* (1979)

Birch, A & Cole, M., *Captive Years – The Occupation of Hong Kong 1941-1945* (1982)

Bosanquet, David, *Escape Through China* (1983)

Briggs, Alice, *From Peking to Perth* (1984)

Briggs, Christopher, *Farewell Hong Kong 1941* (2001)

Bruce, Philip, *Second to None* (1991)

Bush, Lewis, *The Road to Inamura* (1972)

Cambon, Kenneth, *Guest of Hirohito* (1990)

Carew, Tim, *The Fall of Hong Kong* (1960)

Coates, Austin, *A Mountain of Light* (1977)

Collingwood-Selby, Richard, *In Time of War* (2013)

Corrigan, L. B., *A Hong Kong Diary Revisited* (2008)

Crouch, Gregory, *China's Wings* (2012)

Dew, Gwen, *Prisoner of the Japs* (1943)

Ebbage, Victor, Edited by Robertshaw, Andrew, *The Hard Way Surviving Shamshuipo POW Camp 1941-1945* (2011)

Emerson, Geoffrey, *Hong Kong Internment 1942-1945* (2008)

Endacott, G. P., Edited by Alan Birch, *Hong Kong Eclipse* (1978)

Fairclough, Gordon, *Brick Hill and Beyond* (2005)

Ferguson, Ted, *Desperate Siege* (1980)

Gandt, Robert L., *Season of Storms* (1982)

Garneau, Grant S., *The Royal Rifles of Canada in Hong Kong 1941-1945* (1980)

Greenhous, Brereton, *'C' Force to Hong Kong – A Canadian Catastrophe 1941-1945* (1997)

Hahn, Emily, *China to Me* (1944)

Harrop, Phyllis, *Hong Kong Incident* (1943)

Heywood, Graham, *It won't be long now* (2015)

Kase, Toshikazu, *Eclipse of the Rising Sun* (1951)

Kennedy, Alexander, *Hong Kong Full Circle 1939-1945* (1969)

Kwong, C. M. and Tsoi, Y. L., *Eastern Fortress: A Military History of Hong Kong 1840-1970* (2014)

Leiper, G. A., *A Yen for My Thoughts* (1982)

Lindsay, Oliver, *The Lasting Honour* (1978)

Lindsay, Oliver, *At the Going Down of the Sun* (1981)

Lindsay, Oliver, *The Battle for Hong Kong 1941-1945 Hostage to Fortune* (2005)

Linklater, Andro, *The Code of Love* (2000)

Luard, Tim, *Escape from Hong Kong* (2012)

Luff, John, *The Hidden Years* (1967)

MacDonell, George S., *One Soldier's Story 1939-1945* (2002)

Macri, Franco David, *Clash of Empires in South China* (2012)

Marsman, Jan, *I escaped from Hong Kong* (1942)

Meagher, Terry, *Betrayal Canadian Soldiers Hong Kong 1941* (2015)

Muir, Augustus, *The First of Foot the History of the Royal Scots* (1961)

Proulx, Benjamin, *Underground from Hong Kong* (1943)

Rollo, Dennis, *The Guns & Gunners of Hong Kong* (1991)

Stewart, Evan, *Hong Kong Volunteers in Battle* (1953)

Vincent, Carl, *No Reason Why* (1981)

Wait, Carol Briggs, *Taken in Hong Kong – Memoirs of Norman Briggs* (2006)

Wiseman, Bill, *Hong Kong Recollections of a British Prisoner of War* (2001)

Wright-Nooth, George, *Prisoner of the Turnip Heads* (1994)

Other references:

Barton, Thomas, Unpublished report (courtesy family)

Lai, L., Davies, S., Ching, K., & Wong, C., 'Decoding the enigma of the fall of the Shing Mun Redoubt using line of sight analysis', *Surveying & Built Environment*, Vol. 21, Issue 2 (December 2011)

Potts, A. H., Diary (HKU Special Collections Library 940.547252P87 and on www. Gwulo.com

Waters, D. & McEwan, A., 'Colin McEwan's Diary', *Journal of the Royal Asiatic Society HK Branch*, Vol. 45 (2005)

Websites

www.battleforhongkong.blogspot.hk
www.cwgc.org
www.grs.gov.hk/en/
www.gwulo.com
www.hkvca.ca
www.hongkongwardiary.com
www.iwm.org.uk
www.nationalarchives.gov.uk
Facebook Page Battle of Hong Kong

NB: Considerable reference was made to official war diaries, private papers and personal diaries. Where quotes have been taken from these sources a reference is made in Notes providing file number and custodian.

Abbreviations

AA: Anti-Aircraft

ADC: Aide-de-Camp

ADS: Advanced Dressing Station

AIS: Aberdeen Industrial School (used as Aberdeen naval base)

ANS: Auxiliary Nursing Service

AOP: Artillery Observation Post

APVs: Auxiliary Patrol Vessels

ARP: Air Raid Precautions

BAAG: British Army Aid Group

Bn: Battalion

BOP: Battery Observation Post

BOR: British Other Ranks

BQMS: Battery Quarter Master Sergeant

BRMH: Bowen Road Military Hospital

CERA: Chief Engine Room Artificer

Coy: Company

CMC: Chinese Maritime Customs Service

CPO: Chief Petty Officer

CRASC: Commander RASC

CSM: Company Sergeant Major

CQMS: Company Quarter Master Sergeant

DWB: Deep Water Bay

DR: Defence Reserve

DSO: Distinguished Service Order

EOD: Explosive Ordnance Disposal

ERA: Engine Room Artificer

EXCO: Executive Council

FDL: Forward Defended Locality

GDL: Gin Drinkers Line

GOC: General Officer Commanding (British troops in China)

GSO: General Staff Officer

HA: High Angle gun

HE: High Explosive

H.E.: His Excellency

HKE: Hong Kong Electric

HSBC: Hongkong Shanghai Banking Corporation

HKRNVR: Hong Kong Royal Naval Volunteer Reserve

HKSRA: Hong Kong Singapore Royal Artillery

HKVDC: Hong Kong Volunteer Defence Corp

HQ: Headquarters

IJNS: Imperial Japanese Navy Ship

ILS: Indicator Loop Station

IOR: Indian Other Ranks

IWM: Imperial War Museum, London

KMT: Kuomintang

LEGCO: Legislative Council

LG: Lewis gun

LMG: Light Machine Gun (i.e. Lewis gun or Bren gun)

MC: Military Cross

MCS: Mine Control Station

MCSL: Mine Control Station (Lamma)

MCST: Mine Control Station (Tathong)

MiD: Mention in Dispatches

MM: Military Medal

MMG: Medium Machine Gun (i.e. Vickers)

MO: Medical Officer

MT: Motor Transport

MTB: Motor torpedo boat

Mx: Middlesex Regiment

NAAFI: Navy Army Air Force Institute

NCO: Non-Commissioned Officer

ND: Nursing Detachment

PB: Pillbox

PO: Petty Officer

POW: Prisoner of War

PRO HK: Public Records Office Hong Kong

Pte: Private

PWD: Public Works Department

QMS: Quartermaster Sergeant

RA: Royal Artillery

RAMC: Royal Army Medical Corps

RAOC: Royal Army Ordnance Corps

RASC: Royal Army Service Corps

RCASC: Royal Canadian Army Service Corps

RCOC: Royal Canadian Ordnance Corps

RBH: Repulse Bay Hotel

RNR: Royal Naval Reserve

RRC: Royal Rifles of Canada

RV: Rendezvous

SAA: Small arms ammunition

SJAB: St. John Ambulance Brigade

SNO (A): Senior Naval Officer (Aberdeen)

SSP: Sham Shui Po

Tel.: Telegraphist

TSMG: Thompson Sub Machine Gun (Tommy Gun)

UKNA: UK National Archives

US NARA: US National Archives and Record Administration

VAD: Voluntary Aid Detachment

VCC: Vehicle Collection Centre

WDV: War Department Vessel

WG: Winnipeg Grenadiers

WNC: Wong Nai Chung

X-Roads: Cross roads

Acknowledgements

I am grateful to Amberley Publishing for taking on this project, guiding me through the process, and bringing this book to print. I received a lot of help and encouragement from many people. I would like to thank the following who have helped me in different ways, some by allowing me to quote from the personal diaries or memoirs of their family members, some by answering questions and providing information, and some by reviewing content and giving me advice on how to bring the idea of the book to fruition.

Don Ady, Christopher Allanson, Bill and Janice Anderson, Barbara Anslow, Tony Banham, Ken and Kirk and Katherine Barton, David Bellis, Judith Bercene, Paul Bonney, Les Bowie, Mark Burch, Eleo Carson, Judy Chan, Steve Denton, Barbara Durbin, Brian Edgar, David Eldon, Geoff Emerson, Tony Fallon, Hugh Farmer, Conner Hackett, Martin Heyes, Ann Hutson, Ian Gill, Elizabeth Harris, Rebecca Hudson, Gillian Johnston, Kwong Chi Man, Gray Laite, Bill Lake, Susan Lange, David Macri, Vic Marsh, Craig Mitchell, Amanda Parkes, Sheila Peacock, Chris Potter, Helen Hutton Potts, Allan Proulx, the late Richard Neve, John Penn, Charles Porter, Elizabeth Ride, Helen Sheridan, Jan Summers, Bob Tatz, Ronald Taylor, Jim Trick, Tsoi Yiu Lun ('Rusty'), Peter Weedon, Robin Weir, Catherine Baird Williams, Dave Willott and Stuart Woods.

I would like to express my appreciation to the following institutions. The UK National Archives, Hong Kong Public Records Office, the Imperial War Museum, National Army Museum, Royal Logistics Corps Museum, Royal Corps of Signals Museum, Hong Kong University Special Collections Library and Rhodes House Library at Oxford University.

Last but not least, I would like to thank my wife, Marianne, and my son, Christopher, for their encouragement during the research and writing of this book. They patiently put up with me dragging them around battlefields and war sites, and on occasion bringing the war home, for example in the case of war relics found in the hills.

Index

Index